The Seductiveness of Jewish Myth

Challenge or Response?

Edited by

S. Daniel Breslauer

State University of New York Press

Published by
State University of New York Press, Albany

For information, address State University of New York Press,
State University Plaza, Albany, N.Y., 12246

Production by Marilyn Semerad
Marketing by Dana E. Yanulavich

Library of Congress Cataloging-in-Publication Data
The seductiveness of Jewish myth : challenge or response? / edited by
S. Daniel Breslauer.
    p. cm. — (SUNY series in Judaica)
    Revised versions of papers delivered on March 6 and 7, 1994 during
"Myth in the Biblical and Jewish Traditions: An Interdisciplinary
Conference."
    Includes bibliographical references and index.
    ISBN 0-7914-3601-2 (hc : alk. paper). — ISBN 0-7914-3602-0 (pb :
alk. paper)
    1. Judaism—Congresses. 2. Myth in literature—Congresses.
3. Jews—Intellectual life—Congresses. 4. Aggada—Congresses.
I. Breslauer, S. Daniel. II. Series.
BM30.S43   1997
296—dc21   97-7430
                                                         CIP
                                                         r97

The Seductiveness of Jewish Myth

SUNY Series in Judaica: Hermeneutics, Mysticism, and Religion
Michael Fishbane, Robert Goldenberg, and Elliot Wolfson, editors

Contents

Preface

The essays in this volume are revised versions of papers delivered on March 6 and 7, 1994, during "Myth in the Biblical and Jewish Traditions: An Interdisciplinary Conference." This was one in a series of annual conferences sponsored by the Department of Religious Studies and the Kansas School of Religion at the University of Kansas. All of the papers have been revised for this volume. None has been published previously.

The editor is grateful to those who are particularly responsible for the appearance of this volume. The conference participants themselves are commended for their rigorous work in preparing these essays for publication. The sponsoring organizations of the conference provided excellent facilities and a welcoming atmosphere. Acknowledgement is made to Oxford University Press for the appearance of the essay "The Mythology of Judaism" by Howard Schwartz. It is the basis for the Introduction to his forthcoming book, *The Mythology of Judaism*. I am especially indebted to Ms. Jean Gelbart, graduate student in Religious Studies at the University of Kansas, for her careful assistance in editing the essays.

Introduction
S. Daniel Breslauer

The Problematics of Myth in Judaism

The proposition that myth plays an essential role in Judaism from its biblical foundations through the modern period often provokes controversy, denial, and debate. In the early twentieth century Jewish scholars proclaimed that Jews, no less than Aryans, possessed ancient and valuable myths. The work of Ignac Goldziher illustrates these efforts. Myths, he claimed, expressed certain patterns inherent in the human mind. By showing that Jews had invented myths exactly comparable to those of the Europeans, he hoped to prove the common humanity linking them. As Maurice Olender puts it "In asking the Christian West to recognize the `mythology of the Hebrews,' he was asking his contemporaries to assimilate the Jews into European culture."[1] While Goldziher pointed to myth as a common expression shared by Jews and non-Jews, the theologian Martin Buber argued for monotheistic myth as a distinctive form of Jewish religiosity. Buber evolved a complex and challenging definition of myth within Judaism to highlight what he felt to be some obscured characteristics of Jewish faith.[2] Each of these scholars points to the problematics involved in seeking to discover myth in Judaism.

Both Goldziher and Buber encountered resistance and opposition. The idea of "myth" in "Judaism" challenged established views of "monotheism" and the "faith of ancient Israel." In a way, Goldziher's task was easier than that facing either Buber or modern Jewish scholars. Goldziher had a ready made content for "myth," the results of nineteenth and early twentieth century study of European folklore. Wherever he could find traces of lore resembling that identified by scholars of myth in Europe, he would proclaim the presence of Jewish myth. Secondly Goldziher had a limited subject matter. He focused on "the Hebrews." Certainly no nineteenth or early twentieth century thinker could read that word without seeing it as a code name for "Jews." Nevertheless, Goldziher limited his investigation to evidence from the Hebrew Bible. He had a clearly defined textual arena in which he worked. These two advantages certainly helped Goldziher in his attempt to present a coherent theory. Yet his clarity did not prevent challenges. Many scholars claimed that the Hebrew Bible could not, by its very nature, contain myth. Others argued that Aryan myth by its very nature was intrinsically distinctive from Jewish myth. His definitions of both Judaism as the Hebrew Bible and myth as a common body of human arch-narratives was opposed from various sides.

Buber's task was even more difficult than Goldziher's. Buber constructed a new vision of both myth and Judaism. The task he set himself, that of "the discovery and raising of an ancient treasure, the unveiling and freeing of a folk-religion that has grown beneath the surface" demanded a creative approach to religious data.[3] Buber redefined Judaism in terms of his own philosophy of I and Thou and, unlike Goldziher, drew on biblical, postbiblical, medieval, and modern resources alike. While acknowledging that he was not a traditional or observant Jew, Buber sought to transmit the "spirit" of Israel. He looked to the "internal history" of the Jewish people rather than to some external expression to teach him the meaning of Jewish religion.[4] Buber's task in defining the sources in which he would discover "Jewish myth" far exceeded the limited scope that Goldziher set for himself.

Buber's approach to the idea of "myth" was equally ambitious. He generated a typology of myth, tracing what he saw as the natural evolution of human myth-making. He declared unequivocally that "the rationalist's definition of myth is too narrow, too petty."[5] In contrast, his exploration of types of myths, of the development of myth, and of its relationship to history and memory ranges across a variety of genre and forms. Indeed, for Buber, what distinguishes myth is less a matter of formal definition than of inner power. That power springs from the memory of an event; it evokes the originating moment in which humanity meets with the divine. Buber insists that a "living monotheism" requires myth for its continued vitality, for its continuity with the life-giving spirit that brought it into being.[6] While he proclaims that "The Jews are a people that has never ceased to produce myth," he also suggests that the "stream of myth-bearing power" flowed unevenly, sometimes in one expression of Judaism and sometimes in another.[7] The task of discovering "myth" in Judaism means discovering that Jewish expression in which one of the various forms of mythic power becomes incarnate. This vision of a variety of Jewish mythic expressions means that Buber will not impose a predetermined formal definition of myth on the data that he studies. Unlike Goldziher, Buber did not bring to his research a preconceived list of "myths" which he expected to find in his Judaism. He was as open to a variety of myths as he was to a diversity of Judaisms. Where Goldziher sought to define myth and Judaism precisely, Buber sought to open the floodgates to churning waves of

Judaisms and mythologies. He hoped to show how creative diversity enhanced the vitality of various Judaisms in the past and might do so once again in the present.

Naturally many modern thinkers find that Buber did not succeed in his attempt. Even in his own time thinkers as sympathetic to Jewish folk material as M. Y. Berdichevsky objected to Buber's use of the term "myth" to describe such works as Hasidic tales.[8] Despite his insight and creativity, using Buber's views of both Judaism and myth in modern research raises many problems. Modern Jewish scholars need to combine Buber's sensitivity and flexibility with the precision that Goldziher achieved. A contemporary study of myth in Judaism must provide a more specifically delineated definition of myth that communicates with the research on myth being pursued in religious studies generally. It must also work with a definition of Judaism that corresponds to contemporary studies of the history, literature, and development of Jewish religion.

Contemporary Jewish thinkers have given priority to a discussion of "myth" in Judaism. The work of scholars like Buber and Goldzhier have legitimized the discussion of several possible ways "myth" might be considered an aspect of Jewish religiousness. The fact that many students of Jewish religion recognize the essential ambiguity of the subject they study combines with an openness to "myth," making current discussions lively and diverse. Such scholarly conversation has implications for both academics and non-academics. How should Jews regard "myth?" Can they define it in ways appropriate to monotheistic religion? Can they create a definition of "Judaism" in which myth plays a central role? Can they integrate Jewish religion into the models scholars use for religion in general?

The Scope, Plan, and Purpose of this Volume

This present study does not provide a definitive answer to any of these questions. It offers, instead, a panorama of options—diverse definitions of myth, divergent understandings of "Judaism," competing evaluations of the "mythic" project. The very title of the book bristles with such ambiguities. Is "myth" "seductive?" Is it a "danger" threatening "Judaism?" Is it a challenge or an opportunity? The idea of "myth" seduces students of Judaism in at least three ways. First, it may seduce scholars who, fascinated by the allure of "myth," use the term to cover a multitude of their interests. Secondly, it seduces practitioners of

Judaism from a purely rationalistic approach to their faith to pursue one of several non-rational avenues of religious life, and finally it may seduce those interested in a particular tradition such as Judaism to revise their definition of it. The various chapters in this book not only define Judaism differently from one another, but define the seductiveness of myth differently. That diversity might leave this book a tissue of tensions and contradictions. The challenge for readers is to discover their own unity. The next section offers one example of how a reader might construe the book. The combination of chapters is, itself, pluralistic. A particular chapter might prescribe a scholarly method, a practical Jewish response, a view of history. Taken together each prescription counterbalances the other. Yet a reader might search the chapters to find whether or not myth serves a positive function in Judaism or not.

Discovering that means choosing definitions of myth and Judaism, then deciding which of the data presented seems most persuasive. Assuming a reader seeks to evaluate the place of myth in Judaism, how does this volume develop? The volume opens by considering the meaning of myth in Jewish scholarship. Two camps seem to emerge from the discussion. Some scholars, represented by Howard Schwartz, take a positive approach to Jewish mysticism, emphasizing its value and importance not only as a presence in the data but as a beneficent one. Others, like Joel Gereboff, warn against its power to distort meaning and actuality. A third group, represented here by S. Daniel Breslauer, suggests that the recognition of myth requires a rethinking of usual categories for understanding religion.

Howard Schwartz, who in his work as poet, as anthologizer, reteller of tales, and creator of new tales has helped vitalize Jewish myth for modern Jews begins with a mystical story which, he argues, contains within it examples from every type of Jewish myth. He proceeds by sketching that typology in association with the narrative he recounts. After that typological survey he urges the importance and value of myth for modern Jews and invites modern Jews to reappropriate their forgotten heritage.

This section of reflection on the value of myth continues as S. Daniel Breslauer expands the meaning of the term to any narrative which conveys messages about eternal patterns of life and history. Understood that way, Breslauer finds such myth surfacing in the secular poetry of Saul Tchernichowsky. This discovery of secularized myth requires a rethinking of what scholars should consider as "religious" or indicative of the "sacred."

Whereas Breslauer expands the meaning of myth and thereby transforms what counts as "Jewish religion," Joel Gereboff warns against the power of myth to alter facticity. He declares that again and again scholars are misled by myth and follow it, rather than historical fact, to reconstruct the past. Thus he finds that the so-called "historical" presentations of Judaism devised for school children actually recount myth. This use of myth is insidious because it stunts the critical faculties of students and prevents them from learning the historical method of sifting evidence and drawing conclusions. Gereboff does allow for a positive view of myth from the "postmodern" or "deconstructive" method, but approves of it only because it leads both teachers and students to acknowledge the inadequacy of all "scientific" methods and to confess that all reconstructions of the past are partial, incomplete, and mythic. His warning serves as a fit conclusion to this section which has celebrated both myth and its power.

The following section recognizes that "myth" is a modern category. The essays seeking to define myth focus on Jewish thinkers in the modern period. The essays agree in rejecting an earlier stage of scholarship which declared Judaism bereft of myth. Given that Judaism does retain mythology, however it might be defined, then scholars must understand by Judaism a different entity than that considered by previous generations. Michael Berkowitz affirms myth, even and especially in the modern period. Jewish myth when actualized by Zionist ideology, he claims has a positive and salutary effect on Jewish life. His investigation of the Zionist myth of the "New Man" claims that it animated a positive approach to Jewish tourism as a new Jewish ritual This myth enabled the members of the Yishuv to create bridges between themselves and the Jews of the diaspora, thus acting as a benign influence on world Jewry. Such a view is paradigmatic for the virtues of any myth. Even in pre-modern Judaism, myth may have function in this positive way, creating rituals that improved Jewish life. Berkowitz, however, does not identify the mythic Judaism he describes with any abstracted "Judaism."

Steven Wasserstrom goes beyond this to claim that any recognition of myth in Judaism requires a rethinking of the meaning of Jewish religion itself. Wasserstrom shows how an early attraction to myth arising from a fascination with Nietzsche led the disciples of Hermann Cohen toward mythic Marxism (as in the Frankfort school), or theology (Franz Rosenzweig), or to a critical use of history, as in Gershom Scholem. Only Scholem who managed to critique myth from within through his historical approach succeeded in continuing to use myth as a viable category after the rise of Nazism. Wasserstrom, then, takes a cautious approach to myth in Judaism, showing how some ways of construing Jewishness and myth are useful while others are not.

David Norman Smith reviews the more consistently darkside of myth. Smith focuses primarily on that demonic side of myth when showing how Lev Pinsker recognized in "Judeo-Phobia," particularly as expressed by such Romantic thinkers as Ernst Renan, a dangerous entity that could place Jews in an untenable position. The new Judaism conceived of by myth may engender disaster rather than promise progress.

The next, and longest, section of this book looks chronologically at classical Jewish myths from the Bible through the Sabbatian movement that some scholars at least see as the beginning of modernity. The six chapters in this section offer case studies of myths in Jewish history. Ronald Hendel shows how a positive attention to different mythic frameworks can help distinguish one biblical textual tradition from another. He follows that distinction out through later Jewish traditions as well. He seems to imply that given the ubiquity of myth the important question is that of deciding which myth becomes dominant. A particular Jewish period, then, can be distinguished by its mythic world view. Hendel's work confirms the insights of previous scholars by reinforcing textual analysis with attention to literary expression.

Deborah Sills also has a positive view of myth, claiming that because scholars have ignored Philo's use of the Joseph story as a myth of the politician in his recounting of In Flaccum, they have been unable to explain his positive view of Joseph in his cycle of patriarchal allegories and his negative view of Joseph in another work. Discovering the mythic dimension of stories does not weaken their significance, but rather makes that importance more transparent. Sills shows that noting the unexpected presence of myth where illuminates valuable insights.

In contrast, Richard A. Freund studies the case of an absent myth. He reviews the data available for the "Jewish myth of Jesus," wondering if such a myth exists. He discovers that it is absent from all the earliest strands of rabbinic material, only insinuating itself in the medieval period. He suggests that Christians, not Jews, seek a Jewish myth of Jesus and warns against inviting it into the academic circle.

This warning, of course, does imply that the presence of myth is an important positive discovery. James R. Davila suggests that myths may be suppressed for good reason. His study of Melchizedek as King, Priest, or God shows why both the earliest pre-biblical material and later Gnostic references to this figure may have disturbed orthodox religionists. He finds that the Deuteronomistic editors of the Hebrew Bible self-consciously eliminated myth only to have it creep back into various heterodox movements represented by the Dead Sea Scroll material and some Gnostic texts. The former reintroduce the mythic themes eliminated from the Hebrew Bible and the latter transform the innocuous material of Hebrew 7:2-3 into a Gnostic myth. His paper suggests a condemnation of myth without explicitly expressing it.

Elliot Wolfson shows attentiveness to myth reshapes the way scholars must view a historical period. The masculinization of the feminine moon through transformations in medieval Jewish liturgy must cause scholars to reconsider their characterization of Jewish mysticism. As the community of pious men drew closer to each other, they created a myth that reinforced their social cohesion. Implicitly, Wolfson's positive portrait of this community of males which myth supported, paints a negative portrait of previous scholars whose blindness to the intricacies of myth led to over simplifications.

David Halperin, in this collection's concluding essay, offers an outspoken criticism of myth in Judaism that goes even further than the caution offered by Davila. He shows how the messianic claimant Sabbatai Zvi appropriated the coronation myth of Metatron "whose name is like his master's" for his political purposes. He also shows how Sabbatai's own experience with the changing fortunes of the Sultanate in Turkey shaped his self-image and receptivity to that myth. Halperin reveals the demonic potential within myth and its ability to undermine social stability. Jews caught in a trap of false integration seized on myth as the solution to their problems. Mythic solutions, Halperin warns, are illusory and cannot achieve their promised results.

Readers need not accept this interpretation of the organization of the book as their own. Much has been overlooked to provide a consistent point of departure. Clearly Breslauer and Schwartz do not share a single view of myth. Breslauer uses a more literary definition, while Schwartz focuses on narratives of the supernatural. Berkovitz and Gereboff demonstrate another alternative definition, one that makes myth closer to ideology than to a particular genre or literary form. Both Halperin and Wolfson focus on what has been called "Jewish mysticism." The "Judaism" each posits, however, looks different. Perhaps this influences how they view the place of myth. All these differences will, undoubtedly, influence how a reader reads each chapter and may make the question of whether myth is a positive or negative factor irrelevant. Nonetheless, readers may, however, find approaching each chapter with such a question in mind a useful organizing principleas they seek to place the diverse essays into a single framework. The chapters resist such a unification, but daring readers may find the challenge rewarding.

Notes

1. M. Olender, *The Languages of Paradise: Race, Religion, and Philology in the Nineteenth Century*. Trans. A. Goldhammer (Cambridge, MA: 1992), 134.
2. See S. D. Breslauer, *Martin Buber on Myth: An Introduction* (New York: 1990).
3. M. Buber, *On Judaism*. Ed. N. N. Glatzer (New York: 1967), 155.
4. Ibid., 39.
5. Ibid., 102.
6. See M. Buber, *Israel and the World: Essays in a Time of Crisis* (New York: 1948), 22, 119-120.
7. M. Buber, *The Legend of the Baal Shem*. Trans. M. Friedman) New York: 1955), 11.
8. See M. Buber, *Briefwechsel*, Band I: 1897-1918. Trans. J. Amir and G. Stern [Hebrew] (Jerusalem: 1982), 224-225. 237.

Part One:
What is Jewish Myth?

The Mythology of Judaism
Howard Schwartz

It is said that Rabbi Isaac Luria, known as the Ari, had great mystical powers. By looking at a man's forehead he could read the history of his soul. He could overhear the angels and knew the language of the birds. He could point out a stone in a wall and reveal whose soul was trapped in it. So too was he able to divine the future, and he always knew from Yom Kippur who, among his disciples, was destined to live or die. This knowledge he rarely disclosed, but once, when he learned there was a way to avert the decree, he made an exception. Summoning Rabbi Abraham Beruchim, he said: "Know that a heavenly voice has gone forth to announce that this will be your last year among us—unless you do what is necessary to abolish the decree."

"What must I do?" asked Rabbi Abraham.

"Know, then," said the Ari, "that your only hope is to go to the Western Wall in Jerusalem and there pray with all your heart before God. And if you are deemed worthy you will have a vision of the *Shekhinah*, the Divine Presence. That will mean that the decree has been averted and your name will be inscribed in the Book of Life after all."

Rabbi Abraham thanked the Ari with all his heart and left to prepare for the journey. First, he shut himself in his house for three days and nights, wearing sackcloth and ashes, and fasted the whole time. Then, although he could have gone by wagon or by donkey, he chose to walk to Jerusalem. And by the time Rabbi Abraham reached Jerusalem, he felt as if he were floating, as if his soul had ascended from his body. And when he reached the Wailing Wall, the last remnant of Solomon's Temple, Rabbi Abraham had a vision there. Out of the wall came an old woman, dressed in black, deep in mourning. And Rabbi Abraham suddenly realized how deep was the grief of the *Shekhinah* over the destruction of the Temple and the scattering of her children, Israel, all over the world. And he became possessed of a grief as deep as the ocean, far greater than he had ever known. It was the grief of a mother who has lost a child; the grief of Hannah, after losing her seven sons; the grief of the Bride over the suffering of her children scattered to every corner of the earth.

At that moment Rabbi Abraham fell to the ground in a faint, and he had a vision. In the vision he saw the *Shekhinah* once more, but this time he saw her dressed in a robe woven out of light, more magnificent than the setting sun, and her joyful countenance was revealed. Waves of light arose from her face, an aura that seemed to reach out and surround him, as if he were cradled in the arms of the Sabbath Queen. "Do not grieve so, my son Abraham," she said. "Know that my exile will come to an end, and my inheritance will not go to waste. And for you, my son, there shall be a great many blessings." Just then Rabbi Abraham's soul returned to him from its journey on high. He awoke refreshed, as if he had shed years of grief, and he was filled with hope.

When Rabbi Abraham returned to Safed he was a new man, and when the Ari saw him, he said at once: "I can see that you have been found worthy to see the *Shekhinah*, and you can rest assured that you will live for another twenty-two years." So it was that Rabbi Abraham did live for another twenty-two years, years filled with abundance. And all who saw him recognized the aura that shone from his face, for the light of the Divine Presence was always reflected in his eyes.[1]

In just this one sixteenth-century tale, "A Vision at the Wailing Wall," we find a constellation of many of the primary Jewish myths, including those of the *Shekhinah*, of the Messiah, of the Holy Land, and of Yom Kippur. Further, this tale takes the form of a divine test, for unless Rabbi Abraham has a vision of the *Shekhinah*, that year will be his last. So too does it involve a quest, like many a myth or fairy tale in which the hero seeks to find a wise old woman or a lost princess or queen. At the same time it recounts a powerful mystical experience. But it is important to remember that this revelation takes place within the context of an extensive, fully developed mythical system.

Indeed, there is a profound mythical dimension in Judaism, which is beginning to be recognized. The earliest of these myths that we know of are found in the Bible, but it is likely that pre-biblical myths existed, drawn from Near Eastern mythology. This earlier mythology seems to have fueled the continuing evolution of Jewish myths as new ones arose to fill the void created by the loss of the old. These myths involve not only God, but also God's Bride, the *Shekhinah*, and like the Greek myths of Zeus and Hera, they sometimes converge and sometimes diverge, and often give birth to additional myths. So too are there other mythical figures, including that of the Messiah, along with angels, demons, spirits and fabulous creatures of the air and sea, such as the Ziz or Leviathan.

The sources for these myths include the Bible and the translations of the Bible; the Jewish apocryphal and pseudepigraphical works, especially the Hekhaloth texts describing heavenly journeys; the rabbinic texts of the Talmud and Midrash; the kabbalistic literature; medieval Jewish folklore, and hasidic texts. Some mythic material can also be found among the tales collected by Jewish ethnologists. It is the nature of this literature that its sources are widely scattered, but, once gathered, myths of remarkable coherence emerge.

The primary biblical myths are found in the stories of creation, of the Garden of Eden, the Tower of Babel, the sons of God and the daughters of men, the great Flood, the covenant with Abraham, the parting of the Red Sea, the Exodus and the Giving of the Torah. So too is there the vision of Ezekiel, which is the basis of one major branch of Jewish mysticism, *Ma'aseh Merkavah*, The Mysteries of the Chariot. (Creation is the basis of the other branch, *Ma'aseh Bereshit*, concerning the Mysteries of Creation.) And these are only the major biblical myths. There are others that grow out of key episodes such as the death of Enoch: *And Enoch walked with God, and he was not, for God took him* (Gen. 5:24); or Isaiah's vision of the Throne of God, which begins *I saw the Lord sitting upon a high and lofty throne and the train of His robe filled the Temple* (Isa. 6:1). Finally, the importance of the Song of Songs in the mystical tradition must not be overlooked. Rabbi Akiba's reading of this erotic love poem as an allegory of the love between God and Israel, where the male figure is identified as God and the female figure as Israel, transformed the Song of Songs into one of the most important mystical texts.

In some later texts the relationship between God and Israel is directly identified as a marriage. One of these is a hymn for Shavuoth written by Israel Najara that takes the form of a *ketubah*, or wedding contract, between God and Israel.[2] This liturgical poem, which is found in the Sephardic prayerbook for Shavuoth, is based on the verses *And I will betroth thee unto Me in lovingkindness, and in compassion. And I will betroth thee unto Me in faithfulness; and thou shalt know the Lord* (Hos. 2:21-22), and *I will make a new covenant with the house of Israel* (Jer. 31:31). The text of this *ketubah*, read on Shavuoth, describes the Giving of the Torah at Mount Sinai as the wedding between God and Israel, as follows:

> Friday, the sixth of *Sivan*, the day appointed by the Lord for the revelation of the Torah to His beloved people, the Invisible One came forth from Sinai. The Bridegroom, Ruler of rulers, Prince of princes, said unto the pious and virtuous maiden, Israel, who had won His favor above all others: "Many days wilt thou be Mine and I will be thy Redeemer. Be thou My mate according to the law of Moses and Israel, and I will honor, support and maintain thee, and be thy shelter and refuge in everlasting mercy. And I will set aside for thee the life-giving

Torah, by which thou and thy children will live in health and tranquil-
ity. This Covenant shall be valid and established forever and ever."
Thus an eternal Covenant, binding them forever, has been established
between them, and the Bridegroom and the bride have given their
oaths to carry it out. May the Bridegroom rejoice with the bride whom
he has taken as His lot, and may the bride rejoice with the Husband of
her youth.

Here the use of allegory is readily apparent, with God representing
the groom and Israel the bride. Although daring, the allegorical nature
of this text is never in doubt, for the personification of Israel is clearly a
metaphor. But other kabbalistic texts describing a union between God
and the *Shekhinah* are harder to dismiss as mere allegories, especially
those that attribute a mythic independence to the figure of the *Shekhinah*.
The figure/ground nature of these texts, where myth and allegory often
reverse roles, is apparent. So too is it intentional. For as long as the rabbis
were able to present mythic material that could also be understood in
allegorical terms, they were spared the danger of undermining Monotheism, the central pillar of Judaism. In this way Jewish mythology was
able to exist and even thrive, but within a monotheistic framework.

At this point it might be appropriate to define our use of "myth" in
terms of Jewish tradition. "Myths" refer to a people's stories about
origins, deities, ancestors, and heroes. This is precisely what the Torah
recounts for the Jewish people. Within a culture, myth also serves as the
divine charter, and this is certainly the case in Judaism, where the Torah
serves both as a chronicle and covenant. Furthermore, myth and ritual
are traditionally linked in an integral and mutual fashion, and this is also
true in Judaism, where they are inextricably bound. All of these primary
aspects of mythology find expression in Jewish tradition. So too have
individual myths exercised great power over Jewish life. Even to this
day Jews relive the Exodus at Passover and receive the Torah anew on
Shavuoth. Nor, in some Jewish circles, has the longing for the Messiah
subsided.

There are two primary objections to the use of the term "mythology"
in relationship to Judaism. The first is that the term suggests a constellation of gods rather than a single, all-encompassing, omnipotent God.
From the perspective of Jewish theology, where the central principle is
Monotheism, it seems impossible for there to be a Jewish mythology.
However, just as supernatural practices, such as using divination or
consulting a soothsayer, were commonly performed despite the biblical
injunction against them, so an extensive Jewish mythology evolved,

especially in mystical circles, where it was believed possible to preserve a monotheistic perspective while simultaneously employing a mythological one. Here it is understood that all mythological figures, especially the *Shekhinah*, were ultimately aspects of the Godhead, despite their apparent mythological independence. Indeed, it sometimes seems as if all of Jewish myth (and perhaps all of existence) was the epic fantasy of one divine being, or a kind of divine illusion, similar to the Hindu concept of *maya*. For what sometimes appears to have mythic independence can also be understood as an emanation of the Godhead. Here the divine emanations take the form of the Ten *Sefirot*, as symbolized by the kabbalistic Tree of Life. But the *Sefirot* also serve as an antidote to mythology, as they are entirely conveyed through allegory and symbolism, and may have been created to contain the unbridled mythic impulse released in Jewish mysticism, as well as to define its underlying archetypal structure. Certainly, this system of divine emanations is as complex and comprehensive as that of the Jungian theory of archetypes. And while the essence of myth is archetype, it is much harder, if not impossible, to mythologize a system as abstract as the Sefirot. Yet underlying these abstractions are the living forces of myth.

The second objection to the use of "mythology" in terms of Jewish tradition is that it implies that the beliefs under consideration are not true. Even the mere identification of a culture's beliefs as mythological indicates that they are being viewed from a distance, rather than from the perspective of a believer. That is why there has been such great reluctance to identify any of the biblical narratives as myths, or to bring the tools of mythological inquiry to bear on Judaism or Christianity. While it is true that the study of these religions from a mythological perspective does imply the distance of critical inquiry, it does not mean that the traditions being examined are therefore false. Mythological studies are now commonly linked with psychological ones, and scholars such as C. G. Jung, Joseph Campbell, and Erich Neumann have demonstrated how it is possible to recognize psychological truths underlying mythic traditions. Myth itself is the collective projection of a people. In the case of Judaism, many generations of rabbis received and transmitted the sacred myths and traditions, sometimes radically transforming them, as well as imparting their own human and mythic imprint.

The body of these myths, multiplied over the generations, is substantial. The heavenly pantheon is as extensive as that of the Greeks, but with a host of angels playing a role equivalent to the Greek gods. Thus, instead of Poseidon, there is the angel Rahab, who likewise rules the sea.

Or just as Hermes is the divine messenger, so this role in Jewish mythology is played by the angel Raziel, among others. Yet, despite strong parallels with other mythic systems, Jewish mythology is in many ways unique. The primary difference is that instead of consisting of a constellation of many gods, it is dominated by the presence of an all-powerful God who, seated on a throne in Paradise, has ultimate control over all events in heaven as well as on earth. That being said, God often seems to delegate this power to other figures, such as the angel Metatron, who was once Enoch, and is said to be the heavenly scribe, the attendant of the Throne of Glory, the prince of the treasuries of heaven, the ruler and judge of all the hosts of angels, and the executor of the Divine decrees on earth. Of course, the more God's power is delegated in this fashion, the greater the mythic pantheon.

Over time, as the number of supernatural figures in this pantheon increased and interacted, an abundance of mythological narratives emerged. These stories describe events such as the transformation of Enoch into the angel Metatron, the Giving of the Torah, the separation of God's Bride from her Spouse, the chain of events that has so far prevented the coming of the Messiah, and the attempts of Satan to gain inroads in the world of men. They also map out the realms of heaven and hell in great detail. By a process of accretion, these mythic realms were embellished and further defined, giving birth to additional narratives. In this way Jewish mythology has evolved into an extensive, inter-con-nected—and often contradictory—mythic tradition.

At the heart of Judaism there is one universal, all-consuming myth, which contains within it all the other major myths. This is the myth of God's covenant with Israel. Since this one mega-myth serves as a framework for all the others, and since it finds its basis in Monotheism, Judaism can be said to have a monotheistic mythology. Such a conception best describes Jewish myth, which is its own unique kind of mythology. Its most distinctive characteristic is that all mythical divine figures can ultimately be viewed as an emanation of the Godhead, and thus can be contained within a monotheistic structure.

I have identified what I perceive to be the ten major myths contained within the framework of the fundamental myth of God's convenant with Israel. All of these find their source and point of reference in this fundamental myth, but each has evolved into a fully developed mythic constellation. These are: 1) Myths of God and the Bride of God, 2) Myths of Creation, 3) Myths of Heaven, 4) Myths of Hell, 5) Myths of the Holy

Book, 6) Myths of the Holy Time, 7) Myths of the Holy People, 8) Myths of the Holy Land, 9) Myths of Exile, and 10) Myths of the Messiah.

These ten myths contain at least four hundred submyths that are found in widely scattered sources. These submyths can be viewed independently, or, when taken as a whole, they define the overall pattern of the larger myth. In almost every case there is evidence of mythic evolution, with fragmentary myths of biblical or talmudic origin transformed into far more extensive mythic narratives, especially in the kabbalistic era, which represents the culmination of this process.

By way of example, the category of Myths of Creation includes myths of prior worlds, of how God consulted the Torah to create the world, of the seven days of creation, the rabbinic notion of the primordial light created on the first day, when God said "Let there be light" and other myths of the sun and moon and stars, as well as myths of cosmology and cosmogony, myths of sacred waters, including the upper waters and lower waters, the waters of eternal life, and the kingdom of the deep, and the late Lurianic myths of Adam Kadmon and of the Shattering of the Vessels and the Gathering of the Sparks. All of these creation myths find their origin in the account of creation in Genesis and embellish some aspect of it.

One of the most remarkable aspects of Jewish mythology is that it continued to flourish long past the periods in which it took its final form in other cultures. In most cultures the development of myth occurs during an early period, long before being written down, and once committed to writing, the mythic narrative generally remains fixed. But Jewish tradition does not follow this pattern. One reason for this is the existence of the Oral Law, which encouraged this kind of mythic embellishment. Of all the factors that permit the mythic impulse in Judaism to express itself, this is the most important. Judaism is unique in that it recognizes both a written and an oral tradition. The Written Law is, of course, the Torah, and the Oral Law is the oral commentary linked to it. As one midrash puts it, God gave the Torah to Moses during the day, and at night He explained it to him.[3] And whenever a question arises as to the authority of a statement out of the Oral Law, it is always attributed to Moses at Mount Sinai.

Drawing on this extensive oral tradition, which reached back for a thousand years, the rabbis proceeded to reimagine the Bible, and in the process substantially developed its mythic elements. This makes it possible to witness the actual evolution of Jewish myths. Early myths, primarily those found in the Bible, were embellished in the oral tradition and later recorded in the rabbinic texts. These rabbinic myths were themselves transformed in the kabbalistic and hasidic periods. The most fertile period of Jewish myth took place between the thirteenth and seventeenth centuries. This is a remarkably late period in human history for such extensive mythic development. It is then that the major myths of the nature of God and of His Bride took form, along with further myths of creation and of the Messiah. But in every case these kabbalistic myths are rooted in earlier sources and undergo a process of evolution until they achieve full expression. It is important to note that the mythic transformation that takes place between the early periods of Jewish myth and their later evolution is considerable, almost constituting a new set of myths based on the old ones.

While the varied periods of Jewish religion are characterized by their own predominant myths, there is a continuity among them that is reflected in the rabbinic axiom that "there is no earlier or later in the Torah."[4] Commenting on this statement, Rabbi Shlomo be-rabbi Yitzhak ha-Levi adds: "That is to say, every part of it is both first and last like a sphere...and where it ends, there it begins, for behold it is like a circle or a sphere."[5] This principle is certainly reflected in the midrashic method of reimagining the Bible, which draws on one episode, such as the childhood of Moses, to fill in a narrative gap in another, such as the missing childhood of Abraham. This results in a distinctly myth-making process, which contributes in no small part to the ongoing mythic evolution.

Because of the considerable differences between these various phases, it is difficult to speak of a single or definitive Jewish mythology. Yet it is also clear that the seeds of all the major myths are found in the earlier texts, where they are often the subject of a profound evolutionary process, a dialectic that alternates between the tendency to mythologize Judaism with an inclination to resist such mythological impulses.

Perhaps no Jewish myth undergoes as radical a transformation as does that of the *Shekhinah*. In its earliest usage in the Talmud, *Shekhinah* refers to God's Divine Presence, thus the presence or indwelling of God in this world. This presence was linked, in particular, to the sense of holiness experienced on the Sabbath. In time this term came to be identified with the feminine aspect of the Divinity. Myths emerge in the kabbalistic and Hasidic literature that portray the *Shekhinah* as the Bride of God and the Sabbath Queen, personifying her as an independent mythic figure. Indeed, there are several other mythic identities linked to the *Shekhinah*, who is sometimes also portrayed as a princess, a bride, an old woman in mourning, a dove, a lily, a rose, a hind, a jewel, a well, and the moon. These multiple facets of the *Shekhinah* suggest that as a mythic figure, the *Shekhinah* has absorbed many types of feminine roles that are incarnated as several different goddesses in other traditions.

One other subtle identity of the *Shekhinah* is suggested in the talmudic tradition of every Jew receiving a *neshamah yeterah*, a second soul, on the Sabbath: "Rabbi Shimon ben Lakish said: 'On the eve of the Sabbath the Holy One, blessed be He, gives man an extra soul, and at the close of the Sabbath He withdraws it from him'."[6] This extra soul is believed to depart after *Havdalah*, the ritual of separation performed at the end of the Sabbath. This second soul functions as a kind of *ibur*, literally "an impregnation," which is the spirit of a holy figure that fuses with the soul of a living person, bringing greater faith and wisdom. But in this case it is a divine soul that fuses with the souls of Jews on the Sabbath. It is not difficult to identify this second soul with the presence of the *Shekhinah*, the Divine Presence, who is also the Sabbath Queen. Certainly, the arrival and departure of the Sabbath Queen and that of this mysterious second soul are simultaneous. Identifying the second soul with the *Shekhinah* is a way of acknowledging the sacredness of the Sabbath both from within and without.

So too is a cycle of myths linked to the *Shekhinah*. Some of these portray the unity of God and His Bride, while others concern their separation. The key myth, as noted, is that of the Exile of the *Shekhinah*, for at the time the Bride goes into exile, the mythic figure of the *Shekhinah* becomes largely independent of the Divinity and takes on a separate mythic identity. This myth has its origin in the Talmud, in the passage "Come and see how beloved the children of Israel are to the Holy One, blessed be He. For wherever they are exiled the *Shekhinah* is with them....and when they are redeemed in the future the *Shekhinah* will be with them, as it is written *And the Lord, your God, will return with your captivity* (Deut. 30:3)."[7] One of the earliest midrashic references to the *Shekhinah's* own exile is found in the *Mekhilta*: "Wherever Israel went into exile, the *Shekhinah* was exiled with them. They were exiled to Egypt; the *Shekhinah* was with them. They were exiled to Babylon; the *Shekhinah* was with them."[8] Note that what was previously Israel's exile has now become the exile of the *Shekhinah* as well. It is in this kind of incremental fashion that the concept of the *Shekhinah* evolved into an independent mythic being.

As the concept of the *Shekhinah* further evolved from God's immanence in this world to the mythic feminine figure of the *Shekhinah*, the following myth appeared in the Zohar:

When the Temple was still standing, Israel would perform their rites, and bring offerings and sacrifices. And the *Shekhinah* rested upon them in the Temple, like a mother hovering over her children, and all faces were resplendent with light, so that there was blessing both above and below....When the Temple was destroyed the *Shekhinah* came and went up to all those places where she used to dwell at first, and she would weep for her home and for Israel, who had gone into exile, and for all the righteous and the pious ones who used to be there and had perished....At that time the Holy One, blessed be He, questioned the *Shekhinah*, and said to her "What ails you now, that you have gone up entirely to the roofs?"....And she said to Him: "My children are in exile, and the Temple is burnt, so why should I remain here?".... Now the Temple is destroyed and the *Shekhinah* is with Israel in exile....and there is no joy to be found, above or below.[9]

While many of the myths promulgated in the Zohar are couched in allegorical terms, this passage is clearly mythological in its intent. The dialogue unmistakably resembles that between a husband and wife at odds. The tension between them is apparent in the words of the Holy One, "What ails you now?" and in the Bride's reply: "My children are in exile, and the Temple is burnt, so why should I remain here?" Above all, it is apparent that this confrontation takes place between two independently mythic figures.

Note that the myth of the Exile of the *Shekhinah* is a two-part myth. In the first stage the Bride of God goes into exile at the time of the destruction of the Temple, while in the second stage the *Shekhinah*, identified as the *Sefirah Malkhut*, is reunited with the male aspect of God, identified by *Sefirah Tiferet*. This reunion, which is described in the Zohar as a marriage,[10] is brought about through the activities of Israel in fulfilling requirements of the *mitzvot*, and through the intensity, or *kavvanah*, of prayers. When this reunification becomes permanent, the exile of the *Shekhinah* will come to an end. This development is linked to the coming of the Messiah, in that one of the consequences of the messianic era is that the Temple in Jerusalem, which was the *Shekhinah's* home in this world, will be rebuilt. Since the *Shekhinah* went into exile because of its destruction, the rebuilding of the Temple would surely represent the end of her exile. In this way the myths of the *Shekhinah* and the Messiah became linked, as is indicated in the tale of "A Vision at the Wailing Wall." The supernatural figure that Rabbi Abraham encounters there is clearly in exile. This is indicated by her being portrayed as an old woman dressed in black—she is mourning by the *Kotel*, the last remnant of the Temple in Jerusalem that was once her home. And even when the *Shekhinah* reveals her joyous aspect as a bride, she is still in exile, and her assurances to Rabbi Abraham that it will come to an end are a clear reference to the messianic era, when, it is said, the Temple will be rebuilt.

This tale derives from the city of Safed in the sixteenth century, and is one of a cycle of tales about the Ari. The two appearances of the *Shekhinah* that Rabbi Abraham envisions at the Wall, that of the old woman in mourning and of the bride in white, represent the two primary aspects of her nature, one grieving over the destruction of the Temple and the exile of Israel, and other representing the ecstatic feminine, as symbolized by a celestial bride. Indeed, these multiple faces suggest that the figure of the *Shekhinah* contains within it a host of other goddess figures, all of which have been subsumed in one mythic figure.

The entire framework of this tale is based on rituals. It begins with Yom Kippur, the most solemn holy day, when God decides if a person will live or die during the next year. Rabbi Abraham precedes his quest to Jerusalem with three days of fasting, wearing sackcloth and ashes. And the entire quest to the *Kotel* is itself an extended ritual, one called upon for him to perform by the Ari.[11]

According to the Walter F. Otto, "Myth demands ritual."[12] This is the central premise of the Myth and Ritual school of mythological studies, which probably has more advocates than any other. Certainly, the close relationship between Jewish myth and ritual more than fulfills the requirements of this approach, and therefore it can be said that Jewish myth possesses both of the primary elements of a mythic system: myth and ritual.

As in other traditions, Jewish myth and ritual reaffirm and validate each other, for as long as they remain linked, the ritual keeps the myth alive. But as soon as the ritual falls into disuse, the myth loses its primary purposes: linking the past and the present through the acting out of the ritual. Without the ritual, the myth is no more than a story, albeit a powerful and compelling one. For observant Jews, the stories that accompany Jewish rituals have retained the status of absolute truth, which is how a myth appears in the eyes of a believer. Indeed, the key test in our time for whether one holds Orthodox views is whether one believes that God dictated the Torah to Moses at Mount Sinai. For without this belief, the seal of truth that binds the Torah and makes every detail fraught with infinite meaning would be called into question. Thus, for believers, the ultimate truth of the Torah is self-evident and beyond any doubt. This is the essential condition for a mythic system to flourish. However, even for those in our time for whom Jewish myth no longer represents the primary way of viewing the universe, the myths themselves retain their inherent power. Like all myths they are not arbitrary creations, but projections from the deepest levels of the self. From this perspective, the myths can be read as psychic maps, archetypes of the collective Jewish unconscious.

At the same time, much of the evolution of Jewish mythology seems to have had a distinctly conscious element. So too does it diverge from the anonymous nature of most mythology in that it is possible to pinpoint the authors of mythic transformation, especially Moshe de Leon, the primary author of the Zohar, and the Ari, who was not only a great rabbi, as recounted in the opening tale, but a great myth-maker as well.

Drawing on the form and method of rabbinic commentary found in the midrashim, Moshe de Leon created a mystical commentary on the Torah that became its central and most sacred text. It is in the Zohar that the key myths about the Exile of the *Shekhinah* emerge, along with many others. The mythic daring found in this text was considered so extreme that it was forbidden to study the Zohar or other kabbalistic texts unless one was forty years old and was married. These barriers were erected to guard against the mythological impact of the Zohar and other mystical texts, and to limit access to those best suited to interpret them allegorically. The great fear underlying these restrictions is that the text would be misread in a way that would undermine belief in the principle of Monotheism. At the same time, for the select few who gained entrance to these mystical texts, there was the opportunity to achieve a profound level of mystical knowledge and spiritual attainment.

Among those mystics for whom the Zohar became a text as sacred as the Torah was the Ari. He was said to have purchased a manuscript of the Zohar from a wanderer, and this event was the turning point in his life. Not only did the Ari devote the rest of his brief life to mystical contemplation and study, but he modeled himself and his disciples on the portrayal of Rabbi Shimon bar Yohai, the hero of the Zohar, and his circle. This pattern of master and disciples became, in turn, the model for the Baal Shem Tov and subsequent Hasidic rabbis and their Hasidim.

It was the genius of the Ari to have such a deep understanding of Judaism that he was able to create the myth of the Shattering of the Vessels, the last major myth to enter Jewish tradition. This is the most cosmological of the Jewish creation myths. Its central teachings concern the mysteries of creation: How God had to contract Himself in order to make space for the creation of the world, in a process known as *Simsum*. How God then sent forth vessels of primordial light that somehow split apart, scattering the sparks of holy light all over the world, but especially in the Holy Land. And how gathering these sparks can restore the broken vessels, returning the world to its primordial condition.

This myth of the Ari is essentially an original myth drawn from Gnostic themes, yet at the same time it is a remarkable commentary on *Ma'aseh Bereshit*, has discernible links to the system of the *Sefirot*, and also links two other primary Jewish myths, those of the creation and of the Messiah. For the broken vessels initiated the cosmic Fall, and the restoration of the vessels will initiate a messianic era that will resurrect the dead, rebuild the Temple in Jerusalem, and restore the world to its primordial state. Thus this combined myth serves as a framework for all of Jewish history.

The deepest mystery of all among the students of the Ari concerns the true reason for the Shattering of the Vessels. The most important consequences of it, however, are apparent: it shifts the responsibility for the fallen state of existence from man to God, and it also sets the stage for the second phase of the myth, that of the Gathering the Sparks. Here the scattered sparks are sought out and gathered in the belief that when enough have been raised up, the broken vessels will be restored and the world returned to its prelapsarian state. The Ari identified this gathering of the sparks with fulfilling the *mitzvot*, the divine commandments, which endowed these ritual requirements with a divine purpose. This myth also gives a positive explanation to the problem of Jewish exile, especially after the expulsion of the Jews from Spain in 1492. While there is currently a scholarly debate about the extent of the impact of the expulsion in the mystical theories of the Ari, this event, which took place only thirty years before his birth, cannot be ignored. For the myth of the Ari proposes that there was a divine purpose behind the exiles that have haunted Jewish history, and that the Jews are the chosen people in the sense that they were created to search for and raise up the scattered sparks.

This myth, in its apparent simplicity, conveyed kabbalistic principles in a way that could be readily understood. As a result, it was taken up by the Jewish community at large, breaking the grip on the mystical tradition that had been the domain of a select circle of rabbis since ancient times. This myth spoke to the people, turning the curse of exile into a blessing. It gave meaning to their wandering in the Diaspora, for the scattered sparks had to be found and raised up wherever they were hidden. And it held out hope for a messianic era that could be brought closer by acts of human piety.

The most essential feature of the Ari's myth is its two-part nature. Here it is understood from the first that the complete myth requires both parts; it is not possible to consider one without the other. The first part of this cosmological myth is destructive, the second part creative. The archetypal pattern is that of shattering and restoration. But instead of shifting the blame for the Fall to Adam and Eve, here it can be directly linked to God, Who, after all, is the ultimate creator and therefore responsible for any flaws in creation.

Note the remarkable parallels between the Ari's creation myth and that of the Exile of the *Shekhinah*. Both are two-part; both involve separation and reunion, exile and return; both attribute to the prayers of Israel the power to accomplish the necessary *tikkun* or repair. Indeed, it is possible to view the myth of the Ari as a mystical restatement of the Exile of the *Shekhinah*.

It should also be noted that the myth of the *Shekhinah* finds its ritual expression in the ceremony known as *Kabbalat Shabbat*, which was also created by the Ari. In this ritual the Ari would lead his disciples out of Safed to greet the *Shekhinah* at the beginning of the Sabbath. The Ari found the basis for this ritual in the Talmud, where it is recounted that Rabbi Hanina would put on his robes and stand at sunset on the eve of the Sabbath and say, "Come, let us go out to greet the Sabbath Queen."[13] Of course, by the time the Ari created this ritual, the concept of the Sabbath Queen had evolved into an independent mythic figure, and the ritual itself can be recognized as a kind of goddess worship, but, paradoxically, within a monotheistic structure.

Thus the kabbalists did as the rabbis had before them: they received one myth and transformed it into another, which more closely mirrored their view of the world. For them this meant resurrecting the lost goddess, but doing so in a context that appeared to preserve the monotheistic basis of Judaism. So it is that the myths about God, the Bride of God, and the Messiah converge, diverge, and ultimately come together in the messianic vision of the End of Days. For when all of the holy sparks have been liberated, the Messiah will come, the Temple will be restored, and God's Bride will come out of exile, restoring the Godhead to wholeness. In this convergence we can finally see in perspective the ultimate Jewish myth, that of the long-standing covenant between God and Israel, in all its mythic permutations.

Notes

1. *Shivei ha-Ari*. Ed. Shlomo Meinsterl (Jerusalem: 1905). Variants are also found in *Kav ha-Yashar* by Tsvi Hirsh Kaidanover (Livorno: 1837, chap. 92), and in *Ma'assiyot Noraim ve-Niflaim* (Cracow: 1896). For an oral variant see Israel Folktale Archives (IFA) 2632.
2. I. Najara, "Ketubah Shavuoth" in *Sephardi Mahzor*, the Sephardic prayer book for Shavuoth. (Sixteenth century.)
3. *Pirkei de-Rabbi Eliezer* 46: "Rabbi Joshua ben Korchah said: 'Forty days was Moses on the mountain, reading the Written Law by day, and studying the Oral Law by night.'"
4. B. Pesachim 6b and Sifre Numbers, Sec. 64.
5. S. b. Y. HaLevi, *Divre Shlomo*. (Venice: 1596), 68b.
6. B. Betza 16a. It is interesting to note that in the Laws of Shabbat in *Mishneh Torah*, Maimonides changed this passage to read "Comes, let us go out to greet the Sabbath King." *Mishneh Torah*, chap. 30.
7. B. Meg. 29a.
8. *Mekhilta de-Rabbi Ishmael*. Ed. Horovitz. (Frankfort: 1931), Massekhta de-Pisha 14:51-52.
9. Zohar I: 202b-203a.
10. Zohar II: 133b-134a.
11. Marriage is forbidden on the Sabbath because it involves acts, such as the signing of the *ketubbah*, that are violations of Sabbath and Festival laws. See Maimonides, *Mishneh Torah*, Hilkhot Ishut 10:14, Hilkhot Yom Tov 7:16.
12. W. F. Otto, *Die Gestalt und das Sein; Abbandlungen uber den Mythos und seine Bedeutung fur die Menschheit*. (Duseldorf-Koln: 1955), 73-78.
13. B. Shab. 119a. Another early echo of the ritual of *Kabbalat Shabbat* is also found here, where it is said that Rabbi Yannai attired himself on the eve of the Sabbath and said, "Come, O bride, come, O bride."

Poetry, Allegory, and Myth in Saul Tschernichowsky

S. Daniel Breslauer

Poetry, Allegory, and Myth

Some investigators might want to confine a study of Jewish myth to pre-modern periods of Jewish history. Secularization and rationalism may seem to preclude the presence of myth in modern Jewish writing. An exclusion of the modern period, however, overlooks some of the most striking evidence for Jewish use of myth, that found in modern Jewish poetry. Taking that poetry as a point of departure leads to a definition of myth, a delineation of its dimensions and the discussion of myth in Judaism, and finally to a better comprehension of the complexity of the modern Jewish poet. Before looking at the mythic work of one of the major modern Jewish poets, this study considers the general shape of myth in relationship to both allegory and history. It reviews the often ambivalent approach taken by students of Judaism, and only then decodes a complex poem by the celebrated Hebrew poet Shaul Tchernichowsky.

When understood as allegory, Jewish myth influences the content and images found in modern Jewish poetry. Robert Alter has commented on its presence throughout modern Jewish poetry. He suggests that "One may speculate whether allegorizing is a particularly Jewish mode of thinking, perhaps an overdrawn legacy from the Middle Ages."[1] His recognition that in even the most personal poems a modern Hebrew writer may insert nationalistic elements certainly applies to many contemporary texts. The identification of myth with allegory, however, needs refinement since allegory, itself, has many meanings.[2] David Dawson provides one useful definition. For him allegory must always take the form of a narrative, of a story. It represents an extended metaphor that moves beyond a simple symbol or imate into a developed narration.[3] Allegory, then, is recognized by its extended form, its narrative shape.

While this emphasis does limit the category of allegory formally, attention to content will distinguish between two types of allegorical narratives. One type of narrative points beyond itself to specific historical conditions. The extended metaphor of the story translates into facts about the social, political, and experiential world in which the author lives. A second type of narrative suggests what Friedreich Nietzsche calls "the myth of the eternal recurrence of the same." This myth, which he sees as fundamental to his philosophy, emphasizes the recurrent patterns in human life. What is happening now has already occurred and will reoccur incessantly. The human being is trapped in an endless repetition of the same events.[4] Nietzsche's "myth of the Eternal Return" is actually a distinctive type of allegory. In contrast to historical allegories, a second type of extended narrative metaphor emphasizes the eternal and unchanging. Raymond Scheindlin, for example, shows how medieval Jewish authors discovered in the biblical Song of Songs a variety of allegorical models.[5] Sometimes allegory describes the correspondence between a text and some specific historical experience. This experience may be the psychological character of the poet; it can also be a specific historical event or a putatively supernatural one such as the encounter between the people of Israel and God at the time of revelation. Sometimes, by contrast, allegory points beyond any historical or specific referent to enduring patterns within reality. In the case of the Song of Songs this might be the parallel between the cosmic soul and the individual soul (the macrocosm and the microcosm) or the pattern of cosmic love that, in a Neo-Platonic philosophy, acts as the motive force for existence itself. One striking example of the difference between these two forms of allegory appears in relationship to the idea of the messiah. One paradigm describes the messiah as a sleeping king, waiting for the historic moment of awakening. The messianic appearance will occur as one specific act, a deed taking place within the framework of historical change. A second paradigm sees the messiah as a leperous beggar whose coming depends on how Jews act. Any moment can be the messianic time. Bringing the messianic time depends on a process of compassionate living rather than on any specific historical act. While in the first case one must wait for the specific messianic event, in the second all eternity consists of messianic events.

These different types of allegory require different terms. Walter Benjamin suggests such a vocabulary distinction. He regards as allegory only those interpretations that focus on the historical, the specific, the individual. Those interpretations that evoke the eternal, the ever recurrent, and the enduring he calls myth. With this in mind, he recommends allegory as a means of retaining a tie to the concrete and factual. For him allegory was an antidote to myth because it refused to allow mythic generalization to swallow the specific and particular historical expression. It can be considered "the mind's response" to a world bereft of meaning, a world of things deprived of significance. It infuses those things with historical purpose, with specific content.[6] A medieval Hebrew poet, for example, would write of the desert, a garden, or sexual desire as allegories for the poet's personal experience. Even a poet's battles and political encounters often took on an allegorical form. Intentional exaggeration and elaboration drew attention to the actual (or assumed) traits of the poem's author or hero.

Myth, on the other hand, points beyond the specific facts of history. It uses images to evoke eternal patterns, recurring motifs animating every historical period. Allegorical poetry draws attention to the historical facts that differentiate one age from another, one person from other people. Mythic poetry reveals the unchanging reality that lies behind apparent evolution; it uncovers the hidden identity that unites all people as part of a single organism. Students of myth recognize this characteristic as an important trait imputed to certain stories in a particular context. Claude Levi-Strauss, for example, claims that what makes myths "operational" is that they present themselves as "timeless," as articulating a pattern equally appropriate for the past, present, and future.[7] The point, of course, is not that myths are in fact unbounded by their contexts; since Levi-Strauss sees them as the elements of a greater system, their meaning is contingent on the entire "language" in which they appear. Nevertheless, myths have their unique significance only when perceived as eternally valid.[8]

Understood as allegory, poetry complements and expresses history. Understood as myth, poetry challenges history and defies it. Greek philosophers perceived the tension between historical writing and poetry conceived as myth. They recognized in poetry a significant challenge to their rational perspective. Plato devoted attention to the powers and limitations of poets when constructing his putatively ideal republic (*The Republic* 337a-383c, 393c-395b). Plato's rendering suggests that the likely tales spun by poets compete with those of the philosopher and must be treated as dangerous rivals. Precisely because he knows the power of poets, Plato warns against giving them too free a license. In contrast, Aristotle looks more favorably on poets. He notes the inevitable conflict between poetry, which concerns hypothetical things that might have been or might be in the future, with history, which concerns itself to a faithful description of what has been. Unlike Plato, he concludes that poetry is therefore both more philsophical and more valuable than history. The poet moves from the plane of specific events to the realm of universals (*The Poetics* 1454a37-b14).

European thinkers inherited an awareness of the tension between poetry and history from this Greek tradition. For them, it took the form of a contrast between history and myth. Transferring the contrast between allegory and myth into a conflict between history and religion highlights a problematic dichotomy within modern consciousness. Some moderns exalt rationality and science. For them the rejection of myth represents a valuable advance from primitive fantasy. Those who see myth as "false science" hail the advent of history as the dawn of a new age. In opposition to those who celebrate history's vanquishing of myth, other scholars launch a defense of myth.[9] These theorists lament the loss of myth in modernity. They claim that without myth humanity has lost an essential link to the holy and the sacred. From this perspective to "demythologize" is to "desacralize," to transform the holy and the religious into the secular.[10]

Myth, History, and Judaism

The same tension between supporters of myth and those celebrating its demise arises in discussion of Judaism. Martin Buber, for example, encountered opposition, especially from biblical scholars such as Yekezkiel Kaufmann, when he exalted the myths of Judaism.[11] Buber worked to renew Judaism by reconnecting it with its mythic elements. He rooted his renewal in a study of the Hebrew Bible and an affirmation of its mythic dimensions. A furious objection to Buber's contentions could only be expected. Indeed, biblical scholarship has often glorified the "advance" from myth to history demonstrated by the Hebrew Bible. According to this perspective, myth presumes an unchanging "eternal return" of the same. Myth is characterized, in this view, as imagining divinites as unchanging forces working inexorably throughout time. The present, according to the theory attributed to myth, recapitulates the past in an endless cycle. The theory then contrasts biblical religion to this myth of eternal recurrence. The Bible, this theory claims, focuses on history and progress. Biblical narrative, on this account, traces a series of unique events. The story the Bible tells, as interpreted by these critics, begins with a nascent humanity and works steadily upward following the evolution of human beings and human communities. Every new event, according to the biblical view imagined by these scholars, propels the divine plan forward toward a utopian conclusion. Thus G. Ernest Wright, a theologian and archeologist, wrote of Israel against its environment, unique because of its understanding of history, championing progress, a rational and non-mythic view of reality. History, he declares, suddenly appears in Israel against a background of mythopoetic thinking. He sees it revolutionizing human thought.[12]

   More recently Jonathan Z. Smith has rejected the dichotomy between history and myth that so dominated biblical theology. He considers the distinction tendentious, based on preconceived religious beliefs, and unhelpful in understanding the religious dynamics involved. He calls the theological argument "apologetic" and "uninteresting." Instead he seeks an understanding of myth in its historical setting and seeks to show "the utility of concern for such context in the interpretation of texts by historians of religion."[13] Such an approach does seem more promising than that of imposing a static dichotomy on any narrative: either the narrative evokes an eternally recurrent pattern or it moves in linear progression to an ideal conclusion. In Smith's reading, a mythic story takes on meaning from its historical context. By decoding the story within that context the scholar grasps the meaning of the myth in its particularity. Myths need have no single meaning. Placed within different contexts the same stories may convey different messages. In the same way a set of diverse stories from a single historical context may reveal a single meaning. The study of myth has a double function: from a comparative perspective it enables a scholar to note the way a single motif functions in distinctive systems. Such study also provides insight into the distinctiveness of a single context.

Myth in Jewish Scholarship

   Several disciplines in Jewish studies have investigated the meaning of myth: students of the Hebrew Bible debate whether and to what extent the Bible contains myth; scholars of modern Jewish thought examine the impact of myth on social, political, and literary movements in modernity. By far the greatest attention to the idea of myth, however, appears in studies of Jewish mysticism, of the *Kabbalah*. One of the most straightforward definitions of myth comes from Yehuda Liebes. He provides a narrow, but precise, way of understanding myth. Myth, he claims, consists of "a sacred story about the gods expressing that which the abstract word, or Logos, cannot express."[14] This definition emphasizes the narrative form of myth.

Gershom Scholem also implies that myth takes the shape of a narrative, but adds that such narrative exposes eternal, recurring patterns. He suggests that even the main event of Jewish history—the Exodus of the Jews from Egypt and their liberation into freedom and the promised land—appears to the mystics as a recurrent event: "The historical aspects of religion," he remarks, "have a meaning for the mystic chiefly as symbols of acts which he conceives as being divorced from time, or constantly repeated in the soul of everyman." The mystic, Scholem notes, transforms the Exodus from an external event that has "come to pass once only and in one place" into "an event which takes place in ourselves." This provides a mythic rather than historical meaning to the story. As such, Scholem claims, the Exodus can "cease to be an object of learning and acquire the dignity of immediate religious experience."[15]

Scholem goes beyond defining the distinctive form of myth. He also suggests its function: that of providing an alternative to rational monotheism. He identifies mysticism with "a definite stage in the development of religion," the stage in which a formerly demythologized tradition reintegrates the mythical into its substance.[16] He associates this occurrence with the resolution of the problem of over intellectualization. When a religious tradition eliminates myth, he thinks, it runs the risk of losing contact with the emotional, immediate, and spontaneous aspects of life.

Scholem tends to locate the anti-mythic aspects of Judaism with rabbinic rather than biblical religion.[17] Despite narratives in which God plays some role, the rabbinic perspective, Scholem claims, emphasizes divine transcendence. Human beings come into relationship with the divine only through the mediation of Torah, only by means of revelation. He asserts that rabbinic and philosophical Jewish writings saw God as non-mythological, unable to be the subject of stories. As such, Scholem approvingly notes, a medieval mystic declared that the God of the philosophers who is "an absolute Being and therefore by His very nature incapable of becoming the subject of a revelation to others" cannot be the God intended in the "canonical writings of the Bible and in the rabbinical tradition."[18] The God of monotheism cannot be mythic; the stories in Jewish texts are mythic. The mystics, Scholem claims, renew the plausibility of myth—making stories about the divine, not just about the Torah and its scholars—essential theolgical material for Jewish religion. Mysticism, by reintegrating myth into religion, refuses to allow faith to dissolve into abstract ideas. Philosophers, Scholem argued, had denigrated myth in favor of abstractions. Without mythic immediacy, however, Scholem suspects that religion would lose its appeal. Philosophers, by abandoning myth, he claimed, "came dangerously near to losing the living God."[19] With the danger of abstraction arising, mysticism emerges, Scholem suggests, to answer the threat it brings.

Scholem's definition of myth comprises two related ideas. Myth, negatively understood, refuses to reduce religion to abstract ideas. Positively stated, myth consists of vivid stories that by their very nature cannot be explained away as merely metaphors for philosophic concepts. In substance, then, myth is a story that reveals a recurrent or ongoing pattern in reality. Myths differ from one another in so far as they point to different, sometimes even contradictory, patterns. Scholem, however, wants to go farther than this substantive definition. He wants to suggest that the patterns which myths demonstrate cannot be communicated in any other way. Only myth, not abstract language, can convey the structures that the mystic seeks to present. He claims that mystics could not help but use myth because "failing this mythical element, the ancient Jewish mystics would have been unable to compress into language the substance of their inner experience."[20]

Other analysts of Jewish mysticism seem to agree with Scholem's definition of myth, even while they disagree with his evolutionary model for the emergence of mysticism. Moshe Idel disputes Scholem's claim that myth arises as a particular stage in religious development, that it reintroduces immediate experience after the introduction of antimythic rationalism. "Scholem," Idel claims, "created a simplistic division between a defeated mythical Gnosticism and a triumphant nonmythical rabinism."[21] Any vibrant religious tradition, he contends, requires the experiential component. According to such a view, rabbinic Judaism possessed myth no less than its gnostic opponents; medieval Jews who resisted the Kabbalah also possessed myth. If, as Scholem suggests, myth transmits an essential religious message that can be communicated in no other way, then all forms of Jewish religion must include it. The basis of Judaism must include truths available only through myth. Idel comments that, "The need to understand the ultimate meaning of the central Jewish activity—the commandments—moved the Kabbalists to elaborate upon and reconstruct the implicit myths or theosophies that had once motivated and offered an organic significance to the commandments."[22] While agreeing with Scholem that substantively myth provides a narrative communication of that which cannot be transmitted by other means, Idel adds a functional definition. Myth functions to explain the basic elements of religion that philosophy cannot understand.

A third view argues that myth functions as a criticism of non-mythic approaches to truth. The function of myth, on this reading, is to communicate what a particular author thinks is most adequately conveyed by story rather than by any other mode of expression. Pinchas Giller suggests a social or political resonance to this choice. The practicioner of myth is the true "enlightened one." Those who do not use myth but work on the level of normative legalism, he thinks, are construed as abusers of the divine manifestations in the world. While legalism may have effective theurgic power, myth alone expresses the ontological truth behind that effectiveness.[23]

Scholem, Idel, and Giller agree that the use of narratives expressing recurring patterns functions as alternatives to or criticisms of other modes of communication. With that in mind, the study of myth in a literary work must ask two questions: How do the sacred stories told convey a recurring pattern, and how does the work use those stories as alternatives to, or criticisms of, other forms of communication. Turning to modern Hebrew poetry one can ask these two questions of its use of myth.

History, Myth, Allegory, and Modern Hebrew Poetry

What, then, characterizes modern Hebrew poetry—myth or allegory, a concern for the historical and unique, or a concern for the recurrent and unchanging? This question demands greater specification; rather than generalize about all modern Jewish poetry or even all the poems of a single modern Hebrew poet, it is better to focus on one particular poem and discover the dynamics of symbolization within it. The poetry of Shaul Tchernichowsky promises to provide a useful sample for such discovery. Tschernichowsky has been described as "the only myth making poet in the history of Hebrew poetry." His affinity for myth has been traced to "the texture of his personality—a mixture of depth and innocence" which, it is claimed, "corresponded in some way to that of an ancient myth-maker."[24] This rather exaggerated praise suggests that Tschernichowsky identifies himself with ancient myth makers. Discovering the form and function of ancient myth may provide a key to learning what Tschernichowsky infused into his poetry. Certainly it will offer a standard against which to measure what the poet achieved and to determine whether it can best be described as myth or as allegory.

Tchernichowsky's "I Have Absolutely Nothing of My Own"

One of Tchernichowsky's final poems, written just six years before his death in 1943, combines allegory and myth in the sense defined here. The poem is entitled "I Have Absolutely Nothing of My Own," and is subtitled "Stanzas."[25] That designation suggests that the poem is a set of disparate reflections which are only tangentially related to one another. At first glance, this description seems accurate. The poem begins as the narrator, the poet's persona, laments his impoverished condition. The first stanza is introspective. With nothing, not even a table, the poet communes with his own suffering heart, hoping for some sign in this time of diminuation (the translator's term "petty sphere" misses the kabbalistic overtones to the term "period of *qatnut*). The next stanza focuses on the lack of material possessions bearing the imprint of the poet—no poignant keepsakes or intimate artifacts remain to remind the narrator of his past. The next two stanzas skip to a still different idea: the poet claims that he can achieve nothing—he neither builds a house for himself, contributes to the upbuilding of the Jewish homeland, or plants seeds that will bear fruit in the future, that is to say, trees, flowers, or even children. This first section of the poem, episodic as it might seem, actually constitutes a unity. The poet considers the various material possessions he might have accumulated or produced and declares that he has achieved none of these.

The poem then interrupts the progression of ideas with a long interlude which critics often neglect to consider but which bristles with kabbalistic overtones. Here the poet considers his own talent and field of production and wistfully wishes that he had succeeded in it. He draws images from Jewish mysticism which suggest that the apparently autobiographical musings are, in fact, intimations of a cultural heritage. Even the song the poet feels "buzzing in the heart" derives not from immediate experience but rather with the sound attributed in the Talmud to the whirring of the solar orb (see Yoma 20a). This confluence of the personal and images drawn from Jewish tradition reinforce the identification that Michael M. Fischer suggests between "individualistic autobiographical searching" and what he calls "revelations of traditions, recollections...of the divine sparks from the breaking of the vessels."[26]

> As for me, would that I had a table! With its own modest place
> Wherein a man retires regularly to unite with the light issuing from all his worlds
> Liberating sparks of light that seek dissolution in the Eyn Sof...
> Occurring in that blessed hour of influx from poetry,
> Pouring forth like a wave from a mute melody
> Which hums in the heart, demanding expression...

After this wistful interlude the poet accepts the lack of a table and seeks only something wholly his own to place upon the table. He wants only one thing to place on the table, a silent statue to act as his muse to "pour on me dream ointment from its master's garden." The poet calls this statue an "andartta." The term itself is strange. It recalls a talmudic passage which debates whether one can worship in a synagogue in which an "andretta" has been set up (See Rosh Hashana 24b, Sanhedrin 62b). The rabbis conclude that if one bows without intent to worship a foreign deity, then such statues are permitted. The poet, then, wishes to set up statues not for idolatrous prayer but as reminders of the true God. The list of possible inspirations, however, draws only on Western Civilization. Great poets, prophets, and philosophers dominate the poet's writing. His spiritual life, no less than his material one, depends on borrowings from others. Even as a poet he has nothing he can call absolutely his own. Such a lament confirms Baruch Kurzweil's understanding of Tchernichowsky's critique of the culture of liberalism which he represented.[27]

The second part of the poem offers several possibilities for the statue that the poet will erect.[28] Some of the options fall within the Jewish sphere—Moses and Isaiah; some are the Greek heroes with whom most interpreters identify Tchernichowsky—Homer and Plato; some are drawn from world literature—Shakespeare and Goethe; the last represents Tchernichowsky's interest in pagan Canaan and its religion—the goddess Astarte. Of these only two appear as fully realized characters—Shakespeare and Astarte. The poet describes the others by referring to one or another quality associated with them. Moses is the iron man of discipline and the law; Homer is the bronze prophet who sees most truly with sightless eyes; Goethe is the poet who also masters the science of colors; Plato is the cool rationalist whose symposium banishes the inflaming quality of wine. Shakespeare, however, is a poet who is also a man of flesh and blood; Astarte appears in "full flesh" and "sun-tanned" as the goddess of life.[29] None of these possibilities, even Shakespeare and Astarte, satisfy the poet. They are all cultural relics which the poet has inherited and not constructed for himself. They cannot serve as his image of self-expression. The poem concludes as it began: As for me, I have nothing that is mine not even a table. The poet lacks both material and spiritual possessions.

The search for the mythic in this poem usually focuses on the last section. Critics decode the significance of each alternative suggestion for the statue the poet wishes to erect. As Alter and Walter Benjamin would realize, however, these images are allegorical and not mythic. They point to aspects of civilization just as each stanza in the first part of the poem points to a different aspect of the human personality. Each of the several parts of the poem stand for some real entity in the world, not a recurring pattern outside of it. The key allegory, however, is found in the interlude. The interlude evokes the kabbalistic myth as an allegory for the life of the poet. The poet seeks an influx from the supernal light of the higher worlds by investigating the mundane sparks found in life itself.

This stanza tells a story and intimates the narrative line of the poem as a whole. The poet goes in search of a muse. He surveys all reality; he plumbs the resources of tradition and culture. And yet, according to the story told in this poem, he emerges with empty hands. Here Tchernichowsky employs a familiar myth found in nineteenth- and twentieth-century poetry—the poet's dedication to his muse.[30] As with several other poets, including Hayyim Nahman Bialik, Tchernichowsky uses the myth ironically. Tchernichowsky tells the story of a poet endlessly seeking for something of his own, hoping to derive it from his experience of the world. The poet turns to material phenomenon, to objects humanly produced, to the exertions by which people usually claim to leave their imprint on the world. Yet none of these succeeds in providing the poet with a "table," with a possession of his own on which to erect his poetry. The poet turns to spiritual mentors, to cultural guides whether literary or religious, and hopes to find in them an inspiration so as to develop his own unique voice, even if he cannot possess a concrete platform of his own from which to speak.

Both efforts are doomed. The true story of the poet is that no matter where he looks he must await the free influx of power that flows from the spirit of poetry itself. The story of the failed poet is the story of a poet who because he lacks a concrete home, a table on which to set his wares, can find no authenticity in either material or spiritual things. Tchernichowsky fashions the substance of myth by relating his tale of the questing poet. As he tells the story, he uses it to convey the sense of anomie felt by poets without a home, without a material or spiritual foundation of their own. This myth recapitulates the idea of the Jews as a phantom people. The poet, like the prototypical Jew, cannot find a place in the material or spiritual world because he lacks a secure foundation on which to stand. Tchernichowsky, even while living in Jerusalem, sees himself as a man without a country, as a ghost without rooting in either the physical or cultural realms. His personal myth expressed in the poem metaphorically evokes the national myth of the Jewish people in the diaspora. Certainly this message is not esoteric; Zionists from Leo Pinsker onward voiced it in logical and philosophical terms. Yet by turning it into myth Tchernichowsky gives it a poignancy and immediacy. A master of prose such as Ahad Haam might use a different means to transmit the same idea, that of the philosophical essay. A master of poetry like Tchernichowsky, however, might well feel more comfortable personalizing the message by transmuting it into myth. Certainly, as Giller seems to understand, the use of myth denotes the author as an enlightened one who sees more clearly than others the perils lying before them.

Shimon Halkin misreads Tchernichowsky's poem, taking the allegories as serious options, he concludes that "only on the basis of the best in humanity can the poet seize the greatest of poems for himself, for thus and only thus does he see the basis of humanity which comes from the world of the creative spirit."[31] Halkin has read the allegories correctly. The poet does indeed evoke the best and greatest of Western thought. The allegories, however, are not identical to the myth the poet spins. The myth, given the definition with which we began, must be the story that the poet tells. In that story the hero does not seize the former great works for himself. Instead the substance of the myth tells of repeated failure. The recurrent pattern is that of the unsuccessful quest. The poem describes the impossibility of such appropriation of the great works of the past.

This myth functions clearly and logically, in contrast to those theorists who claim that myth cannot be reproduced in coherent language. The myth of the poem, as Robert Alter has already intimated, is a nationalistic one and expresses a familiar image in Zionist literature. The choice of myth as the means for transmitting the message reflects the personal preferences of the poet, the way the poet understands his audience, and the impact that he wants to make upon that audience.

Realizing that this Zionist myth lies at the heart of the poem transforms the way one should understand it and obviates the universalism which Halkin imputes to Tchernichowsky. By focusing on the poem's allegories and not on its myth, Halkin fundamentally misconstrues the poet's intention. Only by thinking through both the substance of Tchernichowsky's myth and its message about the recurring pattern of failure without nationalism does the meaning of the poem emerge. With this understanding in mind the poem presents itself as both myth and allegory, as a statement concerning both the historical situation of the Jewish people and the eternal nature of Jewish existence.

Notes

1. R. Alter, *After The Tradition: Essays on Modern Jewish Writing* (New York: 1969), 234.
2. See the introductory discussion of this term and the long footnote on its variety of uses in J. Clifford, "On Ethnographic Allegory," in J. Clifford and G. E. Marcus, eds. *Writing Culture: The Poetics and Politics of Ethnography.* Experiments in Contemporary Anthropology: A School of American Research Advanced Seminar (Berkeley: 1986), 98. The entire essay, 98-121, shows sensitivity to the use and meaning of allegory in modern texts.
3. D. Dawson, *Allegorical Readers and Cultural Revision in Ancient Alexandria* (Berkeley: 1992), 6.
4. See F. Nietzsche, *Basic Writings of Nietzsche.* Trans., ed., Walter Kaufmann (New York: 1992),714,729-30,751,762. Compare the discussion in M. Buber, *The Eclipse of God: Studies in the Relation Between Religion and Philosophy* (New York: 1952), 110-111.
5. See R. Scheindlin, *The Gazelle: Medieval Hebrew Poems on God, Israel, and the Soul* (Philadelphia: 1991), 38, 49, 88, and compare his introductory remarks and his interpretation of love poetry in his earlier *Wine, Women and Death: Medieval Hebrew Poems on the Good Life* (Philadelphia: 1986).
6. See the discussion of Benjamin's view of allegory and myth in S. Buck-Morss, *The Dialectics of Seeing: Walter Benjamin and the Arcades Project* (Cambridge, MA: 1989), especially pp. 78, 103-109, 116, 146, 159-165, 242-246, 257, 293, 339; S. A. Handelman, *Fragments of Redemption: Jewish Thought and Literary Theory in Benjamin, Scholem, and Levinas* (Bloomington: 1991), 36-42; and in C. Norris, *The Deconstructive Turn: Essays in the Rhetoric of Philosophy* (London: 1984), 107-127.
7. C. Levi-Strauss, *Structural Anthropology.* Trans. C. Jacobson, B. Grundefest Schoepf (New York: 1963), 209.

8. For Levi-Strauss' view of myth within its entire system of "language" see J. D. Culler, *Structuralist Poetics: Structuralism, Linguistics and the Stuy of Literature* (London: 1975), 40-54.

9. See the discussion of early interpreters of myth, including those like Edward Tylor and Sigmund Freud who rejected it and those like Mircea Eliade and Levi-Strauss who celebrate it, in R. A. Segal, "In Defense of Mythology: The History of Modern Theories of Myth," *Annals of Scholarship* 1:1 (1980), 3-49.

10. G. A. Larue, *Ancient Myth and Modern Man* (Englewood Cliffs, NJ: Prentice-Hall. 1973), x.

11. See my *Martin Buber On Myth: An Introduction* (Garland Press, 1990).

12. See G. Ernest Wright, *Israel Against Its Environment*. Studies in Biblical Theology 2 (Naperville: Allenson, 1950), 19-21.

13. J. Z. Smith, *Imagining Religion: From Babylon to Jonestown* (Chicago: 1982), 66; see the entire article "The Unknown God: Myth in History." 66-89.

14. Y. Liebes, *Studies in Jewish Myth and Jewish Messianism*. Trans. Batya Stein (Albany, NY: SUNY Press: 1993), 2.

15. G. G. Scholem, *Major Trends in Jewish Mysticism* (New York: 1963), 19.

16. Ibid., 7.

17. Eliezer Schweid comments on this aspect of Scholem's thinking and suggests that by ignoring the biblical record, Scholem has misunderstood Jewish myth entirely. What Schweid calls the "historical myth" of Judaism, however, might well be what this present essay calls historical allegory. Whether the prophets or indeed the rabbinic tradition thought of their narratives about God as articulating unchanging and recurrent patterns of human experience deserves special treatment in itself. See E. Schweid, *Judaism and Mysticism According to Gershom Scholem: A Critical Analysis and Programmatic Discussion*. Tr. from the Hebrew with an introduction by D. A. Weiner (Atlanta, GA: Scholars Press: 1985), especially. 72-73. 98-99. 158-159.

18. Ibid., 11.

19. Ibid., 37.

20. Ibid., 35.

21. M. Idel, *Kabbalah: New Perspectives*. (New Haven: 1988), 156.

22. Ibid., 157.

23. See P. Giller, *The Enlightened Will Shine: Symbolization and Theurgy in the Later Strata of the Zohar* (New York: 1993), See in particular Chapter 3, 21-32.

24. E. Silberschlag, *Saul Tschernichowsky: Poet of Revolt*. Trans. S. J. Kahn and others (Ithaca, NY: 1968), 39.

25. The poem is found in S. Tschernichowsky, *Shirim* (Tel Aviv: 1966), 440-445. A rather wooden and sometimes misleading translation appears in Silberschlag, *Poet of Revolt*, 173-177.

26. M. M. J. Fischer. "Ethnicity and the Post-Modern Arts of Memory," in Clifford and Marcus, *Writing Culture*, 198.

27. See B. Kurzweil, *Bialik and Tchernichovsky : Studies in Their Poetry* [Hebrew] (Tel Aviv: 1967), 289-295.

28. A common exegetical error in studying this poem is to think of the poet as wishing to have all seven figures erected. Yosef Haefrati makes the actual situation clear—the poem raises, and ultimately rejects, seven possible statues for consideration. See Y Haefrati. *Saul Tchernichowsky: A Selection of Critical Essays of His Writings* (Tel Aviv: 1976), 255-258.

29. See the discussion in H. Barzel, *Poets on Poetry* I [Hebrew] (Tel Aviv: 1970), 93-94.

30. See the discussion of this myth in Bialik's poetry and Russian poetry generally in Y. Ben-Yeshurum, *Hashirah HaRusit Vehashpaata al Ha Shirah Halvrit* [Hebrew] (Tel Aviv: 1955), 116-117. Ben Yeshurun, however, does not mention it in relationship to this poem of Tschernichowsky; see 66-74.

31. S. Halkin, "World and Man." in Ha'efrati, *Tchernichowsky*, 162.

Can the Teaching of Jewish History be Anything but the Teaching of Myth?

Joel Gereboff

In his book *Zakhor*, Yosef Hayim Yerushalmi brilliantly explores the tension between two highly typical modes of relating to the past, myth (collective and sacred memory) and modern historiography.[1] He concludes that these two modes of recollection stand in radically different relations to the past. According to Yerushalmi, the attempt by many modern Jewish historians to use the findings of their endeavors to define the inner character of Judaism and to foster modern Jewish identity is utterly misplaced. Yerushalmi's position, however, seems not to have been subscribed to by North American Jewish educators. Many of these pedagogues, who see the developing of positive Jewish identity as one of the chief goals of Jewish educational activities, have designed extensive materials for teaching Jewish history. Drawing upon an examination of a wide range of American and Canadian Jewish educational materials (curricula, textbooks, workbooks)[2] I will demonstrate in the first two parts of this paper that while most of the authors of these works conceived of themselves as teaching "history," they were, in Yerushalmi's terms, really constructing myths and formulations of collective memory. Now although this analysis of Jewish educational materials is of value in revealing their character and messages as "myth," this part of my investigation, which works within Yerushalmi's definition of the nature of historical inquiry, however, is somewhat problematic. This is because Yerushalmi still portrays historical inquiry in modernist, largely objectivist terms, and he does not consider the significant implications for historiography of postmodernist and deconstructionist thinking. In the final part of this paper, utilizing this latter type of historiographical discussions, especially as they appear in recent writings exploring the relationship between collective memory and history, I will suggest how history, in a postmodernist sense, and myth might intersect within Jewish education.

Yerushalmi's usage of the term collective memory and myth to characterize the way in which most premodern societies referred to the past draws upon the writings of Maurice Halbwachs and Pierre Nora. For all three writers, collective memory provides large scale narratives, or more properly meta-narratives, that selectively and uncritically integrate reports about the past, which thereby provide a sense of identity and self evident legitimacy to the community telling them. In Nora's words:

> [Collective memory] is an integrated, dictatorial memory, unself-conscious, commanding, all powerful, spontaneous, actualizing a memory without a past, that ceaselessly reinvents traditions, linking the history of its ancestors to the undifferentiated time of heroes, origins, and myth. Memory is life, borne by living societies founded in its name. It remains in permanent evolution, open to the dialectic of remembering and forgetting, unconscious of its successive deformations, vulnerable to manipulation and appropriation. Memory is a perpetually actual phenomenon, a bond tying us to the eternal present.[3]

By contrast to collective memory and myth, for Nora, the historical mode of thought:

> is the reconstruction, always problematic, incomplete, of what is no longer. History is representation of the past. History, because it is an intellectual and secular production, calls for analysis and criticism. At the heart of history is a critical discourse that is antithetical to a spontaneous memory. History is perpetually suspicious of memory and its true mission is to suppress and destroy it. History's goal and ambition is not to exalt but to annihilate what has in reality taken place.[4]

Three propositions can serve to summarize the criteria that differentiate collective memory (myth) from history:

> 1. Collective memory relates a meta-narrative that depicts a sequence of events with a clear pattern, generally one of repetition or progression. The narrative discloses the meaning of the emplotted events. These events self-evidently appear to be the only significant occurrences from the past. Criteria for their selection, or comments disclosing that selections have been made, are not included in such accounts. By contrast, critical historical research does not posit that the totality of events neatly fit together to yield a singular story. For historians, occurrences are not inevitable, nor do they reveal one, or necessarily, even any lesson. Historians must explain their selection of certain events and factors as significant. Appeals to theoretical models often reveal the reasons for these choices.

2. Collective memory defines and justifies the community of memory that reports it. Historians fundamentally address other professional historians, and are in search of historical knowledge. Accordingly, historians do not begin their investigations with a vested interest in any particular finding. They are not concerned with the implications that their conclusions may have for the identities of the peoples they are discussing.

3. Collective memory is created, recreated and transmitted through a large complex of interlocking societal institutions that function organically. Most often these narratives about the past are "declared" in various ritual settings in which there is little *analysis* of whatever evidence may be cited in support of the recollections.[5] On the other hand, the conclusions of historians emerge from the careful dissection of data, an approach that does not presuppose the veracity of any type of information. Historical results, therefore, are generally tentative and incomplete; often a matter of probabilities rather than complete certainty.[6]

These distinctions, which convey Yerushalmi's distinctions between myth and history, allow for an investigation of the historical materials produced by North American Jewish educators.

The Classical Paradigm for Teaching Jewish History[7]

By the middle of this century, there had emerged among Jewish educators a commonly shared set of views regarding the teaching of history. This position, which I shall label "the classical paradigm," was evidenced in the educational materials and theoretical discussions produced by these educators. This paradigm has continued to shape a significant portion of the educational endeavors of American Jewry even after the 1950s, though from that time onwards a number of new directions began to be evident. But despite their claims to be works of "history," pedagogic materials reflecting both the classical and newer theories are in fact vehicles for conveying collective memory and for advancing the Jewish identity of students. Works of this sort offer apologetic narratives of Jewish history that are meant to instill pride in the Jewish student; they do not present primary evidence and do not indicate the criteria and theories that stand behind their presentations.

The classical paradigm saw the teaching of Jewish history as an indispensable component of Jewish education, and it advocated a cyclical structure for teaching this subject. That is, it divided the instruction according to three broad age groups, K-3(4), 4 (5)-8 and 9-12,[8] and assigned different general goals to each segment, such that the student completing the entire sequence would cover Jewish history in three different ways. Textbooks were the predominant instructional medium in the actual teaching. As Walter Ackerman remarks, "The teaching of history in Jewish schools relies heavily on the textbook. Whatever the method used by the teacher, a textbook is usually at its core and serves as the basic instructional aid. What a child learns of Jewish history, then is largely a function of the text the school has chosen."[9] The textbooks, such as those of Pessin, Soloff, Gamoran, Isaacs and Klaperman[10] were written in a highly dogmatic, didactic style.[11] They told students what they needed to know, including "*the* message of Jewish history." They generally presented history within a chronological order, and oversimplified the past. They tended to eliminate conflict, and clearly labelled who are the "good guys" and the "bad guys" and presented people as non-complex, non-conflicted persons. The author's methodological and ideological perspective was rarely stated; hence, the criteria governing selections and emphases were not evident. Series designed for use of students over the course of years were not adequately responsive to developmental changes, especially those from the primary age to early adolescence. Ackerman captures the character of many of these works by stating, "They present history as a 'rhetoric of conclusion,' rather than as a method of weighing conflicting evidence and forming independent judgement."[12] The purpose of these works, and of the teaching of Jewish history in general, was to reveal the continuity of Jewish history, the essential unchanging facts about Jewish values and Judaism. This was done with the goal of instilling pride in the student toward Judaism and inspiring the young Jew to engage in positive acts of Jewish identification.[13]

In sum, the designers of instructional materials for teaching Jewish history bought it into a historicistic perspective, for they contended that the critical study and teaching of Jewish history provides a succinct, inspiring and obligating statement of what it means to be a Jew. As Ackerman states, these authors select and present as "what is important in Jewish history, and thus deserving of attention, those events which contribute to the making of the 'myth', the usually traditional story of ostensibly historical events that serves to unfold part of the world view of a people or explain a practice or belief, the texts are eager to teach."[14] Here, and throughout his several articles, Ackerman articulates the view that while the study of Jewish history might allow one to discern how earlier developments shape the present situation of the Jewish people and Judaism, it is not self-evident that such inquiry can either reveal the enduring elements and patterns of Judaism,[15] or isolate those values of Judaism that represent the best and highest ideals of humanity.

Excellent examples of writings that express this theory of instruction in history are contained in works from the mid 1950s by Azriel Eisenberg and Abraham Segal: *The Teaching of Jewish History*, a pamphlet containing their own positions, and *Readings in the Teaching of Jewish History*, an anthology of articles on the topic.[16] Eisenberg's and Segal's detailed presentation of the aims to be pursued in the teaching of Jewish history combines ambitious cognitive goals with desired affective and behavioral outcomes. The following presents the key elements of their position:

Aims of Teaching Jewish History

I.   Knowledge of the Jewish People as individuals and as Members of a Group—This knowledge allows for generalizations about Jews, about interrelationships among Jewish groups and non-Jews; for understanding social organization and processes; for comprehension of motives, causes, results of individual and group behavior.

A. Knowledge of the fact that social problems, conflicts, needs of Jews have always existed; that the basic reason adjustments were made necessary was because of changing conditions. This knowledge contributes to developing a sense of continuity in the development of Jewish life.

B. This knowledge allows one to distinguish those characteristics of Judaism which have changed little or not at all and those that have changed a great deal.

II Appreciation of the role of the past in our lives today.

A. Knowledge of our great movements, leaders, literatures, triumphs and failures and their lasting contribution.

B. Understanding the role played by Jewish individuals and the Jewish group in general world affairs.

C. Appreciation of the contribution of non-Jews to Jewish life.

III. Appreciation of current Jewish events and problems.

A. Understand how these develop out of past situations.

B. Appreciation of the unique position of the Jewish people in democratic lands.

IV. Belief in the ideas of the dignity of the individual and democracy, yielding the acquisition of a reasoned basis for Jewish group loyalties.

A. Ability to distinguish between aspects of Jewish life representing the best and highest ideals of mankind and those representing throwbacks, superstitions, and imitations of lesser people.
B. Knowledge of the common core of tradition, belief, accepted practice by most Jews.
C. Awareness of the harmony between the best in Judaism and in modern scientific thought.

V. Carrying out in daily life the learning acquired from the study of Jewish history.

A. Develop wholesome character traits.
B. Expand interests and sympathies, including those toward history and current events.
C. Develop a well rounded Jewish personality and the desire to participate in all aspects of modern and Jewish life.[17]

This statement represents one of the clearest proposals of the goals of teaching Jewish history, and contains some very ambitious objectives. These theoreticians treat historical events as the result of multifactorial causes, realize the importance of identifying processes and not merely reporting details, and seek to determine connections between the past and the present. But the pursuit of this last goal points to some illegitimate aspects of their objectives. As already noted, the study of Jewish history may not reveal enduring elements and patterns of Judaism, nor can it isolate those values of Judaism that represent the best and highest ideals of humanity.[18] Eisenberg's and Segal's endorsement of this last goal, in fact, indicates that they must use criteria that are grounded in notions established on the basis of the study of something other than the history of the Jews, in order then to use the results of those endeavors to determine a reasoned basis for Jewish group loyalties. Moreover, section V shows that the cognitive pursuits ultimately should translate into specific actions; they should contribute to the socialization of the students.

We noted above that in order to reduce a sense of repetition, to limit boredom and to be age appropriate in the instruction, the advocates of the "classical paradigm" called for a cyclical approach to the teaching of Jewish history. A clear statement of this methodology is provided by William Chomsky:

Modern schools prefer the cycle program in the teaching of history. In such a program the entire range of Jewish history may be covered by varied approaches at different levels of the pupil's maturity. Thus the first cycle would consist of biographies of representative heroes in Jewish history, beginning with Abraham down to modern times. The second cycle would comprise a chronological account of Jewish history centering around the Jewish people. In the third cycle, Jewish movements and institutions may be traced back to their origins, thus bringing into purview once more the total panorama of Jewish history.[19]

The manner in which the cyclical approach was actually implemented, as evidenced particularly by the textbooks from this period, underscores our claim that collective memory, myth, turned out to be the actual content of the instruction. The choice of heroes as the focus of the teaching for young children initially signals this tendency. Chomsky explains this emphasis in the following remarks:

Young children are naturally egocentric. As they grow and mature, their conception of self extends and broadens, projecting itself on fictional and historical heroes with whom they identify themselves. Hence, children are hero worshippers. They are interested in activities and events only insofar as they happen to the hero or are occasioned by him. They live his life, think his thoughts, experience his emotions and emulate his examples in the degree to which they are attracted or repelled by him.[20] History in the primary grades should, therefore, be centered around a hero who is to serve as the embodiment of the age, its customs, its happenings, its spirit. He symbolizes and epitomizes the group and the epoch, the national hopes of the people, its struggles, sacrifices, sorrows, joys. The child's world is thereby enlarged and integrated with that of his people.[21]

What is especially important for our purposes are Chomsky's further observation regarding the tension between the desire to enhance the story, by embellishing and enlivening it through the use of legendary elements, and the concern to relate only accurate historical facts. He endorses the former approach:

Some over-sensitive teachers doubt the advisability of telling children traditional stories and legends, the veracity of which is not established. These doubts are however unfounded. In the first place, young children are known to possess such vivid imaginative powers as to be unable to distinguish between the real and the fictitious. Secondly the actual facts may be so confusing and devitalized as to be less real to him than the mythical and legendary ones. We are still far from possessing the historical details necessary for reconstructing the environment and character of some of our historical heroes and events. This is particularly true in the case of the Biblical period. Young children should be permitted to enjoy such Bible stories without subjecting them to rational analysis or didactic dissection. *The emotional deposit left by an effective story will in itself serve to fortify the young child and to cushion him against the shock of discovering the 'fictitious' character of the story later on* [emphasis added].[22]

These lengthy citations from Chomsky reveal that he thinks one can isolate certain matters as representative of Jewish history and that can convey such information to young people, even through the purposeful misstatement of facts. Additionally, he seeks to achieve these ends by *telling* stories to students but not by actively involving them in thinking out how such information is known and without having them try to correlate the context of the characters with their deeds.

The actual textbooks from this period largely subscribe to this approach, though they seem to emphasize the Jewish values characters communicate more than the teaching of history A typical acknowledgement and justification for the compromises this approach raises for instruction in history is presented by Rose Lurie in *The Great March*.[23] This book for eight through ten year olds was first published in 1931, and was reissued for the nineteenth time in 1966. Emanuel Gamoran states in the introduction:

> Since this book was not written as a history, it was not deemed necessary to include certain historical events. The chief aim in teaching Jewish stories of the post-biblical period to third and fourth graders is not so much to convey information as to give inspiration. The cultivation of favorable Jewish attitudes is one of the important aims in any such course of instruction. Whatever information the children may obtain should be considered quite incidental. While we expect them, as a result of study of this book to know some outstanding Jewish names, and some important Jewish events, the primary end is the cultivation of a love for Jewish heroes, for the Jewish people and for Jewish idealism.[24]

Ackerman summarizes, in his typical pithy and critical manner, the problems that ensue when history or even "proto-history" is used for such external aims as the building of Jewish character:

It seems reasonable to argue, as regard both the earlier and later works, that the discipline of history as such interests them less than the uses to which history may be put. Without exception the texts before us view history as a means to an end. They rest on the assumption that the child's identity is not yet completely formed and the study of history is an avenue to that self-discovery.[25]

After citing typical comments by the authors of textbooks that adhere to this objective, Ackerman concludes:

When the study of the past is clothed in such moral tones, history is transformed from an attempt, however imperfect, to order and interpret a complicated mass of conflicting data into a *guided tour through a museum of virtue"* [emphasis added].[26]

The textbooks developed for teaching older students for instruction in the second and third cycle similarly end up conveying myth, not history. Those for the second cycle especially offer chronological surveys of the history of the Jewish people that in the end glorify selectively chosen matters. The deeds of great individuals are a favorite focus. While workbooks were also written to complement these books, they and the textbooks did not involve the student in discovery of historical information. Nor did they disclose to the student the criteria that governed the selection of narrated events. Finally, students were not asked to express their own evaluations of the deeds and thoughts of earlier generations of Jews. Their role was to assimilate the critical information and to absorb the overall message it conveyed about the history of the Jewish people and the value of Judaism. Thus what is presented as history, is actually the manipulation of the details, sometimes even legendary ones, about *certain* Jews so as to contribute to what Ackerman labels, "the making of the myth, the traditional story of ostensibly historical events that serves to unfold part of the world view of a people."[27]

The overall character of instruction in Jewish history within the classical paradigm can be summarized as follows: It focused upon heroes and great Jews in the primary years. This emphasis is primarily meant to be an introduction to the study of Jewish history. But in the end emotional, not cognitive goals are key. During the intermediate years, the Jewish people is allegedly the topic of study. Great figures, though not labelled as such, however, fill the pages of the actual works designed for teaching Jewish history to children between ten and thirteen. In the final analysis, most of these works teach neither critical history, nor do they set aside that goal and overtly substitute the study of the complex personalities and lives of specific Jews for the purposes of having students deal head on with questions about Jewish values and Jewish character traits.

For the third cycle, the one for high school age students, the classical paradigm calls for a focus upon movements, institutions and recurrent trends, or as Grayzel puts it, "students after their fourteenth or fifteenth year, if they stay with us that long, can be asked to integrate all their information. They will then be ripe to understand how life moves simultaneously on many fronts and how one front affects the others."[28] According to Grayzel and others, when the true task is to teach history to "mature minds," there is little place for hero worship and storytelling. But in the end, for Grayzel and for other Jewish educators, the actual instruction involved the use of the use of a heavily ideological textbook, not the careful analysis of primary texts done with an attention to the implication of the use of historical theories and methodologies. Moreover, the goals of the instruction remain, in Grayzel's words, "giving the Jewish student a consciousness that his roots in civilization are ancient and go very deep, and by taking him to the present step by step, make him feel that his Jewishness and the institutions which nourish it were dearly purchased and dare not be treated cavalierly."[29] The tendency for instruction in Jewish history to serve largely as vehicle for declaring, or at least, for conveying collective memory continues in the period after the 1950s. But in terms of the three contrasting features between myth and history we noted above, in some cases modifications in emphasis and methodology result in instruction that is far more historical in character. Let us now turn to these more recent developments.

New Approaches to Teaching Jewish History

Beginning in the 1960s, developments in the sociological conditions of the American Jewish community and in American society, new pedagogical views in American education regarding teaching history and social studies, and negative assessments of the results of adhering to the classical paradigm gave rise to a variety of new theories and instructional materials for teaching Jewish history.[30] Nearly all of these newly created works did not change instruction in Jewish history from having features typical of items designed for the transmission and development of collective memory. In many cases, however, they did exhibit fewer of these traits. This is obviously not true in the case of instructional resources and curricula that largely adhered to the classical paradigm. These items still displayed all three of the characteristics typical of myth. Textbooks like Abba Eban's *My People* offered grand theories of the course of Jewish history; it did so, as its concluding words show, in order to instill positive Jewish feelings; and did not actively involve students in the exploration of primary sources in accordance with a well articulated methodology.

A number of works from this more recent period modify the classical approach primarily by eliminating this last noted feature.[31] That is, these items utilize inquiry based learning. Students are asked to arrive at conclusions regarding the history of the Jews (or more typically, the history of Judaism) by means of analyses of original sources. But these books still present myth, for their overall purpose is to reveal certain overarching features, messages of Jewish history, for the purpose of motivating Jewish identification. These generally chronologically organized works ultimately want students to buy into certain continually exhibited, and therefore essential values that define Judaism or the values of the Jewish people. Although these values often are detected based on an analysis of contextually located events, the uncovering of their recurrence provides the learners with a strong sense of the *continuity* of Jewish history. This is also achieved by not revealing to students the criteria that determined the selection of events, personalities and writings from the past to which they were exposed.

Many of the curricula of the Conservative Movement, especially the *Experimental Edition of a Curriculum for the Afternoon Jewish School*, display these attributes. The editor of this very large volume states, "There is a unifying element which is common to all four branches [of the curriculum] and which serves as the underpinning for each. That unifying principle can be described as *qedushah*. The term *qedushah* as employed here implies the 'uniqueness' or 'specialness' or 'otherness' and 'difference' of the Jew."[32] Specifically with regard to the history branch the editor declares:

> The History/community Branch is perhaps the most ideological of all.... The branch seeks to develop within the student a growing sense of pride in his/her Jewishness.... In sum the curriculum has the conscious goal of convincing the student that to be a Jew is to be different. To be *qadosh*, one must know certain things, must believe certain things, must stand for

certain things in societal interplay, and must, in his or her personal life, do
certain things and do them on a regular and consistent basis.[33]

Before turning to other types of developments in instructional materials,
it is critical to comment upon the objectivist assumptions that undergird
this curriculum, as well as most other materials utilizing inquiry based
learning. These works do not introduce students to hermeneutical
matters, to the limitations of representation and interpretation. They
speak of the *discovery*, rather than the *construction* of historical information. While these works are a vast improvement over those instructional
resources which narrate the past without the citation and analysis of
texts, they either fully overlook, or significantly underplay, the interac-
tive process between interpreter and text that results in the generation
of historical assertions.

The largest single grouping of more recent texts and curricula are
those which have similar goals to the above materials, but which achieve
them through a topical approach to the study of Jewish history. The
range of topics covered is extensive in those curricula that cover all
phases of education, and more limited in those items, especially textbooks, that deal with only a specific issue for a particular age group.
These materials have cognitive, affective and behavioral objectives, and
advocate inquiry based learning. The chief cognitive goal is the gaining
of knowledge of those values and ideas that have typically defined
Jewish personalities or have sustained Jewish communities. Students
gather these insights through analysis of primary evidence and through
activities that call for role playing and other methods requiring personal
involvement. The discovered information, in turn, should lead to the
development of a Jewish personality that is either a replication of earlier
Jewish types or an authentic reformulation of them in that it draws upon
as precedents. Educational materials from more liberal Jewish groups
are of the latter sort. In these instances, for example, in resources
produced by the Reform movement, students discern Jewish values,
correlate them with the historical conditions and finally are invited to
respond to these examples. The last task involves determining which of
these values may be personally meaningful to them or to the Jewish
community by contributing to contemporary, vibrant Jewish way of
living. Several books on women in Judaism, similarly, invite student
response to what they may consider problematic aspects of past Jewish
roles for women. The larger goal, however, is to encourage and enable

the learners to develop Jewish personalities and communities that grow out of an engagement with examples from the past.

Typical of this approach are curricula and materials advocating the substitution of social studies for the previously, more common courses in Jewish history. Several articles in a special issue of the *Pedagogic Reporter* from 1978 illustrate this position. Martin Cohen identifies as an objective of this mode of instruction, "[To] seek the distinctive values of the Jewish tradition arising from Jewish experience. The constellation of Jewish values, with their particular nuances and implications must be the goal of our teaching. Otherwise we have neither taught nor helped preserve the Jewish faith and tradition."[34] Cohen also notes the instruction should not didactic. He remarks, "Do not force values down students' throats. It is difficult to jog a youngster into considering the possibility of a Jewish value over the obstacles of inherent human apathy, natural human reluctance and the American tendency to withhold judgement about anything authority figures are trying to put over."[35]

Emil Jacoby's views are quite similar. After citing the Bruce Joyce's position on three dimensions of social studies, the intellectual, the social and the personal, Jacoby explains how these are to be achieved in a Jewish setting:

> In Jewish schools the intellectual dimension is expressed in our efforts to introduce the student to the cognitive domain of his/her studies and provide him/her with the necessary skills for further exploration. The goal of the social dimension is to focus on involving the pupil in the Jewish community and developing in him/her a concern for its welfare. Finally, the objective of the personal dimension is to help the child find meaning and purpose in his/her present life as a Jew. This latter objective is an absolute mandate. [For] the development of an ethical personality and the training of a community conscious Jew it is imperative to integrate the various components of Jewish social studies and prepare cohesive units of instruction.

Having briefly noted the basic features of this type of material, we proceed to evaluate them in terms of the criteria differentiating myth from history. Two weaknesses of these items are their failure to reveal to students the criteria determining the choice of topics and their not providing adequate discussion of the implications of the use of certain historiographical methods. Furthermore, those items that call for student reaction buy into a simplistic view of "the autonomous decider."

They do not help students understand the range of factors shaping and limiting their decisions. These features of these items result in their serving, to some extent, as mechanisms for the molding of Jewish students in terms of Jewish "myths."

A third category of newer materials have students interact with past Jewish history for the purpose of understanding the responses of a variety of Jews to recurrent situations Jews have faced in the past and which are also significantly operative in the present.[36] The emphasis in these items is predominantly on the cognitive side. Their premise is that such insights would enable those Jewish students, who choose to be part of the Jewish people, to interpret better present conditions and to construct a meaningful and viable personal and collective Jewish identity. Because these courses analyze the past in order to address the contemporary situation of Jews, they generally deal with only the modern period. To achieve their results they do not minimize the complexity of history—they tend to note the multiplicity of ways Jews lived in the past. They seek to understand these matters through a careful analysis of their larger historical contexts. Most of these materials are for adolescent age students.

The authors of one example of this approach, *Dilemmas and Adaptations: Spotlights on Jewish History*, indicate that the course focuses upon a few key episodes in the history of the Jewish people in order for students to have the time to realize that the questions Jews faced and the answers they gave were not simple. These writers' underlying conviction is that "the experiences of other Jews who faced the dilemma of adapting to different societies and cultures may help contemporary Jews find ways of surviving creatively as a people. Understanding historical processes may help you as you attempt to define how to be Jewish in a contemporary society."[37]

A second work, that of Alex Pomson, makes similar claims. He comments that the history he teaches is one "encountered from the world of adolescent turbulence—full of crises, conflict and uncertainty with ordinary people making choices, facing dilemmas and taking risks."[38] This is the exact type of instruction that Ackerman asserts has been missing in Jewish education. Pomson asserts the content of his course, "Jews in Modern World," "attempts to make sense of a confusing Jewish present by exploring previous Jewish responses to the modern world and emancipation. It intends that students investigate how the modern world is characterized by the necessity of making choices and resolving dilemmas. This is an openended history."[39]

On the surface, these two courses, and others like them, are more historical than any other previously discussed types. There are, however, some aspects of these pedagogic efforts that still make them conveyors of myth. First, while they do not enforce one definition of Jewish identity, their primary goal is to help students develop meaningful and effective Jewish identities. Second, they inescapably predetermine which features from the past can best enable Jewish students to confront their contemporary situation. Third, they implicitly legitimatize only certain definitions of Judaism: above all, they see Jewish identity as a product, or more accurately a series of formulations, resulting from choices made by Jews. Judaism or Jewish identity is not unchanging and transcendent in origin.

The final type of recent course materials to be examined are those that eschew any interest in matters of the identity of their Jewish students. I have found two instances of this sort, *You Are an Historian: An Introduction to Medieval Jewish History and Historiography* and *Panorama of Jewish History.*[40] The title of the former work indicates that its authors, Brier and Ingall, see as a primary goal the cultivation of an understanding of the character of historical research. This work has students develop hypotheses about Jews on the basis of each introduced primary text. They are to check and reformulate these propositions throughout the course. Little attention is given to personal response to the content, for beyond the issues of methodology, the other objectives of this course are for students to learn about 1. Jewish events, personalities and problems which shaped the lives of Jews during the Middle Ages and 2. the interdependence between the Jews and their environment. "The primary source documents are not an arbitrary collection of facts, but a selected focus or "lens" through which students can view Jewish history."[41]

Blank's work is a well thought out, scathing attack upon the teaching of Jewish history for purposes of identity formation. He presents philosophical and practical objections to courses with such an objective. In their place he advocates that:

> The teaching of Jewish must include the mastery of factual material as a goal itself. *Panorama of Jewish History* has as its primary objective the attainment of factual knowledge by the students. A well presented dynamic lesson on a Jewish topic can be as effective in terms of teaching facts and skills as is a lesson on any number of other topics that the student studies during the week. The result of not stressing the attainment of factual knowledge is that the teaching and learning are regarded as essentially non-academic.[42]

These two works represent significant corrections of the deficiencies found in most other instructional works for Jewish history. Yet they do not adequately deal with the role that theories and methods play in shaping the selection and analysis of historical data. Although Brier and Ingall discuss the difficulties that accompany attempts to use historical evidence to arrive at conclusions, they do not sufficiently reveal how theoretical paradigms and other sorts of interests shade the interpretation of primary sources. Nor do they comment upon the rhetorical quality of the narrative reconstructions of historians. Finally, while their selections show an effort to rectify the usual emphasis given to "great" Jews, for they assert that their intention is to make known "everyday life" of medieval Jewry, they do not begin to present the diversity of Jewish life of that era. Neither an introductory work like theirs, nor for that matter, even an advanced work, can manage to discuss the rich variety of Jews from that period. But authors must provide to their readers, especially to students, a statement and explanation of the criteria determining the selected topics and documents. The omission of such remarks obfuscates the impact that values and theories have upon the reconstruction of history.

Blank also does not entertain these matters in a serious manner. Throughout the essay in which he explains his curriculum he contrasts subjective approaches to history with those that have the academic objective of teaching factual knowledge. Although he concedes that "subjectivity in history is to some extent unavoidable," and cautions that "when there is an alternative purpose [such as promoting group identity and loyalty] this purpose and value should be clearly identified,"[43] he never identifies the subjective elements of his own course. It seems, that for him, there are some forms of subjectivity that lead to "the sacrifice of objectivity," and other, less critical types that do not. He never presents the considerations shaping his choices of "factual knowledge that disclose *the* sequence of Jewish history" [emphasis added].[44]

The review of writings by Jewish educators on the teaching of history closes with an examination of the work of two Israeli educational theoreticians, Walter Ackerman and Oded Schremer.[45] Their works are the only philosophical discussions that seriously consider the pedagogic and epistemological ramifications of historians' theoretical models and value commitments. We have already seen that Ackerman requires that the instruction in history should disclose the complexity of past events and people, not present a rhetoric of conclusion. Ambiguities and doubts of personalities, conflicting viewpoints held by Jews in the past on the same issue, including alternatives that did not come to dominate, and contradictions within societies should all be brought before the student for their analysis. Ackerman also comments upon the two matters that compromise most severely the teaching of history—doing so for purposes of promoting identification and doing so from an undisclosed point of view. He contends that these are inescapable components of all historical instruction, but also offers suggestions on how these matters should be introduced to the students:

> The issue is not whether or not the [instructional] text is without a particular point of view—that is impossible and perhaps even undesirable—but rather whether or not it states its position clearly and enables the student to understand the implications of the stance it has adopted.[46]

The conclusion of his paper presents a succinct comment on the matter of promoting identity:

> The manner, style and tone—unfortunately all too typical of most of the texts—foreclose options in place of suggesting alternatives for thought and careful consideration. History is undeniably an essential element in the development of identity; when used for that purpose—as it is by all our books—it must be taught not as a series of closed chapters of already determined significance, but as a continuous search for meaning which permits the student the freedom of his own conclusions.[47]

Schremer offers an extremely cogent review of the impact of the "logic of the disciplines" approach on the teaching of history. He criticizes several recent Israeli history textbooks, and proposes a nuanced set of objectives for teaching history. He thus notes that while the logic of disciplines approach identified five tasks for teaching history, including understanding causes of historical events, knowing sources upon which claims are made and knowing how historians analyze them, it disallowed the sixth goal of discerning the "lessons" to be learned from the past. He concludes his piece by suggesting that since education inevitably serves as a vehicle for socialization, it must in some way attend to discussing the significance of events. In Schremer's words:

> Society cannot afford not to address values and just be scientific. It also cannot indoctrinate. The solution to this dilemma perhaps is in an approach to teaching history that reveals to students the point of view and principles from which it investigates the past, that reveals the existence of alterative

conceptions and their implications, and that focuses upon the differences between the approaches and does not simply endorse one of them.[48]

Schremer's remarks here move in the direction of tracing some of the implications of postmodernist and deconstructionist views for educational theory. A brief examination of such views, particularly as they appear in recent conversations about the relationship between collective memory and history, will reinforce the position of Ackerman and Schremer, that to an extent, the teaching of history inevitably involves the teaching of myth.

Conclusions

Yerushalmi and several other writers drawing upon the notion of collective memory adhere to a rigid distinction between this mode of relating past occurrences and history. For these thinkers historical research done by professional historians cannot and should not attempt to produce collective memory. In Yerushalmi's view, literature and ideology have been and will be the wellsprings of contemporary Jewish collective memory.[49] Yet in the end, he thinks that historiography may be able to make two contributions. First, despite the tentativeness of its conclusions, it can be a means of countering the patently false historical claims made by a host of ideologues and hate mongers. "Against the agents of oblivion, the shredders of documents, the assassins of memory, the revisers of encyclopedias...only the historian, with the austere passion for fact proof, evidence which are central to his vocation, can effectively stand guard."[50] Second, the historian can utilize the information learned about the ruptures of history, its lack of simplistic continuity, in order to imagine alternatives to the present:

> The modern Jewish historian must understand the degree to which he himself is a product of rupture. Once aware of this, he is not only bound to accept it; he is liberated to use it...The very ability to conceive a time when men and women think differently than we, be it in the future or in the past, is the fruit of that historical consciousness which is ours in the present. We cannot avoid it without an inner violence and betrayal. But that is alright. In the terrifying time in which we live and create, eternity is not immediate concern.[51]

In *Time Passages, Collective Memory and American Popular Culture*,[52] George Lipsitz reaches similar conclusions, though he does so in the context of a wholehearted acceptance of a postmodernist understanding of historiography. He remarks:

> Poststructuralist and deconstructionist critics recognize that the 'crisis of representation' stems from the 'inevitability of representation,' from the ways in which all facts are also interpretations singled out for notice because of some subjective judgements.[53]

For Lipsitz, this means that:

> Competing [historical] narratives are not just fights about the past, they also serve to transform cultural identity and political dialogue in the present. What we choose to remember about the past, where we begin and end our retrospective account, and who we include and exclude from them—these do a lot to determine how we live and what decisions we make in the present.[54]

Unlike Yerushalmi then, Lipsitz does not think one can fully extract political interests from historiography. But according to Lipsitz, these inevitable incursions have implications for how and for what purposes one should research and teach history:

> The very cornerstones of historical research [are the] appreciation of difference, understanding of context and the ability to make critical, comparative judgements on the basis of empathy and evidence… Historical accounts do not have to presume final and fixed meanings, they can become important mechanisms for opening up and understanding the multiple possibilities contained in any one account. History can be a way of opening up the present, of seeing its multiple possibilities by exploiting the roads not taken from the past.[55]

Teachers of history are inescapably agents of the institutions and social groups that employ them. They cannot flee entirely from serving some political and ideological interests. But in this regard they are no different from anyone else. Discourse by its nature is tinged with a rhetorical hue. Helping students understand this "fact," and seeing how it shapes the accounts we render of both the roads taken and not taken in the past may enrich and enliven all of our individual and collective pursuits of constructing myths we can live by. We cannot teach history without teaching myth. The issue is only how we do it.

Notes

1. Y. H. Yerushalmi, Zakhor, *Jewish History and Jewish Memory*. (New York: Schocker, 1989). He seems to treat "collective memory" and myth as synonyms, though he uses the first term in the opening portion of the book and the second, in its latter pages.
2. I have examined the holdings for history and curricula of the largest Jewish educational resource center, The Pedagogic and Resource Center and Library of the Melton Centre at the Hebrew University. See two studies by R. Firer (*The Agents of Zionist Education* [Hebrew] (Tel Aviv: Hakibbutz Hameuchad, 1985); *Agents of the Holocaust Lesson* [Hebrew] (Tel Aviv: Hakibbutz Hameuchad, 1989); for the impact of ideology on the teaching of history in Israel.
3. P. Nora, "Between Memory and History: *Les Lieux de Memoire*," *Representations* 26, (1989), 8.
4. Ibid., 8-9.
5. Here I utilize much of Yerushalmi's formulation in *Zakhor*, 94.
6. Below we shall suggest that what most differentiates modernist historians like Yerushalmi from postmodernist ones are additional aspects of matters of method. Specifically, postmodernists see significant limitations to the conclusions of historians due to the representational quality of all discourse, including historical narrative. The situatedness of historians within particular time, place and modes of inquiry all structure and restrict their insights, and moreover, encode these assertions with political, ideological significance. The literary aspects of historical accounts cannot be treated as insignificant, for as Hayden White has argued, their tropological features are themselves part of the message. The meanings of history conveyed by structure and literary features of historical narratives are products of the historians; they are not inherent within the selected events.
7. The following sections of the paper use and recast some of my remarks in a forthcoming companion essay, "Heroes and History in American Jewish Education." In *Crisis and Reaction: The Hero in Jewish History*, Ed. M. Mor (Omaha: Creighton University Press). Two essays by W. Ackerman, "'Let us Now Praise Famous Men in Their Generations': History Books for Jewish Schools in America" (*Dor LeDor: Studies in the History of Jewish Education* 2, x, 1984), 1-35. "The State of the Art: History" in *A World Survey of Jewish Educational Curricula: The State of the Art*, Ed. W. Ackerman, E. Shohamy, J. West and D. Zisenwine, (Tel Aviv: Tel Aviv University, The Israel Institute, 1984), 3-14) provide detailed and very insightful analyses of a significant portion of the curricula and textbooks (especially those published by the early 70s) related to instruction in Jewish history. I have used many of Ackerman's comments on the history of the teaching of this subject area, and on the goals and quality of the instructional materials. D. Bernstein, *Two Approaches to the Teaching of Jewish History in Orthodox Yeshiva High Schools*.

Unpublished Dissertation, (New York: New York University, 1986); D. Goldflam, *Survey of Current Practices and Attitudes of Jewish History Teachers in High Jewish Day Schools in the United States*. Unpublished Dissertation, (Coral Gables: University of Miami, 1989)) provide the only recent data on the actual instruction in Jewish history. Bernstein's is a qualitative work comparing two approaches, integrated curriculum *vs.* separate course, used by several Orthodox Jewish secondary schools in the greater New York city area. It is rich in its interviews of the classroom instructors, and also contains detailed examinations of the most commonly used instructional works. Goldflam's study is a quantitative work based on 38 responses, by a variety of Jewish schools, to his survey on teaching Jewish history. H. Hochberg and G. Lang, ("The Jewish High School in 1972-73: Status and Trends," *American Jewish Yearbook* 75, 1975), 235-76 provide figures for 1973 based upon a small sample of high schools.

J. Fitzgerald, "History in the Curriculum: Debate on Aims and Values," *History and Theory Beiheft* 22/4, 1983), 81-100 provides a historical survey of the general teaching of history in western society. Additional comments on this subject appear in S. Grayzel, "Jewish History as a Subject of Instruction in the Jewish School," in *Readings in the Teaching of Jewish History*. Ed. A. Eisenberg and A. Segal, (New York: Jewish Education Committee of New York Press, 1956), 97-104, and the two already cited articles by Ackerman on the teaching of history.

8. Throughout this paper I offer two ages for dividing the first two groupings because there is some variation on this matter. Some educators place the breaks at grades 3, others at the conclusion of grade 4.

9. Ackerman, "Let Us Praise," 5.

10. D. Pessin, The Jewish People (New York: United Synagogue Commission on Jewish Education, 1951); M. Soloff. *When the Jewish People Was Young* (Cincinnati: UAHC, 1934); M. Gamoran, *The New Jewish History* (New York: UAHC, 1953); J. Isaacs. *Our People: History of Jews, A Textbook of Jewish History for the School and Home* (Brooklyn: Merkos L'Inyone Chinuch, 1970); G. and L. Klaperman, *The Story of the Jewish People* (New York: Behrman House, 1956).

11. These characterizations of the textbooks are a brief restatement of many of Ackerman's observations in his article on these works.

12. Ackerman, "Let Us Praise," x.

13. In his article on textbooks Ackerman remarks, "All the texts, regardless of date of publication, are clearly less interested in the intrinsic merits of history than in the use of the discipline for the fostering of identification and the cultivating of allegiance to the Jewish people." ("Let Us Praise," x).

14. Ibid., 27.

15. While most authors of textbooks order their presentations so as to reveal the key messages of Jewish history, they differ regarding the actual content of that message. Those subscribing to a religious interpretation of Jewish history focus upon certain great Jewish values which are presented as the

essence of Judaism and as the cause that explains the mystery of Jewish survival. Zionist, nationalist approaches note the centrality of the land of Israel as either a reality or a hope in the lives of Jews throughout the centuries. All writers depict the history of the Jewish people so as to legitimate a particular approach to Jewish behavior in the present. They also seem quite confident that their analyses, but what in most textbooks turn out to be "recitations" of the past, will as Soloff remarks, "show us what fine things Jews have done in the past, make us loyal to our people, inspire us, as Jews, to do even greater things in the future" (*op. cit.*, 4).

16. A. Eisenberg and A. Segal, *Teaching Jewish History* (New York: Jewish Education Committee of New York Press, 1954); *Readings in the Teaching of Jewish History* (New York: Jewish Education Committee of New York Press, 1958).

17. A. Eisenberg and A. Segal, *Teaching Jewish History*, 3-4.

18. Eisenberg's and Segal's view is that a certain approach to the world, a willingness to adapt and change, yet a commitment to preserve that essence, is the recurrent feature of Jewish history. Orthodox writers such as Isaacs object to many of the available textbooks, and instead accentuate the role of God, of great Jewish sages, and of obedience to Torah as the determinative factors in the survival of the Jews.

19. These criticisms are not meant to imply that Eisenberg and Segal lack a sophisticated understanding of the complexity of history and historical inquiry. Their program, as I have stated, is one of the most developed proposals. Furthermore, they appreciate that the findings of historians are based upon the use of specific methodologies. Unlike nearly all of the actual textbooks, as Ackerman has shown, they even seem to advocate that students be informed about how theoretical commitments, the points of view of historians, impact upon the results of their endeavors. Yet the following remarks suggest they do not permit their willingness to engage students on these matters to impede the ultimate goal of socialization:

> Jewish history is similar to other in having many causes. In the case of Jewish history religious, cultural, literary and spiritual factors stand out. Objectivity, impartiality and neutrality are neither possible nor desirable. The teacher should develop a positive point of view which serves the best interests of Judaism as he sees it. He should be frank and open about his point of view and should be tolerant of other points of view, but not afraid to criticize or oppose any point of view inimical to Jews (5).

20. While the four theoreticians, S. Grayzel, J. Starr, W. Chomsky and A. Eisenberg, whose papers appear in the anthology *Readings in Teaching of Jewish History*, agree on the basic structure of cycles, there are some disagreements on the details. Grayzel, for example, calls for a chronological approach only for the "mature mind" of the fifteen or sixteen year old. He

suggests that the second cycle, therefore, focus upon the structure of the present and earlier Jewish communities.

21. W. Chomsky, "Varied Approaches in Teaching History," in *Readings in the Teaching of Jewish History* Ed. A. Eisenberg and A. Segal, (New York: The Jewish Education Committee of New York, 1956), 183-84.

22. Ibid., 185.

23. Ibid.

24. Ibid., 185-86.

25. R. Lurie, *The Great March. Post Biblical Stories I,II* (New York: UAHC, 1931).

26. E. Gamoran, "Introduction" In *The Great March, Post Biblical Jewish Stories I* (New York: UAHC, 1966), 1-2.

27. Ackerman, "Let Us Praise," 11.

28. Ibid.

29. Ibid., 27-28.

30. Grayzel, "Jewish History as a Subject of Instruction in the Jewish School, in *Readings in the Teaching of Jewish History*, Ed. A. Eisenberg and A. Segal, 103-04.

31. Ibid., 100.

32. Since this paper seeks to detail the actual pedagogic approaches and the particular importance they assign to discussions of heroes, I here merely allude to the causes of these changes. No effort is made to describe them in detail or to correlate specific causes with individual works. Much has been written on the changes in American society and in the sociology of America, including the impact of such developments on American Jewish education. Ackerman, "Strangers to the Tradition: Idea and Constraint in American Jewish Education," in *Jewish Education Worldwide, Cross-cultural Perspectives*. Ed. H. Himmelfarb and S. DellaPegola (Lanham: University Press of America, Jewish Educational Service of North America, 1988), 70-111, and B. Chazan, *The State of Jewish Education* (New York: Jewish Educational Service of North America, 1988) provide good surveys of these matters. Regarding the negative assessment of the classical paradigm as a whole, or portions of it, one need only to look at many of the materials developed from the 60's onwards for teaching Jewish history. These resources often justify their publication by decrying the frequently called abysmal failure of the classical approach. The studies of Bernstein and Goldflam provide quantitative and qualitative evidence of poor conceptualization, implementation, and results of the classical paradigm.

33. In his analysis of several textbooks published after 1960, Ackerman ("Let Us Praise") details some of these continuities. He comments upon the more recent works by A. Eban, *My People, History of the Jews* (New York: Behrman House, 1978)); F. Hyman, *The Jewish Experience, Books One and Two* (New York: United Synagogue of America, 1974); and E. Charry and A. Segal, *The Eternal People: The Story of Judaism and Jewish Thought through the Ages* (New York: United Synagogue Commission on Jewish Education, 1967); to which

one could add books by S. Rossel, *Journey Through Jewish History* (New York: Behrman House, 1981); and R. Samuels, *Pathways Through Jewish History* (New York: KTAV, 1970). All of these books offer chronological surveys, though they greatly differ in their focus and sophistication.

The curricula designed by Torah U'Mesorah, the national body for Orthodox Day Schools, for several schools (Seattle Hebrew Academy, Hillel Academy of Milwaukee, Hebrew Academy of Suffolk County, Hebrew Academy of Great Kansas City, Akiva Day School of Southfield, Ida Crown Jewish Academy), adhere to the classical paradigm. The curriculum for diaspora education of the Department for Torah Education of the World Zionist Organization *Takhnit Av LeHoraat Toldot Yisrael BeVeyt HaSefer HaYehudi B'Tfusot* (Jerusalem: W.Z.O., Torah Education Dept., 1975) mandates three fairly traditional cycles, though its first cycle is for grades 4-6 and not K-4.

A. Egozi's curriculum *The Hebrew Curriculum for Day Schools and Yeshivot for Grades 7-9* (Toronto: Associated Hebrew Schools of Toronto, 1982), that of the Boston Bureau of Jewish Education *Curriculum for Talmud Torahs* (Boston: Bureau of Jewish Education, 1968) and *The Curriculum Outline for the Hebrew Afternoon Schools in Ontario* (Toronto: Canadian Jewish Congress, 1989); S. Isseroff's curriculum for Orthodox Talmud Torah's *Course of Study and Teacher's Guide for the Talmud Torah* (New York: Metropolitan Commission of Talmud Torah Education and national Commission on Torah Education, 1970); and the curriculum of the Rabbi Alexander Gross Day School in Miami, *Self Study*, (Miami: 1989) also call for a "classical" structuring of instruction in Jewish history.

Providing an answer, often a succinct one, to the "mystery of Jewish survival" frequently serves as the overall message of textbooks and curricula. Eban's book opens and closes with such remarks. Other books that offer the clues to Jewish survival, the lessons from the past for the future include: Samuels, Rossel, B. Chazan and Y. Poupko, *Guide to Jewish Knowledge for the Center Professional* (New York: Jewish Welfare Board, 1990); and S. Copeland, *A Modern Jewish History Chinuch and Hadracha Source Book* (New York: Hashachar, 1978).

Numerous books, including Eban, Samuels, A. Eisenberg, *Eyewitness to Jewish History* (New York: UAHC, 1973); D. Karp, *Heroes of Jewish Thought* (New York: KTAV, 1965); *Heroes of Modern Jewish Thought* (New York: KTAV, 1966); *Heroes of American Jewish History* (New York: KTAV, 1972) stress the importance of instilling pride in Jewish youth. Strengthening Jewish identity through the acquisition of knowledge about Jews and through approaches that focus upon the affective side of the learners continues as a prime goal of nearly all works.

34. A. Eisenberg, Eyewitness to Jewish History (New York: UAHC, 1973); *Curriculum for the Small Jewish Religious School in English Speaking Communities* (New York: United Synagogue Commission on Jewish Education, 1973); E. Grad, *The Teenager and Jewish Education* (New York: Education Assembly

of the United Synagogues of America, 1968); R. Chazan, *A Jewish History Syllabus-High School Curriculum Series* (New York: United Synagogue Comission on Jewish Education, 1975); J. Stern, Ed., *A Curriculum for the Afternoon Jewish School, Experimental Edition* (New York: United Synagogue Commission on Jewish Education, Board of Jewish Education of New York, 1978); Board of Jewish Education of New York, 1978. *Integrated Course of Study in Jewish and General History for Grades 9-10 in Yeshiva and Day High School* (New York: Board of Jewish Education, 1978); J. Blumberg, "The Study of Jewish History in the Jewish Day School," *Ten Daat* 6/1, (1992), 31-32, and A. Labovitz, *Secrets of the Past, Bridges to the Future* (Miami: Central Agency for Jewish Education, 1984).

35. Stern, *Curriculum*, 10.

36. Ibid., 10-12. The above brief references to this work should not be taken to mean that it is a simplistic project. This curriculum is one of a few carefully detailed educational blueprints. It contains one of the most elaborate presentations regarding instruction in Jewish history. In ten tightly type written pages, the authors explain ten components of their definition of history, list five caveats that must be kept in mind in order that these goals be achieved, and offer nineteen pedagogic suggestions for teachers. Moreover, because they allow only for a complex instructional approach, they do not mandate that all schools adopt this branch of the curriculum. They require that all students be exposed only to two or three units, Holocaust, Israel or American Jewish history.

37. H. Adelman, *The Jewish People: Teaching Jewish History, Social Studies, Israel and the Holocaust in Religious Schools, An Introduction to the KTAV Curriculum* (Hoboken: KTAV, 1983); B. Bacon, *Rambam: His Thought and His Times* (New York: Melton Research Center, Jewish Theological Seminary of America, 1993); E. Baum, "The Place of Social Studies in the Jewish School," *Pedagogic Reporter* 29/2 (1978) 2; A. Bennett, "The Place of Social Studies in the Jewish School," *Pedagogic Reporter* 29/2 (1978) 3-4. H. Bogot, Ed, *To See the World Through Jewish Eyes*, (New York: CCAR-UAHC, 1982-88); M. Cohen, "The Place of Social Studies in the Jewish School." *Pedagogic Reporter*. 29/2, (1978) 4-5; A. Friedman,. *Rocky Mountain Curriculum Planning Workshop, A Second Change for Change. All New Experimental Curriculum for Grades K-12 for the Jewish Religious School* (Colorado Springs: Rocky Mountain Curriculum Planning Workshop, 1971); Z. Grumet, "Another Perspective on the Avot and Imahot," *Ten Daat* 6/1, (1992), 25-27; C. Ingall, *Rashi and His World* (New York: Melton Research Center, Jewish Theological Seminary of America, 1987); Jacoby, "The Place of Social Studies in the Jewish School," *Pedagogic Reporter* 29/2 (1978) 6-7; Jewish Educational Service of North America, *Unified Jewish Religious Education Curriculum Guide for the Armed Forces* (New York: Jewish Educational Service of North America, Department of Pedagogic Services, 1983); D. Kaskove and K. Olitzky, *Hebrew, Holidays and Heroes* (New York: UAHC, 1992); S. Leiman, *A New Integrated Social Studies Curriculum for Yeshivah Day Schools Grades 2-6* (New York: Board of Jewish

Education, 1984); M. Lewittes, "Teaching Social Studies in Jewish Schools," *Pedagogic Reporter* 29/2 (1978) 9-12; S. Goldberg Loeb and B. Binder Kadden, *Jewish History: Moments and Methods, An Activity Source Book for Teachers* (Denver: ARE, 1982); J. Moline, *Jewish Leadership and Heroism* (New York: United Synagogue of America, Department of Youth Activities, 1987); F. Reichwald. *Eighteen Lives* (New York: 1981); S. Siegman, E. Weinstein, D. Schapiro and C. Chanover, *Ideas and Activities for Teaching Jewish History* (Baltimore: Bureau of Jewish Education, 1983); C. Ellowitz Silver, *Pass the Torah Please: Jewish Leaders from Mattathias to Saadia* (Denver: ARE, 1990); F. Zeldin, *The Importance of One* (New York: KTAV, 1980).

38. L. Garber, "Teaching Jewish Herstory," in *Issues at Irvine August 27-31, 1978: A Sampler of Jewish Education and Teaching, The Western Conference*, Ed. S. Dorph, (Irvine: 1978); S. Eisenberg Sasso and S. Levi Elwell, *Jewish Women: Preserving Life, Studying, Teaching, Seeking God, Building Community, Making Connections* (Denver: 1983).

39. M. Cohen, To *See the World*, 5.

40. Ibid.

41. Jacoby, *Rashi and his World*, 6.

42. H. Cohen, *Our Struggle to Be: A Course in Four Units for Grades 8-10* (New York: UAHC, 1977); Jewish Educational Service of North America, *Unified Jewish Religious Education Curriculum Guide for the Armed Forces, Guide for Adolescents and Adults* (New York: Jewish Educational Services of North America, Department of Pedagogic Services, 1988); J. Kaye and N. Towvim, *Dilemmas and Adaptations. Spotlights on Jewish History* (Boston: Bureau of Jewish Education, 1982); A. Pomson, "Jewish History: Going Back to the Future." *CAJE Jewish Education News* (1990), 20-21.

43. Kaye and Towvim. *Dilemmas.*, iv.

44. Pomson, "Back to the Future."

45. Ibid.

46. E. Brier and C. Ingall, *Your are the Historian: An Introduction to Medieval Jewish History and Historiography* (Providence: Bureau of Jewish Education, 1982); Paul Blank, "Teaching Jewish History, 'Panorama of Jewish History.'" *CAJE Jewish Education News* (1990), 15-19.

47. Brier and Ingall, *Historian*, 2.

48. Blank. "Panorama," 17.

49. Ibid., 15.

50. Ibid., 17.

51. Ackerman, "Let Us Praise"; O. Schremer, "Historiah uMechqarah MiPerspeqtivah shel Sifre Limud VaHoraah Chadashim," Zion [Hebrew] 57/4, (1992), 451-65.

52. Ibid., 9.

53. Ibid., 33-34.

54. Schremer, "Historian," 465.

55. The literature on collective memory is expanding, with much of it addressing the relationship between that phenomenon and historical accounts.

Informative discussions of these matters appear in J. Fentress and C. Wickham, *Social Memory* (Oxford: Blackwell, 1992); D. Middleton and D. Edwards, *Collective Remembering* (London: Sage, 1990); P. Connerton. *How Societies Remember* (Cambridge: Cambridge, 1989); D. Lowenthal, "The Timeless Past: Some Anglo-American Historical Preconceptions. *The Journal of American History* 75 (1989), 1263-1280; J. Nerone, "Professional History and Social Memory," *Communication* 11 (1989), 89-104; D. Thelen, "History and American History," *The Journal of American History* 75 (1989), 1117-19; P. Burke, "History as Social Memory," In *Memory, History, Culture and the Mind.* Ed. T. Butler (Oxford, Blackwell, 1989), 97-111.

56. See his comments in Yerushalmi, *Zahov*, 96,98.

57. Ibid., 116.

58. Ibid., 101-03.

59. G. Lipsitz, *Time Passages: Collective Memory and American Popular Culture* (Minneapolis: University of Minnesota Press, 1990). My thinking on the implications of postmodernism, deconstruncionism and hermeneutical theory for the status of history have been shaped by many recent works. Two excellent discussions are: D. MaGaughey, "Through Myth to Imagination," JAAR 56/1 (1988), 51-76; and H. White, "The Question of Narrative in Contemporary Historical Theory." *History and Theory* 23 (1984) 1-33; "'Figuring the Nature of the Times Deceased': Literary Theory and Historical Writing," in The Future of Literary Theory. Ed. R. Cohen (New York: Routledge, 1989), 19-43. In these and other writings, White notes the disinterest on the part of many practicing historians in matters of theory.

60. Ibid., 28-29.

61. Ibid., 34.

62. Ibid., 24, 30. Thelen concludes his article ("History and American History, 1129) by commenting upon the implications of his views for teaching:

> If we wanted a history curriculum that taught people how to use memories, we would focus upon how memories are constructed. We would help students to learn how to get honest and accurate feedback for their own constructions even as they followed their natural wishes to find support from their conclusions. We would encourage them to learn how to challenge, adapt and construct memories instead of accepting interpretations that others seek to impose on them, how to test appeals to the past instead of accepting them on faith and authority. We would explore the social and communal contexts in which memories are created, reshaped, and forgotten. We would illustrate how their memories can lead as naturally to progressive constructions and ideologies as to conservative ones.

Part Two:
Modern Uses of
Myth in Judaism

The Invention of a Secular Ritual: Western Jewry and Nationalized Tourism in Palestine, 1922-1933

Michael Berkowitz

Before 1933, it was unusual for a Jew from Western Europe or the United States to consummate his or her participation in Zionism by settling in Palestine. The cases of those who attempted to do so, such as the *Blau-Weiss* youth from Germany, were truly exceptional, as indicated by the vociferous debate surrounding their decision. In the interwar years, although Western Jews making aliya never constituted more than a trickle, the rush of German, British, and American Jewish tourists to Palestine became increasingly significant. Over 70,000 total visitors came to the country from the West during 1924, and in the spring of 1925, 1,200 were present on a single day.[1] Some 40,000, including an estimated 4,000 Jews, saw Palestine in 1930,[2] despite the ongoing Arab revolt and the deepening worldwide economic crisis.[3]

The steady increase of the tourist trade in Palestine resembles that of other Near Eastern and European locales in the interwar years, as the "holiday-taking patterns of the privileged few" were embraced by an ever broader range of people.[4]

There are aspects of the evolution of Palestine tourism, however, which make it distinctive; it does not neatly fit European models or those derived from "less developed countries." Perhaps this helps explain why Jewish tourism to Palestine and the State of Israel is usually absent in the literature on travel.[5] "Tourism," one critic notes, "is a practice of considerable cultural and economic importance; yet despite the pervasiveness of tourism and its centrality to our conception of the contemporary world, it has been neglected by students of culture."[6] It is not surprising, then, that within Zionist scholarship, there is hardly any notice of the tourist trade.[7]

A tradition of Jewish, Christian, and Islamic pilgrimage to their respective holy places in Palestine, especially Jerusalem, was well established by the 1880s when the Zionists arrived on the scene.[8] Travelers motivated by Islam, however, do not seem to have been within the ken of the movement's leaders. Especially after the British gained control over Palestine in the wake of World War I, Zionist officials asserted that the movement stood to gain in various ways through a western-oriented tourist trade. Zionists were elated to show off the fruits of their efforts to non-Jews, including Christian pilgrims to the Holy Land, and they aspired to convert non-Zionist Jewish travelers to Zionism.[9] Most of the movement's energy exerted on tourism, however, came to be channeled toward enticing Jews—who were already inclined to support the movement—to come to Palestine, and if they made the journey, to assure that they carried away a favorable impression of the Zionist enterprise. What the Zionists attempted to do, and to a large extent accomplished by 1933, was establish a secular-Jewish pilgrimage ritual,[10] to endow the ancient historical sites with new national-Jewish meanings, and delineate a secularized "sacred geography" for Jews in Palestine.[11] The movement sought to cultivate the reception of this space, so it would be "venerated as a fount of communal identity" for all Jews.[12]

To be sure, regardless of Zionism, Jewish travelers were inspired by the same core sentiments that had propelled Western Jewish tourists eastward since the early nineteenth century: to see Eretz Israel, the birthplace of Judaism, the bedrock of antiquity, the veritable "cradle of civilization"[13]—in particular, to connect to their own primordial, religious tradition, and to take in sites of historical interest. The Zionist movement invigorated and then overtook this phenomenon by actively encouraging Western Jews, even in places where Zionism was dormant, such as Switzerland and France,[14] to see the movement's work in Palestine first-hand. Despite intermittent pronouncements that tourist trips to Palestine were a prelude "to permanent settlement,"[15] any such pretension was subdued as tourism was integrated into the ideology and practice of Diaspora-Zionist nationalization. Further, a visit to the country was fashioned into the climactic ritual of the process of becoming a complete Zionist.[16] Indeed, this ceremonialized tour, which was both less and more than a pilgrimage, had been precipitated by the dissemination of Zionist artistic and photographic images in the West since Theodor Herzl wielded the techniques of mass politics in the upstart movement in 1897, helping to provide a richly textured view of Jewish life in Palestine.[17]

As opposed to a comprehensive treatment of the interwar tourist trade in Palestine,[18] what follows is a discussion of the attempted appropriation of tourism by the Zionist movement, and its reception by Western Jews.[19] In particular, the focus is on institutional efforts to draw Western Jews, who had not been very involved in Zionism, into the movement's orbit, and to intensify the commitment of those already aligned with the movement by shaping their experience in Palestine. At first, the Zionist movement sought to add some exposure to the new Yishuv for those Jews who made their way to Palestine, mainly in the form of excursions to Jewish settlements. Such trips were made optional, or added to the preexisting schedule of visits to markets, historical venues, and holy places. Eventually Zionist officials made common cause with touring companies to include the sites of the Zionist project as regular stops on the Palestine, or Egypt-Palestine itinerary.

By the early 1930s, the movement so succeeded in fitting tourism into their general attempt to promote the movement among Jews, that the earlier religious-historical impetus for seeing the country was subsumed into the greater scheme of showing off the Zionist efforts. Tourism was quickly enshrined as a marvelous device of propaganda and fund-raising. It furnished assimilated Jews with a way to connect with Jewish Palestine which made them feel as if they knew the inside story, and left some taste of the breadth of Jewish experience in the country. Zionist tourism fostered an ongoing information and propaganda network that for the most part worked to expand knowledge and sentimental attachment for the national project, and furthermore encoded paradigms for perceiving and grasping the Zionist movement which would prove to be remarkably resilient.

In addition to the easily understood economic motives, the use of tourism to bolster national pride, and to demonstrate a nation's claims to legitimacy and greatness are not unique to Zionism. "National and communal efforts to recall and refashion a praiseworthy if not a glorious past," writes historian David Lowenthal, are

> similar to the needs of individuals to construct a viable and believable life history. In reviewing alterations of the past, students of nationalism and psychoanalysis and literary criticism share an awareness that individuals, like states, must continually confront the competing pulls of dependence and autonomy, following and leading, tradition and creativity, infancy and maturity.[20]

But along with these common traits is a distinctive variation on the familiar nationalist tune.

Regarding Western Jews who would come as visitors to Palestine, Zionist officials were not simply interested that money be spent, perhaps invested, and that their spirits be buoyed by the national achievements. The movement was committed to devising means to connect European and American Jews with the place, to create bonds that would lead to specific behaviors, including future visits and greater donations to the Zionist cause. Seeing Palestine was extolled as a more persuasive instrument for gaining adherents and promoting solidarity than any ideological argument. "Above all," it was proclaimed in the German Zionist organ *Juedische Rundschau*, "it is important that every returning tourist from Palestine be an apostle for the idea of the building-up of Erez Israel," to establish "a personal connection of Diaspora Jewry with the new Jewry." Once home, they should instinctively "arouse new Jewish life and a willingness to sacrifice for the purposeful construction of Palestine."[21]

To be sure, any pleasant visit to a foreign country might evoke curiosity, empathy, and sustained interest and good feelings toward the people and the place. The Zionists demanded no less, though, than for a Jew's visit to Palestine to become "the high point" of his or her life.[22] Included in this was the imperative that Jewish visitors feel that they had visited the true home of the depths of their souls. Palestine was not to be another home away from home, or just a superb vacation spot—but the place Western Jews would recognize as their most authentic home.[23] Ideally, an inversion would occur, or at least the boundaries would be blurred in their mind's eye between concepts of "home" and "away," "we" and "they," "here" and "there."[24] Although after the establishment of the State of Israel, the concept "making aliya" (literally, "ascending") would be understood as permanently settling in the country, earlier the notion was more vague; for instance, tourists, along with Chaluzim ("pioneers" to Erez Israel), were said to comprise the "aliya from Germany" in 1923.[25] In effect, all one had to do was visit Palestine in order to undergo this spiritual transformation.

The first attempts to modify Palestine tourism to fit the needs of the movement arose from complaints against the European-based tour industry in the early 1920s. Palestine was already a chief destination for travel,[26] but there was virtually no attention paid to any of the specific "Zionist addresses." One writer grumbled that "not a single Jewish colony or settlement is visited by the large tourist expeditions; they see nothing of the new Jewish life." This was attributed to the "antisemitic tendencies of the great international travel bureaus, especially [Thomas] Cook,"[27] which had been running tours to Egypt and Palestine since 1869.[28] It seems, however, that in the 1920s the touring companies began to sense that it was to their advantage to warm up to the Zionist Organization.[29]   By 1924, Thomas Cook & Son, in its promotional literature for Egypt and Palestine tours, gave special prominence to "the Jewish colonies in Palestine." Apparently the company had taken to heart the dissatisfaction expressed by Jewish tourists and Zionist authorities.[30] Simultaneously, the Zionist Organization sought to attract greater numbers of Jews and Zionists to the country by lowering the cost of travel through assembling larger parties and by partially subsidizing the journey for selected persons and groups.[31] Generic tours were indeed becoming more "Zionistic."[32]

An essential undergirding mythology in tour promotions was that visiting the Promised Land constituted a mitzvah for Jews. In conjunction with the Zionist Organization, the Thomas Cook company instituted a Palestine tour during the Passover holiday in 1929. A British Zionist journal promoting the tour wrote that

> Pesach is a delightful season to pay a visit to the country. In the bright sunshine, with the land budding forth in luxuriant growth and the very atmosphere breathing the spirit of the Jewish Festival of Freedom, the Jew can see the New Palestine he has created under the most favorable climatic, economic, and psychological conditions. We are pleased to note that so universal a touring agency as Cooks should have found it advisable to arrange a special Jewish tour for this year.[33]

Overall, though, in the interwar years there is little evidence of long-range planning concerning tourism within world Zionism or the formative infrastructure of the Yishuv—despite the creation of a bureau with Fritz Loewenstein at its head in 1925. Rather, Zionist tourism emerged as a series of measures to improve on that which existed and to respond to complaints of those whose visits to Palestine had been unpleasant or otherwise disconcerting.[34]

On a material level, the standard many Zionists seemed to have in mind was Switzerland; they wanted facilities in Palestine to be as cheery and efficient as Alpine pensions, and thereby for Palestine to be considered a "Jewish Switzerland," or a "Swiss Corridor to Asia."[35] In 1925, "on the basis of a four-week stay in Palestine," a correspondent for the *Juedische Rundschau* wrote that "the hotel industry in Palestine" was in need of "drastic reform and improvement." He noted a disposition among hotel proprietors that compounded the problem: they did not seem to care about the level of comfort or service, as long as they gave clients a room.[36] Another writer warned that due to guest-house and transportation frustrations, Palestine was acquiring a reputation as an irksome destination. Worse, there were still tour groups that would leave ignorant of the modernization taking place under Zionist auspices and of "the new type of Jewish man" preeminent in the Yishuv. This was not, as previously alleged, due primarily to the ill-will of the touring companies; the Chaluzim shared the blame, as Jewish visitors were only infrequently welcomed by them "with a joyful heart." It was desirable that Jewish tourists, in substantial numbers, should spend a few days in a collective settlement, to afford them more than a "fleeting glance"—so they could be won over to the system which counted many skeptics among middle-class Western Jews. Ironically, Christian visitors seemed to be treated more amicably than Jews, and there was occasional outright hostility toward non-Hebrew speaking Diaspora Jews.[37]

There is little doubt that the brusque handling of eager tourists, and the repeated phenomenon of the inhabitants of Jewish settlements vanishing upon the arrival of their brethren from abroad,[38] helped to mold the programs intended to edify and cultivate the warm feelings of the next waves of Western Jewish visitors. In many of the settlements complaints were apparently acknowledged. As testimony to the rectification of such problems, one young Dutch woman wrote about her experience at a kibbutz, where she delighted in getting to know the Chaluzim: "After dinner, spontaneously, somebody started to sing. Soon everybody joined in, and a few minutes later all were dancing the horrah, the Palestinian round-dance. It was an infectious, simple gaiety, coming naturally at the end of a hard day's work, without the help of alcohol or other stimulants."[39] This sort of experience, which might be characterized as "staged authenticity,"[40] became more and more typical; it represented a radical change from how Zionist tourists were treated, and the face of the Yishuv to which they were exposed. The memoirist recalled: "I was really sorry to leave the colonies, although I felt that for the rest of my life I never wanted to look at another cow again. They are so proud of their livestock that every visitor has to spend a lot of time in the stables, just admiring cows."[41]

Clearly, a main impetus for the Zionist engagement in tourism had been to show off the Jewish settlements that had formerly been off the beaten track. A number of such communities would be visited, emphasizing the Jews' newfound prowess in agriculture and land reclamation. This was remembered by many as a "romance" of the cows.[42] What else, though, did the standardized visit entail, which included many characteristics that would persist for over fifty years? Upon arrival (or shortly thereafter) groups were met by a Zionist dignitary—often someone connected with a fundraising body.[43] On March 10, 1928, for instance, some 600 American tourists landed in Haifa, with 278 Jews among them. Henrietta Szold, who was then a member of the Zionist Palestine Executive, addressed the group at a banquet that evening; it is unclear if it included only the Jewish passengers, or the Christians, as well. She spoke about the extensive development of Palestine in the last decade. Szold stressed that their assistance in the Zionist effort did not constitute "an act of charity, but the fulfillment of their duty" as Jews.[44] The duty of welcoming and initiating the Jewish travelers seemed to fall upon Henreitta Szold, at least weekly, as early as 1922, and she tired of it.[45]

Just as exemplary for displaying the human transformations wrought by the Zionist movement were its educational and cultural institutions. The Herzliya Gymnasium, Haifa Technikum, and Mikveh Israel agricultural school, and the Hebrew University, Bezalel Art Institute, and Hadassah hospital in Jerusalem (outside the walls of the Old City) were showcased as the most sparkling jewels of the new Yishuv.[46] The new Jewish youth sprouting in their ancestral land, healthy in body and spirit, was a dominant motif in the presentation of Palestine. It was said that a literal "metamorphosis" could be observed among the children in the colonies; they had progressed from being sickly in the East European Galut, to being robust in their new homeland.[47]

Sites of significance to Greco-Roman culture, Christianity, and Islam were included in Zionist-led tours. Although some recent critics have alleged that the goal of Zionism was to "possess" the treasures of other faiths,[48] the stress seemed to be on Jewry's suitability as a respectful caretaker, and a mediator between the major religions and their sects. On tours and in travel writing, it was wryly observed that Christians in particular were remiss in tending to their holy places, echoing Herman Melville's impression of the Holy Sepulcher as "A sickening cheat."[49] Predictably, the emphasis in Zionist tours was laid on the evidence of Jewry's earlier incarnation as the biblical nation of Israel. Nowhere was this more striking than in the Old City of Jerusalem. The Wailing Wall, the remains of the western retaining wall around the Temple Mount in the Old City, carried the greatest symbolic significance. This was heightened after the riots of 1929, which had ostensibly broken out due to the denial of the Jewish right to pray at their holiest shrine.

Near the Wall, Zionists were able to make use of monumental British excavations which had begun in the mid-nineteenth century. The relationship of archaeology, the tourist trade, and brewing political formulas, which were no small importance, rarely have been acknowledged by scholars.[50] The labors of the European and American archaeologists were tantamount to a gold mine for Zionist ideology, and the ongoing project of mediating the experience of travelers to Palestine. Overall, there can be little doubt that the intensification of archaeology—fomented by the advance of critical biblical studies and the termination of Ottoman restrictions and harassment—facilitated the rise of Zionist tourism.[51]

The British Palestine Exploration Fund had been founded in 1865; it vigorously "encouraged team efforts and sponsored a number of monumental surveys."[52] After the First World War, Britain reasserted its interest in Palestinian archaeology. Phillip King, historian of the American Schools of Oriental Research, writes that "from the perspective of archaeology," the period between the wars was, and still is considered "the 'golden age of Palestinian excavations.'"[53] In 1919 a Department of Antiquities was established by the British, "and the British School of Archaeology in Jerusalem was the first successor of the old-established schools in Athens and Rome for the training of students and for research in countries overseas." More major excavations in Jerusalem were conducted during 1923-25.[54] The unflagging British mania for "Palestinology"[55] was gleefully appropriated by the Zionists for touring purposes.

Predictably, in 1914 Zionists in Palestine established their own Exploration Society, which was tied to the nascent National Museum at the Bezalel Institute, under the direction of Nahum Slousch.[56] For the most part, however, the excavations initiated by the Zionist group were minuscule compared to the those of the British, Germans, and Americans; they likely did not have the money for the undertaking. During this time, though, Jewish archaeologists who would later have a great impact on Zionism's backward glance, such as Nelson Gleuck and Eliezer Sukenik, would receive their training.[57] They apparently learned not just the tools of the trade of archaeology in a technical sense, but its role in nation-building. Later generations of Jewish tourists, particularly students, would therefore be able to include an archaeological dig among their "working" experiences in the State of Israel. Scratching the soil of an ancient site would carry at least the same level of Zionistic prestige as riding atop a tractor or picking fruit at an agricultural settlement.

Remnants of the enduring Jewish presence in Jerusalem, Zion itself, was the most irrepressible physical evidence propping up the movement's ideology. But Jerusalem, for all its inestimable value, was something of an enigma. The decrepit state of the Jewish Quarter, and its mostly religious inhabitants, was used to convey the message that the old

Yishuv bore the ravages of years of neglect and deprivation; it was in drastic need of restoration and rejuvenation. The counter-image, to a certain extent, was represented by the rise of new suburbs to the West of Jerusalem's Old City, accentuated by the erection of the Jewish Agency building.[58] Above all, however, the purest example of the new Jewish life breathed into the Yishuv was the city of Tel Aviv, touted as the world's first modern "Jewish city."[59] The Tel Aviv/Jerusalem dichotomy would assume many forms in the history of Zionist discourse.

Important archaeological finds related to Jewish history certainly were not limited to Jerusalem, although the Old City ruins were the most spectacular. Sites that were sometimes considered by British archaeologists to be "minor excavations" were frequently "of great importance for the history of the Jewish people," and therefore prime Zionist attractions, such as "the ancient synagogues of Galilee" unearthed by the Deutsche Orient-Gesellschaft before the war.[60] The proximity of these ruins to the new settlements was essential in creating a composite of the new Jewish nation that stressed continuity from ancient to modern times, and assisted in endowing secular, domestic space with religious-national meanings.[61] One American visitor wrote, in a published memoir, that the beauty of Palestine was "as great (on its small scale) as Switzerland or Colorado, as brilliant in places as Naples or Geneva, but a beauty, somehow that is infinitely more appealing, especially in its setting of historic associations."[62] It was a great boon for a Jewish settlement to claim that it was located on or near a place where the Zionists' forebears had lived. Traipsing around on Zionist tours implied dizzying turns in time, but in a fairly circumscribed amount of space.

In addition to the man-made features of the environment, tourists also enjoyed the natural wonders of the country—such as the Dead Sea, and the incredibly varied topography. Again, what made this notable was the existence of such a wide range of natural settings in a relatively small territory. Palestine's topography, like its history, metaphorically encapsulated all of the world. Similar to the impact of British archaeology on Zionist tourism, the British development of Palestine's infrastructure during the mandate, such as refurbishing the port of Haifa and constructing breakwaters for the beaches of Tel Aviv, unintentionally served to make possible the ascendance of Zionist touring. Although Great Britain was surely looking out for its own interests, and there was substance to the claim that the mandatory power favored the Arabs over the Jews on economic questions, the fact remained that Zionists relied to no small degree on large-scale British enterprise, and that tourism in particular stood to benefit.[63]

To be sure, those who toured Palestine under the auspices of the movement were strongly predisposed to see the country "Zionistically" due to the proliferation of images since the turn of the century. The flow of such pictures swelled during the interwar years, particularly through richly illustrated Zionist journals such as *The Pioneer* in England, *Young Judaean* in the United States, *Palaestina-Bild-Korrespondenz* in Central Europe, and the ubiquitous promotions of the Keren Hayesod. In Zionist periodicals and newspapers, more and more space was devoted to travel memoirs and notes from Palestine visitors. Travel to witness Zionism in action spawned a genre within Zionist literature of confessional, epistolary accounts of trips to Palestine, often in the form of juvenilia or quasi-scholarly reportage.[64]

Among the more popular Zionist books between the wars were travel memoirs by two women: *The Immortal Adventure* by Hadassah President Erma Lindheim and *A Springtide in Palestine* by Myriam Harry.[65] The ad for Lindheim's book stated that the author

> has looked at Palestine in all its beauty and has gloried in the valiant struggle of her people for the rehabilitation of the soil of their forbears. *Irma L. Lindheim has written "The Immortal Adventure" so realistically that you will feel you are actually with her in the Holy Land.* Mrs. Lindheim takes us into every nook and corner which she herself has visited, and describes the valiant undertaking of the Zionist pioneers who are restoring the ancient tradition, culture, and life of Palestine with modern schools, hospitals, industry, and agriculture.[66]

In terms of descriptions of the place, Lindheim's *The Immortal Adventure* and Harry's *A Springtide in Palestine* are virtually interchangeable. Lindheim's book, possibly due to the general economic circumstances, only had one printing. Harry's memoir seems to have been a relative best-seller, and appeared in French and German, as well as English. It recounts a young Englishwoman's trip to Palestine which results in her conversion to Judaism and enchantment with the Zionist movement. One would expect that the testimony of a convert—in this case a double conversion, to Judaism and Zionism—would be a lopsided paean to the new-found cause. Yet occasionally Harry seems to have removed her rose-colored lenses; her work is at times refreshingly nuanced. It actually raises questions about the core mythology of the movement she fervently embraces. For instance, she asks whether

"Muslim fanaticism" could ever be reconciled with Zionism, and hints that the conflict is not simply over ownership of the land, but impinged on considerations of ethnicity and class.[67] Although it dispensed less saccharine than the fundraising promotions, the leadership of the Zionist movement proclaimed her novel as one of the most successful creative expressions of the interwar movement.[68] To a large extent, both of these travelogues reinforced the impressions cultivated by the movement's policy-makers, except for striking an unusually empathetic tone toward Palestine's Arabs compared to the general run of Zionist travel literature.

However much there was a sincere effort, on the part of some in the movement, to impart an appreciation for the country and Jewish history and culture, for its own sake, Zionist authorities—with their eyes fixed on Western Jewry—continually returned to the implications for fundraising. "Improved tourism," it was widely understood," means improved propaganda, and improved propaganda means improved fundraising."[69] "Propaganda work" which would strengthen the "financial instruments" of the movement was recognized, if not always explicitly mentioned, as one of the great benefits of tourism.[70] In a column "American Tourists Visit Palestine" appearing in the *Hadassah News Letter*, it was reported that "several visitors were so impressed with the work of the [Hadassah] organization that they made contributions toward its support." The fifty-two individual contributors were listed with their amounts given, from $1 to $500.[71] Similar accounts appeared in numerous Zionist and general-Jewish publications.

In fact, the "Zionist Information Bureau for Tourists," established in 1925, was founded under the auspices of not only the Jewish Agency, but also the Keren Hayesod and the Keren Kayemet L'Israel (KKL, JNF, Jewish National Fund). This bureau issued a pamphlet, "Das juedische Palaestina" in hopes that it would replace or supplement the existing guides that ignored Zionism. It was billed as particularly shrewd in its restrained political tone and its "excellent understanding of the psychology of the tourist."[72] In 1931, though, a more extensive clearing-house type agency was suggested as a resource not only for tourists, but for those seeking information about investments, and to organize fact-finding type missions for professionals such as teachers, engineers, doctors, archaeologists, journalists, and artists.[73]

In addition to using tourism to provide a greater incentive for people to give to the movement, fundraising was intertwined with tourism in other ways. It was quite common for tours to be conducted by officials of the Keren Kayemet or Keren Hayesod.[74] Contests were also established in which free trips to Palestine became the ultimate Zionist perquisite. Trips were usually won not by luck of the draw, but by collecting funds. In 1927, for example, twenty-five trips to Palestine were offered to Zionist youth who had been most dedicated to taking care of Jewish National Fund boxes.[75] *Propagandarbeit* and fundraising were always intimately interwoven.

Visits of notable personalities, both Jewish and non-Jewish, were frequently employed to publicize Palestine tourism. All of the various stops on journeys by Lord Balfour and Tomas Masaryk were elaborately documented in the Zionist press.[76] The movement also considered it a minor victory when less well-known personalities, Jews and non-Jews, visited the country. There was no small pride in recognizing that seeing Palestine was worthy of people such as Dr. Emanuel Libmann, a heart specialist from New York, Sir John Russell, an agricultural chemist from Great Britain, Rabbi Max Heller of New Orleans, who was a "Zionist pioneer in among the ranks of Reform Jewry," and businessman Samuel Lamport, who first came to Palestine to represent Brown University at the opening of the Hebrew University, and later returned to establish a loan society. There was no hint of irony in the reports of visits by famous Zionists, such as Max Brod, Martin Buber and Albert Einstein.[77] In addition to judging the strength of the movement by the star quality of the visitors to Palestine, some in Zionism measured the well-being of Diaspora Jewry by the number of tourists coming from their home nations. In other words, tourism to Palestine was perceived as a sign of Jewish vitality.[78]

Different segments of the movement, most often in political, professional, or age-based contingents, tailored tour packages to meet their specific needs.[79] As opposed to being seen as a kind of fragmentation, the movement's center generally condoned, if not applauded, such initiatives.[80] The Hadassah organization, for one, arranged tour packages for its members and their families "to see the comprehensive undertakings of Hadassah, its work in the schools, playgrounds, health centers, and hospitals."[81] Nima Alderblum wrote in the *Hadassah Newsletter* that

> Thomas Cook & Sons have made arrangements with me to give on board their Mediterranean Summer Cruise a course on the history of Palestine, its historic significance, and its present-day development. The itinerary in Palestine will be one that will acquaint the traveler with real Jewish life and will give him a full idea of the romance of the Zionist renaissance as well as of the historic background of the past.

Consistent with Hadassah's endeavor to supply a serious educational component for young Zionists, Alderblum promised that the trip was "like sending the young folks to a Jewish university," and she backed up this claim by stating that attempts were being made for university students to obtain credits for the course. In fact, three levels would be offered—"one for adults, one for young folks, and one for children." Alderblum also informed her readers that "Hebrew speaking clubs will be formed on board the ship so that tourists could become somewhat familiar with the language." And so that no one might think that one would have to rough it like a Chalutz (pioneer) for the whole trip, Alderblum noted that "Cook's cruises are well known for their comforts and luxuries." As opposed to treating Hadassah as marginal within the Zionist project, here "what Hadassah means to Palestine, to the making of Jewish history, and to the women in America" was at the very core of the trip's sensibility, as it was "permeated with the Hadassah spirit."[82] As a result of a similar trip in the winter of 1926, one woman was inspired "to remain in Palestine for six months, another for a year and a third indefinitely."[83] Indeed, the Hadassah tours were remarkable not only in the history of Zionism and tourism, but in women's history. Although the experience of women travelers has gained the attention of historians, this episode stands apart from the journeys of individuals:[84] it is possibly one of the first missions devised to highlight the contributions of women and a specific vision of womanhood and its potential. This may be seen in contrast to the general history of tourism and politicized travel in which anti-feminist stereotypes were more often than not propounded.[85]

Hadassah, like other factions of the movement, asserted that the "crown and climax" to its program of study was "a visit to Palestine." In 1932 it was able to report that "Travel to Palestine, today, can be accomplished with greater convenience and less expense than ever before. Nothing can so clarify one's outlook and stimulate one's interest as a vital and immediate contact with the *Yishub*, no matter what the duration of one's stay." Along with highlighting its own institutions, two other features distinguish the Hadassah travel programs. Hadassah was adamant, and committed greater resources than any other touring group, to their participants gaining some knowledge of Hebrew. Even more exceptional, however, was the importance it accorded to learning about the Arabs in Palestine. "While concentrating our thought upon the Jewish stake in Palestine," a Hadassah reporter urged, we must not lose sight of the fact that in Palestine the preponderating element of the population is Arab and that surrounding Palestine, on all sides, is the great Arab world. It is imperative that we try to understand these neighbors. A course in Islamic culture and history ought to find a place in a complete and well-rounded scheme of Zionist study.[86]

Although all Zionist trips included visits to the Dome of the Rock, Arab markets in Jaffa and Jerusalem, and occasionally, Arab villages, no other part of the movement devoted as much effort as did Hadassah to attempt to understand the Arab world as a viable and valuable civilization in its own right.

The left wing of the movement, Labor Zionism, also instituted its own tours, with an emphasis on participating, in some way, in the "labor" which was said to be invigorating the nation.[87] The brochure from this group proclaimed that "New forms of social existence have developed in Palestine in the course of its rebuilding," referring to the rise of kvutzot, kibbutzim, moshavot, and various cooperatives. "The Seminar under the auspices of the League for Labor Palestine aims to acquaint its members with the new society based on self-labor. It will do more than merely 'tour' the country. The members of the Seminar will *live* the new social order as well as see it." Following the lead of the Thomas Cook Passover tour, the Labor League "Seminar" also took place over the holiday:

> Almost as soon as we set foot on the soil of Palestine, we will celebrate the Passover Seder with the workers of Ain Harod. Then a week traveling through the Valley of Jezreel and through Galilee, living in workers' quarters, eating in community dining rooms, and sharing in all possible ways in the community life. The itinerary will include visits to [several] workers' settlements.

In addition to imbibing the institutions of Labor Zionism, most of the tour consisted of the typical itinerary: visits to "places rich in historic associations," such as "Safed, with its store of Hasidic traditions, the ancient synagogue at Kfar Nahum, Tiberias, the reconstructed synagogue at Beth Alpha, and other significant archaeological excavations." Other stops, among many, included the Jewish colonies Rehovoth, Rishon le Zion, and Ness Ziona; the agricultural school at Mikveh Israel; the famed Ruthenberg power station; Haifa, Old and New Jerusalem, Jericho, the Dead Sea; and Tel Aviv and its environs, particularly "the blossoming orange groves" and sparkling new suburbs of Herzliya,

Ranana, and Kfar Saba. This trip boasted an exceptionally strong political-educational dimension, beginning on the cruise. Noted Labor Zionist leader Dr. Hayim Greenberg was to deliver several lectures on Zionism and "social movements" in Palestine, to be complemented by "lectures, informal talks, and discussions" once the members reached the country. These were arranged in conjunction with Histadrut, the union of Jewish labor federations in Palestine. "Our contacts," it was promised, "will not be those of sightseeing tourists; they will be warm, personal, human."[88] Indeed, the pledge to provide more of a human connection than the average foreign tour, combined with the opportunity to participate in the building of the society and sharing in the lives of its common people, became part of the stock in trade of not exclusively Labor-sponsored tours, but of Zionist touring to Palestine in general.

Along with the sponsorship of tours from the center of the Zionist Organization and by different factions, one of the consequences of the Zionists' efforts was the packaging of entire trips from "a Jewish point of view." These typically included a strong dose of Zionism. Often they were geared for teenagers or young adults, with the added attraction of making acquaintances with those from one's own social background.[89] Although the trend had been to make the journey more economically inclusive, here the incentive was exclusivity. Trips to Palestine could be part of the dating and mating conventions for Jewish young people which were less overt than earlier holiday trips, usually with one's parents, but essentially served the same function.[90] At any rate, a trip to Palestine became for many youth not only a Zionist, but a secular-Jewish rite of passage.[91]

Prior to World War I, Zionism might or might not have made much of an impact on tourists to Palestine. Even those who were in search of a Zionist experience sometimes "would pass by the throbbing life of Palestine, unable to find its pulse."[92] In many respects comparable to the "conquest of the (Diaspora) communities" achieved by the movement, Zionism also persevered in strongly influencing, if not overwhelming, the character of Jewish tourism to Palestine. The movement deemed it vital to its interest to combat the "threat of meaninglessness" and possibility of "disenchantment" for Jewish tourists making the journey.[93] The goal was for Jewish tourists to fall in love with the country, and to see Jewish sovereignty in Palestine as the preeminent means by which Jewry might obtain justice. "One cannot but love this land," an American rabbi wrote in 1927:

it has been martyred, as the age-old victim of war and barbarism; it will yet
be maltreated, it is to be feared, for a long time; but the day must come when
it will shine out, not only to the eye that loves beauty, to the soul that reveres
holiness, but also to the heart which responds to the call of justice.[94]

By the end of the 1920s, it would have been virtually unthinkable for a
Jewish traveler to miss the "pulse" of Zionism in the country; indeed, the
rhythm of the trip was likely to be dominated by Zionism—from
inception to follow-up. Pictures of steam-ships bound for Palestine
became a part of the archive of Zionist images.[95] In 1932, it was said that
even the intense summer heat no longer dissuaded the surge of Zionist-
inspired, Jewish tourists, and commentators were amazed by how many
Americans made the journey.[96] However they might have *shvitst*, their
enthusiasm did not abate.[97]

Travel to Palestine became integral to inscribing "a moving, living
picture"[98] in the mind of Western Jewry. Many layers of Jewish religious
and national associations are evident in the following ad, which appeared in a British Zionist magazine in 1932:

The Jewish New Year is coming!
Make your resolution now.
You must visit Palestine this year.
The historical monuments are attractive.
The religious places are fascinating.
The sunny weather is very healthy.
The Zionist achievements are wonderful.
The modern improvements are amazing.
The trading possibilities are increasing.
The plantations and Industries are developing.
Buildings and settlements are improving.
The Glory of the Past and the Hope of the Future are calling you![99]

A striking features of this ad is its imperative: "You must visit Palestine
this year," which echoed the calls for all Jews to give money to the cause,
as well as the Passover injunction "Next year in Jerusalem." It is
conceivable that one could view the Zionists' deliberate mediation of the
Jewish experience in Palestine as manipulation, or worse, exploitation.
But that would misrepresent their sincere belief in the authenticity of
their claims. This was, in the Zionist imagination, a chief means to attain
national liberation; Jews had to be able to see their potential as a people
and a nation, quite literally, before their eyes—preferably in the best
possible light, as a blossoming flower—in order to perceive themselves

as fully human. The notion of migration, if only temporary, became a functional and symbolic motif of Western Zionism. It was, after all, a reformulation of a central myth of Judaism—exile, return, redemption—that so many non-Jewish peoples had internalized as their own heritage.[100] Zionist tourism in the 1920s, then, was self-consciously constructed as the mediation of a palpable Jewish national space. This helped to move Palestine, as a modern Jewish home, toward the center of Western Jewish discourse—while making it possible to remain a Zionist outside of Zion for most of one's life.

Notes

Research for this project was supported by grants from the Leo Baeck Institute-DAAD, the Rapoport Fellowship of the American Jewish Archives, the Indiana University Center for Research on Philanthropy, the Institute for German History of Tel Aviv University, and the Melton Center for Jewish Studies and Department of History of the Ohio State University.

1. "70613 Palaestinareisende im Jahre 1924," in *Juedische Rundschau*, March 24, 1925, 219; "1200 Personen in einem Tage," in *Juedische Rundschau*, March 31, 1925, 237.

2. Typically, the ships dropped anchor in Haifa and the passengers visited Jerusalem; the bulk of passengers came from the United States and Central Europe; see "Executive der Jewish Agency, Materielien, Palaestina-Touristik, May 1930, 71. JA. 31, D.D. 2/3/4/1/4/, Central Jewish Archives, Jerusalem; "Die palaestinensische Touristensaison 5688," in *Juedische Rundschau*, November 18, 1927, 651. On the basis of limited evidence, it seems that tourism to Palestine and Israel did not usually suffer from internal strife until the 1973 War; see B. Reich and G. Kieval, Israel: *Land of Tradition and Conflict* (Boulder: Westview, 1993), 531; R. W. McIntosh, *Tourism Principles, Practices, and Philosophies* (Columbus, Ohio: Grid, 1972), 41.

3. See N. W. Cohen, *The Year After the Riots: American Responses to the Palestine Crisis of 1929-1930* (Detroit: Wayne State University Press, 1988).

4. G. Young, *Tourism: Blessing or Blight?* (Harmondsworth, Middlesex: Penguin, 1973), 24; see F. Dulles, *Americans Abroad: Two Centuries of European Travel* (Ann Arbor: University of Michigan Press, 1964), 153-4; F. W. Ogilivie, *The Tourist Movement: An Economic Study* (London: P. S. King & Son, 1933), 221; P. Bernard, *Rush to the Alps: The Evolution of Vacationing in Switzerland* (New York: Columbia University Press, 1978), 176 .

5. The history of travel and tourism has generated a significant body of scholarship, much of it dealing with literature of the pre-modern period;

work dealing with contemporary history tends to focus on theoretical implications of tourism and the intersection with imperialism and colonialism; see E. J. Leed, *The Mind of the Traveler: Gilgamesh to Global Tourism* (New York: Basic, 1991); S. Greenblatt, *Marvelous Possessions: The Wonder of the New World* (Chicago: University of Chicago Press, 1991); M. Pratt, *Imperial Eyes: Travel Writing and Transculturation* (London and New York: 1992); N. Howe, *Migration and Mythmaking in Anglo-Saxon England* (New Haven and London: Yale University Press, 1989). The best general, theoretical treatment is J. Urry, *The Tourist Gaze: Leisure and Travel in Contemporary Society* (London: Sage, 1990); Urry is particularly helpful in illuminating the relationships between the increasing attention to tourism and poststructuralist theory; see also D. MacCannell, *Empty Meeting Grounds: The Tourist Papers* (London: Routledge, 1992); L. Vascek and G. Buckland, *Travelers in Ancient Lands: A Portrait of the Middle East, 1839-1919* (Boston: New York Graphic Society, 1981); J. C. Simmons, *Passionate Pilgrims: English Travelers to the World of the Desert Travelers* (New York: William Morrow, 1987); F. W. Ogilvie, *The Tourist Movement: An Economic Study* (London: P. S. King & Son, 1933); J. Krippendorf, *The Holiday Makers: Understanding the Impact of Leisure and Travel.* Trans. V. Andrassy (London: Heinemann, 1987); P. Pearce, *The Social Psychology of Tourist Behaviour* (Oxford: Permagon, 1982); P. E. Murphy, *Tourism: A Community Approach* (New York and London: Methuen, 1985); A. J. Burkart and S. Medlik, *Tourism: Past, Present, and Future* (London: Heinemann, 1974). Along with the general aversion to discussing Jews, Palestine, and Israel, there is almost total ignorance of tourism and travel among Muslims and other non-Christians by those purporting to engage in universal arguments; one of the few exceptions is L. Turner and J. Ash, *The Golden Hordes: International Tourism and the Pleasure Periphery* (London: Constable, 1975).

6. J. Culler, *Framing the Sign: Criticism and Its Institutions* (Oxford: Basil Blackwell, 1988), 153.

7. The explicit discussions relating tourism to Zionism tend to emphasize the contemporary, phenomenological aspects of non-Jewish tourism, as opposed to historical development; see G. Bowman, "The Politics of Tour Guiding: Israeli and Palestinian Guides in the Occupied Territories," in *Tourism and the Less Developed Countries*, ed. D. Harrison (London: Bellhaven Press, 1992), 121-134; E. Cohen, "Arab Boys and Tourist Girls in a mixed Jewish-Arab Community," in *International Journal of Comparative Sociology*, 12, 4 (1971): 217-33; M. Wolffsohn, *Eternal Guilt? Forty Years of German-Jewish-Israeli Relations.* Trans. Douglas Bokovoy (New York: Columbia University Press, 1993), 114-118.

8. See T. A Idinopulos, *Jerusalem Blessed, Jerusalem Cursed: Jews, Christians, and Muslims in the Holy City from David's Time to Our Own* (Chicago: Ivan R. Dee, 1991); D. Eickelman and J. Piscatori, eds., *Muslim Travellers: Pilgrimage, Migration, and the Religious Imagination* (Berkeley and Los Angeles: Univer-

sity of Califronia Press, 1990); J. Campo, *The Other Sides of Paradise: Explorations into the Religious Meanings of Domestic Space in Islam* (Columbia: University of South Carolina Press, 1991), 139-165; Y. Portath, *The Emergence of the Palestinian-Arab National Movement 1918-1929* (London: Frank Cass, 1974), Chapter One.

9. "Palaestina-Reisen," in *Juedische Rundschau*, February 12, 1924, 77; "1200 deutsche Touristen in Palaestina" (Fuehrung durch den Palestine Lloyd)," in *Juedische Rundschau*, June 8, 1928, 325.

10. D. MacCannell remarks, without explanation, that "In 'The Holy Land,' the tour has followed in the path of the religious pilgrimage and is replacing it;" see *The Tourist: A New Theory of the Leisure Class* (New York: Schocken, 1976), 43.

11. See M. Vovelle, *Ideologies and Mentalities*, trans. E. O'Flaherty (Chicago: University of Chicago Press, 1990), 45, 89, for the application of these ideas in different contexts.

12. Lowenthal, *The Past is a Foreign Country* (Cambridge: Cambridge University Press, 1985), xvii.

13. R. Elston, "Travel in the New Palestine," in *The Monthly Pioneer* (February 1929): 17.

14. *La Nouvelle Aurore*, June 20, 1924, 12; "1200 deutsche Touristen in Palaestina" (Fuehrung durch den Palestine Lloyd)," in *Juedische Rundschau*, June 8, 1928, 325.

15. *The New Judaea*, September 26, 1914, 10; F. Loewenstein, "Der deutsche Zionismus und Palaestina," in Jue*dische Rundschau*, August 29, 1924, 493.

16. E. Rosenberg, "Palaestinafahrten des K.J.V.," in *Der Juedische Student* (October 1930): 3.

17. M. Berkowitz, *Zionist Culture and West European Jewry before the First World War* (Cambridge: Cambridge University Press, 1993), 119-164.

18. N. Shepherd, *The Zealous Intruders: From Napoleon to the Dawn of Zionism— the Explorers, Archaeologists, Artists, Tourist, Pilgrims, and Visionaries Who Opened Palestine to the West* (San Francisco: Harper and Row, 1988).

19. Given that tourism "is a complex and highly fragmented activity," many avenues of investigation necessarily remain open; see R. Bar-On, *Travel and Tourism Data: A Comprehensive Research Handbook on the World Travel Industry* (Phoenix and New York: Oryx Press, 1989), 3.

20. D. Lowenthal, xix.

21. F. Loewenstein, "Palaestina Touristik," in *Juedische Rundschau*, January 8, 1926, 14.

22. "Palaestina Touristen-Organisation," in Juedische Rundschay, November 12, 1926, 640.

23. On the question of the "quest for authenticity" see P. L. Pearce, *The Ulysses Factor: Evaluating Visitors in Tourist Settings* (New York, Berlin, and Heidelberg: Springer-Verlag, 1988), 162-193; D. MacCannell, *The Tourist: A New Theory of the Leisure Class* (London: Macmillan, 1976), p.49, cited in Urry, 8-9.

24. See L. Hazleton, *Jerusalem, Jerusalem: A Memoir of War and Peace, Passion and Politics* (New York: Penguin, 1987), 5.

25. "Die Alijah aus Deutschland," in *Juedische Rundschau*, March 23, 1923, 142.

26. Before the Thomas Cook Company organized tours to Palestine, in the 1850s most of the British-based trips to Palestine were conducted by the company of Henry Gaze; in the late 1860s the Middle East was thought to be "the most lucrative travel market yet to appear; see E. Swinglehurst, *The Romantic Journey: The Story of Thomas Cook and Victorian Travel* (New York, Evanston, San Francisco, London: Harper and Row, 1974), 174.

27. "Brief aus Palaestina," in *Juedische Rundschau*, April 27, 1923, 199-200; see Swinglehurst, *The Romantic Journey*.

28. M. Feifer, *Tourism in History: From Imperial Rome to the Present* (New York: Stein and Day, 1985), 188.

29. E. Newman to L. Hermann, May 9, 1924; L. Hermann to L. Lipsky, April 1, 1924; L. Stein to L. Hermann, March 7, 1924; KH 1/273, Central Zionist Archives, Jerusalem.

30. "Cooks Palaestinareisen," in *Juedische Rundschau*, November 7, 1924, 634.

31. "Neue Formen der Palaestina-Touristik," in *Juedische Rundschau*, June 28, 1927, 367; Turner and Ash, *The Golden Hordes*, 56-8; "New Propaganda Features: Cheap Palestine Tour," in *Our Fund* (Tevet 5686 [1926]), 37; "1200 deutsche Touristen in Palaestina" (Fuehrung durch den Palestine Lloyd)," in *Juedische Rundschau*, June 8, 1928, 325; "Die Touristen-Saison in Palaestina," in *Juedische Rundschau*, May 23, 1924, 300; "Fabreline" ad, *Hadassah News Letter* (March 1927): 27; ad in *Juedische Rundschau*, December 20, 1929, 683.

32. "Coronia's Winter Tour," announcement reprinted from the *New York Times* in *Hadassah News Letter* (February 1921): 1; Cunard Line ad, *Hadassah News Letter* (March 1928), back cover.

33. "Editorial Comments: Palestine Tours and Exhibition," in *The Monthly Pioneer* (February 1929): 4.

34. J. Hirsch, "Das Hotelwesen," in *Juedische Rundschau*, December 11, 1925, 813.

35. "Palaestina-Reisen," in *Juedische Rundschau*, February 12, 1924, 77; "Palaestina Touristen-Organisation," in *Juedische Rundschau*, November 12, 1926, 640; see P. Bernard, *Rush to the Alps: The Evolution of Vacationing in Switzerland* (New York: Columbia University Press, 1978).

36. Hirsch, 813.

37. Report of address by Dr. Alfred Apfel, "Die Touristik in Palaestina," in *Juedische Rundschau*, November 28, 1924, 681-2.

38. Apfel, 682.

39. G. V. Tign, "Oh Life of Joy and Sorrow, Laughter and Tears," typescript manuscript, ME 643, 191-92, Leo Baeck Institute, New York.

40. D. MacCannell, "Staged Authenticity: Arrangements of Social Space in Tourist Settings," in *American Sociological Review*, 79 (1973): 589-603.

41. G. V. Tign, "Oh Life of Joy and Sorrow, Laughter and Tears," p.191.

42. Pekarsky, "Avukah: Today and Tomorrow (Pre-Convention Thoughts)," in *The Avukah Bulletin* (December 1931): 3.

43. "Touristenempfang in Palaestina," in *Juedische Rundschau*, April 20, 1928, 221; "Die Touristen-Saison," in *Juedische Rundschau*, March 12, 1926, 149.

44. "Palaestinatouristen," in *Juedische Rundschau*, March 30, 1928, 188.

45. Henrietta Szold to Jessie Sampter, February 25, 1922, folder 44, box 5, record group 7, Hadassah Archives, New York.

46. For the place of these institutions within the greater scheme of Zionist settlement, see D. Penslar, *Zionism and Technocracy: The Engineering of Jewish Settlement in Palestine, 1881-1918* (Bloomington: Indiana University Press, 1991); Berkowitz, *Zionist Culture*, 144-164.

47. "Tochter eines juedischen Kolonisten vom Rechoboth im Orangengarten ihres Vaters," in *Palaestina-Bilder-Korrespondenz* (May 1931), cover; "Eine Metamorphose," in *Palaestina-Bilder-Korrespondenz* (June 1932): 67; photo "Schechunath Borochov, Kindergarten," in Erez Israel [publication of Keren Hayesod, probably around 1925].

48. S. Greenblatt, *Marvelous Possessions*, ix.

49. H. Melville, *The Writings of Herman Melville*, vol. 15, eds. H. Hayford, H. Parker, and G. T. Tanselle (Evanston: Northwestern University Press and the Newberry Library, 1989), [journal entry for January 1857], 88. E. Renker traced this reference.

50. In the accounts of different schools of archaeology, there is little attention to larger issues outside the framework of the discipline; see P. King, *American Archaeology in the Mideast: A History of the American Schools of Oriental Research* (Philadelphia: The American Schools of Oriental Research, 1983), 101.

51. King, *American Archaeology*, 15ff.

52. Ibid. 7.

53. Ibid. 55.

54. K. Kenyon, *Digging Up Jerusalem* (London and Tonbridge: Ernest Benn, 1974), 32-4.

55. R. A. S. Macalister, *A Century of Excavation in Palestine* (New York: Arno, 1977 [reprint of 1925 edition]), 21.

56. Macalister, 72; Gideon Oftrat-Friedlander, "The Bezalel Museum," in *Bezalel 1906-1929*, ed. N. Shilo-Cohen (Jerusalem: Israel Museum, 1983), 359.

57. King, 96-108.

58. *Palaestina-Bild-Correspondenz*

59. See Berkowitz, *Zionist Culture*, 157-160.

60. Macalister, 66-7.

61. J. Campo, *The Other Sides of Paradise: Explorations into the Religious Meanings of Domestic Space in Islam* (Columbia: University of South Carolina Press, 1991).

62. M. Heller, *My Month in Palestine: Impressions of Travel* (New York: Bloch, 1929), 26.

63. See R. Owen, *State, Power, and Politics in the Making of the Modern Middle East* (1992).

64. J. Neumann, "My Trip Through Palestine," in *Young Judaean* (November 1914): 1-4; (December 1914): 5-9, (January 1915): 9-12.

65. M. Harry, *A Springtide in Palestine* (London: Ernest Benn, 1924); I. Lindheim, *The Immortal Adventure* (New York: Macaulay, 1928). Harry's book was translated (from the French) into German as *Das kleine Maedchen von Jerusalem* in 1928.

66. Ad enclosed in *Hadassah News Letter* (March 1928), emphasis in the original.

67. Harry, *A Springtide in Palestine*, 147, 110.

68. P. Goodman, "A Springtide in Palestine," in *The New Judaea*, November 7, 1924, 70; *Menorah* [Paris], October 15, 1922, 51-3; "Les Saintes Meres," in *Menorah* (Summer 1931): 83; ad in *Juedische Rundschau*, April 4, 1928, 200;

69. Hirsch, 813.

70. W. Turnowsky, "Werbung durch Reisen," in *Juedische Rundschau*, September 8, 1931, 428; "New Propaganda Features: Cheap Palestine Tour," in *Our Fund* (Tevet 5686 [1926]), 37.

71. "American Tourists Visit Palestine," in *Hadassah News Letter* (October 1927): 11.

72. "Fuer Palaestinatouristen," in *Juedische Rundschau*, January 4, 1927, 12.

73. "Hin-Propaganda oder Her-Propaganda. Beitrag sum Sokolow-Monat der Zionistischen Organisation, 1931," D.D. 2/3/4/1/4, Central Zionist Archives, Jerusalem.

74. "Touristenempfang in Palaestina," in *Juedische Rundschau*, April 20, 1928, 221.

75. "Wer kommt mit? 25 freie Palaestina Reisen fuer die Jugend," in *Juedische Rundschau*, February 11, 1927, 86; "Jugend-Preisausschreiben des Keren Kajemeth Leisrael," in *Juedische Rundschau*, February 18, 1927, 101.

76. "Lord Balfours Empfang in Tel Awiw," in *Juedische Rundschau*, April 4, 1925, 249; "Masaryk in Palaestina," in *Juedische Rundschau*, April 26, 1927, 236.

77. "Touristen in Palaestina," in *Juedische Rundschau*, May 6, 1927, 256; "Einstein in Palaestina," in *Juedische Rundschau*, Febraury 16, 1923, 75; "Touristenempfang in Palaestina," in *Juedische Rundschau*, April 20, 1928, 221.

78. "Kein Palaestina Tourist aus Polen," in *Juedische Rundschau*, February 26, 1926, 117.

79. "In Erwartung der Touristen-Saison," in *Juedische Rundschau*, January 5, 1926, 3; F. Loewenstein, "Palaestina-Jugendfahrt," in *Juedische Rundschau*, July 20, 1928, 414; "Palaestina-Studentreise," in *Juedische Rundschau*, November 25, 1924, 674; "Palaestinafahrt des K. J. V. (Fruejahr 1930)," in *Der Juedische Student* (November 1929): 4.

80. "Summer Cruise," in *Hadassah News Letter* (April 1927): 4.

81. "Come to Palestine" ad of the American Economic Committee for Palestine tour, *Hadassah News Letter* (January-February 1933): 4.

82. N. H. Alderblum, "Palestine on Shipboard. A Unique Summer Trip to Palestine," *Hadassah Newsletter* (December 1926): 10.

83. "American Tourists Visit H.M.O. [Hadassah Medical Organization] Institutions," in *Hadassah News Letter* (February 1927): 3.

84. See B. Melman, *Women's Orients: English Women and the Middle East, 1718-1918: Sexuality, Religion, and Work* (Ann Arbor: University of Michigan Press, 1992); M. L. Pratt, 102-7.

85. Leed, 11-129.

86. M. L. Rubenovitz, "Zionist Education for Hadassah," in *Hadassah News Letter* (March-April 1932): 3, 15.

87. Right-wing tours did not take on a regular form until after the rise of Menahem Begin in the 1970s; see G. Bowman.

88. "A Travel Seminar for Palestine," in Erma Lindheim file, Biographies—Nearprint file, American Jewish Archives, Cincinnati, Ohio.

89. Ad for "Educational Travel Institute," in *Young Judaean* (March 1924), back cover.

90. See M. Kaplan, *The Making of the Jewish Middle Class in Imperial German* (New York: Oxford University Press, 1992).

91. See V. Turner, From *Ritual to Theatre: The Human Seriousness of Play* (Baltimore: Johns Hopkins University Press, 1992), 55.

92. Alderblum, 10.

93. Campo, 159-60.

94. Heller, 29.

95. Postcard, "Ein Dampfer auf der Fahrt nach Palaestina. Zum Andenken an den 14. Zionisten-Kongress 1925 zu Wien," D.D. a, 2/1/1/14, Central Zionist Archives, Jerusalem.

96. 2"Beginn der Touristen-Saison in Palaestina," in *Juedische Rundschau*, January 14, 1927, 27.

97. "Neuer Touristenstrom," in *Juedische Rundschau*, October 28, 1932, 417.

98. Circular letter from Thomas Cook & Son, quoted in Alderblum, 10.

99. Ad for "B.P. Tours—British Pal. and Eastern Tours, Ltd.," in *The Monthly Pioneer* (October 1932): 23.

100. P. Tillich, "Mind and Migration," in *Social Research* 4 (1937): 295-305, quoted in N. Howe, *Migration and Mythmaking in Anglo-Saxon England*, 6. I have borrowed liberally from Howe's use of Tillich.

A Rustling in the Woods: The Turn to Myth in Weimar Jewish Thought

Steven M. Wasserstrom

Die Zukunft wird die Wirklichkeit der Geschichte.
Hermann Cohen[1]

The most influential and brilliant students of Hermann Cohen (1842-1918), the Neo-Kantian Jewish philosopher of Marburg, largely rejected one of his fundamental views on Judaism. Opposing his characterization of Judaism as the religion definitively opposed to myth—Judaism as virtually identical with a demythologized Enlightenment rationality—these post-Cohenian thinkers turned to a view of myth as a creative and living force. At least three Cohen students, Franz Rosenzweig, Ernst Bloch and Ernst Cassirer, wrote revolutionary works which innovatively reassessed the relations between myth, the history of religions and Judaism. These figures were joined by a much larger cohort in an enthusiastic and influential turn to myth, a cross-section of the German Jewish intelligentsia which included Gershom Scholem, Martin Buber, Alexander Altmann, Aby Warburg, Hans Jonas, and others.

In this paper I will assess the post-Cohenian turn to myth. First, I will begin with the year 1923 and its significance. Then I will consider the profound and seriously underestimated impact of the late philosophy of Schelling, with reference to three students of Cohen (Rosenzweig, Bloch and Cassirer) who were explicitly influenced by the late Schelling in their new approach to myth. I will next explore the theory of the *"daimonic"* ("the rustling in the woods"). Finally, I will consider some results for the history of religions, especially for Scholem's epochal rejection of the Cohenian view of Judaism as anti-myth. In each case I will suggest that the turn to myth impelled a return to history in Weimar Jewish thought.

1923

> The world is collapsing
> Behind a thin wall.
> Blood-red are the crossbars of windows
> As shades of night fall.
> "Spring 1923", by F. Sramek[2]

"We are convinced that today a *kairos*, an epochal moment in history, is visible," proclaimed Paul Tillich in 1922.[3] The first line of Albert Schweitzer's *The Decay and Restoration of Civilization*, published in 1923, was: "We are living today under the sign of the collapse of civilization."[4] Sramek's momentous Czech poem, titled "Spring 1923" began, "The world is collapsing and crumbling/ Behind a thin wall." And in the same year, T.S. Eliot, in England, wrote a review of James Joyce titled "*Ulysses*, Order and Myth." Redolent with worry over "the panorama of futility and anarchy which is contemporary history," Eliot concluded with a clarion call: "Instead of narrative method, we may now use the mythical method. It is, I seriously believe, a step toward making the modern world possible for art..."[5] If Virginia Woolf was correct that human nature changed on or about December 1910, then one may be permitted to suggest that human nature—at least in its European high-cultural form—celebrated its Bat Mitzvah in 1923.

This new time was a *quickening*. In Germany, indications were that the old life was dying, and dying fast: by July 1923, $1 = 353, 412$ Marks, but by December 1923, $1 = 4.2$ trillion Marks.[6] Time itself seemed almost to swerve, if not curve fully back on itself; one could not go forward; history had ruptured. At just this time, a debate ensued concerning the very character of temporality. On April 6, 1922, Henri Bergson encountered Albert Einstein in Paris, at which confrontation he "attempted to defend the cause of the multiplicity of coexisting 'lived' times against Einstein. Einstein's reply was absolute: he categorically rejected 'philosopher's time".[7] Other new theories of time, such as Ernst Bloch's eventually influential "nonsimultaneity of simultaneities," blossomed among radical political philosophers.[8] Gustav Landauer (1870-1919), pacifist, anarchist, unaffiliated socialist, and man of letters, was fortunate to have his work *Die Revolution* published posthumously by Martin Buber in 1923.[9] In this work Landauer identified "a qualitative differentiation of time."[10] Along with Landauer, the art historian Wilhelm Pinder (b. 1878), who was developing a theory of "the noncontemporaneity of contemporaries," influenced the generational sociology of Karl Mannheim.[11] Mannheim then fully articulated (in Michael Löwy's words) a "new perception of temporality at variance with evolutionism and the philosophy of progress."[12]

It is inside this sense of "new time," breaking forth in 1923, that the turn to myth must first be framed. This philosophical breakthrough affected other areas of culture, starting with the arts. Thus, the Jewish littératur Rudolf Kayser became the editor of the tastemaking and pacesetting magazine, *Die Neue Rundschau* in 1923—when he also published a work of metaphysical anarchism, *Die Zeit ohne Mythos*.[13] Jews in Frankfurt in 1923 included the young Elias Canetti, a future Nobel Prize winner for literature, who there immersed himself in the study of Gilgamesh. He was later to recall: "In this way, I experienced the effect of a myth."[14] In Frankfurt alone, Jewish Institutes as the Freies Jüdisches Lehrhaus, the Institut für Sozialforschung, and Aby Warburg's Institute (as well as non-Jewish institutions such as Leo Frobenius's Forschungsinsitüt für Kulturmorphologie) were blazing trails backwards into the mythic dimensions of history.[15] In 1923, Aby Warburg delivered a public lecture on the Pueblo serpent rituals he had witnessed some years before. Extolling snakehandling, he concluded that "myths and symbols, in attempting to establish spiritual bonds between man and the outside world, create space for devotion and scope for reason which are destroyed by the instantaneous electrical contact—unless a disciplined humanity re-introduce the impediment of conscience."[16] Warburg's successor was thus accurate in her assessment that "Warburg believed in the power of reason; he was an *Aufklärer* precisely because he knew the heritage of demonic antiquity so well."[17] It was at Warburg's library, not incidentally, that Cassirer was inspired to undertake his monumental *Philosophy of Symbolic Forms*. The turn to myth was a return to history.

Symbolic forms, whether in the thought of Cassirer or Warburg, were not limited to art history, or to the history of myth, but held the key to history itself. Indeed, a reconceptualization of the philosophy of history emerged from this ferment of temporality. A particularly striking result of this new historical reflection was the widely-used image of *history turned backward*. For example, George Lichtheim, distinguished historian of Marxism, and translator of Scholem's *Major Trends in Jewish Mysticism*, observed that in his 1923 classic of Western Marxism, *History and Class Consciousness*, "[the George Lukács of 1923] was in fact returning from Marx to Hegel."[18] The former student of Heidegger, Karl Löwith, eventually wrote his classic treatment of the philosophy of history, *Meaning in History,* chronologically backwards, beginning with Jakob Burckhardt and ending with the Hebrew Bible.[19] One might say, in fact, that the watchword of the age was the epigraph Walter Benjamin placed over his ruminations on *Jetztzeit,* and which he attributed to Karl Kraus: "Origin is the Goal."[20] With almost equal epigrammatic force, Cassirer would cite Friedrich Schlegel to the effect that the historian comprises *"einen ruckwarts gekehrten Propheten,* a retrospective prophet. There is also a prophecy of the past, a revelation of its hidden life."[21] This same passage was also glossed by Walter Benjamin.[22] And just as Cassirer could cite Schlegel, so Bloch quoted Hamann: "The field of history has thus always appeared to me like that wide field full of bones, and lo! they were very dry. Nobody except a prophet can prophesy upon these bones that sinews and flesh will grow on them and skin will cover them."[23]

History turned backward on or about 1923, and it turned back to myth. The turn to myth in Weimar Jewish thought is explicable, in the first instance, against the "nonsimultaneity of simultaneities" of 1923. For students and young associates of Cohen, including Franz Rosenzweig, Ernst Bloch, Ortega y Gasset, and Ernst Cassirer, published importantly innovative works in that *annus mirabilis,* in each of which the turn to myth was discernible.[24] But unlike proto-Nazi myth-infatuation, their myth-studies pointedly were not regressive. By the sharpest of contrasts to fascist primitivism, the Jewish turn to myth was comprised of historical flights out of time, pathways into deepened history, re-entrances into historical meaning: *myth as history reborn.* In 1923, Gerhard Scholem remained in Germany only until *Yom Kippur,* after which he immediately made *aliyah* and changed his name to Gershom.

From Cohen to Schelling

The ultimate Jewish Kantian of his time, Hermann Cohen, catalyzed a heroic age of remythologization, marked by its reversion from Kant to Schelling.[25] For in the brief interim between Hermann Cohen's death at war's end and the momentous year of 1923, young German thinkers turned to myth, especially through study of Friedrich Schelling's "philosophy of mythology."[26] Cohen's conventional view of Judaism as an enemy of myth was not the only such view then being championed.[27] The new science of sociology, especially that of the neo-Kantian founding sociologist of religion, Max Weber (d. 1920), agreed with Jewish thought that demythologization was set in the Bible itself. Weber strove to demonstrate that the rationality of Biblical Judaism was embodied in the social structures of ancient Israel. This latent rationalization then was made consciously manifest by the Rabbis of late antiquity, and finally institutionalized by the major Jewish philosophers of the middle ages. Weberian sociology of religion thus largely accepted this Jewish self-understanding of the world historical significance of "ethical monotheism."[28] So too, significantly, did Cohen's "admired colleague," Julius Wellhausen, the dean of the new Biblical Criticism.[29] On the established Jewish thinking, on the Critical Biblicist reading, and on the new sociological understanding, then, Judaism resisted myth from the outset, and therefore deserved to be seen as the historic pioneer in the disenchantment of the world.[30]

Against the backdrop of this emerging concensus, the sudden popularity of the "reorientation of European Social thought" among young Jewish intellectuals stands out all the more starkly.[31] So great was the attraction of Jews to the new social thought that by 1924 Friedrich Gundolf could disparage German sociology as "a Jewish sect."[32] But this flight to social theory, further dramatically impelled by defeat in the Great War, interupted a fantasy. The Jewish dream of a smooth assimilation to Germaness, becoming fully German, suddenly was disrupted. No longer could Jews sententiously claim, as Cohen did during the war, that "as for our own spiritual life, we have already experienced an intimate religious partnership in the accord that exists *between Jewish messianism and German humanism.*"[33] After the Great War, young Jews could no longer unproblematically sustain such optimism. The immediate postwar shattering of Kantian humanism and positivism coincided, ironically, with the ultimate humanistic achievements of Weber and Cohen: the *Religionssoziologie* of Max Weber was published posthumously in 1922; the *Jüdische Schriften* of Herman Cohen were published posthumously in 1924.[34] At the same time, the precipitious decline of Kant even received offical notice. In 1924 the Minister of Education for the Weimar Republic, the scholar of Islam Carl Heinrich Becker, observed that Kant held little appeal in these postwar years, whether for the young or the old.[35] What did hold appeal, for old and young, was social theory, Marxist or otherwise. And it was this social reflection which provided the impetus for a new embrace of myth.

Ernst Bloch, who had completed his dissertation under Hermann Cohen in 1909, is a representative figure of the almost instant transition from Kant to Schelling.[36] Between 1912 and 1914, Bloch "hung out" with

Lukács and other geniuses at the Heidelberg salon of Max Weber. Meanwhile, as the European war was breaking out, the dignified Jewish messianism of Cohen was erupting in this philosophical *enfant terrible*. Frau Marianne Weber saw him in action: "a new Jewish philosopher had just come—a young man with an enormous crest of black hair and a self-confidence equally excessive, who obviously took himself to be the forerunner of a new Messiah and insisted that everyone would recognize him as such."[37] By 1918, less than a decade after finishing his thesis with Cohen, Bloch published *Geist der Utopie*, where he now held that Myth (*Mythos*) revealed "a becoming of God, a disclosure of the God who is now living and sleeping in man alone, an internal monologue within the creature, a self-disclosure of God before himself, in which, however, the transcendent of God is brought to life."[38] Here we are galaxies away from Cohen's professorial moralism, not to speak of his circumspect, Kantian monotheism. Now the leading motifs of Schelling's *Philosophy of Mythology* were re-annunciated. Philosophy is identified with theogony, the becoming of the godhead, which in turn is viewed as world process itself: God unfolds inside history, history inside us.[39] It is not for nothing that Habermas famously dubbed Bloch "The Marxist Schelling."[40]

Bloch was not the only young Jewish social philosopher following Cohen who turned to Schelling during the Great War. The literal rediscoverer of Schelling's lost fragment for a "New Mythology" was Franz Rosenzweig, who in 1914 identified the manuscript of "the Oldest System-Program for German Idealism" as being authored by Schelling.[41] On the very month that Cohen died (April 1918), Rosenzweig wrote to his mother that "before everything else" he saw Schelling as "his patron saint."[42] And the same letter, he saw himself as "destined" to have discovered the *Systemprogramm*.[43] This was just months before he was to begin the *Star of Redemption*, where he proclaimed that

> The Jew alone... possesses the unity of myth which the nations lost through the influx of Christianity... The Jew's myth, leading him into his people, brings him face to face with God who is also the God of all the nations.[44]

Rosenzweig's "New Thinking," like the emerging "New Being"of Paul Tillich, drew deeply on Schelling's original "New Mythology."[45]

Almost simultaneously, between 1916 and 1918, Gershom Scholem and Walter Benjamin engaged in a ferocious discussion of myth. Ben-

jamin, according to Scholem, "accepted myth alone as 'the world'...
myth was everything."[46] Precisely at this time, they together studied
Hermann Cohen, but were disappointed with him.[47] They preferred
German Romantic philosophers, up to and including Nietzsche. Of this
effervescent post-Cohenian moment he shared with Benjamin, Scholem
pointedly observed that "I suppose it was in those days that we especially influenced each other."[48] Much can be said, it is clear, about the
multiple crossfertilizations occurring at that instant. Benjamin, for
example, soon thereafter cited both Ernst Bloch and Franz Rosenzweig
in his "Theologico-Political Fragment" of 1921-1922.[49]

The most complete and influential exposition of the turn to Schelling
was explicated by another Cohen student, Ernst Cassirer, as is well-
known.[50] What is somewhat less well-known, perhaps, is that at roughly
the same time, Heidegger called Schelling's *Of Human Freedom* (1809)
"one of the profoundest works written in Germany and thus of occidental
philosophy."[51] Heidegger, in general terms, resembled Rosenzweig in
underscoring the momentous dimensions of the civilizational shift
(*Kehre*) being undergone. And Rosenzweig, like Heidegger, utilized the
term *Ershutterung*, *Shattering*, to describe the crackup of philosophical
totality.[52] The future Nazi author of *Being and Time* acknowledged, in
fact, that the turn to myth in Weimar thought could be articulated by
Jewish philosophers. Heidegger thus accepted "the merit of [Ernst]
Cassirer's work insofar as it is the first attempt since Schelling to place
myth as a systematic problem within the range of philosophy."[53] It is
interesting to recall that a mortally ill Rosenzweig commented on this
exchange between Heidegger and Cassirer at his life's end. He made
two striking points which are relevant here. First, he noted that the "old
Cohen" in fact did lead to the "new thinking." Second, he observed that
this new thinking was represented by Heidegger and not Cassirer.[54]

These were not the only crosscurrents feeding the interest in Schelling
and the turn to myth. Theorists of religion who also were receptive
readers of Schelling at this time included Otto, Jaspers, Tillich and Barth.
The Schelling-Revival, in short, caught up philosophers and historians
of religion, Jew and non-Jew alike.[55] The turn to myth in Weimar Jewish
thought, then, was at the forefront of a turn to myth in European—or at
least German—thought at large. The Schellingian detour thus signified
a *postKantian*, *postMarxian*, *postWeberian*, *but still dialectical* return to
history. This may explain its promise to Jewish thinkers (with the
unanswered exception of Rosenzweig)—for it promised return to a now
deepened history, by an ironic leap backward over Enlightenment

Reason, into the archaic depths available inwardly for historical reflection.[56]

"A Rustling in the Wood": Daimonic Eruption

In the wake of the Great War, transEuropean *Krisis* was shattering the solidity of Kantian optimism. One immediate result was a reinvigoration of thinking on human origins. The perception of the "collapse of civilization" impelled students of religion with their cohort to return to "The Beginning," the "Primordium." Lévy-Bruhl in France and Otto in Germany, widely read at this time, analyzed Adam as social actor, interpreting primordial mentality or the original encounter with the numinous in terms of the psychology of a percipient individual.[57] In such intimations of a perfectly creative instant, of a eruptive, intitial forming of religious language, one hears echoes from nineteenth-century German philosophy. A formative influence on this view of origins, along with Schelling, no doubt was Nietzsche, who celebrated the "eruptive character" (*Ausbruchcharakter*) of Dionysian release.[58] So too did it become a feature for interwar students of religion as otherwise disparate as Jung, Otto and van der Leeuw, who each utilized some notion of primal form-creation as the basis in their theories of religion, and who each did so explicitly under the sign of Nietzsche.[59]

For some of the new thinkers, the Original Human was a pristine genius. First Speech, accordingly, paradigmatically was *poetic*. Since the Enlightenment, since Hobbes and Rousseau, and since the first explorers' reports from Africa and the New World, the First Man had been seen as a savage, however Noble. Now the First Man was also a Poet of divine language, of the originary moment when speech first pierced the evanescent noises in the primeval glade.[60] This romantic fiction of the primal individual obviously echoed that of the modern individual, preeminently the poetic genius "finding himself." Schelling provided a typical romantic model:

> In all of us there swells a secret marvelous power of freeing ourselves from the changes of time, of withdrawing to our secret selves away from external things, and of so discovering to ourselves the eternal in us in the form of unchangeability. *This presentation of ourselves to ourselves is the most truly personal experience, upon which depends everything that we know of the suprasensual world. This presentation shows us for the first time what real existence is, while all else only appears to be.* It differs

from every presentation of the sense in its perfect freedom, while all other presentations are bound, being overweighted by the burden of the object.[61]

Around 1920, another student of Hermann Cohen, Boris Pasternak, described poetic inspiration this way:

[No] real book has a first page: like the rustling in the woods, it is born Heaven know where, grows and rolls on, waking hidden thickets in its path, and suddenly at the darkest, overwhelming, panic-stricken moment it speaks out from all the tree-tops at once, having reached its goal.[62]

Few Jewish thinkers at this time went as far as Pasternak did, preferring not to cross the line from an aestheticized philosophy of history to poetry as such. Bloch and Benjamin befriended the Dadaist Hugo Ball in Zürich—author of *Flucht aus der Zeit* (*Flight out of Time*)— but they could not follow his 1923 defection from Dada into "the aesthetic conception of the world" (from which position he tellingly joined forces with Carl Schmitt).[63] For most Jewish post-Cohenians, in other words, the daimonic moment of inspiration was less a figure for poetic insight than an emblem of the meaningfulness of time, of seizing the time, of the momentous first creation of something historically new.[64] For Bloch, such moments were the forward motor of history itself:

The kindling place of inspiration lies in the *meeting* of a specific genius... with the propensity of a time to provide the specific content which has become ripe for expression, forming and execution. Not only the subjective, but the objective conditions for the expression of a [Newness] must therefore be ready, must be ripe, so that this [Newness] can break through out of mere incubation and suddenly gain insight into itself.[65]

Rosenzweig, for his part, spoke of a "new thinking," that "knows it cannot have cognition independent of time... one must await the given time; one cannot skip a single moment (*Augenblick*)."[66] Paul Tillich, who published two doctoral dissertations on Schelling, delineated the "ripe moment," *Kairos*. Similar themes are found in Ernst Bloch and Walter Benjamin, both of whom applied the image of *Jetztzeit*, of *Now-Time*.[67] Scholem spoke of "plastic hours, when action is possible," and even of "thrusts" or "breakthroughs" in history.[68] Nor could Cassirer escape his

(Schellingian) sense that events of the spirit unfold at "the right time" and must be understood, therefore, as expressions of that time. He followed Usener in observing a critical transition from "*Augensblickgötter*," "Momentary deities" to daimonic potencies, and then to the first gods.[69]

> The division of the realm of the 'holy' from that of the 'profane' is the prerequisite for any *definite* divinities whatsoever. The Self feels steeped, as it were, in a mythico-religious atmosphere, which ever enfolds it, and in which it now lives and moves; it takes a spark, a touch, to create the god or daemon out of this charged atmosphere. The outlines of such daemonic beings may be ever so vague—yet they indicate the first step in a new direction.[70]

Compare Rosenzweig:

> Thus the self is born in man on a definite day. Which day is this? It is the day on which the personality, the individual, dies the death of entering the genus. This very moment lets the self be born. The self is a *daimon*...[71]

From such a stark beginning, then, bold sketches of world history intuitively could be derived. For Cassirer and Rosenzweig, this originary moment not only let history be born, but the self be born as well. In fact, historical periodizations (worldages) and generational metaphors (lifeages), flourished among the general interest in organic metaphors.[72] The First Age, for Schelling, had consisted of a force "demonic and heteronomous."[73] The late Schelling spoke tellingly of the "other" who breaks forth out of the "dark depths of nature" out of the "will of the deep."[74] Benjamin, as a young man, "distinguished between two historical ages, of the spectral and the demonic, that proceded revelation... [and] the real content of myth was the enormous revolution that polemicized against the spectral and brought its age to an end."[75] The first age of religion, according to Scholem, was a world "full of gods whom man encounters at every step."[76] Cassirer, for his part, minutely imagined this primordial religious experience to be a

> ... whispering or rustling in the woods, a shadow darting over the ground, a light flickering on the water: all these are demonic... but only very gradually does this pandemonium divide into separate and clearly distinguishable figures [or forms, *Gestalten*].[77]

The products of such eruptions out of an initial formlessness were understood as to be Forms [*Gestalten*]. In 1923 Tillich, for example, spoke of the demonic as "an eruption of the irrational ground of any realization of form."[78] Three years later Tillich again asserted, in his famous essay on the Demonic, "the tension between form-creation and form-destruction upon which rests the demonic..."[79] Bloch, as noted above, likewise spoke of the "propensity of a time to provide the specific content which has become ripe for... *forming*." And forms were first words, symbolic forms: more than poetry, they were prophecy, *divine speech*. For Rosenzweig, "Revelation is always present, and if it occurred in the past, then it was in that past which is the beginning of the history of mankind: it is the revelation granted to Adam."[80] This daimonic theory, then, constituted a vision of the First Human—but not Hobbes's brutish First Man. Rather, this was Adam as Prophet.

These confluent retrovisions—philosophical, psychological, sociological, aesthetic, and especially historical—thus transformed fleeting *daimonic* suddeness (*Plötzlichkeit*) into a theory of *revelatory eruption*.[81] It is hard not to recall here the letter Scholem wrote in 1926, in honor of Rosenzweig's fortieth birthday. Sent from Jerusalem, it begins, "This country is a volcano! It houses language!" He continues, "Those who ... mustered the daimonic courage [*den damonischen Mut*] to revitalize a language... walked and still walk above this abyss." Eventually, such imagery was consolidated into a full-blown historical psychology, as Scholem came to characterize his consistently daimonic approach. But these myth-revisionists also understood that with form-creation dialectically came form-destruction. And, indeed, the primal eruption of daimonic forces soon evoked darker expression in Heidegger's extraordinary Nietzsche seminars of the 1930s, in Jung's equally extraordinary Nietzsche seminars of the 1930s; and in the anthropological notion of *Ergriffenheit*, primal ontic seizure, championed in the Leo Frobenius school, also based in Frankfurt. *Ergriffenheit* was a term centrally used both by Heidegger and by Jung in the late 1920s and early 1930s. They applied this image of "being gripped," "being seized," both to the structures of original experience and to the action of an *Ergriefer*, a leader who seizes. *Ergriffenheit* also simultaneously became a founding theorem of the Eranos circle of historians of religion, established in 1933, the year that Weimar died.[82]

Understandably, then, theorists of the Frankfurt School increasingly resisted this "new mythology." On their dissident view, the *damonic* primal scene of *Urreligion* was dangerously regressive.[83] Eventually,

Adorno and Horkheimer spoke of *Mana* as "tautology of terror" and "objectified dread."[84] In fact, Adorno came to find a terrifying epistemological error at the heart of this fantasy:

> The picture of a temporal or extra-temporal original state of happy identity between subject and object is romantic, however—a wishful projection at times, but today no more than a lie. The undifferentiated state before the subject's formation was the dread of the blind web of nature, of myth; it was in protest against it that the great religions had their truth content.[85]

The quest for an *Urreligion* marked Comparative Religion and *Religionsgeschichte* in this period, but was coming under increasingly sharp critique, and not only from Marxists.[86] Of course, even for plodding academics, Durkheim's *Elementary Forms of the Religious Life* and Cassirer's *Philosophy of Symbolic Forms* had already dismantled if not demolished the once-towering theories known as "Naturism" and "Animism", associated with Tylor and Frazer.[87] *Mana* now was outmoded. Both for the avant garde and for the professoriate, a more *true to life* theory of religious origins and development was demanded. Biologistic and especially organismic, metaphors—*palingenesis, pseudomorphosis, symbiosis*, and ultimately *Life* [*Leben*] itself—consequently came into vogue.[88] What mattered now was less Weber's worldviews, than vitality of life itself, a view known as *vitalism*. While not a vitalist as such, Franz Rosenzweig announced at the beginning of the *Star of Redemption* that the "conception of the world [*Weltanschauung*] now has for its counterpart the conception of Life [*Lebensanschauung*]—and he concluded the *Star of Redemption* with the climactic words, "Into Life" [*uns Leben*]." Count Paul Yorck von Wartenberg, whose influential letters to Wilhelm Dilthey were published in 1923—and prominently cited both by Heidegger in *Being and Time* and by Gershom Scholem as the epigraph to his masterwork, *Sabbetai Zevi*—asserted that philosophy "is not science but life, and fundamentally has been life even where it wanted to be science."[89]

All the churning currents of the Weimar *Krisis*—Romanticism, *Lebensphilosophie*, Nietzscheanism, critique of reification, "romantic anticapitalism," vitalism, and apocalypticism—poured into the torrential turn to myth. Perhaps the single strongest stream was Schelling's philosophy of mythology. On this thinking, the daimonic moment unified deep past with projected future. For only out of this instant emanated authentic symbols, which alone linked myth with utopia. The immediate linkage was the living present itself, the "now," the "ripe time." Through this lived immediacy, the daimonic made origins imaginable again. And the reimaginers, during the Weimar years, experienced this revelatory eruption as inciting a new age. By conjuring Adam, they invoked utopia now. Myth thus organically coordinated past, present and future; the artificial splits in time were united in a living being: and so historical life revived.

Conclusion: Judaism in the History of Religions according to Gershom Scholem

Jewish thinkers wrestled the *daimon* of history without losing social consciousness. Starting in the early Weimar years, Gershom Scholem, Martin Buber, Walter Benjamin, Alexander Altmann, Aby Warburg, Hans Jonas, Hans Liebeschutz, Paul Kraus, Leo Strauss, Hans Levy, Henry Pachter, Martin Plessner, Shlomo Goitein, Hannah Arendt, Theodor Adorno, and Max Horkheimer engaged the problem of religion in society largely through historical and philosophical analysis. That is, these scholars turned to the most "irrational" components of their civilization, preeminently myth, and they historicized them. In various ways, they set out, as Schelling had proclaimed, "to discover reason in this seeming unreason."[90]

But this bold turn from Cohen is also inextricably linked to the dire fate of the Weimar Republic. Those Jewish thinkers who experienced or adopted myth as masterconcept in the early Weimar years mostly abandoned it after the National Socialist appeal to myth was actualized, and the Nazi myth became reality.[91] Not all did so, however. In this regard, Scholem, emigrant in Palestine, presented a characteristically paradoxical contrast to his comrades, Cassirer, Bloch, Horkheimer and Adorno, who composed their masterworks in American exile. They no longer championed myth, warning, instead, of the dangers of the dialectic of enlightenment and the looming myth of the state. Scholem the Zionist, meanwhile, continued to champion myth. This is the vision set forth in *Major Trends in Jewish Mysticism*, delivered as lectures in New York in 1938, which we now are finally prepared to reread. To this daimonic vision—in which destruction allows construction—he remained true even in his great Eranos lectures, delivered in German after the War, in Europe.

Scholem's sustained leap, which we can now see was hardly unprecedented in its derivation, was to become, we also know, unparalleled in its impact. For he (perhaps alone) used the category of myth permanantly to relocate Judaism in the history of religions. Nonetheless, the establishment Jewish self-presentation, it must be remembered, remained opposed to this "new thinking." Jewish leadership, intellectual and political, Zionist and non-Zionist, generally continued to portray Judaism as the religion of reason, and therefore as the original and final enemy of myth. Scholem's consistent Schellingian scenario of three worldages of religion, culminating in mysticism as the revival of myth, seemingly was designed to smash the clay feet of this shaky consensus.

However, the real greatness of Scholem's accomplishment, in the end, was not purely iconoclastic, but rather was to have it both ways.[92] On the one hand, he could resurrect myth as the generative principle of religion. On the other hand, he rejected regression to the archaic, recognizing that the only viable vantage point for the dialectician is ever at the front of the social process. Therefore, he had to work "inside history," even to act, in a sense, as its furthermost incitement onward. In an almost unknown testimony, Adorno strikes the right note. Reminiscing over thirty years of friendship, Adorno observed the following:

> If I am not totally mistaken, Scholem became a historian of Kabbala…
> because he understood its contents to be in essence historical and
> therefore believed that its discussion had to be a historical one. This
> kind of historical truth can only be seized at the furthest distance from
> its origins, that is exactly in complete secularization.[93]

George Steiner's recent offhand observation that Scholem was "a master of disenchantment" similarly may not be wide of the mark.[94] My specific concern has been to place this "disenchanted" history of religions—Scholem's theory of Judaism—into its intellectual context. It was, finally, a *successfully* post-Schellingian theory of myth. Like Cassirer's *Philosophy of Symbolic Forms*, Scholem's *Major Trends* retrofitted myth to the history of monotheism. In both cases, the *"Urgeschichte des Bedeutens,"* "the original history of meaning" (in Benjamin's pregnant phrase) initiated cycles of creation and destruction, and thus subsumed the intitially disruptive daimonic into a continuing historical dialectic. This continuing vision meant, for one thing, that Scholem (and Cassirer) could then utilize this theory of history as the basis for an applied, practical scholarship. Such academic domestication was possible neither for the revolutionary theories of the Frankfurt School nor for the revelational theology of Franz Rosenzweig.[95] Still, in all these disparate cases, with all their constitutive differences registered, the turn to myth opened a dialectical vision of history as symbolic process. Rosenzweig stressed that revelation "brings an absolute symbolical order into history."[96] Scholem followed Schelling in describing his own symbolic shaping of history as a "narrative philosophy."[97] Beginning at the eruptive moment of the revelation to Adam, these narrative philosophies allowed Judaism to be understood in symbolic terms common to all religions. It too had a myth. It too could pass through cycles of devastation and regeneration; and it too could be reborn. Scholem's worldages—lifted from Schelling's *Weltalter*—then, mark the *Weltgeschichlicher Moment*, the world historical moment, when Judaism reentered the history the religions, if not history as such.

Notes

1. *Religion der Vernunft aus den Quellen des Judentums* (1919; 2nd ed., Frankfurt am Main: 1929), 294.
2. *The Penguin Book of Modern Verse Translation*. Ed. George Steiner, (Penguin: Harmondsworth, Middlesex, 1966), 258. The chronological simultaneity explicated in the following discussion of the year 1923 may seem flagrantly to conflict with the thesis of nonsynchronism documented here. For a justification of this procedure, see H. Blumenberg, The *Legitimacy of the Modern Age* (Cambridge, MA: 1991) 478, on the "reciprocal interaction of synchronicity and nonsynchronicity".
3. Reprinted as "Kairos" in *The Protestant Era* (Chicago: University of Chicago Press, 1948) 32-55, at 48.
4. Black: London, 1923, reprinted 1961.
5. *The Dial* 75 (1923) 480-483.
6. For effects of the insane inflation of 1923, see *The German Inflation of 1923*. Ed. F. Ringer (New York: Oxford University Press, 1969); W. Benjamin, "A Tour of German Inflation," in Reflections, (New York and London: Harcourt Brace Jovanovich, 1978), 70-76; and especially now Gerald Feldman, *The Great Disorder: Politics, Economics and Society in the German Inflation, 1914-1924* (New York: Oxford University Press, 1993). Note George Steiner's "intriguing suggestion," from Elias Canetti, that "the ease of the holocaust relates to the collapse of currency in the 1920s... The same large numbers tainted with unreality the disappearance and liquidation of peoples." (*In Bluebeard's Castle. Some Notes Towards the Re-definition of Culture* (London: Faber and Faber, 1971) 45. See also Canetti's vivid memories in *The Torch in*

my Ear (New York: Farrar Straus Giroux, 1982), "Inflation and Impotence, Frankfurt 1921-1924," 3-55.

7. Recalled by Bergson in *Mélanges* (Paris: 1972), 1340-46; cited by I. Prigogine and I. Stengers, *Order out of Chaos* (Bantam: 1984), 294.

8. For this notion of so-called "Neo-Riemannian time" see, for example, W. Hudson, *The Marxist Philosophy of Ernst Bloch* (London: Macmillan, 1982), 146-148.

9. Volume 13 of the series *Die Gesellschaft* (Frankfurt-am-Main: 1923).

10. Discussed in M. Löwy, *Redemption & Utopia: Jewish Libertarian Thought in Central Europe: A study in elective affinity* (Paris, 1988; ET, Stanford: 1992) 203-206. Löwy notes that Landauer's anarchism strongly affected Scholem at the time (65).

11. Wohl, *Generation*, 74.

12. Ibid., 3.

13. Discussed by M. Löwy, *Redemption & Utopia*, 163.

14. *Torch in my Ear*, 49.

15. W. Schivelbusch, *Intellektuellendämmerung. Sur Lage der Frankfurter Intelligenz in den zwanziger Jahren: Die Universität. Das Freie Jüdische Lehrhaus. Die Frankfurter Zeitung. Radio Frankfurt. Der Goethe-Preis und Sigmund Freud. Das Institut für Sozialforschung* (Insel Verlag: Frankfurt am Main, 1982).

16. "A Lecture on Serpent Ritual," *Journal of the Warburg and Courtauld Institute* 2 (1939) 277-292, at 292. This was his only English-language lecture to be published in the *Journal of the Warburg and Courtauld Institute*.

17. G. Bing, cited by P. Gay in *Weimar Culture: The Outsider as Insider* (New York, etc.: Harper and Row, 1968), 33.

18. *From Marx to Hegel* (New York: The Seabury Press, 1971), 20.

19. (Chicago: University of Chicago Press, 1949).

20. "Theses on the Philosophy of History," #XIV, in *Illuminations*, (London: Collins/Fontana, 1973), 263.

21. *An Essay on Man* (New Haven: Yale University Press, 1946).

22. *Gesammelte Schriften I*, 1237, cited by I. Wohlfarth, "On Some Jewish Motifs in Benjamin," in *The Problems of Modernity. Adorno and Benjamin.* Ed. Andrew Benjamin (London and New York: 1989), 157-215, at 164.

23. *The Principle of Hope* (Cambridge, MA: MIT Press, 1986) vol. 1, 134.

24. Bloch's *Durch die Wüste* and the second edition of *Geist der Utopie* were published in 1923. See the overview of this period in R. H. Roberts, *Hope and its Hieroglyph, A Critical Decipherment of Ernst Bloch's Principle of Hope* (Atlanta. Scholars' Press: 1990), 12-19. O. Y. Gasset published *The Theme of Our Time* in 1923, on which see R. Wohl, *The Generation of 1914* (Cambridge, MA: Harvard University Press, 1979), 134-142. For Ortega's perennial debt to Cohen, see S. Schwarzschild, "The Theologico-Poltitical Basis of Liberal Christian-Jewish Relations in Modernity," in *Das Deutsche Judentum und der Liberalismus—German Jewry and Liberalism* (Sankt Augustin: Comdok-Verlagsabteilung, 1986), 70-95, at 90. Ernst Cassirer published *Language and*

Myth in that year. Martin Buber's *I and Thou*, also published in 1923, marked a watershed in his career. So too his *Lectures on Judaism* as David Novak writes," [Buber's] lectures of 1938 simply elaborate the argument of 1923 (indeed, one could say this about everything Buber wrote after 1923)." D. Novak, "Buber's Critique of Heidegger," *Modern Judaism* 5 (1985), 125-140, at 132.

25. On Cohen's rejection of Schelling, see W. Kluback, *The Legacy of Herman Cohen* (Atlanta: 1989), 58-63.

26. Of course, Cohen's original success itself may be the really surprising fact. As M. Schwarcz put it, "One of the most surprising phenomena in connection with Jewish thought in Germany is the conceptual subservience of all thinkers, no matter to which current in Judaism they belonged, to the philosophy of Kant." M. Schwarcz, "Religious Currents and General Culture," *Yearbook of the Leo Baeck Institute* 16 (1971) 3-17, at 7.

27. In fact, "[the] dichotomy for or against *Mythos* already characterized Jewish thinking (especially in the German cultural sphere) in the first decades of this century." Z. Levy, "Über Franz Rosenzweigs Auffassung des Mythos," in *Der Philosoph Franz Rosenzweig (1886-1929) Bd. II. Das Neue Denken und seine Dimensionen.* Ed. W. Schmied-Kowarzik (Verlag Karl Alber: Freiburg/München, 1988) 287-299, at 288 [my translation].

28. W. Schluchter, *The Rise of Western Rationalism. Max Weber's Developmental History* (Berkeley: University of California Press, 1981). "Ethical monotheism" was itself, it would seem, a neologism coined by German Jewish Reformers, but I have been unable to identify its coinage.

29. See Schwarzschild, "The Theologico-Poltitical Basis," 81.

30. This view has remained persuasive for decades. See for example, N. Elias, "The Sociologist as a Destroyer of Myths," in *What is Sociology?* (Columbia University Press, NY: 1978), 50-70.

31. H. S. Hughes, *Consciousness and Society. The Reorientation of European Social Thought 1890-1930* (2nd ed., New York, 1977).

32. W. Lepenies, *Between Literature and Science: The Rise of Sociology* (Cambridge, etc.: Cambridge University Press, 1988), 292.

33. H. Cohen, "Deutschtum und Judentum," in *Jüdische Schriften*, vol. II, (Berlin 1924), 312. Schwarzschild angrily insisted, however, that "Cohen is often accused of some sort of fatuous historical as well as philosophical optimism. This accusation displays real psychological and conceptual insensitivity." ["'Germanism and Judaism'—Hermann Cohen's Normative Paradigm of the German-Jewish Symbiosis," in *Jews and Germans from 1860-1933: The Problematic Symbiosis.* Ed. D. Bronsen (Carl Winter: Heidelberg, 1979), 129-157, at 139].

34. Wirtschaft und Gesellschaft (J.C.B. Mohr/ Paul Siebeck); Cohen in 3 vols., Berlin.

35. *Kant und die Bildungskrise der Gegenwart* (Leipzig, 1924) 13, cited in *Max Scheler 1874-1928. An Intellectual Portrait*, J. R. Staude, (New York and London, 1967), 146.

36. P. Mendes-Flohr, "'To Brush History Against the Grain': The Eschatology of the Frankfurt School and Ernst Bloch," *Journal of the American Academy of Religion* LI (1983) 631-650, at 636-640. For more on Bloch and Cohen, see Mendes-Flohr, "'The Stronger and the Better Jews': Jewish Theological Responses to Political Messianism in the Weimar Republic," *Jews and Messiah in the Modern Era: Metaphor and Meaning [= Studies in Contemporary Jewry VII]*. Ed. J. Frankel (1991) 159-196.

37. *Max Weber—ein Lebensbild* (Tübingen: 1926), 476, cited in R. H. Roberts, *Hope and its Hieroglyph, A Critical Decipherment of Ernst Bloch's Principle of Hope* (Atlanta: Scholars' Press, 1990), 8. Roberts also cites an amazing letter of Bloch to Lukacs from 1911 ("Ich bin der Paraklet..."), 8, n. 20. This immediacy of the messianic was sustained for some time. Between 1917 and 1919 at least three revolutions (Russia, Bavaria and Hungary) were partly spearheaded by Jews. As noted shortly thereafter, some Jews experienced revolution as a "collective messiah". See P. Honigsheim from 1924, cited in M. Löwy, "Jewish Messianism and Libertarian Utopia in Central Europe (1900-1933)," in *New German Critique* 20 (1980) 105-115, at 105.

38. Ibid., p. 9-10.

39. The fullest treatment of the viscissitudes of Schelling in Jewish thought is W. J. Cahnmann, "Schelling and the New Thinking of Judaism," *Proceedings of the American Academy for Jewish Research* 48 (1981), 1-56.

40. *Philosophical-Political Profiles* (Cambridge, MA: MIT Press, 1984).

41. Published in 1917, and republished in Rosenzweig's *Kleine Schriften* (Berlin: 1937).

42. Cited in Cahnmann, "Schelling," 50, from *Briefe*, 299. Compare Scholem, "In Memory of Hermann Cohen," *Modern Judaism* 5 (1985) 1-3 [dated April 5, 1918].

43. The debate over the identity of the author of the *Systemprogramm* continues. The fullest treatment of the problem is *Mythologie der Vernunft*. *Hegels altestes Systemprogramm des deuteschen Idealismus*. Ed. C. Jamme and H. Schneieder (Frankfurt: 1984). X. Tilliette continues to defend Rosenzweig's argument for Schelling's authorship: "Rosenzweig et Schelling," in Ebraismo Ellenismo Cristianesimo II [=*Archivio di Filosofia* LIII/2-3] (1985), 141-152. For Rosenzweig and Schelling, see M. Cacciari, "Sul presupposto. Schelling e Rosenzweig," *Aut Aut* 211-212 (1986), 43-65, and more generally, *l'Ange Nécessaire* (Paris: 1988).

44. *Star of Redemption*, 329. For a fine treatment of the unresolvable tension between Cohen and Rosenzweig with regard to Schelling's philosophy of myth, see W. Kluback, "Time and History: The Conflict between Hermann Cohen and Franz Rosenzweig," in *Der Philosoph Franz Rosenzweig (1886-1929) Bd. II. Das Neue Denken und seine Dimensionen*. Ed. W. Schmied-Kowarzik (Verlag Karl Alber: Freiburg/München, 1988), 801-813.

45. In his "New Thinking: Notes on *The Star of Redemption*," Rosenzweig choose the Schellingian slogan "absolute empiricism" for his system: *Franz Rosenzweig, His Life and Thought*, presented by N. N. Glatzer, (2nd edition,

New York: Schocken, 1967), 207. For the "new thinking" more generally see the comments of Löwith: "The 'new thinking' was a phenomenon characterizing a whole generation deeply impressed by the bankruptcy of the bourgeois-Christian world and the emptiness of the academic routine." [*Nature, History and Existentialism* (Evanston: Northwestern U. Press, 1966), 53]. For the "New Being" of Tillich, see *The New Being* (New York: 1955) and "The Importance of New Being for Christian Theology," originally in *Eranos Jahrbuch* 1954, translated in *Man and Transformation: Papers from the Eranos Yearbooks 5* (Pantheon, NY: 1964), 161-179.

46. *Walter Benjamin, the Story of a Friendship*, (Philadelphia: Jewish Publication Society, 1981), 31.

47. Ibid., 59.

48. Ibid., 61.

49. Discussed by M. Löwy, *Redemption & Utopia*, 101-102.

50. In the opening pages of his *Mythical Thought* [=*Philosophy of Symbolic Forms*, volume 2] (New Haven: Yale University Press, 1955), Schelling is given full due.

51. Cited by N. Tertulian, "The History of Being and Political Revolution: Reflections on a Posthumous Work of Heidegger," in *The Heidegger Case: On Philosophy and Politics*. Ed. T. Rockmore and J. Margolis (Philadelphia: Temple University Press, 1992), 208-231, at 209. This work was also crucial in the development of Tillich's theology. See J. L. Adams, Paul Tillich's *Philosphy of Culture, History, Science and Religion* (New York: Schocken Books, 1970), 7.

52. D. F. Krell, "Shattering: Toward a Politics of Daimonic Life," *Graduate Faculty Philosophy Journal* 14-15 (1991), 153-183. And for Rosenzweig, *Star of Redemption*, [from Part I to Part II] "Transition, Retrospect: The Chaos of the Elements," which begins, "Mythic God, plastic world, tragic man—we hold the parts in our hand. Truly we have smashed the All.... the unity of the All [is] shattered for us." *The Star of Redemption*, Trans. W. Hallo (Boston: Beacon Press, 1972), 83.

53. "Review of Ernst Cassirer's *Mythical Thought*," (1928), Trans. by J. C. Hart and J. C. Maraldo, *The Piety of Thinking, Essays by Martin Heidegger* (Indiana University Press: Bloomington and London, 1976), 32-45, at 45. It should be noted that Heidegger was not entirely accurate here. Usener, for example, had already laid the groundwork, as Cassirer himself scrupulously observes in *Language and Myth*, (New York: Harper & Brothers, 1946), 15.

54. Schwarzschild published a precis of this forthcoming work as "Franz Rosenzweig and Martin Heidegger: The German and the Jewish Turn to Ethnicicism," in *Der Philosoph Franz Rosenzweig (1886-1929) Bd. II. Das Neue Denken und seine Dimensionen*. Ed. W. Schmied-Kowarzik (Verlag Karl Alber: Freiburg/München, 1988) 887-889. Other convergences of these two thinkers are noted by K. Löwith in "M. Heidegger and F. Rosenzweig or

Temporality and Eternity," in *Philosophy and Phenomenological Research* (1942-1943), 53-77; and by M. Theunissen in *The Other. Studies in the Social Ontology of Husserl, Heidegger, Sartre, and Buber* (Cambridge, MA, and London: 1986), especially 263.

55. It also included, for example, such French Jewish scholars of religion in the 1920's as M. Mauss: "Il ne nous suffit pas de décrire le myth. Suivant les principes de Schelling des philosophes, nous voulons savoir quel être it traduit." Oeuvres II (Paris: 1969), 161, cited by M. Detienne, "Une mythologie sans illusion," in *Le temps de la reflexion* I (1980), 29.

56. For "Civilisation" vs. "Kultur" at this time, see, for example, A. Schweitzer, *Verfall und Wiederaufbau der Kultur* and *Kultur und Ethik*, both published in 1923. For a general orientation to the terminology, see N. Elias, "On the Sociogenesis of the Concepts 'Civilization' and 'Culture'", in *The History of Manners* [= *The Civilizing Process vol. 1*] (New York: Pantheon Books, 1978), 1-35.

57. For example, R. Otto claimed that the primordial, prereligious *daimonic* arises from "intuitions of persons of innate prophetic powers." [*Idea of the Holy* (London: Oxford University Press, 1939), 122] It is important to remember that early sociology was still forming in the tension between literature and science. See W. Lepenies, *Between Literature and Science: The Rise of Sociology*, (Cambridge, etc: 1988).

58. K. Kerényi, "Dionysus, the Cretan: Contributions to the Religious History of Europe," *Diogenes* 20 (1957), 1-21, at 13.

59. They did much to revive the moribund "primal" scenario. M. Müller (a student of Schelling) had already said, in 1885, that the "devil-savage, however, of the present anthropologist is as much as a wild creation of scientific fancy as the angel-savage of former philosophers. The true Science of Man has no room for such speculations" [reprinted as "Reflections on Savage Man," in *Ways of Understanding Religion*. Ed.. W. H. Capps (New York: 1972), 70-77, at 73]. By 1965 E.E. Evans-Pritchard could flatly observe that such theories were "for anthropolgists at least, as dead as mutton, and today are chiefly of interest as specimens of the thought of their time" (cited in Capps, *Ways*, 127).

60. For contrasts between Benjamin and Rosenzweig on the "Revelation of Adam," see S. Moses, "Walter Benjamin and Franz Rosenzweig," *The Philosphical Forum* XV (1983-1984), 188-206, at 198-199. For an insightful characterization of this "semiotic of the prelapsarian" and its implications, see G. Steiner, "The Scandal of Revelation," in *Salmagundi* 98-99 (1993) 42-71, at 67-68.

61. Schelling, *Philosophical Lettters upon Dogmatism and Christianity*, cited in A. P. Mendel, *Vision and Violence*, (Ann Arbor: University of Michigan Press, 1992), 139. Emphasis added.

62. "Random Thoughts," in *Selected Writings and Letters* (Moscow: Progress Publishers, 1990), 88 [dated 1919/1922]. For Benjamin's corrosive rejection

of such "primeval forest" scenarios, see Menninghaus, "Walter Benjamin's Theory of Myth," in *On Walter Benjamin: Critical Essays and Recollections*. Ed. G. Smith (Cambridge, Mass., and London: 1991), 292-329, at 298.

63. As discussed by R. Faber, "Einleitung: 'Pagan' und Neo-Paganismus. Versuch einer Begriffsklärung," in *Die Restauration der Götter: Antike Religion und Neo-Paganismus*. Ed. R. Faber and R. Schlesier (Würzberg: Königshausen + Neumann, 1986), 10-26, at 15.

64. This was true of those non-Jewish thinkers who turned to this new orientation to immediacy: "Heidegger had baldly appropriated the *kairological*—the *kairos*, the appointed time, the "moment" (*Augenblick*) of truth and decision in *Being and Time* (§ 67a)—and kerygmatic conceptions of human existence that he had first learned from biblical Christianity, and gratuitously attributed them to the Greeks, to whom they were quite alien." [J. D. Caputo, *Demythologizing Heidegger* (Bloomington, Indianapolis: 1993), 181]. Related idioms were appropriated into the notion of "decision" [*Decizion/ Entschiedung*] used for the Conservative Revolution by C. Schmitt, and by P. Tillich in the interests of religious socialism [*The Socialist Decision* (New York: Harper and Row, 1977, first edition 1933)].

65. *The Principle of Hope* (Cambridge, MA: MIT Press, 1986), vol. 1, 124.

66. "The New Thinking," notes [1925] on the *Star of Redemption*: Glatzer, *Franz Rosenzweig*, 196-197. For metahistorical implications, see *Star* 110-11 ["The Moment"]. See also Meinecke's final statement, *Historism. The Rise of a New Historical Outlook* (ET New York: Herder and Herder, 1959, 1972).

67. See the discussion by Hudson, 148. See also, for a comparison of Benjamin and Rosenzweig on this point, Löwy, 58-59. S. Kraucauer also used the notion of Kairos. See his unjustly neglected *History, The Last Things before the Last* (New York: 1969).

68. See, for example, his interesting interview with I. Howe, in *Present Tense*. See also "Reflections on the Possibility of Jewish Mysticism in our Time," *Israel Yearbook*, 134.

69. In his 1928 review of Cassirer's *Mythical Thought*, Heidegger applied the thinking of his *Being and Time*, published just the year before, to his Jewish colleague's approach to myth. Heidegger asserted here that "all disclosed beings have the ontological feature of overwhelmingness (*mana*)... [and] *mana* discloses itself in a specific present "moment of vision" ("*Augensblicklichkeit*"). See "Review of Ernst Cassirer's Mythical Thought" [1928] in *The Piety of Thining: Essays by Martin Heidegger*. Trans. J. G. Hart and J. C. Maraldo (Bloomington and Indianapolis: 1976), 43. This passage is glossed in Krell, *Daimon Life: Heidegger and Life-Philosophy* (Bloomington: Indiana University Press, 1992), 167. One also thinks of Rosenzweig's essay of 1917, "Zeit ists. Gedanken über das jüdische Bildungsproblem des Augenblicks".

70. *Language and Myth*, 72.

71. *Star of Redemption*, 71.

72. In part due to the vogue for depicting historical development in terms of an organism's development. For generational metaphors, see R. Wohl's admirable *The Generation of 1914* (Cambridge, MA: Harvard University Press, 1979). Note that Scholem never lost the sense of his generation as a youth movement [*From Berlin to Jerusalem*, 166]. For Schelling's revolutionary notion of "organism" see K. Mannheim, "The Concept of the State as an Organism," in *Essays on Sociology and Social Psychology* (London, 1953, repr. 1966), 165-185. Nor did Scholem forgo his own "organicism": "his works contain numerous instances of the key terms 'organic', 'organism', 'original', 'sovereign', and 'spontaneous.'" [A. Funkenstein, "Gershom Scholem: Charisma, *Kairos* and the Messianic Dialectic," *History and Memory* 4 (1992) 123-139, at 130].

73. *The Construction of the History of Religions in Schelling's Positive Philosophy: Its Presuppositions and Principles* (Breslau: 1910, ET 1970), 16.

74. Cited in Kluback, *The Legacy*, 63.

75. Scholem, *Walter Benjamin, The Story of a Friendship*, 61. Much remains to said about triadic schemes in this milieu. They were used by Cassirer, Rosenzweig, and Scholem. Behind them echo the portentous Schelling. For some observations on triadic myth in Benjamin, see I. Wohlfarth, "On the Messianic Structure of Walter Benjamin's Last Reflections," in *Glyph* 3 (1978), 148-212, at 174-184.

76. *Major Trends in Jewish Mysticism*, (Schocken: New York, 1942), 7. This passage echo Vico, paragraph 379, "All things are full of Jove," which in turn derived from Vergil. Alternatively, a source may have been Thales of Miletus, "Everything is full of gods."

77. *Philosophie* 3:84 / *Philosophy* 3:72, cited in J. M. Krois, *Cassirer, Symbolic Forms and History*, (New Haven and London: Yale University Press, 1987), 86.

78. Cited in H. F. Reisz, Jr. "The Demonic as a Principle in Tillich's Doctrine of God: Tillich and Beyond," in *Theonomy and Autonomy*. Ed. J. J. Carey (Macon, GA: Mercer University Press, 1984), 135-156, at 148.

79. "The Demonic. A Contribution to the Interpretation of History," [1926] in *The Interpretation of History* (New York and London: 1936), 80. See also Reisz, "The Demonic," 138-143, for the roots of this image in Schelling.

80. "The New Thinking," notes [1925] on the *Star of Redemption*: Glatzer, 202. One sees here the concern which Benjamin called *Urgeschichte des Bedeutens* ("The original history of meaning"), a phrase which well could have been used by Cassirer. See Wohlfarth, "Jewish Motifs," 160.

81. Note that Gustav Landauer—who developed this theory of "demonic depth"—conceived "Revolution" as "an irruption in the world." See Löwy, "Jewish Messianism", 108, following K. Mannheim. For *Plötzlichkeit* and the "aesthetics of horror," see K. H. Bohrer, *Asthetik des Schreckens* (Munich: Carl Hanser, 1978), 334ff, and the discussion in R. Wolin, "Carl Schmitt. The Consevative Revolutionary Habitus and the Aesthetics of Horror," *Political Theory* 20 (1992), 424-447.

82. W. Cutter, "Ghostly Hebrew, Ghastly Speech: Scholem to Rosenzweig, 1926," *Prooftexts* 10 (1990), 413-433, at 417. For more on this text see R. Horowitz, "Franz Rosenzweig and Gershom Scholem on Zionism and the Jewish People," in *Jewish History* 6 [= *Frank Talmadge Memorial Volume II*] (1992), 99-113; M. Brocke, "Franz Rosenzweig und Gerhard Gershom Scholem," in *Juden in der Weimarer Republik*. Ed. W. Grab and J. H. Schoeps (Bonn: 1986), 127-153 (text published on 148-150).

83. For Jung, see the statements made in *Nietzsche's Zarathustra. Notes of the Seminar Given in 1934-1939 by C.G. Jung*. Ed. J. L. Jarrett (Princeton, NJ: Princeton University Press, 1988), vol. 2, 1030 [June 24, 1936]. Also in 1936, Jung's issued his best known pronouncement on *Ergriffenheit*, in his ambivalent response to J.W. Hauer: "Wotan", in *Civilization in Transition* (= *Collected Works, vol. 10* (New York: Pantheon, 1964). See also Jung, *Letters*, vol. 1, 1906-1950, 211-212. For Hauer's side of the *Ergriffenheit* controversy see M. Dierks, *Jakob Wilhelm Hauer 1881-1962. Leben. Werk.Wirkung. Mit Einer Personalbibliographie* (Verlag Lambert Schneider: Heidelberg, 1986), 283-299, 289-293.

For Scholem, see his "Identifizierung und Distanz. Ein Rückblick," in *Eranos Jahrbuch* 1979, 463-467, at 466. Adorno pointedly applies the notion of *Ergriffenheit* to Scholem: "Der objektive Gehlat dessen, woran gerade einem wie Scholem bis ins Innerste Ergriffenen alles liegen mußte, schien gefärhrdet durch rhetorische Insistenz auf Ergriffenheit." ("The rhetorical insistence on being stirred (*Ergriffenheit*) endangered the objective contents of that which matters in particular to someone like Scholem, who is moved (*ergriffen*) through and through"). "Gruß an Gershom G. Scholem. Zum 70. Geburtstag: 5 Dezember 1967," in *Neue Zuricher Zeitung* 136 (# 5199, Dec. 3, 1967, n.p.): I thank Frederika Heuer for her translation of this difficult text.

For Heidegger's extensive use of *Ergriffenheit/Ergriefer*, see *Being and Time*, (first English edition, London: SCM Press, 1962), 565, s.v. "seize upon". For the usage in the Frobenius school, see A.P. Kriel, *The Legacy of Leo Frobenius* (Fort Hare, South Africa: Fort Hare University Press, 1973), 2-3, and 19. Frobenius's successor, Ad. E. Jensen, also centrally used this idea: "Spiel und Ergriffenheit", *Paideuma* 2 (1942) 124-139, and *Myth and Cult among Primitive Peoples* (Chicago: University of Chicago Press, 1963), 3-4, 53, 56. The Frobenius/Jensen usage has been powerfully critiqued by J. Z. Smith: "No Need to Travel to the Indies. Judaism and the Study of Religion," in *Take Judaism for Example. Toward a Comparison of Religions*. Ed. J. Neusner, (Atlanta: Scholar's Press, 1992), 224-225, and "Sacred Persistence," 42-43, and "A Pearl of Great Price," 96-100, both in *Imagining Religion. From Babylon to Jonestown* (Chicago: University of Chicago Press, 1988).

84. It should be noted, however, that even some of these revolutionaries were taken up with the idea originally. Near the end of his long life, Leo Lowenthal wittily recalled: "My first publication [in 1923] was an essay

'The Demonic. Outline of a Negative Philosophy of Religion.' It was a terribly ambitious thing, and earned me a great deal of criticism at the time from Siegfried Kracauer and Franz Rosenzweig, but also excited praise from Ernst Bloch... 'The Demonic' was a mix of Marxist theory, phenomenology, psychoanalysis and religious-mystic-Jewish themes. It all seemed to go very well together." ["We Never Expected Such Fame," conversation with M. Greffath [1979] in *Critical Theory and Frankfurt Theorists* (Transaction: New Brunswick [USA] and Oxford [UK] 1989), 240]. This dissertation was published in 1923—but before the decade was out Lowenthal had converted with his friends to a *mélange* of Marx and Freud. His turn to myth and the daimonic, in other words, was a brief affair, typifying its Weimar moment. *The Demonic. Outline of a Negative Philosophy of Religion*, moreover, specifically concerned the reactionary Catholic theosophist F. von Baader, colleague of Schelling and major influence on G. Scholem. A. Momigliano noted that the specifically Catholic influence on Scholem's early thought has been almost entirely unappreciated. See his brilliant review, "Gershom Scholem's Autobiography," The New York *Review of Books*18, December, 1980, 37-39, reprinted in *Settimo Contributo alla Storia Degli Studi Classici e del Mondo Antico* (Rome: Edizioni di storia e letteratura, 1984), 350-359.

85. *Dialectic of Enlightenment*, (1944; reprint, New York: 1989), 15-16, and 20-21. Vico and Durkheim had both invoked the Lucretian maxim that "fear is the beginning of the gods", though Durkheim criticizes Lucretius for it.

86. "Subject and Object," in *The Essential Frankfurt School Reader*. Ed. A. Arato and E. Gebhardt (New York: 1988), 497-511, at 499. It should be noted that Cassirer, like Adorno in this passage, also locates the first spark of monotheism at this daimonic moment: "Here it is but a single step to the fundamental idea of true monotheism," (*Language and Myth*, 76). Again, a certain common connection to Schelling is at work here, though the link is much more attenuated in the case of Adorno. See K. Baum, *Die Transzendierung des Mythos. Sur Philosophie und Äesthetik Schellings und Adornos* (Würzberg: Königshausen & Neumann, 1988). With regard to the origins of monotheism, on the other hand, they retained a (largely unacknowledged) similarity to Cohen.

Adorno, like Scholem, explicitly denied that such statements should be taken as evidence for an affinity which he might be seen to share with the archbourgeois Cassirer; but the filiation is unmistakable. D. Biale, for one, recognized Scholem's similarity to Cassirer with regard to his theory of symbolism: *Gershom Scholem. Kabbalah and Counter-History* (2nd ed., Cambridge, MA: Harvard University Press, 1982), 68. I would add other examples. Compare Scholem from 1938 with Cassirer from 1946: "The attempt to discover the *hidden life* beneath the external shapes of reality and to make visible that abyss in which the symbolic nature of all that exists reveals itself: this attempt is as important for us today as it was for those ancient mystics." (*Major Trends*, 38), "There is also a prophecy of the past, a revelation of its *hidden life*." (Cassirer, *Essay on Man*,) [emphasis added].

One should not underestimate the impetus of anti-bourgeois passion in Scholem's denial of Cassirer's influence. After all, Scholem, in his first published essay, had defined Jewish tradition itself as "unbürgerlich" (Löwy, *Redemption & Utopia*, 62). Such sentiments were common in this milieu. See the remarkable letter of Ernst Simon to Martin Buber [11.2.23], where he castigates Buber for pandering to the same audience which celebrated Hermann Cohen: "We will only half understand him—and his historic place within German Jewry not at all—unless we see what kind of people he was condemned to speak to. Who sustained his reputation among Jews in his lifetime...? The lazy and fat bourgeoisie of the B'nai Brith lodges." [*The Letters of Martin Buber: A Life of Dialogue*. Ed. N. N. Glatzer and P. Mendes-Flohr (New York: 1991), 307].

87. E. Hieronimus, *Der Traum von der Urkulturen* (München: 1975); and *Die Restauration der Götter. Antikereligion und Neo-Paganismus.* Ed. R. Faber and R. Schlieser (Würzberg: 1986), esp. K.-H. Kohl, "Naturreligion. Zur Transformatinsgeschichte eines Begriff," 198-215.

88. For "life", see Krell, *Daimon Life*. For Cassirer's views in 1930, shortly after his encouter with Heidegger, see "'Spirit' and 'Life' in Contemporary Philosophy", in *The Philosophy of Ernst Cassirer*, Ed. P. A. Schilpp (New York: Tudor, 1949).

89. Letter of 6 October, 1885, cited in Lepenies, *Between Literature*, 206. For more on Yorck in the context of the milieu under discussion here, and with reference to the metaphor of "eruption", see G. Lichtheim, "On the Rim of the Volcano. Heidegger, Bloch, Adorno," *Encounter* xxii/4 (April, 1964), 98-105, at 102. Lichtheim, in his youth, was responsible for the English translation of Scholem's *Major Trends in Jewish Mysticism*.

90. Cited in Biale, *Gershom Scholem*, 67, who notes that this was also cited by Cassirer, *Philosophie*, vol II., 5.

91. Three works composed by emigrant German Jews in the United States during the Third Reich present a important follow-up to the earlier turn to myth. Adorno and Horkheimer's *Dialectic of Enlightenment* (written in Southern California) and E. Bloch's the *Principle of Hope* (composed largely in Cambridge Massachusetts, 1938-1947) are masterpieces in which, as the *Dialectic* epigrammatically declares, "myth is already enlightenment; and enlightenment reverts to myth" (*Dialectic*, xvi). Cassirer's *The Myth of the State*, (New Haven and London: Yale University Press, 1946, reprint, 1973), produced at Yale during the war, likewise reflects this subsequent, disillusioned phase of the dialectic. Now *Mythos* is a darker daimon, the realized nightmare of maturity and not some youthfully dreamt anticipation of a more potent future.

92. See, preeminently, "Religious Authority and Mysticism," in *On the Kabbalah and its Symbolism*, (New York: Schocken, 1969), 5-32, which remains among the most important theoretical statements in the history of religions to be written in this century.

93. "Gruß an Gershom G. Scholem." Note that in Scholem's letter to Rosenzweig in 1926, his ferocious anti-bourgeois loathing of "secularization" is obvious: "The ghastly gibberish which we hear spoken in the streets is exactly the faceless lingo that 'secularization' of the language will bring about; of this there cannot be any doubt!" [Cutter, "Ghostly Hebrew", 417].

94. "The Remembrancer. Rescuing Walter Benjamin from his Acolytes," *TLS*. October 8, 1993. One may say that, just as Schelling espoused an "absolute empiricism," and a "higher realism," so too did Scholem argue an "ultimate disenchantment".

95. See the letter of Rosenzweig [11.14.23], chiding Buber that Simon will get over "the great hangover from his [dreamy faith] in the power of form to save a person." [*The Letters of Martin Buber*, 310.]

96. A. Altmann, "Franz Rosenzweig on History," in *Studies in Religious Philosophy and Mysticism*, (Ithaca, NY: Cornell University Press, 1969), 275-292, at 288.

97. Also "absolute empiricism": Glatzer, *Franz Rosenzweig*, 207. I. Heinemann, in his introduction to the *Kuzari*, saw Halevi's view of truth as "radical empiricism" (20).

Judeophobia, Myth, and Critique*

David Norman Smith

For myth-makers the eternal and the historical are sharply opposed, an opposition which is characteristically expressed in terms of antinomies between the immutable and the immediate, the transcendental and the transient, the essential and the ephemeral. Heraclitean flux is foreign, even antithetical to the mythic thinker, who thrives, instead, in the realm of the absolute, whether this absolute is conceived as Pythagorean harmonics, the Parmenidean One, Platonic *eidos* or Stoic *logos*.[1]

In myth, the everlasting seems to be nothing less than a miracle, the passing moment little more than a mirage. Even when myth assumes a structured chronological form to narrate the origin of a social order, it is not thereby converted into "history." Origin myths legitimate the status quo by pseudo-historical means. They embed the reigning social relations in an unfolding dynamic which is said to spring inexorably from an "eternal yesterday," thereby reducing the present to an incarnation of eternally recurrent manners and morals. Rather than telling the literal truth about the past, myths create a collective pseudo-memory, a figurative history, which subserves the present by subverting the past.[2]

It is certainly true that the most sophisticated mythic thinkers, such as Hegel and Heidegger, have often shown great ingenuity in seeking to reconcile the eternal and the empirical, but they, too, ultimately harness truth to myth. In Heidegger's hands, for example, *Zeit* falls under the spell of *Sein*, while history masks "historicity" and existence finds its truth in "destiny."[3] Even Hegel, whose sensibility was deeply historical, nonetheless treated history as the shell of an ultimate inner reality. "Objective spirit," that is, the realm of institutions and folkways in which "spirit" finds an embodied social and historical form, is ultimately reduced to "absolute spirit," which Hegel posits as the immanent reality "manifest" in history.[4]

In this way Hegel and other myth-makers treat phenomenal reality as if it were epiphenomenal, and conceive history as an emanation of the noumenal (which is often the numinous as well).

After Hegel's death in 1831 the historical critique of myth came to play an increasingly large role in European intellectual life. This was due, in part, to the powerful if contradictory influence of Hegel's logic, which inspired mythologists and historians alike. It is hence no accident that the new critical spirit was especially plain in neo-Hegelian circles, where Strauss, Baur and other "higher critics" of the New Testament waged a campaign of demystification against Biblical miracle stories in the name of a "higher," historically oriented ethical religiosity.[5] The critique of myth also played a major role in the neo-Hegelian *"Völkerpsychologie"* of Lazarus and Steinthal, which became influential after 1860, and in the kindred fields of ethnology (which crystallized in the works of Tylor and Bastian, among others) and comparative mythology, as represented by Kuhn, Schwartz, Müller, and the early Goldziher.[6]

Another rich vein of critical thinking appeared somewhat later in the comparatively neglected writings of Lev Pinsker, Ahad Ha'am and other early critics of modern antisemitism, or "Judeophobia." Pinsker in particular drew attention to the fact that mythical thinking about "the Eternal Jew," which had been rife in Europe for centuries, had now begun to assume more sharply demonological forms than ever. The uncanny survival of the Jews after untold trials made them appear increasingly surreal.[7] To many non-Jews, in fact, it now appeared that the Eternal, Wandering Jews had become literally immortal, an aberrant people suspended above history, with an inborn taste and talent for evil—indeed, radical evil.

This mythos, expressed in racial and conspiratorial terms, was the crux of the status conferred on Jews by antisemites in the latter years of the nineteenth century. Reflection on this mythology led Pinsker and his successors (most notably Ahad Ha'am, Peretz Bernstein and Maurice Samuel) to formulate a subtle perspective on ethnic myth in the years after 1880. In this paper I will probe the origin and social-theoretic implications of this perspective, with primary emphasis on Pinsker and his immediate forebears. I will argue that Pinkser's classic text, *Auto-Emancipation*, is a seminal, representative essay which draws together many of the most penetrating trends in nineteenth-century ethnology, psychology, folklore and historiography (not always intentionally). The result is a complex synthesis, which is often deftly and acutely elaborated, yet is at times naive, even uncritical in outlook. In all these ways *Auto-Emanicipation* is a classic text, the nucleus of many later insights; it merits careful attention.

The Eternal Return of Hatred?

It appeared, in 1870, that the impending *fin de siècle* would mark the beginning of an era of emancipation for European Jews. The walls of the ghetto had been breached and civil rights had been won in region after region: in Avignon in 1790, Holland in 1796, Frankfurt in 1811, Belgium in 1830, France in 1831, Denmark in 1848, Austria-Hungary in 1867, Saxony in 1868, and North Germany in 1869. Even Heinrich Graetz, the most impassioned chronicler of the afflictions of the Jews, was confident that a new day was dawning. In the preface to the final volume of his vast history of the Jews, Graetz proclaimed himself "happier than any of my predecessors." Continuing progress had inspired the "joyous feeling that in the civilized world the Jewish tribe had at last found not only justice and freedom but a certain recognition. Now at long last it had unlimited freedom to develop its talents, not as an act of mercy but as a right acquired through thousandfold sufferings."[8]

This freedom was the ultimate, revealed destiny of a people whom Graetz had once called an "immortal nation." Such nations, he professed, have "a diamond core" and cannot be injured—"neither iron nor fire can harm [them], and even less so corrosive acids." They "defy the chemical decomposition of history,...do not succumb to catastrophes, [and] have the elasticity to pull themselves together and rise again."[9] Eternally reborn, like the Phoenix, "the Jewish people is heading before our very eyes toward a process of rejuvenation which previously was scarcely imagined. The enemies of the Jews observe it in bitter rage, ...everyone is amazed by this phenomenon. Is this incredible stirring a true heart-beat or the galvanized twitch of a corpse? Can deceased and scattered bones live again?"[10] Jubilantly, Graetz answered his own question with Messianic certainty. The Jews, he announced, are indeed eternal.

This radiant optimism was the fruit of a stunning reversal in the fortunes of European Jews which had seemed almost unthinkable less than a century before. Moses Mendelssohn, the symbol of Enlightenment Jewry, had been diplomatic to a fault in his efforts to promote tolerance; no one had cherished more liberal or universal hopes for the future. Yet Mendelssohn had remained less than sanguine about the ultimate prospect of success in this endeavor. "You may cut all the roots of an age-old prejudice without wholly depriving it of nutriments," he wrote in 1782. "It will suck them out of the air, if need be. In short: reason and humanity raise their voices in vain, for grey-headed prejudice is deaf."[11]

The fatalism of this *cri de coeur* no longer rang true in 1870. It seemed, indeed, that history had proven Mendelssohn wrong. In the final volume of his *magnum opus* Graetz showed that the curve of egalitarianism and tolerance had risen steadily since 1782, marred only by a few cloudbursts of apparently anachronistic hatred (most notably the German "hep hep" riots of 1819 and the infamous ritual murder affair in Damascus in 1840).[12] Age-old prejudices seemed to be senescent, and Jews, welcoming the newborn spirit of enlightenment, found a new spiritual home in the nascent liberalism of the era. In France, Jews embraced "the rights of man" and "the principles of 1789"; in Germany the *Humanitätsidee* of Humboldt and Goethe offered a framework for a new liberal identity, founded on the ideal of *Bildung*, or humanistic self-cultivation; and even in obdurately conservative Russia "enlightenment" *(haskala)* became the watchword of a liberalizing movement.[13]

Nowhere, it seemed, was enlightenment beyond reach. By 1828 the movement to grant Jews civil rights had assumed such breadth and momentum that it came to be hailed as "emancipation," pure and simple.[14] Jews were emboldened to believe that enlightenment and emancipation would soon be victorious in every arena. Yet, soon after Graetz gave lyrical expression to this hope, the moral and political climate changed drastically. An "anti-emancipatory" movement of great force and scope appeared on the scene, fueled by a new kind of rage against Jews.[15]

Anti-Jewish feeling was, of course, nothing new. A dogmatic religious animus, which had fired Catholic theology since Justin and Tertullian, had attained canonical form in the writings of Chrysostom and Augustine,[16] while various economic grievances became common after the advent of the mercantile revolution in the eleventh century, when money lending and related issues began to loom large in public consciousness. Specifically demonological complaints, including charges that Jews murder children, poison wells, and practice black magic, became familiar in the twelfth century. A few centuries later, in imperial Spain and Portugal, it became common to stigmatize Jews in terms of race and "blood."[17] But the radical Jew-haters of the period after 1870 were obsessed by racial and demonological concerns to an unprecedented degree. They were fiercely proud of their "progress" beyond mere religious prejudice, and the social movements they led were indelibly marked by a new kind of racial fury.[18] This first became evident in the *Trendperiode* after the crash of 1873, when the continental European economy sank into a long and traumatic depression lasting (save for a few minor upswings) until 1896.[19]

Shortly after the crash the pendulum of public sentiment began to swing in an anti-Jewish direction. In Austria, the arch-reactionary Catholic publicist Sebastian Brunner unleashed a stream of vitriolically anti-Jewish manifestos and articles, "...many pitched at the level of the barely literate"; swollen by contributions from others, this stream was soon a virtual flood.[20] In Germany, the journalist Otto Glagau published a series of landmark articles in the *Gartenlaube*, a hugely popular family magazine with a readership of nearly two million. These articles, alleging Jewish political domination and financial chicanery, enjoyed a *succes de scandale* and were soon echoed by a chorus of anti-Jewish writers.[21] It was hence no longer novel, in 1878, when an ultra-conservative polemicist declared that Bismarck's regime had fallen prey to Jewish intrigues and would soon "not even be able to mint coins, but will have to leave this, too, to the bankers and in [the] future Bleichröder or Rothschild will appear on our currency... Indeed, it might be best if this were already so, for then everyone would know who governs in present-day society."[22]

This theme—the notion of occult Jewish domination, achieved by financial wire-pulling—became perhaps the leading motif in anti-Jewish writings in this period. It was soon supplemented, however, by expressly racial claims as well. Marr, Fritsch, Nietzsche's brother-in-law Förster, and many others were instrumental in advancing a racial doctrine in which the Jews were "explicitly denied human status."[23] Eugen Dühring gave the Wandering Jew a new, expressly racial identity when he wrote, for example, "The Jews remain collectively a single Eternal Jew {*Ewiger Jude*} who persistently defies all nobler things by reason of his inherited nature."[24] Claims of this type had become so pervasive that in 1879 and 1880 alone critics published no fewer than three refutations of the "new Germanic" racism.[25] But as the depression deepened after 1880, racism sank ever-deeper roots in public consciousness. "Standing on the brutal fact of race," the Pan-German agitator Schönerer declared in 1883, "...we will never accept a Jew as a German just because he speaks the language or gives himself out to be a German nationalist and urges intermarriage of Germans and Jews."[26] A slogan adapted from Schönerer's paper became a rallying cry for a growing mass movement of racial antisemites: "What matters is not the Jew's faith—his swinishness lies in his race."[27]

Historians agree, however, that the most galling and damaging blow to Jews in the *Bismarckzeit* came not from obscure conspiracy theorists or racist journalists but from Bismarck's inner circle. In 1878, Bismarck's court chaplain Adolf Stöcker founded the Christian Social Workers Party, after leading a stridently anti-Jewish campaign among Berlin's workers.[28] Soon afterwards the historian Heinrich von Treitschke, the poet laureate of Prussian nationalism, wrote a four-part polemic in which he insulted German Jews as "our misfortune," a phrase that won instant notoriety.[29] Treitschke, who had been called to the University of Berlin by Bismarck in 1874, spoke with unmatched authority when he insisted that there had "always been an abyss between Europeans and Semites, since the time when Tacitus complained about the *odium generis humani.*"[30]

In 1870, Graetz had concluded that this abyss had been bridged at long last. A decade later this conclusion was in ruins. Mendelssohn's "ancient prejudice" had sprung to life once again—and it was now visibly fiercer and less compromising than ever.

The Riddle of the Hydra

A great deal of the anti-Jewish sentiment of the Bismarck era was plainly delusional, but Treitschke, at least, was eager to denounce real as well as fantasy Jews. He was particularly incensed, above all, by the partisan spirit of the final volume of Graetz's history, which he singled out for special criticism. Graetz's vehement attack on modern Jew-haters and his proud affirmation of Jewish life and culture roused Treitschke's ire: "...the Jews, who talk so much about tolerance, [must] become truly tolerant themselves and show some respect for the faith, the customs, and the feelings of the German people." He drew a sharp dividing line between "*unser Judentum*" (who could redeem themselves by "mak[ing] up their minds without reservation to be Germans") and "*Herr Graetz und sein Judentum,*" whose stiffnecked pride doomed them to live eternally beyond the pale.[31]

Treitschke's solution to the problem of antisemitism—a concept he helped popularize[32]—could not have been simpler. Jews could never escape the "odium" of humanity as long as they remained unapologetic Jews—indeed, as long as they remained Jews at all. The specter of the Jews had haunted Europe for millenia, and now Treitschke wanted to exorcise it. To make this possible he called upon the Jews to voluntarily melt away, thus conceding what their enemies had been unable to coerce.

Treitschke's polemic ignited a firestorm of debate, in which, remarkably enough, Graetz was almost alone in categorically rejecting Treitschke's premises. The vast majority of Jewish intellectuals who replied to Treitschke, either privately or publicly, willingly endorsed his assimilationist logic and defended positions which were, in essence, "undignified attempts at ingratiation."[33] Bresslau, the historian, was characteristically conciliatory: "If you would have…indicated to us the means by which this transformation process of the Jew into a German could be speeded up, you would have made every unprejudiced and open-minded Jew grateful to you…" Even humbler was the neo-Kantian philosopher Hermann Cohen, who felt he could "confidently assert" that all German Jews yearned to have an "absolutely German-Germanic appearance" and who rebuked Graetz, his former teacher, for the "frightful perversity of [his] emotional judgments."[34]

A few intellectuals, such as the influential Berlin psychologist Moritz Lazarus, showed greater self-respect, but few indeed were willing to question Treitschke's ultimate assumptions.[35] Nor were they willing to speak up for the unbending Graetz, who answered Treitschke with vigor but with very few allies.[36] Viennese chief rabbi Adolf Jellinek and the board of the Beth Ha-Midrash, unhappy that Graetz "has recently been attacked by his own co-religionists in harsh, often insulting words," were among the few to defend his honor.[37] Yet no one rallied to defend Graetz's central thesis—namely, that the Jews owe their prolonged survival to the fact that they are not simply "co-religionists," but rather a kind of dispersed nation, a people unified by a proto-national culture into something far less perishable than a "confessional fellowship" (to use Max Weber's phrase).[38] This contention, which Graetz's great successor Simon Dubnow later called the heart of a sociological perspective on Jewish history, earned Graetz only anathemas from this contemporaries.[39]

Graetz's isolation was due, ultimately, less to his unrepentant pride than to the uncongeniality of his convictions. Since Mendelssohn, it had become the norm among both Orthodox and Reform Jews to assert that Jewish identity revolved primarily around Judaism. Jews were not "a state within a state," a nation dispersed among nations, but rather individuals of many nationalities who shared a common creed (and a painful history). Hence Jews could be truly French, German or Russian and remain Jews as well. All that was needed was to keep the faith, to avow the God (and Torah) of their fathers.

Graetz dissented. He insisted that the Jews are not individuals united by faith, but a people whose identity is ultimately national and historical, not simply doctrinal. And Judaism itself is the religion of a people, not of individuals alone: "The existence of every individual Jew," he argued, "is premised upon the existence of a Community of Jews (*Klal Yisrael*)...."[40] Repudiating the claims of Reform Judaism, Graetz spurned Treitschke as well.[41] The Prussian ideologue had demanded that Jews trade their national identity as Jews for a purely German loyalty; most Jewish luminaries vainly protested that they had already done so. But Graetz denied that *Judenthum* could be so easily dissolved.

He returned to this issue in his parting reflections on the new antisemitism. Striking a quasi-mystical note, Graetz rejoiced over the apparent immortality of the Jewish people. It seems, he exclaimed, that "even if thousands upon thousands of its members are rubbed out, death enjoys no power over this race."[42] What accounts for this imperishability? The Diaspora, Graetz says, with all its rigors and travails: "if the Jews had managed to preserve somewhere a modicum of political independence down to our own day, would their existence still represent something extraordinary? Certainly not! They had to be harassed, humiliated, and spat upon; they had to become serfs of the royal chamber, pariahs, almost gypsies to be viewed as a miraculous phenomenon defying the natural laws of national development..."[43]

Yet hate springs eternal as well: "In all parts of the civilized world a Jew-hatred long thought dead raises its Hydra-like head, organizes an international league against the Jews, and deliberates in congresses on how to effect their humiliation. Some use the pretext of race, others religion, and still others the rise and alleged power of the Jews in journalism and the money market. The enemies of the Jews are as unlikely to die out as the Jews, and they seem to renew themselves along with the Jews from generation to generation. Doesn't this tenacious, indestructible, unnatural hatred and contempt provoke reflection? If it be a riddle, it is worth seeking the solution."[44]

It was reflection on this riddle which led Graetz's contemporary, Lev Pinsker, to posit the first "scientific" hypothesis about the nature and orign of anti-Jewish feeling. For centuries this sentiment had been familiar as *Judenhass* ("Jew-hatred") and *Rish'es* ("wickedness"),[45] but it had not prompted inquiry or analysis. The wickedness of the Gentiles was simply taken for granted, and endured. It was not until *Judenhass* itself became "scientific"—anchored in pseudo-ethnological notions of "Aryan" and "Semite"—that reflection turned scientific as well. Pinsker, like Graetz, was riveted by the mystery of an ancient yet ever youthful hate. His theory of *Judophobie*, and his ideal of Jewish "auto-emancipation," were the twin results of an intensive effort to understand this phenomenon well enough to undermine it, at long last.[46]

The Specter of the Jews

Auto-Emancipation appeared in Berlin in late 1882, just as the tempest over Treitschke began to fade into memory.[47] Pinsker's initial impetus, however, came from the fateful anti-Jewish pogroms in Russia the year before. Signing his manifesto "a Russian Jew," Pinsker had long been a leader of the Russian-Jewish enlightenment. Since 1861 he had co-edited the influential *haskala* journal *Sion*, and he was well-known as an ardent defender of Western science and liberalism. A physician, Pinsker had served in the Crimean War, and he entertained no doubts about the authentically Russian identity of Russian Jewry.[48]

This faith was first shaken in 1871, when Pinsker's home town of Odessa was rocked by fierce anti-Jewish riots.[49] A decade later, in the aftermath of the assassination of Tsar Alexander II in March 1881, anti-Jewish programs ravaged 160 cities and villages, leaving more than 20,000 Jews homeless and another 100,000 reeling from serious property losses.[50] It was in the crucible of this trauma that Pinsker forged his analysis of the eternal return of *Judenhass*. Unsatisfied with the conventional wisdom which he had long purveyed, Pinsker came to three overlapping conclusions: that the Jewish people, lacking a territorial home, had become hopelessly uncanny in the eyes of *Nichtjuden*; that anti-Jewish feeling is a kind of inherited mass psychosis; and that Jews can rely only on themselves for their emancipation.[51]

To publicize his new ideas as widely and effectively as possible, Pinsker went on a pilgrimage to Western Europe, where he visited many of the leading figures in the European Jewish community. On the whole his reception was chilly. *Oberrabbiner* Adolf Jellinek of Vienna, who had extended a hand of sympathy to Graetz just a few years earlier, was shocked by Pinsker's pessimism. "You exaggerate the importance of antisemitism," he told his stunned guest. "This poisonous plant which sprouted on the banks of the Spree will wither faster than you imagine, since it has no roots in history."[52] Later that year *Auto-Emancipation* fell on equally deaf ears.

Complacency of this kind had been sharply criticized a year earlier by the writer Moshe Leib Lilienbaum: "We tend to think that the troubles Israel suffered in the Middle Ages have passed away, that German antisemitism is only an ape created by Bismarck the German for his political purposes."[53] Hence people imagine that "when Bismarck achieves his set purpose...these hardships will come to an end... But if we remember the well-known rule that anything that comes into the world by a historical process has profound roots in the society in which it has emerged, ...we may come to a different conclusion, albeit a very sad one."[54]

Pinsker could not have agreed more. Indeed, his theory of Judeophobia marked a new departure precisely to the extent that it sought to explain modern *Judenhass* in terms of its "profound roots" in society and history. *Auto-Emancipation* contains echoes of many leading schools of thought, including the *Völkerpsychologie* of Lazarus, Tylor's ethnology, Kuhn's comparative mythology, Charcot's neuropsychiatry, and the "higher criticism" of the New Testament. Pinsker's synthesis of these ideas is not always wholly successful, but it is incisive, rich in implications, and remarkably fertile. Some of the most subtle later critics of antisemitism (including Ahad Ha'am, Maurice Samuel, Peretz Bernstein, Otto Fenichel, Theodor Adorno, and even Jean-Paul Sartre) are unmistakably Pinkser's heirs. *Auto-Emancipation* is thus a kind of intellectual prism, refracting (and at times refocusing) a spectrum of initially independent themes. This gives Pinsker's thinking a representative quality which has not been widely noticed.[55]

Unlike most "enlighteners," Pinsker had always believed that the Jews form a nation, rather than a denomination. "Our task," he wrote in *Sion*, "...is to revive in [our] hearts the real meaning of the great past of the Hebrew nation as well as the purport of its present."[56] Answering a Ukrainian paper which warned that the Jews form an alien "nation within a nation," Pinsker asked rhetorically: "Doesn't this imply that in every land there should be one nation which rules over and devours the rest, one nation to which all other nationalities must cleave, or else [risk] extermination or expulsion?"[57] His answer is that a "multiplicity" of nations is vastly preferable to an ethnic monolith, and that Jews do indeed form one nationality among others.

In 1882, however, Pinsker changed his tune. He now argued that the Jews are only *potentially* a united people, while they remain, in reality,

just what the Westernizing "reformers" wanted them to be—a fragmented remnant of ancient Israel, united only by ephemeral religious
bonds. In reply to an imagined interlocutor who deems the Jews lacking
in "national self-respect," Pinsker waxes ironic: "National self-respect!
Where can we obtain it? It is truly the greatest misfortune of our tribe
(*Stammes*) that we do not constitute a nation, that we are merely Jews."[58]

At what point did the Jews cease to be a nation? Not, Pinsker says,
when they first ceased to have a directly territorial, political identity. It
is doubtless true that "under the crushing weight of Roman domination" the Jewish state "vanished before the eyes of the peoples (*Völker*)"[59]—
but they did not immediately lose their national status at that instant,
since nationality, for Pinsker, does not require the existence of a state.
Like Lazarus and other *Völkerpsychologists*, Pinsker insists that nations
are ultimately spiritual rather than biological or geographic entities.[60] It
was hence readily possible for the Jewish people to exist "spiritually as
a nation" (*geistig als Nation*) long after the exodus from Palestine. But this
spiritual survival was as mysterious to non-Jews as it was rare. Few if
any other "nations" have been reduced to their spiritual essence; they
have, on the contrary, remained incarnate in tangible local sites, popu-
lations and traditions. "Thus the world saw in this people the uncanny
form of one of the dead walking among the living. This ghostlike
apparition of a people without unity or organization, without land and
ties (*Land und Band*), no longer alive and yet moving among the living—
this eerie form, which has scarcely any historical parallels, without a
model (*Vorbild*) or a copy (*Abbild*), could hardly fail to have a wondrous
effect on the imagination of the peoples."[61]

Scattered before the four winds, the Jews "are everywhere guests,
and nowhere at home."[62] These uncanny guests seem like wandering
ghosts; dispersed, they are also despised. Rather than forming a living
nation, they have been transformed into a living myth. As such they have
become "eternally alien" and "eternally despised."[63]

In the Mirror of the Peoples

This argument reveals Pinsker's keen awareness of the folkoric
aspect of public opinion about the Jews. Like Heine, who also spoke of
"this ghost of a people," Pinsker alludes directly to what Heine called
"the myth of the Eternal Jew."[64] This myth was a veritable obsession in
the nineteenth century, represented by the legendary figure of Ahasverus,

who had sprung to mythic life as the Eternal or Wandering Jew (*Judæus non mortalis, Ewige Jude, Juif Errant, l'Ebreo Errante*) during the Protestant Reformation, especially under the influence of Martin Luther in Germany.

Tales of undying vagabonds had circulated for many centuries, often mixing motifs from the Biblical stories of Cain and St. John with elements of the Germanic and Nordic legends of Woden, the Wild Huntsman, and the Flying Dutchman.[65] But not until 1602 was this vagabond defined as a Jew or given the curious name of "Ahasverus."[66] In that year a tiny *Völksbuch*, published in Danzig as *A Brief Account and Description of a Jew Named Ahasverus*, reported that the Lutheran cleric Paul von Eitzen had met Ahasverus in a church in 1542, where he learned at first hand that this repentant Jew—who had jeered Christ at Golgotha—still roamed the earth, a deathless vagrant who had been condemned to wander interminably until Judgement Day.[67] In 1694, in a late edition of this *Völksbuch*, the phrase "Eternal Jew" was applied to Ahasverus for the first time, and in 1714 this rubric was extended to the Jewish people as a whole.[68] Still later, in the century after the French revolution of 1789, the accursed, wraith-like Ahasverus came to personify the Jewish people for widening circles of public opinion, prompting an outpouring of art, artefacts, literature, and criticism (including nearly 1,500 publications in the period from 1775 to 1930).[69]

In a few classics of the era, including epic poems by Shelley and Mosen, the "*neue Ahasver*" was equated with wandering, striving humanity as a whole. Ahasverus was portrayed as "a kind of Prometheus, …who rebels against God for the sake of humanity."[70] But more often the Wandering Jew was viewed as a malign force. This notion became especially common after the failed revolutions of 1848, when "an intensification of the alienation of the Jewish image" bore fruit, in part, in what Graetz in 1887 called an "envenomed application of the myth" of the Eternal Wanderer to the Jewish people *en bloc*.[71] In the words of Schoepenhauer, "Ahasverus, the Wandering Jew, is nothing but the personification of the whole Jewish race," whose punishment will be as bitter and perpetual as his sin "against the Savior and World-Redeemer."[72] A chorus of critics chimed in to accuse the Jews of the quintessentially modern sins of egoism, arrogance, and money-love.[73] Ultimately, in the final third of the century, "demagogic… antisemitic agitators began to conjure up the fantastic figure of a Jewish demon of darkness as a contrast to the Germanic Siegfried- or Baldur-type. They equated this demon with the eternal enemy of the Nordic race, the

Eternal Jew."[74] Constantin Frantz was just one of many antisemites to forecast a dire fate for the living bearer of this myth. New eruptions of "popular rage," he wrote in 1882, will precipitate a "great Jewish catastrophe," including a forced exodus from Europe. "Where the first blow [will] be struck, the place from which the movement will rapidly spread abroad, is the German empire. …Is it not a premonition that from their earliest history the Jews have been wandering"? And so they shall wander, for "they themselves are Ahasverus to whom no peace is granted…"[75]

The opponents of *Judenhass* in this period were well aware of the dangers of the Ahasverus myth, and several of them tried to explore and explode it. In "The Unconscious Ahasverus, or the Thing Itself as You Like It" (1878), Fritz Mauthner took satirical aim at Richard Wagner's antisemitic obsessions, which he also sought to combat in an account of the history of the myth.[76] In 1880 Karl Blind went considerably farther on the same path in an essay dedicated to "dispelling the dark shadows of present bigotry" which shroud "the phantom figure of the Wandering Jew."[77] Applying Kuhn's new methods of comparative philology and mythology, Blind hoped to show exactly how a variety of old Nordic gods, ghosts and gnomes had been turned by popular fancy into "demoniacal spirits of an 'accursed race'," and how, as a result, "the flame of fanaticism was lustily fed."[78] "If the science of comparative mythology had no other use," Blind concludes, "it would still be valuable as a means of overthrowing prejudice,"[79] since it allows us to decode even those "cruel fancies in which the human mind seems to have gone most wildly astray."[80] The myth of the Wandering Jew is just such a cruel fancy, the effect of which has been to spur an "unjust prejudice against an inoffensive class of fellow citizens."[81]

Pinsker takes a very similar position. The Jews, he insists, must refuse the "role of the 'Wandering Jew'," so repeatedly thrust upon them by *littérateurs* and the credulous public. "This role is truly hopeless; it is enough to drive one to despair."[82] Yet Pinsker also sees that this role cannot be simply wished away. The status of eternal, infernal ghost has been conferred on Jews by the mythopoetic power of public imagination, and its grip on this imagination is demonstrably real. However false, the Ahasverus myth is objectively, socially effective. It has consequences. "The time has come for a sober and dispassionate realization of our true position. Without bias or preconception we must recognize in the mirror of the peoples (*im Völkerspiegel*) the tragicomic figure of our people, which, with maimed limbs and distorted countenance, helps to make world history without even properly managing its own little national history (*Völksgeschichte*)."[83]

The spectral Jews of myth are real for the antisemite—and antisemitism is all too real for Jews. Hence, though the living Jews of history have nothing in common with tragicomic Ahasverus except longevity, they are treated and regarded as if they were a single ghostly Wanderer. "Fear of the Jewish ghost," Pinsker explains, "has been handed down and strengthened for generations and centuries."[84] This fear has given rise to a psychosis, "Judeophobia," and to a psychotic mythology, peopled with sorcerers, eternal Wanderers and ritual Murderers. Both the psychosis and the myth invite further analysis.

Judeophobia, Myth, and Critique

Pinsker defines "Judeophobia" as a kind of "abstract" hate-complex, in which all Jews are reduced to a devilish stereotype: "It is the fear of ghosts (*Gespensterfurcht*), the mother of Judeophobia, which has evoked that abstract—I might call it Platonic—hatred, because of which the whole Jewish nation is held responsible for the real or supposed misdeeds of its individual members, and is libeled in so many ways, and is buffeted about so disgracefully."[85] For the fearful Judeophobe, Jews are not real, living individuals, but one-dimensional vessels of evil, Platonic Ideas, eternally One and Unchanging. Living Jews are reduced by this unbalanced logic to spectral figures of myth, who are loathed not for their real individual or communal qualities but for the abstract Idea they are presumed to personify. The object of this hatred is an anonymous, ethereal *Geist*, a faceless spirit or spook, which is superimposed upon the Jewish people; while the Platonic hatred itself, Pinsker says, is a kind of *psychose*.[86] "Judeophobia is a form of demonopathy, which is unique by virtue of the fact that the Jewish ghost has become familiar to all of mankind, not just certain peoples, and that it is not disembodied, like other phantoms, but is a being of flesh and blood..."[87]

The abstract hatred which this demonopathy focuses on the Jews has effects which are far from abstract. As a living specter, "ghostly" only to the superstitious, the Jewish *Völk* is far from immune to fleshly ills. Indeed, it "suffers the most excruciating pain from the wounds which the fearful mob inflicts when it feels menaced."[88] Thus does "abstract hate" cause real pain. It also spurs *mythos*: "Friend and foe alike have tried to explain or to justify this *Judenhass* by bringing all sorts of charges against the Jews. They are said to have crucified Jesus, to have drunk the blood of Christians, to have poisoned wells, to have taken usury, to have exploited the peasant, and so on."[89]

The power of these accusations is not logical but psychological.[90] Logically they are almost entirely without merit—"made up out of whole cloth, based to a certain extent on *á priori* reasoning, and true, at most, in individual cases, but untrue as regards the whole people."[91] Yet these fabulous charges are *believed*. The abstract hatred arising from psychotic fright finds its "justification" in myth. In this way, *Judenhass* inspires *Judenmythos*; demonopathy engenders demonology. And though this myth has a psychological origin, it has a physical object. "These charges against an entire people, and a thousand and one like them, …had to be trumped up wholesale to quiet the evil conscience of the Jew-baiters, to justify the condemnation of an entire nation, to prove the necessity of burning the Jew, or rather the Jewish ghost, at the stake."[92]

Here, as elsewhere, demonology inspires the wish to exorcise de-mons—in this case, the wish "to burn the Jewish ghost." But since ghosts do not burn, Jews serve as surrogates. Pinsker's irony is biting: "He must be blind indeed who will assert that the Jews are not *the chosen people*, the people chosen for universal hatred."[93] For milennia, he argues, Judeophobes have "desired to strike in each of us the whole Jewish people."[94]

Can this demonopathy be defeated? Will hate yield to tolerance? Pinsker answers in the negative. Enlightenment rationalism, he insists, is powerless in the face of psychosis. Skeptics may refute the claims of deluded Judeophobes, but they cannot deny that actions flowing from these claims have injured Jews for more than two milennia in cultures the world over. Why? What gives these claims such lasting power? For Pinsker, the violence and persistence of anti-Jewish feeling reflects its character as an engrained psychosis with deep roots in European mentality and culture. Like other "subconscious and superstitious ideas…Judeophobia, too, has become rooted and naturalized" among the peoples with whom the Jews have dealt.[95] And once "rooted and naturalized," Judeophobia resists all the vain efforts of skeptics, ratio-nalists, and others who live by the word: "…against superstition even the gods fight in vain."[96]

For Pinsker, in other words, Judeophobia is not merely a personal psychosis but is, rather, a mass demonopathy, which gives rise to an enduring popular demonology. This mass psychosis is deeply rooted in what Pinsker, like Lazarus and Steinthal, calls the *"Seelenleben der*

Völker." Seamlessly woven into the fabric of the *Völksgeist*, it has an *"ethnologische"* ground. It is a cultural phenomenon with roots in the encultured psyche. And this, in turn, gives it the semblance of an age-old, changeless folkway.[97] "Like the Jewish people, the real 'Wandering Jew'—antisemitism—is seemingly immortal as well."[98]

Although Pinsker gives few details about the specific historical forces which produced this new *Judenhass* and *Judenmythos*, he stresses the cardinal role of the Diaspora. It is the prolonged dispersion of the Jews which renders them uncanny. "There is something unnatural," he wrote in a letter to Leo Levanda, "about a people without a territory, just as there is about a man without a shadow."[99] The Jews are so evanescent that they seem to ideally embody what Tylor called "the fundamental thought of the stories of shadowless men still current in the folklore of Europe"; they resemble Shelley's "woe-worn" Ahasverus, whose "inessential figure cast no shade upon the golden floor"; like the dead in Dante's Purgatory, they know that only the living cast a shadow.[100] As energy, rather than matter, they have velocity but no mass.

This metaphor of the shadowless shade was probably borrowed from Chamisso's *Peter Schlemihl*, which was then the most renowed exemplar of this theme.[101] Pinsker also seems to have been influenced by Chamisso in formulating his famous summary epigram, which shows just how contradictory *Judenmythos* can be: "To sum up what has been said, for the living the Jew is a dead man, for natives an alien and vagrant, for property-holders a beggar, for the poor a millionaire and an exploiter, for patriots a man without a country, for all classes a hated rival."[102]

"The Jews," in short, are anything the public imagines them to be. As figures of myth, "Jews" are infinitely plastic. They can be typecast as Judas or Ahasverus, Marx or Rothschild, Abraham or the Elders of Zion. Literally anything can be imputed to these bizarre, hapless scarecrows—and all such imputations carry social weight, however false they may be. For the mythic imagination, in other words, living Jews are little more than screens for projection.[103] And such mythic, projected Jews can excite abstract fear and hatred even when no actual Jews are present.[104] They live in the mind's eye of the ghost-fearing public—that is, in the collective fantasy of demonopaths.

Mythos and *Ethnos*

Understanding the problem in these terms puts Pinsker on the same spectrum with Lazarus, Steinthal, Bastian, Goldziher, Tylor, Blind, and other early critics of *Judenmythos*. Steinthal appears to have been the pioneer in this field.[105] In 1860, in the first issue of the *Zeitschrift für Volkerpsychologie und Sprachwissenschaft*, which he co-edited with his brother-in-law Lazarus, Steinthal published a withering critique of the pseudo-scientific racism of Ernest Renan's "Aryan" philology.[106] It is perhaps not coincidental that myth and race were the dual focus of this essay, or that it was Steinthal's phrase *"Semitismus"* which led Steinschneider to coin the neologism "antisemitic prejudice" later the same year (speaking of Renan).[107]

It was no secret that Renan took pride in his prejudice: "I am... the first," he wrote about his *Histoire générale et système comparé des langues sémitiques* (1855), "to recognize that the Semitic race, compared with the Indo-European race, represents an essentially inferior type of human nature."[108] Steinthal censured Renan for invoking the "half-animal" notions of "race" and "instinct," which he regarded as a fatal departure from social analysis.[109] He also indicted Renan for his mythic thinking. It was apparent that, beneath the surface novelty of Renan's rhetoric— the "scientific" vocabulary of philology and race, adapted from Bopp and Gobineau—there lurked the familiar figure of the Eternal Jew. Renan had argued, for example, that the "Semitic intelligence," imprisoned by a static and sterile language, is fatally dry and abstract. As a vehicle for the message of the One True God, the Semitic mind can allegedly grasp nothing else—now or ever. For Semites, the living world of change and color is forever sealed. "The Semitic language," in Maurice Olender's apt paraphrase of Renan, "is distinguished for its capacity to convey what is immutable." And it, too, is immutable: "This unalterability, regarded as an objective linguistic fact, of course matches the image of the Hebrew people as unchangeable, allegedly impervious to history..."[110]

Steinthal was acutely aware of the dualistic tendencies of mythic thought, which so often inspire Manichaean distinctions between blessed deities and evil anti-gods, who are "hostile at once to men and gods."[111] He noted, for example, that many German deities had been "converted into devils and monsters, ...into night-hags and witches"; this typified what he called "the conversion of mythical actions...into terrestrial history," or, more succinctly, "myth transformed into legendary history."[112] Real history is thus "unconsciously falsified."[113]

Plainly, Renan's account of the eternal "Semite" is a classic example of the fabrication of just this kind of legendary history, in which "the Eternal Jew" is lifted from the realm of folklore into that of ersatz history. In this way immortality was conferred on mere morals, who were thus exalted "from the limited to the illimitable."[114]

Steinthal's critique of Renan's *Rassenmythos* was soon extended by many others, including Delbrück and Cohen.[115] Ignaz Goldziher, who sought to develop and apply Steinthal's outlook on a large scale, was scornful of Renan's "scheme of race-psychology" which led him to treat the Hebrews as "a people quite apart, and not to be measured by the standard of History and Psychology"—"for history is just what this scheme disregards."[116] For the "ingenious" Renan, Goldziher protested, the Jews "were not born into life as infants, and never saw the sunlight till they were men, or even old men."[117]

A vision of this kind is entirely meaningless, Goldziher adds, "unless we...speak of whole races...as psychologically pathologic, and make the whole Semitic race thus pathologic..."[118] This, of course, he could never concede. Nor was such a vision congenial to Bastian, Tylor, or any of the other great myth-critics of this period. "It is always his self-created world of spirits with which man surrounds himself," Bastian proclaimed.[119] Chimeras, ghosts and "ideas of demonic possession" spring from mystical visions, which normally arise amid "psychically contagious" communal processes. And such processes frequently inspire xenophobia and demonology: "Foreigners are often conceived of as the embodiment of evil..."[120]

Tylor, who is now widely regarded as the founder of ethnology, was equally perturbed by "the relapse of parable into pseudo-history," which often takes the form of what he calls "myths of observation."[121] Such myths "attach themselves to real persons, places, or objects, as strongly as though they actually belonged to them," and thus falsely "assume the appearance of real history."[122] Warmly avowing his debt to Steinthal, Bastian and Lazarus, Tylor declared war on all "myths presenting themselves in the dress of historical narrative, and historical facts growing into the wildest myths."[123] It is the primary "office" of ethnology, he wrote, "to expose the remains of old crude culture which have passed into harmful superstition, and to mark these out for destruction."[124] Every demonology (and angelology) must yield to science, which Tylor hopes will be the engine of "a new reformation."[125]

Ethnology, a vital part of this new reformation, is hence "essentially a reformer's science."[126]

Pinsker's critique of Judeophobia clearly belongs to the same intellectual current which swept up Steinthal, Bastian and Tylor, but Pinsker is far less sanguine about the prospect of "reforming" myth and bias.[127] This, then, is why Pinsker urges "the auto-emancipation of the Jewish people as a nation."[128] And this is why, in later years, Pinsker was able to find common ground with Heinrich Graetz, despite their many differences.[129] Both were compelled by unhappy experience to recognize that Judeophobia is a stubborn social reality which gives Jews a demonized status they cannot simply wish away. "The mere fact of belonging to this people is a mark of Cain on one's forehead, an indelible stigma which repels non-Jews and is painful to the Jews themselves."[130]

This stigma, Pinsker argued, ultimately reveals little or nothing about the Jews themselves—but it speaks volumes about the Judeophobe. "Myth," as Tylor explains, "is the history of its authors, not of its subjects…"[131]

Notes

* Thanks to Dan Breslauer for helpful suggestions. I am also grateful to the Office of Research, Graduate Studies and Public Service of The University of Kansas for financial support.

1. Logos is the conceptual starting point for a line of thought which culminated in the familiar Stoic notion of the *ius naturale*, the *lex naturae*. See É. Bréhier, *Études de philosophie antique* (Paris: 1955) and O. von Gierke, *Natural Law and the Theory of Society* (Cambridge: 1934).

2. M. Weber, "Politics as a Vocation," in H. H. Gerth and C. W. Mills, eds., *From Max Weber* (New York: 1946), 78-79.

3. We can regard myths of this kind as "meta-narratives" which negate the facts they purportedly convey by forcing them into a Procrustean framework. "Traditional culture," F. Allan Hanson writes, "is increasingly recognized to be more an invention constructed for contemporary purposes than a stable heritage handed on from the past." ("The Making of the Maori: Culture Invention and Its Logic," *American Anthropologist*, 91 [4], 1989, 890). Cf. R. Hendel's treatment of the Aristotelian notion of the nexus of myth and tragedy, elsewhere in this volume.

4. See H. Marcuse, *Hegel's Ontology and the Theory of Historicity* (Cambridge, MA: 1987, first published in German in 1932). Cf. C. B. Guignon, "The Twofold Task: Heidegger's Foundational Historicism in *Being and Time*," in

Tulane Studies in Philosophy, 32, 1984; and J. A. Barash, *Martin Heidegger and the Problem of Historical Meaning* (Dordrecht: 1988).

5. This point is plain not only in Hegel's *Phenomenology of Spirit* and *Science of Logic*, but in his stunning critique of Schleiermacher's theology, which appears as "Hegel's Foreword" (to a book by H. Hinrichs) in E. von der Luft, ed., *Hegel, Hinrichs, and Schleiermacher on Feeling and Reason in Religion: The Texts of Their 1821-22 Debate* (Lewiston, NY: 1987), 245-68.

6. D. N. Smith, *Authorities, Deities and Commodities* (Ph. D diss., University of Wisconsin: 1988), Chap. 10, "The Disenchantment of the Word".

7. Folk psychology and the early Kuhnian study of mythology are now nearly forgotten. For further data, see the references cited in Notes 92ff.

8. Perhaps surprisingly the concept of the Eternal Jew is relatively modern. Radically delusional anti-Jewish sentiments had first become widely common in the twelfth century, but it was not until the seventeenth century that the legend of the eternally wandering Jew, Ahasverus, began to take shape. The phrase "the Eternal Jew" (*die Ewiger Jude*) was first applied to Ahasverus in 1694, and before long Ahasverus became the defining figure in the Christian mythology of the Jewish people. For details see the discussion, below.

9. H. Graetz, *Geschichte der Juden*, cited by W. Laqueur, *A History of Zionism* (New York: 1972), 27.

10. "The Rejuvenation of the Jewish Race," in H. Graetz, *The Structure of Jewish History and Other Essays*, ed. I. Schorsch (New York: 1975), 143.

11. Ibid., 143-44.

12. Moses Mendelssohn, *Vorrede zu Manasseh Ben Israel, Rettung der Juden*, 1782, cited by R. Rürup, "Jewish Emancipation and Bourgeois Society," in the *Leo Baeck Year Book* (hereafter *LBYB*), 14, 1969, 77. This line, translated from the foreword to the German edition, has been slightly altered to correspond to the rendering given in the English edition of Graetz's *History of the Jews from the Earliest Times to the Present Day*. Trans. B. Löwy (London: 1892), Vol. 5, 382.

13. Graetz devoted nearly 100 pages of Vol. 11 to an account of Mendelssohn's role as the architect of a "paradigmatic" reconciliation between modernity and Judaism. Cf. J. Guttmann, *Philosophies of Judaism* (New York: 1964), 330ff. "Hep hep" was the rallying cry of the anti-Jewish movement in post-Napoleonic Germany and is the colloquial name given to the riots of 1819. See E. Sterling, "Jewish Reaction to Jew-Hatred in the First Half of the Nineteenth century," *LBYB* 3 (1969).

14. See E. Shmueli, *Seven Jewish Cultures* (Cambridge: 1990), 168ff.; M. R. Marrus, *The Politics of Assimilation* (Oxford: 1971); G. L. Mosse, *German Jews Beyond Judaism* (Bloomington: 1985) and L. Greenberg, *The Jews in Russia. The Struggle for Emancipation*, Vol. 1: *1772-1880* (New Haven: 1944).

15. See, e.g., J. Katz, *Jewish Emancipation and Self-Emancipation* (Philadelphia, New York and Jerusalem: 1986); *Out of the Ghetto: The Social Background of Jewish Emancipation, 1770-1870* (Cambridge, MA: 1973), 191ff.; and "The

Term 'Jewish Emancipation.' Its Origin and Historical Impact," in A. Altmann, ed., *Studies in Nineteenth-Century Jewish Intellectual History* (Cambridge, MA: 1964).

16. See especially S. Volkov, *The Rise of Popular Antimodernism in Germany* (Princeton: 1978); and cf. W. Mohrmann, *Antisemitismus. Ideologie und Geschichte im Kaissereich und in der Weimarer Republik* (Berlin: 1972).

17. See, e.g., the valuable recent studies by H. Conzelmann, *Gentiles, Jews, Christians: Politics and Apologetics in the Greco-Roman Era* (Minneapolis: 1992), and W. Nicholls, *Christian Antisemitism: A History of Hate* (London: 1993).

18. See G. I. Langmuir, *History, Religion, and Antisemitism* (Berkeley: 1990); H. Maccoby, *Judas Iscariot and the Myth of Jewish Evil* (New York: 1992); R. Po-Chia Hsia, *The Myth of Ritual Murder: Jews and Magic in Reformation Germany* (New Haven: 1988); R. I. Moore, *The Formation of a Persecuting Society: Power and Deviance in Western Europe, 950-1250* (Oxford: 1987); and V. Newell, "The Jew as a Witch Figure," in V. Newell, ed., *The Witch Figure* (London: 1973).

19. "There must be no question...of parading religious prejudices," W. Marr wrote, "when the issue is race...." This line appeared in an 1879 pamphlet— *Der Sieg des Judenthums über das Germanenthum, vom nicht konfessionellen Standpunkt aus betrachtet*—which was reprinted 12 times that year! Also in 1879 Marr founded the *Antisemitenliga*, the first openly racist anti-Jewish organization. The next year E. Dühring published *Die Judenfrage als Racen-, Sitten- und Culturfrage* (Leipzig and Karlsruhe: 1880), which, he later boasted, definitively put race ahead of religion. "My work was the first presentation of the racial standpoint in the Jewish question in contrast to the religionism that was the sole authority at that time." (cited in Alex Bein, *The Jewish Question: Biography of a World Problem* [London: 1990], 609).

20. See H.-U. Wehler, *The German Empire, 1871-1918* (Leamington Spa: 1985) and H. Rosenberg, *Grosse Depression und Bismarckzeit* (Berlin: 1967).

21. A. G. Whiteside, *The Socialism of Fools: Georg Ritter von Schönerer and Austrian Pan-Germanism* (Berkeley: 1975), 82. Brunner was editor-in-chief of the *Wiener Kirchenzeitung* until 1874.

22. Glagau's series started in December, 1874, and was later republished as *Der Börsen und Gründungsschwindel* (Berlin: 1876). See F. Stern, *Gold and Iron: Bismarck, Bleichröder, and the Building of the German Empire* (New York: 1977), 501f. and U. Tal, *Christians and Jews in Germany: Religion, Politics and Ideology in the Second Reich, 1870-1914* (Ithaca: 1975), 260ff.

23. C. Frantz, *Der Untergang der alten Parteien und die Parteien der Zukunft* (Berlin: 1878) cited in P. G. J. Pulzer, *The Rise of Political Anti-Semitism in Germany and Austria* (New York: 1964), 78. Bleichröder was Bismarck's Jewish banker; the French-Jewish Rothschilds were the most renowned bankers of the era. All were stock characters in the anti-Jewish dramaturgy of this entire *Trendperiode*.

24. T. Fritsch, *Leuchtkugeln* (Leipzig: 1881). Fritsch, who remained a leader of the racist *avant garde* well into the twentieth century, "claimed that God had created the Jew as a buffer between man and ape." (G. L. Mosse, *The Crisis of German Ideology: Intellectual Origins of the Third Reich* [New York: 1964], 143). Förster collaborated with Marr in founding the *Antisemitenliga* in 1879.

25. The charming Dühring called for a "Carthaginian" solution to the Jewish problem, thus inviting the Holocaust. See Dühring, *Die Judenfrage als Racen-Sitten- und Culturfrage*, cited by P. L. Rose, *German Question/Jewish Question: Revolutionary Antisemitism in Germany from Kant to Wagner* (Princeton, NJ: 1990), 39. (I've slightly altered the translation, rendering *"Ewige Jude"* as "Eternal Jew" rather than "Wandering Jew.")

26. See W. Z. Bachrach, "Jews in Confrontation with Racist Antisemitism, 1879-1933," in *LBYB* 25, 1980, especially 197ff.

27. Whiteside, *The Socialism of Fools*, 96. Schönerer led a major antisemitic movement in Austria which prefigured the later successes of Karl Lueger and Adolph Hitler (who praised him in *Mein Kampf*). Schönerer was an early disciple of Dühring, which puts in doubt Niewyk's claim that Dühring's influence at this time "was limited even within racism's lunatic fringe." (Donald Niewyk, "Solving the 'Jewish Problem': Continuity and Change in German Antisemitism, 1871-1945," *LBYB* 35: 1990, 361).

28. The original of the couplet cited is: *"Was der Jude glaubt ist einerlei; in der Rasse liegt der Schweinerei."* (Whiteside, *The Socialism of Fools*, 96). For other translations, see S. Ragins, *Jewish Responses to Anti-Semitism in Germany, 1870-1914* (Cincinnati: 1980), 19, and K. Kautsky, *Are the Jews a Race?* (New York: 1926), 11.

29. See the essays collected in G. Brakelmann, M. Greschat, and W. Jochmann, *Protestantismus und Politik: Werk und Wirkung Adolf Stoeckers* (Hamburg: 1982); and W. Frank, *Hofprediger Adolf Stoecker und die christlichsoziale Bewegung*, Aufl. 2 (Hamburg: 1935).

30. Historians have conjectured that Treitschke might have adapted this phrase from the poet Heine, whose reference to Judaism as "a misfortune" was well-known. This hypothesis is plausible, but it seems just as likely that Treitschke was echoing Luther, who wrote, in 1542, that "the Jews...are a heavy burden on us, a scourge, a pestilence and misfortune for our country." (Luther, "On the Jews and Their Lies," cited by M. Weinberg, *Because They Were Jews* [New York: 1986], 86). See also Gerhard Falk, *The Jew in Christian Theology. Martin Luther's Anti-Jewish "Vom Schem Hamphoras," Previously Unpublished in English...* (London: 1992). The term "Die Juden sind unser Unglück" was later the slogan of Julius Streicher's Nazi newspaper, *Die Stürmer*.

31. Tacitus had said that Jews had earned "the universal hatred of humanity." Treitschke agreed, saying that "Jews who are nothing else but German speaking orientals" will always be "odious" for the Prussian patriot. (Treitschke, "A Word About Our Jewry." Trans. H. Lederer, in P. Mendes-

Flohr and J. Reinharz, eds., *The Jew in the Modern World: A Documentary History* [New York: 1980], 283).

32. Ibid., 283. "Herr Graetz und sein Judentum" is the title of the second of the articles which Treitschke published in his own *Preussische Jahrbücher*. The whole series, which began in November 1879, was reprinted as a pamphlet under the title *Eine Wort über unser Judentum* (Berlin: 1880).

33. Marr is usually credited with coining the word "antisemitismus," but this is inexact. Steinthal broached the concept and Steinschneider introduced the word in the 1860's; it first appeared in print on November 11, 1879, when the *Allgemeine Zeitung des Judentums* reported on the "ridiculous" activities of Marr's newly-formed *Antisemitenliga*; and on November 15, 1879, the first of Treitschke's articles made use of this category as well. See Bein, *The Jewish Question*, 595.

34. Bein, *The Jewish Question*, 658.

35. M. Meyer, "Great Debate on Antisemitism: Jewish Reactions to New Hostility in Germany 1879-1881," *LBYB* 11, 1966, 149-50, 152 and 156. Treitschke found Cohen's position congenial, praising him in his final article: "In much that is essential I am in agreement with him, for he demands that our Jewry dispense with a special national status inside the German nation" (Treitschke, *"Zur Judenfrage"* [February: 1880]).

36. See the documents collected by W. Boelich in *Der Berliner Antissemitismusstreit* (Frankfurt: 1965); and cf. J. Doron, "Classic Zionism and Modern Anti-Semitism: Parallels and Influences (1883-1914)," *Studies in Zionism*, 8, 1983, 175. On Lazarus, see I. Schorsch, *Jewish Reactions to German Anti-Semitism, 1870-1914* (New York: 1972).

37. In 1868, while writing Vol. 11, Graetz told his friend Moses Hess that he was finding pleasure in "scourging the Germans and their leaders—Schleiermacher, Fichte, and the whole wretched Romantic school." See Graetz, *Tagebuch und Briefe*. Ed. R. Michael, cited by Meyer, "Graetz and Treitschke," 9.

38. See the statement by A. Jellinek *et al.*, cited by Meyer, "Great Debate", 158. Others who took Graetz's side in this debate included rabbis Moritz Eisler and Leo Glück.

39. "No one in any camp suggested," *á la* Graetz, "that the Jews were a nation." Viennese rabbi Moritz Güdemann, for example, who later succeeded Jellinek, "limited himself to an indictment of those who abandoned Graetz" (Meyer, "Great Debate", 158). For data on Graetz's historiography, see S. Sniderman, "Bibliography of Works About Heinrich Graetz," in *Studies in Bibliography and Booklore*, 14 (1982).

40. S. Dubnow, *Nationalism and History* (New York: 1958), 352. Graetz is still a remarkably obscure figure though he was a university lecturer, editor and writer, whose great history appeared from 1853 to 1870. As recently as 1968, Reuven Michael could entitle an article "The Unknown Heinrich Graetz" and express curiosity about "why very little is known so far about Heinrich

Graetz, the Jewish historian" (*LBYB* 13, 34). For more information, see Josef Meisl, *Heinrich Graetz. Eine Würdigung des Historkers und Juden* (Berlin: 1917).

41. S. Avineri, *The Making of Modern Zionism* (New York: 1981), 27.

42. Ibid., 26.

43. "I say thousands? Millions have been slain on this road of suffering; but the race as a whole cannot be liquidated." (Graetz, *The Structure of Jewish History*, 211)

44. Ibid., 210.

45. Ibid., 209. According to Schorsch, Graetz's comment about an "international league" refers to the First International Anti-Jewish Congress in Dresden in late 1882, organized by Alexander Pinkert-Waldegg. See Schorsch's notes and introduction, "Ideology and History in the Age of Emancipation," in Graetz, *The Structure of Jewish History*.

46. *Rish'es* is the Yiddish pronunciation of the Hebrew *Rish'ut*. See S. Na'aman, "Social Democracy on the Ambiguous Ground between Antipathy and Antisemitism," *LBYB* 36, 1991, 229ff. Louis Jacobs argues that most prayers sought to undo "wickedness" rather than "the wicked" *per se*—"*kol ha-rish'ah* not *kol ha-resha'im*"; see "Praying for the Downfall of the Wicked," in *Modern Judaism* 2, 1982, 301.

47. Na'aman is not persuasive when he says that Pinsker's concept of *Judophobie* and the conventional notion of *Rish'es* refer to "the same feeling," "a feeling of loathing or even hatred towards Jews" (Ibid., 229). As we will see below, Pinsker's "Judeophobia" is not simple antipathy or *Judenhass*, but rather a psychologically aberrant belief in specters and shades.

48. Written in German and published in Berlin, Pinsker's *Autoemanzipation* (a 36-page pamphlet) was plainly directed to a German audience.

49. Yehuda Leib Pinsker (known as Lev, Leo or Leon) was born in Poland in 1821, the son of an eminent Hebrew scholar. He studied law and medicine, received a medal from the Tsar for his services in the Crimean war, and later devoted himself to the Russian Jewish community. See B. Netanyahu's "Introduction" to Leo Pinsker, *Road to Freedom, Writings and Addresses* (New York: 1944). See also D. Vital, *The Origins of Zionism* (Oxford: 1975), 122ff.

50. Riots had occurred in 1821, 1849, and 1859, but the pogroms of 1871 were far more serious. See J. Klier, "The Pogrom Paradigm in Russian History," in J. Klier and S. Lambroza, eds., *Pogroms: Anti-Jewish Violence in Modern Russian History* (Cambridge: 1992).

51. See A. Orbach, "The Development of the Russian Jewish Community," in Klier and Lambroza, *Pogroms*, 143ff., and "The Modern Character of Nineteenth-Century Russian Antisemitism," in S. Gilman and S. Katz, eds., *Anti-Semitism in Times of Crisis* (New York and London: 1991).

52. L. Pinsker, "Auto-Emancipation: An Appeal to His People by a Russian Jew," in *The Zionist Idea*. Ed. A. Hertzberg (New York: 1960). The two main editions of *Auto-Emancipation*, edited by Netanyahu and Hertzberg, use nearly identical versions of a translation by David Blondheim. Since this translation is not always accurate or complete, I emend it as needed (and I

quote from whichever variant is closest to the original from Leo Pinsker, *Autoemanzipation: Ein Mahnruf an Seine Stammesgenossen von Einem Russischen Juden* [Berlin: 1917].) I will cite these editions, respectively, as "Netanyahu" and "Hertzberg.

"The phrase "auto-emancipation," which became *"Selbstemanzipation"* in the hands of Nathan Birnbaum, echoes or parallels Marx's phrase "self-emancipation of the workers." Meanwhile Flora Tristan, whose *Union ouvrière* (Paris: 1843) anticipated Marx's ideal of working-class unity, grounded her notion of proletarian solidarity in the historical example of Jewish ethnic solidarity. And so the wheel turns.

53. Jellinek's report of this conversation (which appeared in his house organ, *Neuzeit*), is summarized in detail by Netanyahu in Pinsker, *Road to Freedom* (1944), 47ff.

54. M. L. Lilienblum, "Obshcheyevreiski vopros i Palestina," in *Rasvyet*, 1881, cited by Vital, *Origins of Zionism*, 117, n. 9. The quotation is a play on the popular Russian saying that "the ape was invented by a German" (*Nemets obez' yanu vydumal*).

55. Ibid., 117. In 1883 Lilienblum argued that specifically modern antisemitism arises from "the overall trend toward nationalism" among Germans and others (in Hertzberg, ed., *The Zionist Idea*, 174). This argument parallels the recent claim by Hans-Ulrich Wehler in *The German Empire* that German antisemitism was spurred in part by the drive to achieve "national integration" in the rough years after Bismarck brought Germany together under Prussian leadership.

56. Pinsker's influence on Ahad Ha'am is generally acknowledged. The psychoanalyst Rudolph Loewenstein also directly avowed Pinsker's influence, pointing out that the reactions of many non-Jewish psychiatric patients confirm Pinsker's observations and adding that a number of psychiatrists (such as Erik Erikson) had formulated parallel theories. (*Christians and Jews: A Psychoanalytic Study* [New York: 1951, 14-15], 30-31) For data on Adorno, Samuel, Fenichel, and Sartre, see David N. Smith, "The Social Construction of Enemies," a paper presented to the annual meeting of the American Sociological Association in 1992. Cf. Peretz Bernstein, *Jew-Hatred as a Sociological Problem* (New York: 1951); first published in Germany in 1926, Bernstein's work is a finely-nuanced synthesis of Simmelian and Pinskerian themes which repays careful reading.

57. Indeed, few writers outside Zionist circles have noticed Pinsker at all. Even in these circles, while he is ritually praised as a precursor of Herzl and Weizmann, Pinsker seldom wins more than faint praise for his theoretical acuity. Bein is one of the few to credit him with "a genuine touch of genius" (*Theodore Herzl* [Philadelphia: 1940], 175), while Avineri (*The Making of Zionism* (1981), 76) accuses him of circular reasoning: "Pinsker really says that non-Jews fear Jews because they are afflicted by a malady whose main symptom is a fear of Jews." This is less than apt, as we will see.

58. Quoted from *Sion* by Netanyahu in Pinsker, *Road to Freedom* (1944), 34.
59. Ibid., 34.
60. Pinsker, "Auto-Emancipation," 189.
61. Pinsker, *Autoemanzipation*, 7. In Netanyahu's version of the Blondheim translation, this line is oversimplified and Pinsker's reference to *"Römerherrschaft"* ("Roman domination") is missing entirely: "The state was crushed before the eyes of the nations" (77). Though Hertzberg restores this reference, he slightly changes its sense: "The state was crushed by the Roman conquerors..." (184).
62. Lazarus expressed his views on this subject very clearly in his reply to Treitschke: "a nation is...a spiritual product of individuals, who themselves belong to this product. They are not being a nation, rather they are continuously creating a nation..." (M. Lazarus, *Was heisst national?* [Berlin: 1880], cited by Bachrach, "Jews in Confrontation," 199). Ignaz Goldziher, a few years earlier, had credited Schelling with the same viewpoint, which, he said, anticipated the discoveries of Lazarus and Steinthal. See Goldziher, *Mythology among the Hebrews and Its Historical Development* (London: 1877; reprinted in 1967), xxii. The French sociologist Celestin Bouglé later declared this viewpoint to be the crux of *Völkerpsychologie*: "To speak truly, the being of a people ... is the spiritual product of those who compose it, those who create it incessantly." (C. Bouglé, *Les Sciences sociales en Allemagne* [Paris: 1897], 23) Bouglé discovered this idea in Lazarus, *Leben der Seele* (Berlin: 1855), Vol. 1, 372.
63. *Autoemanzipation* (Berlin: 1917), 7-8.
64. "Auto-Emancipation," in Netanyahu, 76.
65. Ibid., 83, and Hertzberg, 192.
66. Heinrich Heine refers to "the myth of the Eternal Jew" in an 1826 letter which appears in his *Briefe* (1950, 284), cited in Bein, *The Jewish Question*, 532. He anticipated Pinsker, Bein says, in his *Memoiren des Herrn von Schabelewopski*, where he called the Jews a "ghost of a people." This metaphor expressed a recurrent theme in Heine's writings, which appeared as early as his undated *Gedanken und Einfälle* ("The Jews—this ghost of a people that ineluctably stood guard over its treasure, the Bible!") and reappeared much later in his *Confessions* as well: "Like a ghost guarding a treasure that had once been entrusted to it—that is how this murdered people, this ghost of a people, sat in its dark ghetto guarding the Hebrew Bible." "A book," he adds, "is their fatherland, their property, their ruler, their good fortune and misfortune." Ibid., 654.
67. See G. Hasan-Rokem and A. Dundes, eds., *The Wandering Jew: Essays in the Interpretation of a Christian Legend* (Bloomington: 1986); E. Knecht, *Le Mythe du Juif errant: Essai de mythologie litteraire et de sociologie religieuse* (Grenoble: 1977); and G. K. Anderson's monumental study, *The Legend of the Wandering Jew* (Providence: 1965).

68. It is still a mystery why the Wandering Jew is called "Ahasverus", a name which, in the Book of Esther, designates a Persian king who ruled over the Jews.

69. The original title of the *Völksbuch* is *Kurtze Beschriebung und Erzehung von einem Juden mit Namen Ahasverus*, etc., which, in the ninth edition and after, is credited to the pseudonymous "Chrysostomos Dudulaeus Westphalus". For data on this *Völksbuch*, see A. Schmidt, *Das Völksbuch vom ewigen Juden* (Danzig: 1927), and A. Schaffer, "The Ahasver-Volksbuch of 1602," in Hasan-Rokem and Dundes, eds., *The Wandering Jew*, 27f. Cf. A. Leschnitzer, "Der Gestalwandel Ahasvers," in *In Zwei Welten: Siegfried Moses zum 75th Geburtstag* (Tel-Aviv: 1962). Leschnitzer argues persuasively that the ethos and worldview of the 1602 *Völksbuch* is wholly Lutheran, expressing a theological anti-Judaism continuous with Luther's diatribes of the early 1540s.

70. The phrase *"ewigen Jud"* was first applied to Ahasverus in the thirty-first edition of the *Völksbuch*, which appeared in 1694. For the first interpretation of Ahasverus as the personification of Jewry, see Book 5, Chapter 14 of the *Jüdischen Merckwürdigkeiten*, a four-volume work (1714-17) by the Lutheran theologian J. J. Schudt of Frankfurt. "This itinerant Jew," Schudt wrote," is not a single person, but the entire Jewish people which has been dispersed throughout the world after Christ's crucifixion..." Cited by Bein, *The Jewish Question*, 532.

71. The magnitude of this cultural phenomenon is difficult to overstate. In addition to a flood of plays, poems, novels and essays dealing with Ahasverus, there were also dolls, puppets, card games, dice games, and coins; artworks of all kinds, including engravings, etchings, and an opera; and even a variety of plants named "Wandering Jews."

72. This is a comment on J. Mosen's epic poem *Ahasver* (1838) by G. Anderson in *The Legend of the Wandering Jew*, 220. Cf. the parallel remark about Shelley's "Wandering Jew's Soliloquy" (1812) and *Queen Mab* (1813) by Rose, *German Question*, 25.

73. A. Leschnitzer, "The Wandering Jew: The Alienation of the Jewish Image in the Christian Consciousness," in *The Wandering Jew*, eds. Hasan-Rokem and Dundes, 233; and Graetz, "Historical Parallels in Jewish History" (1887), in *The Structure of Jewish History*, 259.

74. A. Schopenhauer, *Parerga and Paralipomena: Short Philosophical Essays* (Oxford: 1974), Vol. 2, 261, cited by the editors in Hasan-Rokem and Dundes, *The Wandering Jew*, 227. See also H. W. Brann, *Schopenhauer und das Judentum* (Bonn: 1975).

75. See, e.g., the views of Karl Rotteck, as discussed by Rürup in his *Emanzipation und Antisemitismus: Studien zur Judenfrage der bürgerlichen Gesellschaft* (Göttingen: 1975), 61.

76. Leschnitzer, "The Wandering Jew," 234.

77. C. Franz, *Die Weltpolitik* (Chemnitz: 1882-83), 115-118, cited by Rose, *German Question*, 38. Frantz was a paragon of paranoid consistency on the subject of

the Ahasverus myth. As early as 1844, in a tract opposed to Jewish emancipation, Frantz prophesied that Jewish civil rights, once conferred, would
avail the Jews naught, since "They can neither live nor die, and from this fate
no earthly power can redeem them." (Frantz, *Ahasvers oder die Judenfrage*,
cited by Rose, 37)

78. F. Mauthner, "Zur Geschichte der Sage vom ewigen Juden," in the 1878
Wochenblatt.

79. K. Blind, "Wodan, the Wild Huntsman, and the Wandering Jew" in Hasan-
Rokem and Dundes, eds., *The Wandering Jew*, 188 and 181. (Blind's article
was first published in 1880.) In the 1848 revolution and afterwards, Blind
was a close associate of Marx and Hess in the Communist League. He later
devoted himself to comparative mythology.

80. "We all know, alas! what deeds such fanaticism is capable of doing" (Ibid.,
172). Blind believed that the Wandering Jew was a composite of ancient
Germanic beliefs about eternal wayfarers (most notably the god Wodan, the
legendary Wild Huntsman, and several kindred figures) and Christian
beliefs that were "grafted on" to this "phantom figure." A good number of
others have taken similar positions. See Anderson, *Legend of the Wandering
Jew*, for invaluable data on the literature in this field.

81. Ibid., 188. Blind and his wife, née Friederike Cohen, had long been partisans
of Feuerbach's myth-critical philosophy; Marx even said that they were too
orthodox in this respect!

82. Ibid., 169. Critical inquiry into the myth of the Eternal Jew ran parallel to the
myth itself throughout the nineteenth century. V.-A.-J.-M. Coremans, one
of the pioneers in this field, offered a very appropriate double study of
Ahasverus and the legend of the Unicorn in 1845 (*La Licorne et le Juif Errant*,
Brussels). Notable later studies in this field included contributions from O.
F. H. Scönhuth, G. W. Roeder, and J. G. T. Grässe. It was in Pinsker's day,
however, that myth-critical inquiry into Ahasverus reached its zenith, in the
work of G. Paris, "Le Juif Errant", in the *Éncyclopédie des sciences religieuses*,
VII (Paris: 1880), and above all in the writings of L. Neubaur, *Die Sage vom
ewigen Juden* (Leipzig: 1884) and *Neue Mitteilungen über die Sage vom ewigen
Juden* (Leipzig: 1893).

83. Ibid., 171. A similar indictment of the "*Judenhetze*," "race-hatred," and
"'anti-semitic' venom" of the Ahasverus myth was contributed a year later
by M. D. Conway, whose excellent study, *The Wandering Jew* (New York:
1881), drew upon Blind's "able article" (98) as well as the rich literature
produced by Coremans, Grässe, Tylor, and many others. See Conway,
passim, but especially 83f. and 269f.

84. "Auto-Emancipation," in Hertzberg, 191.

85. Ibid., 91. Cf. *Autoemanzipation*, 19, and the emended translation by Vital,
Origins of Zionism, 131. Pinsker's point here clearly presages Sartre's concept
of "the gaze of the Other."

86. Ibid., 184.

87. Ibid., 185.

88. Blondheim translates *"psychose"* as "psychic aberration" (see "Auto-Emancipation" in Hertzberg, 185; cf. *Autoemanzipation*, 8). Pinsker was not alone in coining neo-psychiatric terms in this period. For example, in *Rome and Jerusalem* (1862), Moses Hess speaks of both "Germanomania" and "Francophobia" (New York: 1945), 33. In fact, by 1893, Max Nordau was positively annoyed about the proliferation of psychiatric terms: "It was unnecessary for Magnan to give a special name to each symptom of degeneration, and to draw up in array, with almost comical effect, the host of 'phobias' and 'manias'." (M. Nordau, *Degeneration* [New York: (1893) 1968], 242)

89. Ibid., 185. The term *"Dämonopathie,"* which had appeared as early as 1865, was defined by the *Sydenham Society Lexicon of Medicine* in 1883 as "a mental disease in which the patient fancies himself, or acts as if, possessed by a demon" (*Oxford English Dictionary*). The term "Judeophobia" may have been original to Pinsker, but it appeared in another 1882 article as well (see H. Adler in *Eclectic Magazine* 35, 196 and 205).

90. Ibid., 185; cf. Netanyahu's variant translation, 53. This echoes Shylock's famous line in Shakespeare's *Merchant of Venice*: "When you prick me, do I not bleed?"

91. Ibid., 185.

92. Steinthal made exactly this point in one of his earliest myth-critical essays, an exposition of Adalbert Kuhn's analysis of the Prometheus myth, which Steinthal extends to Samson and Moses as well. See H. Steinthal, "Die Sage der Samson" (1962), available in English under the title "The Original Form of the Legend of Prometheus: A Review of Ad. Kuhn's 'Herabkunft des Feuers und des Göttertranks,'" in I. Goldziher, *Mythology Among the Hebrews*, 435.

93. "Auto-Emancipation," in Hertzberg, 185.

94. Ibid., 185.

95. Ibid., 185. The allusion to Tacitus in this passage is plain. See n. 31, above.

96. "Auto-emancipation," in Netanyahu, 88.

97. Ibid., 184-85. Pinsker's analysis is vulnerable to serious criticism at this point. While he recognizes that Judeophobia has specific social and historical causes, he also argues that, once "naturalized," it becomes "hereditary," an "incurable disease" which has been "transmitted for two thousand years. His error was to decide that prejudice, formed by history, could turn into a kind of biopsychic destiny.

98. Ibid., 186.

99. Lazarus gave the new *Völkerpsychologie* its first extended exposition in 1855 in his renowned two-volume *Leben der Seele*. Blondheim translates *"Seelenleben"* as "psychology," thus removing all associations with *Völkerpsychologie*.

100. "Auto-Emancipation," in Hertzberg, 184.

101. Cited by Netanhayu in his "Introduction" to "Auto-Emancipation," 54. According to Vital, this line encapsulates the "central message" of *Auto-Emancipation*, "repeated or echoed on every one of its thirty six pages" (Vital, *Origins of Zionism*, 128). Leo (Yehuda Leib) Levanda was a Russo-Jewish writer who advised the governor of Vilna on Jewish affairs in the 1860's; after the 1881 pogroms he supported *Hibbat Zion*.

102. E. B. Tylor, *Religion in Primitive Culture* (New York, [1873] 1958, 14-15), first published as *Primitive Culture*, Vol. 2; Tylor cites the Purgatory section of the *Divine Comedy*, third canto. Vis-à-vis Shelley, see E. Railo, "The Wandering Jew and the Problem of Never-Ending Life," in *The Haunted Castle* (London: 1927), 205; Railo cites the seventh canto of *Queen Mab*. According to Anderson (*Legend of the Wandering Jew*, 184), Shelley was the first to unite the legend of Ahasverus to the theme of the shadowless soul.

103. Chamisso was also the author of *Der neue Ahasverus* (1831), which was one of the most liberal retellings of this tale, emphasizing that suffering humanity is ultimately one.

104. Pinsker's apparent debt to Chamisso has gone unnoticed, though the probable allusion to Chamisso's *Peter Schlemihl* is fairly plain. Equally evident, in my opinion, is the parallel between Pinsker's famous epigram (in "Auto-Emancipation," ed. Netanyahu, 83) and a line from a letter to Madame de Staël: "I am a Frenchman in Germany and a German in France," Chamisso wrote, "a Catholic among Protestants, a Protestant among Catholics, a Jacobin among aristocrats, an aristocrat among democrats." (See the introduction by L. von Loewenstein-Wertheim in A. von Chamisso's *Peter Schlemihl*, 1813 [London: 1957], 11.)

105. Paul Massing makes precisely this point in his superb historical analysis of *fin de siècle* German antisemitism: "'The Jews', who functioned as Conservative scapegoats, were phantoms rather than human beings one knew." (P. Massing, *Rehearsal for Destruction: A Study of Political Anti-Semitism in Imperial Germany* [New York: 1949], 108)

106. For illustrations of this point see D. N. Smith, "The Social Construction of Enemies," a paper presented at the 1992 meeting of the American Sociological Association.

107. Steinthal's work ran parallel in may ways to the ethnological myth-criticism of Bastian, who had studied with Lazarus and was very much a partisan of *Völkerpsychologie*. Bastian's seminal study, *Der Mensch in der Geschichte*, which appeared in 1860 in three volumes, contained a rich neo-sociological analysis of demonology in Vol. 2, subtitled "Psychologie und Mythologie." See, e.g., the highly pertinent selections appended to K.-P. Koepping's *Adolf Bastian and the Psychic Unity of Mankind* (London: 1983).

108. H. Steinthal, "Zur Charakteristik der semitischen Völker," in the *Zeitschrift für Volkerpsychologie und Sprachwissenschaft*, Vol. 1, 328ff.

109. M. Steinschneider, *Hamaskir: Hebräische Bibliographie. Blätter für neuere und ältere Literatur des Judentums*, 3 (Berlin: 1860), 16. Steinschneider was reporting on Steinthal's article, which criticized Renan's article "Nouvelle

considérations sur le caractère général des peuples sémitiques, et en particulier sur leur tendance au monothéisme," published the year before in the *Journal Asiatique*.

110. Cited by S. Wilson, *Ideology and Experience: Antisemitism in France at the Time of the Dreyfus Affair* (London: 1982), 470.

111. Steinthal, "Charakteristik der semitischen Völker", 421, n. 1.

112 See M. Olender, *The Languages of Paradise: Race, Religion, and Philology in the Nineteenth Century* (Cambridge, MA: 1992), for this citation (54-55) and for all others cited in this paragraph. Renan adds that the Semitic mentality is monistic by nature, obsessed with "unity" and blind to "multiplicity." Semites have a monotheistic "instinct" that makes them anti-mythological by nature. They are adamantly iconoclastic, attuned only to the absolute. And they deserve no praise even for their monotheism, which they received as a revelation from God—with no independent effort or insight of their own. Renan, like Schlegel and other romantics, held "the mythopoetic faculty" in high esteem, and hence regarded the allegedly anti-mythological tendency of the Semites to be a fatal flaw.

113. Steinthal, "The Legend of Samson," 390.

114. Ibid., 431, 424, 427.

115. Ibid., 431.

116. This line is from Steinthal's lecture on "Myth and Religion," delivered in 1870, as cited in Goldziher, *Mythology Among Hebrews*, 264.

117. See, e.g., the essays by B. Delbrück and H. Cohen, respectively, in the third and fifth volumes of the *Zeitschrift für Völkerpsychologie* (1865 and 1868). Among the other notable figures who echoed Steinthal in this period, Lazarus, Paulsen, Pott, and Tylor are perhaps pre-eminent.

118. Goldziher, *Mythology Among Hebrews*, 5, 12, 5.

119. Ibid., 11.

120. Ibid., xxi-xxii.

121. Bastian, *Der Mensch in der Geschichte* (l860), in Koepping, *Adolf Bastian*, 188.

122. Ibid., 195, 197, 198, and 186. Bastian illustrates this tendency by pointing out that, "for a long time, the Turks were considered ogres in Germany, and until well into this century the church-bells were sounded every day and a prayer said against the Turks."

123. Tylor, *Primitive Culture*, 415, 306.

124. Ibid., 308, 306.

125. Ibid., 306. For Tylor's debt to *Völkerpsychologie*, see the note appended to the second edition of his *Researches into the Early History of Mankind* (Boston: 1878). Cf. Tylor, "The Survival of Savage Thought in Modern Civilisation," in *Proceedings of the Royal Institute*, Vol. 5, 1869, 527, and J. Leopold, *Culture in Comparative and Evolutionary Perspective: E. B. Tylor and the Making of Primitive Culture* (Berlin: 1980), passim. Lazarus and Steinthal, meanwhile, often cited Tylor as well, and Steinthal favorably reviewed *Primitive Culture* in *Zeitschrift für Völkerpsychologie*, 1875.

126. Tylor, *Primitive Culture*, 539.

127. Ibid., 535.

128. Ibid., 539.

129. In part this pessimism reflects Pinsker's tendency to stray from the neo-sociology of the *Völkerpsychologists* to a kind of residual biological determinism, which warps his theory at critical junctures. In his worst moments, in fact, Pinsker even voices racial and sexual bias. This is not only objectionable but inconsistent with the predominantly ethnocultural thrust of Pinsker's analysis.

130. "Auto-Emancipation," in Netanyahu, p. 104. Avineri (*Modern Zionism*, 79) says that Pinsker "consciously modeled" his nationalist rhetoric on the language of Giuseppe Mazzini, who influenced Hess and many other early Zionists and proto-Zionists as well.

131. Meyer ("Great Debate", 159) gives a good summary of Graetz's relations with Pinsker and the group Pinsker led after 1884, the Hibbat Zion. Evidence of Graetz's continuing sympathy with Hibbat Zion is provided in A. Druyanow, ed., *K'tavim L'toldot Hibbat Zion V'yishuv Eretz Yisrael*, Vol. 1 (Odessa: 1919), and Vol. 3 (Tel Aviv: 1932).

132. "Auto-Emancipation," in Hertzberg, 184.

133. Tylor, *Primitive Culture*, 416.

Part Three:
Case Histories on
Myth in Judaism

The Poetics of Myth in Genesis

Ronald S. Hendel

The problematization of biblical narrative in Judaism, whose seed perhaps begins with Rashi's contesting of traditional rabbinic interpretation in the eleventh century, has come to full flower in recent decades. The emphasis on the meaning of the Bible, with cognizance that meaning and truth need not correspond, has become commonplace, in contrast to Spinoza's time when it was grounds for excommunication.[1] In recent years even the question of the Bible's meaning has been transformed. In the wake of works such as Erich Auerbach's *Mimesis*, Robert Alter's *Art of Biblical Narrative*, and Meir Sternberg's *Poetics of Biblical Narrative*, we now are as concerned to ask "how" the Bible means as "what" it means.[2] In other words, the concept of meaning (Rashi's *peshat*) has also come to be problematized. It has become increasingly a question of rhetoric, ideology, and poetics rather than history or philology. Etymological and grammatical analysis alone cannot tell us what $bĕrē'šît$ means in Genesis 1:1—it requires involvement in the what Sternberg calls the drama of reading, or in Alter's phrase, the pleasures of reading. As Rashi observed to his grandson long ago, it seems that new interpretations for biblical narratives are being found every day.

Many pleasures, including those of the literary kind, gain with practice and relevant knowledge. For some knowledge it is difficult to find a use, as in the minutiae of modern historical-critical work on the Bible. Alter makes a telling distinction between excavative and literary scholarship, and suggests (particularly in his earlier work) that the literary scholar has little to learn from the biblical scholar.[3] Sternberg describes the difference as that between source-oriented and discourse-oriented inquiry, and regards these as distinct yet interdependent modes of inquiry, whose bridge or relationship has yet to be clearly envisaged.[4] For many literary scholars of the Bible (with the notable exception of individuals like Harold Bloom and Frank Kermode),[5] it is almost as if historical-critical work were an embarrassment or an obstacle to the task of reading the Bible.

I offer the following reflections with an eye toward the prospects of constructing a mode of inquiry adequate to the conditions of both history and literature, source and discourse, and their mutual interrela tions. My desire is to complicate our conventional notions of source and discourse in biblical studies, to show that the effects of both inform our readings of the text, as they have in the many readings of Genesis since antiquity. The keys to my inquiry will be the related concepts of myth and plot. My chief claim is that the myths of Genesis are plural in their modes of narrative organization or emplotment, in the intelligible relations that join together the events of the story. In the differences among the poetics of myth in Genesis, we will see that attention to the interplay of source and discourse creates the possibility for more nuanced readings of its multifarious text.

Organization and Insight

Aristotle, whose *Poetics* still manages to inspire literary theorists, defined *mythos* as "the soul of tragedy."[6] By *mythos* he meant what we would call textual organization or emplotment. It is, in Aristotle's phrase, "the organization of events."[7] The way that events are organized constitutes the intelligible aspect of the narrative, that which imparts meaning to the otherwise opaque or ambiguous singularity of events. In this view, the meaning of fictions does not inhere in the mere successiveness of events, but in the ways that the events relate to each other within the discursive structure of the narrative organization. This organization creates a concordance of meaning in which the beginning, middle, and end achieve intelligibility in the light of the whole. From this view of *mythos* Aristotle was able to argue that fiction is more profound than history, since in history events are merely contingent or successive, while in fiction events are seen under the aspect of the universal.[8] The mode of emplotment is hence the soul of the narrative, its intentional design or horizon of meaning.[9]

Recent theorists, such as Arthur Danto, Hayden White, and Paul Ricoeur, have analyzed the ways in which modes of emplotment also serve to organize the meanings of historical texts, such that Aristotle's distinction between literature and history has been largely effaced with respect to their plots.[10] That is to say, the intelligibility of all narratives inheres in their modes of emplotment. For the Hebrew Bible, the differences between myth and history, or between folkloric and historical compositions, thus becomes a matter of degree rather than of kind. To be sure, there are differences with regard to historical reference for the events and characters of the various narratives, but the importance of modes of organization or emplotment is basic to each type of text. In this respect, the plots of the Joseph or Moses story can be compared or contrasted to that of the Garden of Eden story without concern for the differing degrees or types of historical reference that may be attributed to each. Plot and historical reference are distinct though complementary axes, each having its own conditions while also shaping the other.

To illustrate the qualities and varieties of *mythoi* in Genesis—by which I mean both its myths and plots—I have selected some turning points from the middles of Genesis narratives and will draw attention to the modes of emplotment that bind them to their beginnings and ends. My discussion will of necessity be partial and suggestive, but I hope to show the value of this sort of inquiry, and how it can allow for the multiplicities of the text to which its many readers respond. The stories chosen are from the J, E, and P sources, respectively. These sources I regard as sufficiently established such that their existence is generally unproblematic (bracketing the uncertainties concerning dates, provenances, and certain difficult details).[11] To anticipate my results: the major sources of Genesis, J, E, and P, each projects a distinctive mythology and a distinctive mode of emplotment. These clashes of plot create some of the most distinctive features of biblical narrative.

Seeing Differently: Eve, Abimelech, God

The three scenes I have chosen are moments of sight or insight. In the middle of the P creation story, God sees that the various acts of creation are good, and that in sum they are very good (Gen 1:31). In the middle of the E story of the "Matriarch in Danger," King Abimelech perceives God in a dream revelation and receives a divine warning and command (Gen 20:3-7). In the middle of J's story of the Garden of Eden, Eve sees the forbidden fruit as an object of her desire (Gen 3:6). Each of these moments of perception presents a turning or focal point in the narrative, and each relates in distinctive ways to the beginning and end of the story. These moments, I suggest, provide an entry into the different modes of emplotment and narrativity in Genesis.[12]

Eve's moment of perception is depicted in the text as purely subjective. To be sure, she was cajoled by the deceptive speech of the snake, with which she participated with her own shadings of the truth. But her moment of insight is portrayed as a personal or inward turning, which is represented very nearly from her own perspective: "She saw that the tree was good for food, and that it was a pleasure to the eyes, and desirable to make one wise" (Gen 3:6).[13] In this ascending scale of sensation—from bodily appetite to visual aesthetics to intellectual desire—we follow an internal, subjective progression of desire that defines and eventually overwhelms the perceiver. In this turning moment the woman's desire ascends from the belly to the eyes to the mind, coloring her desire as at once animal, human, and quasi-divine (or at least drawn towards it). The consequence of this perception is her decision—which the narrative leaves unverbalized, perhaps nearly instinctual—to hold her desire as more compelling than God's command. Eve's subjectivity is shown directly to the reader, and though what she perceives is not entirely true, she (and the reader) do not know this until her next act of seeing, when she and the man perceive their own nakedness and shame. Eve's perceptions are true to herself with respect to her desire, but since she is human she does not see the whole truth. Notably, Yahweh's perceptions later in the story also follow a progression, by means of interrogation, from which he infers the whole truth.

This turning point in the Eden story depends wholly on the subjective perceptions and actions of the human character, Eve, and secondarily, Adam. The humans choose to eat the fruit and to disobey Yahweh's command, and subsequently suffer the consequences. Though Adam and Eve each attempt to shift the blame to another (Adam to Eve, Eve to the snake), Yahweh straightforwardly metes out the punishment for each. The humans—not Original Sin, not the yētser hārā'—are responsible for their actions, whose outcomes they cannot anticipate. The outcome is dependent on Yahweh's response, which he measures out in proportion to the human misdeeds (note that Yahweh elsewhere changes his mind about the outcome when good reasons are advanced, whether by humans or himself: cf. Gen 4:13-15; 18:23-32; also 8:21). The significance of Eve's perception and her turning of mind are intelligible in the nexus of relations to the beginning condition of existence in the Garden and to the end condition of existence in the all-too-human world. There are abundant ambiguities in this final condition that the humans bring about, wittingly or not, but the story presumes that the humans are the responsible agents for their actions and the consequences they cause. In the workings of the plot, the characters of Eve and Adam, in conjunction with the autonomous character of Yahweh, jointly construct their destiny.[14]

Abimelech's moment of perception in Genesis 20 is initiated by God, and that which is perceived concerns the divine authorship of the king's past behavior. In the complicated rhetoric of the dream-dialogue between God and king, God delivers a threat of death to Abimelech for his putative transgression, yet the knowledge is revealed (to the reader and in part to Abimelech), bit by bit, that the king is innocent, and that God already knows and is indeed the cause of his innocence: "Now Abimelech had not been intimate with her....And God said to him in the dream, 'Indeed I already know that you did this innocently, for I was the one who prevented you from sinning against me'" (Gen 20:4, 6). The reader's perception is guided by these revelations. The death threat is, in retrospect, seen to concern the king's future release of Sarah rather than his past sexual relations with her, now redefined as a false readerly assumption. The king's character too is reconfigured: rather than a savage oppressor, he is now seen as a just man. Similarly and most dramatically, God's character is reconceived as the author of human actions rather than as a deity merely reactive to them.

The way that Abimelech's perception operates in the intelligible organization of the story contrasts strikingly with Eve's perception. In both stories the themes of transgression and the threat of death are present; yet these possibilities are foreclosed in the E story by a mode of emplotment that renders them moot, subject already in the past to God's will. God, as the author of significant human actions, enacts events such that the putative transgression could not possibly have been carried out (note the afflictions laconically mentioned in vv. 17-18). The threat of death, which takes a curious turn in Yahweh's curses in the Garden of Eden story (from a threat of execution to the fact of mortality, perhaps an amelioration of the initial threat), becomes for Abimelech an incentive for future action, not a judgment for past transgression. The end of the story becomes simple to antici-pate the Abimelech story—obviously he will return Sarah to Abraham—while knowledge of the end in the Eden story remains opaque to Eve and Adam after their successive (and ironic) acts of seeing.

The differences in the way events are conceived in the two narratives pertain equally to the characters of the humans and God and the
relations between them. Human autonomy, and the uncertainty and
ambiguity that devolve from it, is in the Abimelech story replaced by
God's revelation of the precision of his divine will, from which humans take their cue, even if unknowingly. One can compare the
overarching conception of human and divine action in the E version
of the Joseph story, revealed to the brothers (and to the reader) by the
interpretive master, Joseph: "As for you, you thought to do me evil,
but God intended it for good" (Gen 50:20, cf. 45:5-8). God's thoughts
and perspective are the only true ones; the human characters—and
the human reader—rely on divine revelations, sometimes mediated
by his inspired representatives, to learn, often retrospectively, the
true significance of human thoughts and deeds.[15]

God's moments of perception in the creation account of Genesis
1:1-2:3 cohere with other events in a manner quite different from that
in the J and E narratives. In the P story the chorus, "God saw that it
was good," echoes after almost every act of creation (though not all,
cf. day two), until its emphatic resumption in v. 31: "God saw all that
he had made, and it was very good." These serialized moments of
divine perception form the focal points in the narration, contrasting
pointedly with the cosmic chaos of the beginning scene (v. 2). What
makes the mode of emplotment distinctive in P is not only the different character of God—a cosmic, transcendent deity, possessing no
explicitly anthropomorphic features—but also the dense intertextual
links that bind the middle and end of this story with the beginnings
and ends of others. There is a different sense of the configuration of
events in P's discourse: the middles and ends of one narrative serve
as the beginnings for others, such that the organizational whole tran-
scends the individual texts into an overarching or transhistorical narrative structure. P's sense of a complicative, serializing plot is, as
Frank Cross has astutely noted, a forerunner of the apocalyptic understanding of time and causality; yet P's plot is far from eschatological—the goal of things is the cosmic order enshrined in the present,
not the irreal future.[16] The object is a cosmic order that warrants
God's perception that it is very good.

The turning point that God's perception in Genesis 1 anticipates
is its inversion in the next P story: the Flood. The beginning of this
story opens with a change in God's perception: "God saw the earth,
and lo it had become corrupted" (6:12). The structure of this sentence

is identical to that in Gen 1:31 ("God saw X, *wĕhinnēh* Y"); only one other sentence in the Bible is so constructed (see below). The corruption of the world is the complication or reversal in P's cosmic plot, that which undermines the perfect beginnings in Genesis 1.[17] The initial resolution of the crisis is signaled at the end of the flood story in God's covenant with Noah and all living creatures. But this is only the first in the great sequence of covenants in P—the Noachic, the Abrahamic, and the Mosaic—each resuming and refining the cosmic order. As many commentators have noted, the process begun with the creation in Genesis 1 concludes only with God's covenant with Moses and Israel at Sinai, and in particular with the last action at Sinai: the completion of the Tabernacle in Exodus 40, when Yahweh's divine presence (his *kābôd*) enters the Tabernacle to dwell among the Israelites.[18] At this moment, according to the narratives sense of the P discourse, Israelite religion, properly constituted, begins.

A series of intertextual signs confirm that these events resume and complete the (re)creation of an orderly and good cosmos, begun in Genesis 1, through the enactment of God's commands.[19] For example, at the moment of the completion of the Tabernacle, the text breaks into rhythmic language redolent of Genesis 1: "Moses saw all the work, and lo they had done it, as Yahweh had commanded, so they had done; and Moses blessed them." (Exod 39:43) Several phrases in this verse echo Genesis 1, not the least significant of which is Moses' perception of the work, that it was now complete, signaling the completion of the process begun in Genesis 1. This is the third of the three sentences of perception with the structure: "God/Moses saw X, *wĕhinnēh* Y," found only in Gen 1:31, 6:12, and Exod 39:43. What was created to be good, then became corrupted, is now complete, according to God's command. The moment when God's presence begins to dwell on earth is introduced by phrases also redolent of Genesis 1:1-2:3 (cf. Gen 2:2): "Moses completed the work; and the cloud covered the Tent of Meeting; the *kābôd* of Yahweh filled the Tabernacle." (Exod 40:33-34) In this event not only is God's presence on earth initiated, but also, at least implicitly, the human participation in God's day of rest. The Sabbath command as the sign of the Sinaitic covenant is closely connected to the construction of the Tabernacle; the command for each adjoins in Exodus 31 and 35. Just as the divine Sabbath is the last act in Genesis 1:1-2:3, so the Sabbath law is God's final command on Mount Sinai, explicitly recalling Gen 2:2-3 (see Exod 31:12-18).

In sum, the mode of emplotment within which God's perception in Genesis 1 is intelligible in its broadest terms is an extended plot in which creation is only a beginning. The sense of organization in the discourse of P is essentially trans- or intertextual. Creation, flood, the series of covenants, the Sabbath, and the "Tabernacling" presence of God are mutually implicated in the overarching design of the story. Creation alone is intelligible in itself, *in nuce*, but its full meaning is disclosed only in the sense of the whole. Gen 1:1-2:3 portrays a point to which the cosmos must return, albeit at another level, impelled by God's commands and the religion of Israel. The beginning and end implicate each other in the verbal texture of the discourse and in the thematic "goodness" of creation/re-creation/covenant, each enacted through God's utterances, whether to the raw matter of creation or to God's chosen humans. The significance of actions, divine and human, is shaped through this intertextual nexus. The recurrent debate on whether P is a continuous narrative source is itself a symptom of this distinctive narrative quality: it is discontinuous, periodic, and intertextual in its nature. Such is, in brief, the mode of emplotment in the discourse of P.

Eve, Abimelech, and God see differently in these three sources *qua* discourses of Genesis. To put it perhaps too bluntly, Eve perceives her own subjective desires; Abimelech perceives God's power over human affairs; and God perceives the state of the cosmos. Each perception creates a point on which the whole narrative will turn, but the manner and implications of the perception differ significantly in each case. By tracing the relations to the beginnings and ends of the narratives, by examining how crises and resolutions, turns and returns, are rendered mutually intelligible, one can perceive more clearly the *mythoi* of the stories, their narratological souls. A richer sense of the dense and diverse textuality of biblical narrative is the issue. Attention to their mythic qualities, in these senses, deepens the drama of reading the biblical texts.

Reading the Myths

Having traced briefly the modes of emplotment in the three dominant discourses of Genesis—those called J, E, and P by modern scholars—one is entitled to ask what difference these perceptions make. Most literary scholars, among them Alter and Sternberg, tend to echo Edmund Leach's sensible rejoinder, "Why unscramble the omelette?"[20] Genesis—and the whole Hebrew Bible (and, for Christians, the Old and New Testaments)—is now a single continuous text, whose significance cannot or ought not be reduced to its sources or constituent parts. This point is a powerful one, and one that historical-minded scholars have not yet sufficiently addressed. (Many interpreters rely on an affirmation of the primacy of "canon" for their response, but, as James Barr and John Barton have shown, this is an answer to a different set of questions, concerning primarily theological or confessional issues.)[21] The difference made by attention to the interplay of source and discourse concerns not only matters of history and textuality, but also (and necessarily) the effects they have and have had on the contemporary reader and on readers in the great traditions of the past.

On the effects of the intrinsically plural textuality of the Pentateuch, Richard Friedman aptly observes that "the effect of the combination of the differing compositions....resulted in a Torah whose theology was neither independent of its sources nor a simple composite of them."[22] He cites as a key example the character of God, who in the Pentateuch encompasses and fuses the traits of deity in each source such that the final composite picture is different than that envisaged by any single source.[23] The reader, as it were, gathers the different concepts of God in various texts and perceives a united deity that shines through them all. The act of reading makes the text a whole, beyond the conception of its constituent parts.

To expand on this understanding of the effects of the plural text, I would emphasize that the interplay between reader and text can also result in other than a composite view or synthesis. In recent literary theory it has become a commonplace, even a banality, to observe that textual meanings often clash or undermine themselves when followed to their theoretical limits. In the case of the Hebrew Bible there is a more explicitly empirical and experiential sense of the intrinsic clash of literary discourse. In Genesis, as sketched above, there is a clash of *mythoi*, and this clash sometimes results in a synthesis, but may also remain unresolved, yielding the sense of an irreducibly problematic narrative, as it were a self-problematizing text.

In a thoughtful essay addressing similar narratological issues in the Bible, Geoffrey Hartmann suggests that the distinctive quality of biblical narrative, that which distinguishes it from other or "mere" literature, is its quality of "frictionality":[24]

> I would like to assert that Scripture can be distinguished from
> fiction by its frictionality: not only its respect for friction, which
> exists also in literary texts, but its capacity to leave traces, which
> incite and even demand interpretation of what it has incorporated.

Hartman explores the frictionality that inheres in some individual
stories, such as the enigmatic tale of Jacob's divine encounter in Gen
32:23-33. I would add that the frictionality extends outward to whole
complexes of stories and whole discourses, in particular to the clashing modes of emplotment and their narratological consequences in
the Pentateuch. Not only are there composite, frictional traditions
preserved in individual narratives, but the compositeness goes all the
way up, to the concepts of God, fate, the human condition, and the
ways that events and their meanings cohere.

To illustrate this condition of biblical narrative with regard to its
Wirkungsgeschichte, its effects through its many readings in the history
of biblical interpretation, I wish briefly to consider some classic
Jewish responses in antiquity and in the present. One of the most famous set of differences among Jewish groups in Hasmonaean and
Herodian times concerns the clashing concepts of God's will and human freedom among the Sadducees, Pharisees, and Essenes.
According to Josephus' description, the Sadducees were adherents of
the doctrine of free will; the Essenes were advocates of pure predesti-
nation; and the Pharisees were somewhere between the two, acknowledging the effect both of human free will and God's providence.[25] The Pharisaic doctrine is later expressed eloquently in the
Mishnah in a famous dictum attributed to Aqiba: "All is foreseen, yet
freedom of choice is given."[26] While the influence of Hellenistic
philosophies undoubtedly colors Josephus' description, commentators have neglected to point out that each of these positions is fully
rooted in the biblical *mythoi*.[27] The Sadducees have adopted in their
creed the mode of emplotment of J; the Essenes of P and E; and the
Pharisees a paradoxical union of them all. The difficulty interpreters
have had with Aqiba's pronouncement illustrates the dilemma of this
interpretive situation:[28] the Pharisaic/Rabbinic view is fully biblical,
but also self-contradictory. To put it differently, in the biblical interpretation of Aqiba the frictionality of biblical narrative is embraced.
In contrast, the Sadducees and Essenes each selected a different set of
biblical discourses as decisive.[29] In sum, these Hellenistic Jewish
groups ordered and justified their beliefs by their readings of the

Bible. The diversity of religious beliefs in this as in other periods is grounded not only by differing hermeneutic claims, but by the diversity of biblical *mythoi*.

A contemporary response by a prominent biblical scholar illustrates similar effects of biblical myths and plots. In a thoughtful and provocative work, *Creation and the Persistence of Evil: The Jewish Drama of Divine Omnipotence*, Jon Levenson investigates the biblical concepts of creation and particularly the conceptuality of the P creation story (Gen 1:1-2:3) in the larger context of priestly theology and its legacies in rabbinic theology. In his last chapter Levenson describes as fundamental to biblical and Jewish theology a dialectic between human freedom and faithful obedience. The narratives that he first presents as illustrations of this dialectic are the story of Abraham's intercession with Yahweh on behalf of Sodom and Gomorrah (Gen 18:23-32), and Abraham's binding of Isaac (Genesis 22). In the former text Abraham is the exemplar of the virtuous human who argues with God; in the latter Abraham is the one who in perfect faith obeys God's command. Levenson describes the resulting theological conception as follows:[30]

> The two perspectives delimit a theology in which human judgment neither replaces the inscrutable God who commands nor becomes superfluous within the life lived in faithfulness to him. In this larger, dialectical theology, both arguing with God and obeying him can be central spiritual acts, although when to do which remains necessarily unclear.

Levenson's description is entirely apt, including his emphasis on the unclarity that remains from this dialectic. What I would underline is that in this response to biblical theology Levenson is perceiving qualities of the clashing *mythoi* of J and E stories of Abraham (Genesis 18 is J; Genesis 22 is E). The theological dialectic is, in other words, a narrative one; the tangled plots create a powerful (and often inscrutable) dialectic of perception and belief. It is ironic that Levenson, in concluding his reflections on the P creation story and its theological implications, at the end supplements his discussion with a response to the clash of *mythoi* in J and E. It is as if the biblical interpretation were incomplete when limited to the riches of P, absent the differing perspectives of J and E. The necessary friction—literary and theological—of the heterogenous biblical discourses is so fundamental to our experience of the Bible that a selective or harmonized view fails to match our cognizance of the Bible's multifarious significance.

The interpenetrations of beginnings, middles, and ends, the *mythoi* of Genesis, constitute an irreducible feature of the poetics of biblical narrative. Attention to their effects may not only provide insight on the relation between literature and history, source and discourse, but may deepen our senses of this text's distinctive hold on our literary and religious imaginations.

Notes

1. On the distinction between meaning and truth in biblical writings, see B. Spinoza, *Tractatus Theologico-Politicus*, Trans. S. Shirley (Leiden: 1989), 143-44; on the *Tractatus* as (among other things) a development of Spinoza's earlier defense against charges of apostasy, see p. 4; and E. Curley, *A Spinoza Reader*, Ed. and Trans. (Princeton: 1994), xv.

2. E. Auerbach, *Mimesis: The Representation of Reality in Western Literature* (Princeton: 1953); R. Alter, *The Art of Biblical Narrative* (New York: 1981); M. Sternberg, *The Poetics of Biblical Narrative: Ideological Literature and the Drama of Reading* (Bloomington: 1985).

3. Alter, *Art*, 13-17; see the more nuanced view in idem, *The World of Biblical Literature* (New York: 1992), 131-52.

4. Sternberg, *Poetics*, 14-23.

5. H. Bloom, *The Book of J* (New York: 1990); idem, *Ruin the Sacred Truths: Poetry and Belief from the Bible to the Present* (Cambridge: 1989), 1-24; F. Kermode, *The Genesis of Secrecy: On the Interpretation of Narrative* (Cambridge: 1979).

6. Aristotle, *Poetics* 50a38. I am indebted for my understanding of the implications of Aristotle's work to his modern successors, especially F. Kermode, *The Sense of an Ending: Studies in the Theory of Fiction* (Oxford: 1967); and P. Ricoeur, *Time and Narrative* (3 vols.; Chicago: 1984-88). On Aristotle, a well-balanced treatment is S. Halliwell, *The Poetics of Aristotle: Translation and Commentary* (London: 1987); see also E. Belfiore, *Tragic Pleasures: Aristotle on Plot and Emotion* (Princeton: 1992).

7. Aristotle, *Poetics* 50a15: *hē tōn pragmatōn systasis*.

8. To be precise, Aristotle's object of inquiry is tragedy; for the extension to all fictions see the works of Kermode and Ricoeur cited in n. 6.

9. On the plot as the "intention" or "desire" of narrative, see P. Brooks, *Reading for the Plot: Design and Intention in Narrative* (New York: 1984).

10. A. Danto, *Narration and Knowledge* (New York: 1985); H. White, *Tropics of Discourse* (Baltimore: 1978); Ricoeur, *Time*, 1. 91-225.

11. See recently, R. E. Friedman, "Torah (Pentateuch)," *The Anchor Bible Dictionary* (New York: 1992) 6. 605-22; and my forthcoming article, "Historical Linguistics and Source Criticism."

12. For complementary discussions of other biblical narratives from this perspective, see R. S. Hendel, "Tangled Plots in Genesis," in *Fortunate the Eyes that See: Essays in Honor of David Noel Freedman*. Eds. A. H. Bartelt, A. B. Beck, C. A. Franke, and P. R. Raabe. Grand Rapids, MI: 1995.

13. Reading without the second *hū 'ē its* with LXX and Vulgate; see the commentaries.

14. Note the numerous stories in the J source in which Yahweh doesn't participate: e.g., Gen 9:20-27 (curse of Canaan); 25:29-34 (Jacob's pottage); 26:1,6-11 (second wife-sister story), 27:1-45 (deception of Isaac), 34 (rape of Dinah), 38 (Judah and Tamar); and others.

15. Cf. the angelic revelation to Abraham in Gen 22:12; the dream revelation to Jacob related in Gen 31:10-12; similarly, the retrospective recognition of God by Jacob in Gen 32:31.

16. See Cross, *Canaanite Myth and Hebrew Epic: Essays on the History of the Religion of Israel* (Cambridge: 1973) 295.

17. Curiously, the relationship between Gen 1:31 and 6:12 is largely neglected in the commentary literature, perhaps due to the atomistic approach of most classical and modern interpreters.

18. See, e.g., Cross, *Canaanite Myth*, 295-300; and the following note.

19. See J. Blenkinsopp, *Prophecy and Canon: A Contribution to the Study of Jewish Origins* (Notre Dame: 1977) 57-66; M. Weinfeld, "Sabbath, Temple and the Enthronement of the Lord: The Problem of the Sitz im Leben of Genesis 1:1-2:3," in A. Caquot and M. Delcor, Eds., *Mealanges bibliques et orientaux en l'honneur de M. Henri Cazelles* (Neukirchen-Vluyn: 1981) 501-12; and J. D. Levenson, *Creation and the Persistence of Evil: The Jewish Drama of Divine Omnipotence* (San Francisco: 1988) 84-86.

20. See Alter, *World*, 69.

21. J. Barr, *Holy Scripture: Canon, Authority, Criticism* (Philadelphia: 1983) 47-74; J. Barton, *Reading the Old Testament: Method in Biblical Study* (Philadelphia: 1984) 77-103; idem, *People of the Book? The Authority of the Bible in Christianity* (Louisville: 1988) 24-35; cf. the affirmation of this theological quality in J. D. Levenson, *The Hebrew Bible, the Old Testament, and Historical Criticism: Jews and Christians in Biblical Studies* (Louisville: 1993) 120-24.

22. R. E. Friedman, "Sacred History and Theology: The Redaction of Torah," in Friedman, ed., *The Creation of Sacred Literature: Composition and Redaction of the Biblical Text* (Berkeley: 1981) 28.

23. Friedman, "Sacred History," 26-28; idem, *Who Wrote the Bible?* (New York: 1987) 234-41.

24. G. H. Hartman, "The Struggle for the Text," in Hartman and S. Budick, Eds., *Midrash and Literature* (New Haven: 1986) 13.

25. Josephus, *Jewish War* 2.162-66; *Jewish Antiquities* 13.171-73; 18.12-22. For a collection of the relevant texts, see G. W. E. Nickelsburg and M. E. Stone, *Faith and Piety in Early Judaism: Texts and Documents* (Philadelphia: 1983) 24-39. The best treatment of Josephus' descriptions and the attendant issues is S. Mason, *Flavius Josephus on the Pharisees: A Composition-Critical Study* (Studia Post-Biblica 39; Leiden: 1991), chs. 6, 8, 12, and appendix A on earlier scholarly interpretations; see also G. Baumbach, "The Sadducees in Josephus," in L. H. Feldman and G. Hata. Eds., *Josephus, the Bible, and History* (Detroit: 1989) 174-78; and T. S. Beall, *Josephus' Description of the Essenes Illustrated by the Dead Sea Scrolls* (Cambridge: 1988) 112-14.

26 *m. 'Abot* 3.19.

27. Even Mason's careful treatment concentrates on Hellenic and Hellenistic antecedents to the exclusion of biblical concepts (e.g., *Pharisees*, 153-56, where he recalls the older scholarly consensus that Josephus' ascriptions "do not sound very Jewish"). Note Josephus' claim that these matters "have been treated philosophically in the Law" (*Antiquities* 16.398). For Josephus, as for other Jews of the period, biblical warrant for beliefs was of paramount importance, even if necessarily portrayed (particularly in an *apologia*) through Hellenistic lenses. Cf. the hermeneutical claims of the recently released Halakhic Letter from Qumran (4QMMT), where the differences between Qumran Essenes and Pharisees are depicted exclusively in terms of the exegesis of biblical law.

28. E.g., E. E. Urbach, *The Sages: Their Concepts and Beliefs* (Cambridge: 1987) 256-64.

29. This is not to limit the biblical discourses only to the Pentateuch, though in this period, as later, the Torah was accorded high authority.

30. Levenson, *Creation*, 153.

Strange Bedfellows: Politics and Narrative in Philo

Deborah Sills

The biblical figure of Joseph, son of Jacob and child of myth, has been variously represented by Hellenistic Jewish authors. In his *Antiquities Judaicae*, Josephus gives us an elaborate narrative that both amplifies and at points contradicts the biblical text.[1] Recasting the biblical material, the Alexandria writer Philo also turns his attention to Joseph. Philo makes Joseph the hero of *de Iosepho*, the villian of *De Somniis* li, and, finally, one could argue, the counterweight for Philo in his critique of Roman political leadership titled *In Flaccum*. How are we to understand these seemingly irreconcilable portaits of Joseph in Philo's work? Is there a logic that informs the various ways Philo recasts Joseph? Does the motive for contradictory reinscription and reinterpretation lay in the biblical narrative itelf? Is the LXX's Joseph so ambiguous, so "multi-colored," that Philo could be comfortable describing him, on the one hand, as one "whose nobility of character and nature ... was under God's directing care" (*de Iosepho* 37-38) and, on the other, then portray Joseph as "one who takes no acccount of the excellence of the soul, but is thoughtful for the well-being of the body and has a keen desire to be well off in outward things" ...and as a result, "is shaken this way and that and can never attain to fixity" (*de Somniis* ii:11)?

These varied portraits might be said to reflect, at least in part, what reader response critics term "the horizon of assumptions" that in-formed, in this instance, the first-century Alexandrian Jewish commu-nity and that shaped in turn the "horizon of expectations" of Philo and his own readers.[2] According to this view, Philo becomes both reader and text, and the peculiar cast he gives to the Joseph story represents a uniquely Alexandrian take on Joseph's life and times. But the issue is unique in what sense? Philo is suprisingly consistent in his representa-tions of the other patriarchs. Abraham, Moses or, for that matter Adam and Eve are not subject to the kind of schizophrenic characterization we see visited on Joseph. Thus, the question becomes, how are we to understand the various uses to which Joseph is put?

Joseph in Biblical Tradition

The story about Joseph (Genesis 37-50) is the longest continuous narrative about one patriarch in the Bible. The fascination it holds for all readers is reflected in its reappearance and reinterpretation in ancient as well as modern literature. Joseph is a plastic figure whose very character is mythic. Part trickster, part fortune-teller, and too good looking for his own good, he is, as Robert Alter describes him, "a magisterial knower...who has a lot to learn at the outset."[3] The biblical narrative itself plays with the motif of true and false knowledge, and the reader, unlike the characters, is omniscient. Joseph's journey to Egypt moves him from a veiled ignorance to a revealed wisdom. As a youth, he dreams dreams of prophecy, but is unable to understand their meaning (Gen. 44:5ff). In Egypt, his rise to power follows on his success in interpreting the dreams of his fellow prisoners and then the dreams of the king. In the story's narrative climax, it is Joseph who reveals his true identity to his long estranged brothers, and as Robert Alter points out, forces his brothers to confront the truth of their own past.[4]

Alter's literary analysis of the Joseph story is deeply psychological. Through the implimentation of specific formal means of composition, the authors of the Bible, he argues, realize their representational purpose. It is to attempt to answer a question about the human and the construction of one's reality in relation to the radically new insight of a monotheistic revelation. "What is it like," Alter writes, "to be a human being with a divided consciousness—intermittently loving your brother but hating him even more; resentful or perhaps contemptuous of your father, but also capable of the deepest filial regard; stumbling between disastrous ignorance and imperfect knowledge; fiercely asserting your own independence but caught in a tissue of events divinely contrived; outwardly a definite character and inwardly an unstable vortex of greed, ambition, jealousy, lust, piety, courage, compassion, and much more"...? Alter concludes by noting that "Fiction fundamentally serves the biblical writers as an instrument of fine insight into these abiding perplexities of man's creaturely condition."[5]

Alter's reading of the Joseph story feels right, morally and psychologically. Yet as readers we are quite willing to enjoy the retelling or recasting of the Joseph saga in, for example, Thomas Mann's 1936 novel *Joseph and his Brother/Joseph in Egypt* or, more recently, Tim Rice's muscial drama "Joseph and his Amazing Technicolor Dream Coat." Critic Giles Gunn suggests that myths, like other narratives, are regarded by people who tell and retell them as ways to understand the meaning of their world and their place in it, and that they are constructed less to entertain or even inform the mind than to indicate in what directions and about what subjects and with what seriousness it should think.[6] In illustrating Gunn's point, James Kugel, in his discussion of rabbinic reflection on the Joseph story, argues that all interpreters or exegetes of biblical stories are really "expositor(s) with an axe to grind."[7] It is in search of this axe and the peculiar slant, when worked, it gives to the story, that we will now turn.

There is, beyond Genesis 37-50, remarkably little reference in the Bible to Joseph or his family. There are, of course, the list of sons of Jacob in Genesis 30:22-25, 35:22-26, and Exodus 1:16, but aside from these, there are only two references to Joseph as an individual: Joshua 24:32 and Psalm 105:16-22. Joshua 24:32 links the Joseph story to the larger biblical narrative, relating how it was that Joseph's bones were "brought up from Egypt and were buried at Shechem." The passage from Psalm 105 places Joseph's rise from slavery to "lord of the King's house" within a larger framework of God's command of history. It is God's plan that the king has made Joseph "ruler of all his possessions" and that Joseph is "to instruct (the King's) princes at his pleasure, and to teach his elders wisdom." Apart from the two passages noted above, all other references to Joseph suggest either the northern tribes or the separate nation of Israel.

In Sirach 49:14-16, Joseph's name appears in a long hymn to past worthies, linked to the likes of Enoch, Shem, Seth, and Adam, who was described as "above every living being in the creation." In I Maccabees 2:53, Mattathias describes Joseph as "steadfast" because he is able to observe all the commandments even in the face of great adversity. In 4 Maccabees 18:11, the mother of the seven martryed sons addresses her children, relating how her husband had "taught her sons the Law and the Prophets,…reading to you of Abel, slain by Cain, of Isaac, offered as a burnt offering, and of Joseph in prison."

At the end of the last century, L. A. Rosenthal suggested that there were notable links between the Joseph narrative and the books of Esther and Daniel.[8] Jewish tradition has long associated Joseph with Esther and Daniel, and it is to these connections that Theodore Gaster turned in his consideration of the festivals of Purim and Hanukkah.[9] Both authors observe that in each of these stories, the narrative is set in a foreign royal court where a Jewish courtier is delivered from a position of obscurity to one of authority and great wealth. In each case, the courtier is able to deliver his family or her people from danger. Following this deliverance, the court then willingly acknowledges God's soverignity. W. Lee Humphreys argues that the authors of Esther and Daniel appropriated the older Joseph-courtier tradition, and used it as a model in constructing their own stories.[10] For Humphreys, the Joseph novella, as he describes it, is constructed from a number of separate tales. The material in Genesis 40 and 41 (along with 47:13-26 and 50-26), which tells of Joseph's remarkable rise and extraordinary success as an Egyptian courtier, can stand alone. It is Humphreys's suggestion that "there is a Horatio Alger quality to this part of the Joseph novella,…it is a delightful success story, complete in itself." For Humphreys, it is precisely Joseph's ability to maneuver in foreign courts that intrigues the authors of Esther and Daniel.[11] It is Joseph's public face, more than the private nature of his intimate familial relations, that concern them.

This concern with Joseph as courtier is particularly striking when one turns to rabbinic reflection on the Joseph story. If one considers only Ginzberg's 1909 collection of rabbinic legends, what one sees is the rabbis' overarching interest in the nature of Joseph's personal character and the changing shape of his relationship to his father and brothers. While the rabbis do consider at length Joseph's rise to power, what proves more compelling are the issues about love and lust, betrayal, jealously, longing, and reconciliation. How culpable was Joseph in the Potiphar's wife affair? How good-looking was he really? Was it necessary for him to be as brash and boastful in relating his first series of dreams to his father and brothers? Who was the worst of the brothers? As a Jew who spends his adult life in Egypt, whom does he marry? Is it a suitable match? What do we make of a weeping Joseph? How is it that the brothers are never really punished?[12]

Turning to the Hellenistic literature of the Jewish diaspora, the questions authors address to the Joseph story are quite different. I am not willing to say that the reasons for these differences lay exclusively in the formal modes of analysis or are ultimately linguistic. Nor am I willing to argue that Jewish authors writing in Greek such as Philo or Josephus invariably treat the material "as a coherent unfolding story," as Alter suggests, "in which the meaning of earlier data is progressively, even systematically, revealed or enriched by the addition of subsequent data."[13] What one does note, however, is a persistent re-examination of the reasons for, and the means by which, Joseph achieves a place in the Egyptian royal house, i.e., why he is so successful in the diaspora. Specifically, what is it in Joseph's nature that enables him to rise twice in

Egypt—first as the master of Potiphar's house, then as the vizier of the whole of Egypt?

Philo in Jewish Tradition

Philo's library is large, and as Colson and Whitaker suggest in the Introduction to their 1929 English translation of his library, "while it is a fault which is rather lovable, Philo is an inveterate rambler." They go on to point out that "in fact this word does not mean that the thoughts are disconnected. In fact it is the mark of the true rambler that his points are always connected, and that he is unable to restrain himself from following up each connexion as it occurs."[14] It is, to paraphrase his translators, an inability to distinguish the essential from the merely important that accounts for the breath of Philo's collected works.

Much of twentieth-century scholarship on Philo has been devoted to problems about identity and classification. Precisely how Jewish was Philo or, alternatively, how thoroughly had he broken with normative Jewish tradition, and in turn, how representative is Philo of Diaspora Judaism in the first-century? What we see is that Philo's library had often been put into service to support inquiries into the cultural origins of Christianity or utilized in debates about the nature and character of identity, Jewish or Christian, in the Hellenistic world.[15]

More recent reflection on the relationship between Diaspora and Palestinian Jews has called into question these modes of analysis. In his 1992 study of nationalism in Jewish Palestine, Doron Mendels looks at the historical appropriation of mythic materials and how these materials are recast and reinterpreted to both reflect contemporary political and cultural issues and at points to shape them. He notes that Hellenistic writers focus not on native rulers but on those, as in the case of Egypt, who have some history there. It is to Moses and Joseph, not to David or Soloman, that the Egyptian Jewish writers turn.[16] Gregory Sterling, using terms taken from genre studies, considers many of the same texts that Mendels examines. Making a related point, Sterling observes that writers on the order of Dementrios, Artapanos, or Philo are all writing national histories, histories that draw primarily from biblical traditions, but also reflect and incorporate Greek and Roman materials. What is distinctive, Sterling argues, is that they write as "national historians...who claim the superiority of the Jewish nation over both other Oriental people and Greeks."[17] They are apologists in the way that Tchikover described Philo,[18] writing for a Jewish audience, but with an eye always turned to the gentile world. For both Sterling and Mendels, the mythic representation of biblical figures reflects current cultural and at times political concerns. David Dawson, in his 1992 *Allegorical Readers and Cultural Revision in Ancient Alexandria*, makes a provocative argument about the uses of allegory.[19] Particularly in relation to Philo, his is a useful distinction which suggests that allegory's decisions of mind are as much social and cultural as they are psychological or aesthetic. Dawson makes an argument that challenges the traditional view of Hellenistic Jewish literature as an exercise in cultural and religious assimilation. For Dawson, Philo's allegorical reading of the Torah brings the Greek world within the interpretive grasp of the Jewish text, by making Hellenistic ethics or cosmology, at least in part, the content of scripture. Allegorical reading transforms Jewish scripture from a closed book into an interpretive lens, capable of permitting readings that construe the wider Hellenistic culture in specifically Jewish terms. Is this simply an apologetic enterprise? Dawson argues that it goes much further, making the suggestion that authentic Greek culture is actually Jewish. What Philo does interpretively, Dawson maintains, is to read on two levels, the literal and allegorical, simultaneously. This kind of reading achieves a twofold effect. First, it protects the integrity of the literal textuality of the scripture, and second, it enables the text to embrace the Hellenistic meanings of its cultural milieu. It follows, then, that Philo's subordination of Greek meanings and Greek sources to scripture enables him to (1) argue that the Bible and Moses antedate and surpass in wisdom the classical authors, and (2) to read the Bible as a master text which has absorbed the whole of Hellenistic culture.[20]

Joseph in Philo's de Iosepho

Students of Philo have located *de Iosepho* among Philo's commentaries on the Law, suggesting that it followed the now lost tracts *Isaac* and *Jacob*, which themselves would have extended the issues raised in *De Abrahamo*. Beginning in *De Abrahamo* and presumably developed further in *Isaac* and *Jacob*, Philo recapitulates a history of the soul. He constructs his analysis of the soul in two parts, each represented by a triad of biblical noteworthies. The first triad, Enos, Enoch, and Noah, suggest Hope, Repentance, and Justice. They are but imperfectly wise. The second triad of Abraham, Isaac, and Jacob, however, represent Wisdom or Virtue as acquired through (1) teaching, (2) nature, and (3) practice.[21] I mention this arrangement because Philo begins *De Iosepho* by noting that Moses has given the place of primacy to these three wise men and that he will now "carry on the series by describing a fourth life, that of the statesman."[22] The prerequisites for the statesman, Philo writes, are three: shepherd-craft, household management, and self-control.

First, one must have been practiced in the art of shephard-craft. Like Moses, who trained as a shepherd with his father-in-law's flock after having fled Egypt, Joseph had recognized, as a very young man, the degree to which the governed react like sheep to crisis and danger. Philo argues that the underlying meaning of the brother's decision to first murder and then, after reflection, to sell their brother into slavery can be traced to the etymology of Joseph's name. "Addition of a lord" reflects the local character of the statesman's authority. While God himself exercises "universal lordship"—"for this world is the Megalopolis"—Joseph's domain is limited and the nature of that limitation requires a "coat of varied colors," inasmuch as the "poltical life is a thing varied and multiple, liable to innumerable changes."[23] Commenting on Joseph's sale to the Ismaelites, Philo notes that "the *politicus* is sold, for when the would-be popular orator mounts the platform, like a slave in the market, he becomes a bond-servant instead of a free man, and through the seeming honors which he receives, he is the captive of a thousand masters."[24] Philo expands the possibilities of Genesis 39:1 ff by comparing the mob which the *politicus* must control to the Egyptian eunuch and his lustful wife. Both the eunuch and the mob "possess to all appearance the organs of generation," but are "deprived of the power of using them."[25]

Philo's second requirement for statescraft is what he calls "household management." Joseph has excelled in this art, initially in the home of his Egyptian master, and then on a much larger scale, when he was put in charge of the King's household, that is, the nation as a whole. According to Philo, "Household management may be called a kind of state management, just as a city too is a great house, and statesmanship the household management of the general public."[26] In fact, Philo charts the development of Joseph's skills, first as he serves the eunuch, then in prison, and finally to his appointment as viceroy to the king.[27]

Thirdly, Philo argues that the politician must exercise self-control. Joseph's ability to do just this is exemplified in his encounter with the eunuch's wife. Potiphar is not named in Philo's narrative. In the dialogue between Joseph and the wife, Joseph emerges as a youth who understands that his first responsibility is to his master. Philo has Joseph declare "the master found me a captive and an alien, and has made me by his kindness a free man and a citizen. Shall I, the slave deal with the master as though he were an alien and a captive?"[28] The rhetorical question suggests the extent to which Philo is quite self-consciously thinking about the formal relations that obtain between master and slave, between ruled and ruler. Joseph's status as a free born Jew, now a slave on foreign soil, will be transformed before the narrative ends, when he will be recreated as both master of the nation and husband to one of Egypt's loveliest daughters.

Yet, inasmuch as Philo creates a Joseph who can transgress social boundaries, Philo remains troubled at the prospect of what is in store for those who would emulate Joseph's journey. In v. 55, speaking directly to Potiphar's wife, Philo argues that self-control, knowing how to control one's self, "forstalls the descent into…licentiousness [which results in] civil strife and war,…[whereas] the results of continence are stability and peace and the acquisition and enjoyment of perfect blessings." Individual license invites social instability. Even in this most private moment, then, Philo's concerns are civic. The true statesman, Philo concludes, knows quite well that the people have the power of a master, yet the true *politicus*, who is master of himself, will not admit that he is a slave, preferring to regard himself as a free man who shapes his activities to please his own soul." It is the ability to achieve "mastery of the self" that enables the statesman to master the multitude.[29]

Finally, Philo suggests, that like Joseph, the true stateman has the ability to interpret dreams. The course of a human life is a dream, full of confusion, disorder, and uncertainty, and men as a whole are incapable of sustained reflection. In v.143 ff., Philo argues that in the face of this "vast confusion and disorder"…the statesman must come forward, and, like some wise expounder of dreams, interpret the day-time visions and phantoms of those who think themselves awake, and, with suggestions commended by reason and probability, show them the truth about each of these visions." The Joseph of *de Iosepho* dies of old age, "unsurpassed in comeliness, wisdom, and power of language." While the experiences of his youth involved "conspiracy, bondage, and painful misfortune, he spent the "other eighty years as a ruler…a most admirable supervisor and arbiter in times both of famine and plenty, and most capable of presiding over the requirements of both."[30]

Joseph in Philo's de Somniis ii: The Problem about Joseph

The problem about Joseph is not a new problem. At the turn of the century, W. Bousset drew attention to the problem by arguing that Philo's inconsistencies and contradictions were the result of his uncritical use of disparate sources. Alternatively, Masebieau and Brehier located the source of the problem in the political climate of first-century Alexandria. Philo's positive evaluation of Joseph actually suggests a period of relative peace in the city while, on the other hand, the negative tone of *de Sommiis* II points to a period of tension between Philo's Jewish community and the Roman government. E. R. Goodenough took a not dissimilar tack, maintaining that the solution to the puzzle hinged on the possibility of discerning the relationship between Philo's literary motives and the audience for whom he wrote. In fact, Goodenough's larger project, the recovery of a Hellenistic Judaism esoteric and mystical in nature, depended in large part on the discriminations he made about Philo's reading public. *De Iosepho*, which characterizes Joseph as a man endowed with the gift for rulership and a "well born mind, one greater than that which is associated with a private citizen," was written, so Goodenough argues, with a single purpose in mind: "to convince its gentile readers that the real source for the highest political ideal of the east, the idea of a divinely appointed and guided ruler, had its original expression in Jewish literature, and its highest exemplification at a time when a Jew was "prefect" of Egypt."[31] Alternatively, Philo's *de Somniis* ii was an allegorical tract, intelligible only to people thoroughly conversant with the LXX and of interest only to Jews who understood the method and objective of mystic allegory. Philo's characterization of the politicus-Joseph in *de Somniis* represents a clever piece of *double entendre* that mounts what Jews would have recognized as a fierce denunciation of Roman character and rule in a form calculated to seem quite innocuous if it fell into Roman hands.[32]

Goodenough's student, Samuel Sandmel, was apparently intent on following his teacher's basic hypothesis with one very significant modification. Sandmel challenged the idea that one can determine with certainty the intended audience for whom a text is written. "There could be conceivably be very little difference in actuality, in the tone of a writing, whether it was aimed at friendly Gentiles or at uninformed Jews on the threshold of apostasy."[33] The sheer size of Philo's library suggests that, over the span of his writing career, Philo may have either modified his views or used the figure of Joseph for another purpose. Arguing that consistency is not a requirement of creative artists, Sandmel posited that while *de Josepho* was a work of Philo's old age, "reflect(ing) fatigue and a lack of zest,"[34] *De Somniis* can be read as an example of Philo's work "from a more robust stage of the scholar's life."[35]

In her summary of the state of the problem, Jouette Bassler reminds us that the various positions noted above all assume that the described inconsistencies and contradictions are real. Following suggestions by R. G. Hamerton-Kelly and Valentin Nikiprowetsky, Bassler proposes that "instead of attempting to explain the lack of coherence in Philo's writings in terms of external or psychological factors,...we [should] look behind the apparent contradictions for deeper levels of literary and theological coherence."[36] Quoting Nikiprowetsky, Bassler notes that "the way to uncover the coherence of Philo's thought is to take him seriously as a scriptural exegete and to focus on his exegetical intentions." This approach would reveal the "deep coherence of Philo's writings" and would also resolve seemingly contradictory details which, as Nikiprowetsky points out, "will prove to be merely the result of the exegetical constraints imposed by the biblical texts."[37] Burton Mack has followed Nikiprowetsky's suggestion and focused on Philo's exegetical methods in order to uncover pre-Philonic traditions and sources in his work.[38] Bassler's conclusions, however, which are much closer to my own, are somewhat different. She assumes, in fact, that there is much more consistency in Philo's treatment of the Joseph material and thus invites a re-exploration of its contents. After carefully comparing the manner in which Philo describes Joseph, first in *de Iosepho* and then in *de Somniis* II, she notes that while the "tractates...are undeniably different,...there lies behind these differences a high degree of congruence."[39] Philo's concern, and hence the motive behind his exegetical methods that moved both stories forward, was the character of the politician, and particularly the statesman's propensity to "desire domination."

What strikes one as particularly interesting in discussions about Philo's Joseph is the fact that while scholars want to enlarge the field of inquiry, their attempt to uncover the deeper exegetical foci in the Joseph stories remains for the most part committed to the consideration of only those tracts that make explicit reference to Joseph. Yet as an allegorist of the first order, Philo himself would never have felt so constrained. If, indeed, Philo's interest in Joseph is primarily in the Joseph who succeeds in Egypt "as a statesman and politician," then it might prove fruitful to examine other texts where Philo addresses the "problem about politicians." Such an examination would reveal where, more specifically, Philo attempts to locate "the politician" in his reconstruction of the biblical narrative and what theological frame of reference he presumably employs to link these different "Josephs" to a deeper exegetical grammar.

Philo's English translators catalogue two of his extant tracts as "historical and political."[40] For historians of the Hellenistic world, both the *Legatio ad Gaium* and *In Flaccum*, together with the testimony of Josephus in his *Antiquities* and *Contra Apionem* and the *Acts of the Alexandrian Martyrs*, are the key documents in reconstructing the religious and political climate of Alexandria during the middle of the first-century C.E.[41] *In Flaccum*, however, is the only one of these documents that narrates the fall of a public man, the Roman Prefect Flaccus. Like Joseph, Flaccus was a foreigner who ruled Egypt, but unlike his biblical counterpart, Flaccus ends his political career in exile and disgrace.

In Flaccum

In the introduction to his translation of *In Flaccum*, F. C. Colson suggests that the treatise not only displays "considerble literary merits" but that it possesses real historical value "in so far as it gives a substantially true account of events of which we know very little from other sources."[42] In the same way, E. Mary Smallwood, both in her translation and commentary on *Legatio ad Gaium* and in her more comprehensive 1976 analysis of Jewish-Roman relations,[43] also reads *In Flaccum* primarily for the light it sheds on the tortured relations that obtained between the various ethnic communities in first-century Alexandria. Yet, when Colson comes to examine Philo's treatment of Flaccus' demise, he is repulsed by the way Philo

> gloats over the misery of Flaccus in his fall, exile, and death....While I have said in the preface, none of the treatises in this volume [he includes *Every Good Man is Free, On the Contemplative Life, On the Eternity of the World, Hypothetica* and *On Providence*] have any great value nor would probably have survived, but for the high esteem given to his main work, this is the only one which those who admire the beauty and spirituality so often shown both in the Commentary and Exposition might well wish to have been left unwritten.[44]

What does Colson find so repulsive? Clearly, it has something to do with Philo's tone, his "vindictiveness" as Colson describes it. In place of Philo the aesthete, whose philosophical ruminations on the human condition and the ascent of the soul seemed to have characterized for Colson the civility of Alexandrian Jewry, we have a narrator whose vivid and bloody tale of human pride and debauchery is told perhaps for the sheer pleasure of relating how low the mightly have fallen. Yet, *In Flaccum*, because it is one of the few sources available that treats the years 38-41 C.E. tends to be read as a descriptive narrative, and historians have often used Philo's analysis of the origins of hostilities as a point of departure in developing a chronology of the period. Both Box and Smallwood have suggested that Philo's Legatio *ad Gaium* and *In Flaccum* relate, with some contradictions, essentially the same story.[45] For both historians, it is a story of political intrigue, of social, and—when the force of Flaccus' policies took effect—political, persecution of Philo's Jewish community. *In Flaccum* recounts the anti-Jewish legislation Flaccus brought to bear against the Alexandrian community as well as the creation of the Jewish ghetto, the desecration of the community's synagogues and the public scourging of community leaders. The narrative takes a dramatic turn with Flaccus' arrest and his subsequent exile to the island of Andros.

It is instructive that about a fifth of the surviving text of *In Flaccum* is devoted to the circumstances surrounding Flaccus' journey to Andros, his miserable life there on the island, and his eventual execution, following what Philo reports to be Gaius' decision that a life in exile is far too contemplative and serene for his political enemy Flaccus. Philo's dramatic narrative of the prefect's last days, the arrival of his assassins, and Flaccus' capture, all of which culminate in a grizzly scene where the murderers "dug a pit, while the others violently dragged him along, resisting and screaming and struggling hard," concludes with Flaccus, who has "had his whole body pierced with wounds. . . [and] cut to bits, [lying] carved like a sacrificial victim." (*Flaccum* 188-191) Yet, even this theatrical scene has become part of the historical record. Anthony Barrett, in his wonderfully readable 1989 biography *Caligula: The Corruption of Power*, reports that indeed

> Flaccus observed their [the assassins] arrival and tried to hide in the wilder interior of the island. They pursued him there and eventually tracked him down, stabbing and clubbing him to death, and depositing his remains in a crude pit.[46]

What scholars have tended to ignore is the imaginative or dramatic character of *In Flaccum*. While historians might read it for the information that they can glean about the political and cultural climate of Alexandria, Philo has written a tale about the decline and fall of a public man. It is not finally tragic, but it does have tragic features. Philo begins the treatise by noting that Flaccus was "the complete master of official business of Egypt," which as Philo points out, was an enormous task.

> He exhibited with a remarkable freedom proof of a more brilliant and kingly nature...filling the city and the country with good order,... for he remembered that it was to maintain peace that he was appointed. vs.4-5

Philo narrates the rapid disintegration of Flaccus' character and will to rule. It begins with the death of Tiberius and the ascension of Gaius. With the execution of his friend and confidant Marco, Flaccus "completely gave up his remaining hope," Philo writes. Fearing for his own life and "no longer capable of paying attention to his duties,...Flaccus, the ruler became the subject and the subjects governors." (vs. 17-19) What enrages Philo is Flaccus' capitulation to the demands of the mob. In place of the state, the mob, lead by such "demagogues like Dionysius, record-porers like Lampo and sedition leaders like Isidorus," rule Alexandria. The Jewish community's situation grows increasingly fragile as the city itself plunges into civil war. Flaccus has created "a man-made famine" while "every other place was full of prosperity and plenty." (v.18) Flaccus no longer rules but is "the slave of the mob." (v.19)

What brings about Flaccus' fall from power and his exile to Andros? Those whom Flaccus had courted now become his accusers. Both Lampo and the "popularity hunter" Isidorus "launch accusations against Flaccus...inventing against him things which had never happened and spinning long lying screeds of ribald doggerel" (v.139). Philo's narrative is confused. He notes that the nationalists, led by Isidorus and Lampo, have bribed "no small number of people...with money and wine" to testify against Flaccus. In reponse, Flaccus appears to have called together "the whole city" to expose Isidorus and his cabal. Convinced by Flaccus' exhortations, the "poor people" of Alexandria "shouted out some for disfranchisement, some for banishment, some for [Isidorus'] death." "Fearing arrest, Isidorus fled, but by this point Flaccus' fate is sealed" (144-149).

Why Flaccus was removed from his position as Alexandrian Prefect and why he was subsequently banished remain issues for debate. Was it simply Caligula's response to Flaccus' inability to control the increasingly factious communities in his city? Was it the threat of civil war that moved Gaius to replace Flaccus with an administrator who in fact did restore order? Did Flaccus have to face poltical accusations steming from his earlier association with those supporting Gaius' enemy Gemellus? Can his exile be linked to his long-standing friendships with Marco and Lepidus, both of whom came to a bad end, falling victim to Gaius' paranoic quest for a conspiracy close to home? Philo does not specify the charges that are brought against Flaccus but, rather, ponders how it is that in the course of human affairs justice inevitably prevails and that Flaccus, once ruler of Alexandria, now stands accused by its citizens. It is this inversion of the social order, where one must endure "the gloating of one's enemies" that "to me is worse even than death," that Philo writes (v.148). Flaccus' miscalculations have reaped him "a rich harvest." Flaccus, a man of great wealth and fine taste, now lives "like a slave." His journey to Andros as a prisoner retraces the course of his initial trip to Alexandria to which he once traveled as the newly appointed "governor of Egypt." Justice is served, Philo observes, as "the cities which then beheld him puffed with pride, parading the grandeur of his good fortune, might once more behold him covered with dishonour instead" (151-154). Upon reaching the island that will be his home in exile, Flaccus "let a stream of tears pour down his cheeks as from a fountain" and laments his humiliating fall into obscurity and the spectre of deportation. Born and educated in Rome, friend of Augustus's grandsons, a confidant of Tiberius and for six years the governor of Egypt, Flaccus now imagines that violent death in his native land would have been preferable to his new "home of exile," which he thinks of as a "tomb." "As I journey in my misery," Philo imagines Flaccus saying to himself, "it is as though I were bearing the corpse that is myself to a sepulchre" (v.159).

Among the more intriguing elements of Philo's narrative are the extensive first-person declarations that Flaccus makes about the course of his life. In a particularly moving passage, Flaccus is reputed to have asked if

> I Flaccus...who was governor of Alexandria...had among his subjects great forces of infantry, calvary, naval, not a mere lot of counters, but all men of the best-proved excellence, now wonder was this then a

phantom, not the truth? Was I asleep and dreamt the light-heartedness of those days, saw but spectres moving in a void, figments of a soul which recorded as may suppose things which had no existence as though they were?

Philo's Flaccus responds, "Yes, I have been deluded. They were the shadow of realities, not the realities themselves, a counterfeit of clear vision, not the clear vision which exposes falsehood to light." Flaccus' growing awareness of the quixotic character of political life, his sense of the illusionary nature of partisan achievement, and his experience of betrayal by "the family" he tried to serve, all torment him. Harrassed and shamed in public, he spends most of his days in solitude. His nights are filled with "weird visions...if ever he chanced to fall asleep." (v.167)

This period of reflection reaches a climax as Flaccus becomes "possessed as in a Corybanic frenzy." In a prophetic trance, "with his eyes to heaven and the stars," he screams,

> King of god and men,...so then Thou doest not disregard the nation of the Jews, nor do they misreport Thy Providence, but all who say that they do not find in Thee a Champion and Defender, go astray, from the true creed. I am clear proof of this, for all the acts which I madly committeed against the Jews I have suffered myself (vs.170-172).

Ironically, God's providence has been turned against him. He has been robbed of his position, exposed to the ridicule of his enemies, and then exiled. Now living as a foreigner abroad, Flaccus, prophetic about his approaching end, notes that "every day or rather every hour I die in anticipation and suffer many deaths instead of the final one" (176). Like "a beast of the field", whose "food and drink are given to me as to animals to keep them for the slaughter," Flaccus describes himself as a "hunted animal" felled by "wild thoughts" which rack his rural solitude. Philo's account pulls out all the stops in recounting Flaccus' end:

> The assassins never lost a moment in pursuing him. Then they caught him and some of them at once dug a pit, while others violently dragged him along, resisting and screaming and struggling hard, the result of which was that as wild beasts do, he ran upon the blows and had his whole body pierced with wounds. For as he clutched hold of the slaughterers and was so entangled in the scramble with them that they had no room to apply their swords directly but dealt their blows downwards and sidewards, he caused himself to suffer more severely,

and with hand, feet, head, breasts and sides slashed and cut to bits, he lay carved like a sacrificial victim.....The whole place was flooded with blood which poured out like a fountain from the many veins which one after the other were severed, while as his corpse was dragged into the pit which had been dug, most of the parts fell asunder as the ligaments which bind the whole body together in one had been rent. Such was the fate of Flaccus, who thereby became an indubitable proof that the help which God can give was not withdrawn from the nation of the Jews (vs. 188-192).

The drama and intensity of Philo's narrative makes it almost seem as though Philo actually witnessed Flaccus's terrible death. Yet this same dramatic intensity, which increases in force precisely because of the example that the narrative intends to make of Flaccus, is precisely what should remind us that the text is primarily a work of historical fiction. Philo's story turns the fall of a Roman politicus into a subject of moral spectacle. At the beginning of Philo's narrative, Flaccus is the ruler of all Egypt with virtually total control over his subejcts. By the end, the absolute ruler has been betrayed by those he once befriended, tried in Rome, and banished to a life of exile on the Isle of Andros. In between, the reader has been invited to contemplate the meaning of this inversion of fortune with the help Flaccus's own imagined reflections. Flaccus cries, laments his fate, and indulges his fears and anxieties, but only at the end does Philo finally permit him to recognize the ephemeral quality of his public existence, the dream-like character of a life lived for self-aggrandizement and selfish gain.

How, then, are we to understand this narrative? Is it, as Joutte Bassler has argued, suggestive of a deeper narrative matrix that runs throughout Philo's work? And if so, how more exactly would one characterize this narrative matrix? It seems to me that Philo's narrative life of Flaccus draws on and is shaped by the same themes that Philo develops in de Iosepho and de Somniis ii, themes concerning the nature of political leadership and the constraints on the political life. The life of the politician who prevails, outlined in de Iosepho, is inverted in Philo's narrative life of the unlucky Flaccus. Unlike Joseph, who was able to confront and succeed in the face of the reversals which beset his career, Flaccus succumbs to them. In all three categories—shepherd craft, household management, and self-control—Philo's Flaccus is a notable failure. As the chief civil and military authority in Alexandria, he is unable to maintain the public order. As a public administrator, he becomes a slave to the mob. Finally, as a moral exemplar, he loses self-control, his increasing anxiety at the thought of what will befall him in exile only confirming Philo's original thesis that those without superior moral fortitude, training, and practice will not succeed in the "dream like" world of power politics. Reinforcing David Dawson's reading of Alexandrian allegory, what we see in Philo's tale about the moral decline of the Roman Prefect Flaccus is actually the inversion of the Joseph story. The Flaccus narrative is rendered a Jewish story, or, more accurately, the narrative movement in *In Flaccum* counters and inverts the tale Philo tells of Joseph in *de Iosepho*. That "deeper level of literary and theological coherence" noted by Bassler that reveals, as she puts it, "the deep coherence of Philo's writing,"[47] turns in these three texts on Philo's interest in, and reflections on, the nature and character of political leadership.

Thus one sees in the three texts we have considered an interpretation of political leadership that is built on a mythic remembrance of the Joseph story in Genesis. Philo reprises the Joseph tale as a tale of political survival and achievement in the land of Egypt. He imagines the figure of Joseph as exemplifying the qualities of self-mastery and self-knowledge; qualities that, as Philo reconstructs it, proved essential to Joseph's success abroad. Philo then reinscribes his own version of the Joseph story in the narrative he creates about Flaccus. *In Flaccum* is the Joseph story told backwards. Flaccus begins as the "prefect of Egypt" and ends his life, cast abroad as a slave, as an exile betrayed by those he imagined his allies. Ultimately, he is thrown into a pit which is, symbolically, the same pit from which Joseph was rescued and sold into bondage. However, in Flaccus' case, Jacob's fears that his favorite son had been torn to pieces by wild beasts, his coat of many colors awash in blood, are metaphorically realized: "...as Flaccus' corpse is dragged into the pit,...the whole place flooded with blood." Here Flaccus's story then ends, just where Joseph's is beginning.

In his reflections on the cultural character of religion, Clifford Geertz argues that for those who believe them, religious narratives provide a model of—and a model for—reality.[48] Nonetheless, Geertz is careful to point out that this recasting and reconstruction of experience in forms of meaning sensed as in some sense sacred should be understood as an ongoing process. Religious traditions change, and because of nothing so much as the new interpretative uses to which we are compelled to put some of the mythological material that informs them. Philo's employment of the Joseph story is just such a case in point. Philo's re-narrativization of the biblical story of Joseph is, at least in part, a response to the political and ethnic violence that overtook Alexandria in the middle of the first-century C.E., a violence that could be religiously contained, so to speak, only by redefining the role and, more important, the character of the political leader. Philo turns the Flaccus story into a Jewish moral allegory by finding the key to its meaning in the contrasts it can be rhetorically made to suggest with the career of a Biblical hero who epitomized, in the traditional scriptural account, the Mosaic ideal of leadership.

Notes

1. Josephus, *Jewish Antiquities*, Book II, 8-200 (Cambridge: Harvard University Press, 1957). Josephus's narrative of Joseph's life is much longer than the biblical story. At several points he makes the narrative more specific: Joseph was 17 years old when he was sold into bondage (II,33), a public festival explains why it was that "there was none of the men of the house within" (Gen 39:ll) when Potiphar's wife, now at home alone with Joseph, propositions our hero (II,45).
2. See H. R. Jauss, *Towards an Aesthetic of Reception* (1982) and *The Aesthetic Experience and Literary Hermeneutics* (1982). For a history and discussion of *Reception Theory, see Robert C. Holub Reception Theory: A Critical Introduction* (1984).
3. R. Alter, *The Art of Biblical Narrative* (New York: Basic Books, 1981), 159.
4. Ibid., 163.
5. Ibid., 176.
6. G. Gunn, *Early American Writing* (New York: Penguin Books, 1994), 3-4.
7. J. L. Kugel, In *Potiphar's House* (New York: Harper, San Francisco, 1990), 251.
8. L. A. Rosenthal, "Die Josephesgeschichte mit den Buchern Ester und Daniel verglichen," ZAW 15 (1895), 278-84; "Nochmals der Vergleich Ester, Joseph, Daniel," *ZAW* l7 (1897), 125-128.
9. T. Gaster, *Purim and Hanukkah in Custom and Tradition* (New York: Henry Schuman, 1950), 70-71. W. Lee Humphreys' 1988 literary analysis of the Joseph story summarizes much of the bibliographical material on the connection between Joseph and Esther and Daniel. *Joseph and his Family: A Literary Study* (Columbia: University of South Carolina, 1988), 214.
10. Ibid., 210.
11. Ibid.
12. L. Ginzberg, *The Legends of the Jews* (Philadelphia: Jewish Publication Society of America, 1913), Volume II, 1-184.
13. Ibid.
14. *Philo*, Vol. 1, xiv.
15. In addition to R. Marcus's bibliographical article "Recent Literature on Philo (1924-1934)," *Jewish Studies in Memory of George Alexander Kohut* (New

York: 1935), see works by E. R. Goodenough and H. Wolfson, each representing two very different assessment of Philo's place in the Hellenistic world, specifically, Harry Wolson, *Philo*, 2 vols. (Cambridge: Harvard University Press, 1947) and E. R. Goodenough, *By Light Light* (London: Oxford University Press, 1935) and *The Politics of Philo Judaeus* (New Haven: Yale University Press, 1938).

16. D. Mendels, *The Rise and Fall of Jewish Nationalism* (New York: Doubleday, 1992), 42.

17. G. E. Sterling, *Historiography and Self-Definition: Josephos, Luke-Acts and Apologetic Historiography* (Leiden: E.J. Brill, 1992), 223.

18. V. Tcherikover, "Jewish Apologetic Literature Reconsidered," Eos 48 (1956), 69-93.

19. D. Dawson, *Allegorical Readers and Cultural Revision in Ancient Alexandria* (Berkeley: University of California Press, 1992).

20. Ibid., 108-114.

21. I am following Colson's General Introduction to the Loeb Library edition of Philo's work in 12 volumes. See Volume VI, ix-xx.

22. *de Iosepho*, 1-2.

23. Ibid., 28-29.

24. Ibid., 35.

25. Ibid., 58.

26. Ibid., 37-38.

27. Ibid., 38-39. Philo's plan for famine relief, as Joseph describes it to the king, includes a plan of action that is extraordinary in its elegance and its attention to detail. There is nothing to equal it in the Genesis story. Joseph begins by telling the king that it is his intention to mimick a traditional harvest during the surplus years, storing one fifth of the harvest to be used during the following seven years of famine. The sheaves should be harvested, but not threshed. Why? Storing hay in this manner will prevent spoilage. Annual threshing during the fallow years will serve as a reminder of more prosperous times. Because unthreshed grain cannot be accurately measured, the citizens will be less likely to grow anxious at the prospect of a dwindling supply. And finally, the discarded ears can be used as cattle fodder. Joseph concludes his presentation by urging the king to make all these preparations in secret, so as to spare his citizens any undo anxiety over the approaching famine. As you can imagine, the king, overwhelmed by Joseph's abilities as both diviner and tactician, appoints him immediately as viceroy of Egypt. Once appointed, Joseph reveals himself to be a conscientious administrator, regularly visiting all the cities of Egypt. As the famine overtakes the whole of Egypt and beyond, Joseph "orders all the stores to be thrown open, thinking that he would thus increase the courage of those who saw (the stored ears of corn), and so to speak, feed their souls with comforting hopes before he fed their bodies."

28. Ibid., 46-48.

29. Ibid., 71.
30. Ibid., 268-270.
31. Goodenough, *The Politics of Philo Judaeus*, 63.
32. Ibid., 21.
33. S. Sandmel, *Philo of Alexandria: An Introduction* (New York: Oxford University Press, 1979), 47.
34. Ibid., 64.
35. Ibid.
36. J. M. Bassler, "Philo on Joseph: The Basic Coherence of De Iosepho and De Somnaiis II" in *Journal for the Study of Judaism in the Persian, Hellenistic and Roman Period*, (Leiden: E. J. Brill, 1985), Vol. xvi, No. 2, 242.
37. Ibid., 242-243.
38. B. Mack, "Exegetical Traditions in Alexandrian Judaism" in *Studia Philonica* 3 (1974-75), 71-112.
39. Bassler, 254.
40. *Philo* vol. ix, 299-301.
41. For an overview of the political and cultural issues that informed this period, see P.M. Frazer, *Ptolemaic Alexandria*, 3 vols. (Oxford: The Clarendon Press, 1972) and, for an analysis of the years 35-42 c.e., E. M. Smallwood, *The Jews under Roman Rule*. (Leiden: E.J. Brill, 1976).
42. *Philo*, vol. ix, 301.
43. E. M. Smallwood, *The Jews Under Roman Rule* (Leiden: E. J. Brill, 1976).
44. *Philo*, vol. ix, 301.
45. H. Box, Philo *Alexandrini, Ad Flaccum*. (Oxford, 1939), xlix, and Smallwood, 235.
46. A. A. Barrett, Caligula: *The Corruption of Power*. (London: B. T. Batsford, 1989), 110.
47. Bassler, 243.
48. C. Geertz, "Religion as a Cultural System" in *The Interpretation of Cultures* (New York: Basic Books, 1973), 123.

The Myth of Jesus in Rabbinic Literature

Richard A. Freund

The understanding of "The Myth of Jesus in Rabbinic Literature" goes much beyond the period of the creation of classical rabbinic texts into the critical studies of rabbinics of the modern period. In the modern period, as *Wissenschaft* scholars of rabbinics began to re-assess the narratives of rabbinic literature in an attempt to reconstruct a critical view of Jewish history, the status of Christians, Jesus and the entire Greco-Roman period began to be reinvestigated. Before the modern period, many late rabbinic texts from the Talmudim (and post-Talmudic works such as *Masechet Sopherim*) to the Zohar used, reused and recombined earlier rabbinic texts relating to Jesus. In the eighteenth and early nineteenth centuries this situation changed as Jews attempted to understand their own history by reinvestigating the historical texts of Judaism. In the early period of *Wissenschaft* scholarship, many of the texts relating to Christianity and Jesus were only partially reinvestigated. Often these texts were reinvestigated with only a minimal commitment to the critical examination of the texts themselves in a rush to determine an overall view of the period. Scholars such as Bost, Derenbourg, Geiger, Graetz, Hoffmann, Holtzmann, Jost, Renan and Wellhausen also contributed to some of the modern misunderstandings of the myth of Jesus in rabbinic literature to occur. Often their work tells us more about relations between Jews and Christians in nineteenth-century Europe than first-century Palestine.

Later Jewish and Christian writers such as Billerbeck, Dalman, Finkerstein, Harnak, Montefiore, Moore, Scheuer, and Strack began to move towards a " dialogue of sorts" in researching rabbinic texts in light of New Testament and early Christian literature (and visa-versa). The goal of this early twentieth century work was to determine parallels for the sake of comparison. Unfortunately, this work was often done with a " higher criticism" or overall ideological model in mind and limited attention was given to the fundamental questions of "lower criticism" or the status of the manuscript readings of the texts themselves.

Later in the twentieth-century, new understandings of Jewish history forced pre-and post-W.W.II scholars such as Bultmann, Daube,

Davies, Flannery, Flusser, Parkes, Rivkin, Sandmel, Schweitzer, Zeitlin, and many other to reassess the work of the nineteenth- and early twentieth-century scholars. Some Christian scholars were more interested in the "historical Jesus" than earlier generations and the discovery of the 1947/8 Nag Hammadi and Dead Sea texts made the comparison of the varying versions of Jesus' life and his historical *Sitz in Leben* more compelling. Unfortunately, the Jewish and Christian reassessments of the historical Jesus in the post-W.W.II era were often done with the Holocaust and its implications looming in the background. What this latter consideration did was to create an atmosphere in which the search for the historical Jesus was a vehicle for the search for reconciliation and dialogue between Jews and Christians in the post-W.W.II era. Often, this latter search was conducted at the expense of the demands of problematics of critical NT and rabbinic textual studies and did not advance our understanding of the mythical status of Jesus in Jewish and rabbinic texts.

One cannot also ignore the deep seated passions which lurked behind this question of the myth of Jesus in rabbinic literature in the minds of the general Jewish and Christian population. On the one hand, the idea of recovering the rabbinic myth of Jesus was prejudged to be negative and problematic because of the perceived role of the rabbis in early Christianity. The gospel's view (albeit not in all gospels—or better—the interpreted view of the gospels) was that the rabbis (in the form of the Pharisees) or Jewish leadership of the period (the Priests) had not only rejected Jesus but were responsible for his crucifixion. Conventional nineteenth- and twentieth-century wisdom held that Jesus was a revolutionary against Rabbinic Judaism and therefore the need to investigate the Jesus myth in rabbinic literature a fruitless search. The use of rabbinic texts by some nineteenth- and early twentieth-century Christian scholars often tended to reinforce stereotypical views known to Christians from gospel interpretations or to gloss over them completely in order to not worsen Jewish-Christian relations.

On the Jewish side, the nearly fifteen hundred year history of disputation, ghettoization and persecution of Jews in Christian Europe and elsewhere *seemingly* in the name of Jesus made the topic of "Jesus" a difficult topic for unimpassioned research for Jewish scholars of European extract. In the twentieth century, one need only mention the controversies created in the Jewish communities of Palestine and later Israel upon the publication of the scholar Joseph Klauzner' s tomes, *Yeshu HaNotzri* and *MiYeshu ad Paulus* and in the United States and Israel over the Yiddish writings of Scholom Asch' s *The Nazarene, The Apostle and Mary,* just before, during and directly after the Holocaust in order to understand how deep the question goes in the Jewish consciousness. Most recently, the rise of groups such as "Jews for Jesus" and other so called Hebrew-Christian groups in the United States and Europe who use such materials to demonstrate one element or another in their group's ideology has complicated the serious research into the topic. In short, it is difficult from many perspectives to write a critical analysis of the myth of Jesus.

The Use of Rabbinic Literature

As indicated above, there are a number of problems associated with the use of rabbinic materials to demonstrate reliable information about fixed historical personalities such as Jesus in Palestine in late antiquity. This chapter cannot fully resolve these problems, but all scholarly literature which uses rabbinic materials to build a case about historical "facts" needs to be aware of some major questions. A major problem is whether rabbinic texts are able to give us any substantive and reliable information about historical personalities in Israel in late antiquity at all. One tradition in modern rabbinic scholarship has generally assumed that rabbinic literature provides reliable information for modern scholarly analysis. Since the beginnings of modern rabbinic studies, writers such as Frankel, Geiger, Graetz, Krochmal, and even contemporary writers such as Lieberman, Urbach, and Weiss Halivni, among many others, generally use critical textual method but fundamentally accept the attributed and unattributed information of rabbinic sources as authentic expressions of historical circumstances.

In the past thirty years, this basic assumption has been challenged by Jacob Neusner and a host of other scholars in a variety of works.[1] Neusner writes:

> The sources of Judaism of the dual Torah, oral and written, accurately and factually testify to particular moments in time. But how shall we identify the right time, the particular context to which the documents and their contents attest—and those to which they do not provide reliable testimony? Using the canonical sources of Judaism for historical purposes requires, first of all, a clear statement of why, in my view, these sources tell us about one period, rather than some other. The

problem, specifically, is that the documents preserved by Judaism refer to authorities who, we generally suppose, flourished in the early centuries of the Common Era. But at the same time, we also know, these documents were brought to closure in the later centuries of late antiquity...At the same time, we cannot show, and therefore do not know, that these sayings really were said by the sages to whom they are assigned, and we frequently can demonstrate that the sayings are attributed by diverse documents of the same canon to two or more figures. Along these same lines, stories that purport to tell us what really happened exhibit marks of stylization that show reworkings, and, more important, we rarely find independent evidence, e.g., corroboration by outside observers, of other views of what happened. Not only so, but where sages' stories about events can be compared to stories told by outside observers, we rarely can find any correlation at all, either as to causes, or as to circumstances, let alone as to actual events.[2]

In this assessment of the rabbinic traditions which are potentially associated with Jesus, a number of questionable attributions will be noted but not investigated and only a smaller number of "better" traditions will be fully analyzed. The "better" traditions are those whose attribution history and other stylistic features suggest that they are "more original" than others. In addition, this is part of a on-going study I am writing about information on places, events and people in particular historical contexts in Ancient Israel where corroboration from outside observers, texts and material culture (about these events, places and people) is available. Although the methodology and suggestions of Professor Neusner will not be cited in every instance in this chapter, some of his conclusions have been driving forces in the elimination from consideration (at least at this stage of investigation) of certain attributed materials.

The problem of "lower criticism" or manuscript reading investigation is another question in the use of rabbinic texts in general. One encounters a special problem in the researching of Jesus in rabbinc literature because many scholars in the modern period did not research the process of rabbinic text transmission to determine whether they were reliable sources or not. Many studies of Jesus and early Christianity in rabbinic literature often bring together sources from differing periods with the assumption that somehow rabbinic literature was one continuous work without differing layers which can be differentiated. An example of a first attempt to investigate the different historical layers of rabbinic texts was made by R. Travers Herford in the now classic *Christianity in Talmud and Midrash*. In this book Herford collected possible references to Jesus and Christianity from the Talmud and Midrash. His work, when it appeared in 1903, was a landmark achievement and established for the English reading public the existence of a new and extensive literature and source of information on Jesus and the origins of early Christianity from a literature contemporaneous with the NT and apostolic teachings. Over ninety years later, it is clear that what this book did was to demonstrate the complexity of the rabbinic literature and understanding of the development of the myth of Jesus in rabbinic literature. This chapter will investigate the myth of Jesus in rabbinic literature by delineating the different layers of rabbinic texts and traditions which are used to support it and the potential sources of this(ese) myth(s) about the life of Jesus in rabbinic literature.

Ancient Sources for the Jewish Myth of Jesus

In his book *Cosmos and History*, Mircea Eliade described the mythological character as one "identified with a category, an archetype, which entirely disregarding his real exploits, equipped him with a mythical biography."[3] He concluded:

> the recollection of a historical event or a real personage survives in popular memory for two or three centuries at the utmost. This is because popular memory finds difficulty in retaining individual events and real figures. The structures by means of which it functions are different: categories instead of events, archetypes instead of historical personages. The historical personage is assimilated to his mythical mode (hero, etc.) while the event is identified with the category of mythical actions....the memory of historical events is modified, after two or three centuries, in such a way that it can enter in to the mold of the archaic mentality, which cannot accept what is individual and preserves only what is exemplary.[4]

The investigation of Jesus in rabbinic literature is important because of the problem of how long the real personage might survive in popular memory. Five contemporaneous sources of potential information present themselves when we begin to investigate the Jewish myth of Jesus. They are the New Testament, Josephus, Philo, Jewish Papyri (and other writings), and the Tannaitic levels of rabbinic literature. Among these

last four sources, there is no specific mention of the actions of Jesus of the
Gospels in the literature at all. The Tannaitic literature has a terminus ad
quem of approximately the mid-third century C.E. and therefore does
have at least the possibility of reflecting the real personage in the
mythological biography of Jesus. Josephus has an interesting place in
this question, since he recorded in great detail the events and figures of
Judaism, especially Galilean Judaism which he intimately knew in the
first century C.E. The use of Josephus' writings by the early Church is
also a matter which affects the understanding of this question. It is well-
known, for example, that the early Church Fathers such as Hippolytus,
Clement of Alexandria, Irenaeus, Tertullian, Origen and Eusebius used
Josephus' *Antiquities* and *Against Apion* as *apologia* in the Roman world
to establish their claims to antiquity.[5] The following is the section in
Josephus' work which describes Christianity. Josephus 18.63-64 states:

> About this time there lived Jesus, a wise man, if indeed one ought to call
> him a man. For he was one who wrought surprising feats and was a
> teacher of such people as accept the truth gladly. He won over many
> Jews and many of the Greeks. He was the messiah. When Pilate, upon
> hearing him accused by men of the highest standing amongst us, had
> condemned him to be crucified, those who had in their first place come
> to love him did not give up their affection for him. On the third day he
> appeared to them restored to life, for the prophets of God had proph-
> esied these and countless other marvelous things about him. And the
> tribe of the Christians, so called after him, has still to this day not
> disappeared (L. Feldman, The *Antiquities*, Book XVIII, Loeb Classics
> Library edition, p. 51).

The arguments for and against the authenticity of this section in
Josephus are cited by Feldman in his translation.[6] The arguments against
authenticity cannot, however be brought solely from the literature of
Josephus, since this section does appear in almost all extant manuscripts
of Josephus (in one form or another).[7] The passage, however, does have
relevance for our study of the myth of Jesus in rabbinic literature, since
often Josephus does record narrative/stories/myth which are reminiscent of if not word-for-word examples of traditions found in rabbinic
literature. One example will suffice. In Josephus (Antiquities 11.8) there
is an account of Alexander the Great's meeting with the Samaritans
during a visit to Israel. The narrative in the BT Yoma 69a actually
parallels the Josephus information and tells us us something about the

common roots of Alexander information among the Jews. Josephus' account contains much greater detail than the rabbinic text, but the general outline of the story line is the same. The general outline is: A dispute occurs between the Samaritans and Jews. Alexander goes to Jerusalem, meets the high priest and prostrates himself before him. Sacrifices in the Jewish Temple are given (the Jews are favored over the Samaritans) and the Samaritans are treated badly by Alexander. Josephus' Jewish Greek account is therefore connection with the rabbinic tradition which indicates some connection between rabbinic redaction of **legendary** materials and circulating Greco-Roman writings.[8] It is important to note that this Alexander narrative occurs in the Babylonian Talmud without a direct indication of Tannaitic source. It may, therefore, like other legendary materials have circulated orally in Babylon before final written redaction.

The context of the Jesus passage in Josephus is important. The terminology and extremely formulisitic language "He was the messiah" and "On the third day he appeared to them restored to life, for the prophets of God had prophesied these and countless other marvelous things about him" is very close to formulas of the early church. Also, the preceding and subsequent sections to the one cited above deal with a sedition against Pilate by a group in Jerusalem and then another sedition in Rome—not exactly the most appropriate context for such an account to appear. Although the language of Josephus is formulistic, it is possible that parts of the language have only been altered to make them fit later church doctrines. Similarly, the formula-like words are found again in *Antiquities*, 20. Josephus writes, "And so he convened the judges of the Sanhedrin and brought before them a man James, the brother of Jesus who was called the Christ, and certain others" (Josephus, *Antiquities*, trans. L. Feldman, p. 497). These two references are the only evidence in Josephus of his knowledge of a "Jesus," since *Wars* and the *Life* lack any references to this "messiah/Christ." This is extremely provocative, since if Josephus did hold him to be the Messiah, he might have been expected to have written more about him in the period. Since Josephus lived almost to the end of the first century and in Palestine and Rome where the influence of the early Christians would have been known, this raises serious questions about whether these references are examples of substantive information about Jesus by Josephus or later glosses on Josephus by Church writers.

Regarding this same subject, R.H. Colson, in the general introduction to the Loeb edition of Philo, page IX-X (vol.1) writes, "It has been generally held that he (Philo) was born about 20 B.C.E. The date of his death is uncertain, but it has been seen that his lifetime covers the lifetimes of Jesus Christ and John Baptist, and much of that of St. Paul. *There is not intimation that he knew anything of their work."* (emphasis my own)

Jewish papyri (and other ancient manuscript information) from Palestine and Egypt of the early Roman period, yield no information concerning a named "Jesus" or any of his disciples. The following, therefore, is a summary of our conclusions concerning Jesus in contemporary Jewish literature:

> 1. From the period of the first century, Philo and early Jewish manuscript information do not reflect any knowledge of "Jesus," his disciples, or Christians.

> 2. Josephus, however, does present a Jewish view concerning Jesus, his disciples, and Christians. His view, if it is to be considered authentic, reflects a formula-like understanding of the role of Jesus by those who accepted him and condemnation (for no apparent reason) by others.

> 3. In light of the entire corpus of Jewish (Greek) material extant from this period, the conclusion is that the Jews were not altogether clear about the "Jesus group."

> 4. The fact that Josephus and Philo do have tractates confuting pagan charges against them or literature debating major theological issues of the period, one might expect such a literature in answer to NT charges against the Jews (Pharisees and Sadducees). The lack of such literature is thought-provoking.

The Textus Receptus: *From Jewish Hellenism to Early Rabbinic Texts*

Of course, all of the above is dependent upon reliable textual traditions. The textual tradition of the major ancient and medieval texts of research themselves (i.e., Bible, Talmudim, Hellenistic literature, commentaries, poetry, etc.) are not as stable as one would like and require significant critical research in order to determine what they say and why. Many of the texts that will be cited in the post-biblical Jewish tradition, for example, are texts which were not maintained, copied, or studied within the classical Jewish and especially rabbinic tradition.

Works which are major sources for our understanding of the lives of the
Jews during the Hellenistic period such as the Apocrypha, the writings
of Philo, Josephus and many others are extremely important to our
understanding of the rise of rabbinic Judaism and early Christianity in
the first century C.E.[9]

The rabbinic tradition itself is divided into different periods of
literary activity extending from the first part of the third century C.E.
with a number of different collections of legal and literary materials:
Tannaitic (early classical rabbinic), Amoraic (middle classical rabbinic),
Saboraic (late classical Rabbinic), Stamaitic (final editorship) and Geonic
sources (until the eleventh century). Each group employed differing
editing and writing techniques and it is this complex textual tradition
which comes into play when one wished to use a rabbinic text.

The instability of the textual tradition of rabbinic literature is also a
major problem since although internal evidence shows the Babylonian
Talmudic text to have been completed in the sixth century, the first
complete copy of the Babylonian Talmud is a fourteenth-century manuscript (Munich, Codex Hebr. 95).[10] All other copies are extant in manuscript fragments from the eighth to ninth centuries C.E. For textual critics
of the Talmud, the question is: How can we be sure what is the correct
reading some eight hundred years after its redaction? As earlier suggested, the subject of this book will not be a search for some "correct" or
"original" text, but an exploration the questions raised by textual differences found in texts. The recognition of the complexity of the textual
traditions of rabbinic literature in the research of topics is fundamental
to the academic credibility of this research.[11] This chapter, therefore, will
adapt some textual criticism techniques in the study of rabbinic texts
concerning Jesus. In particular, differing forms of textual criticism will
be use to investigate how the different "layers" of rabbinc texts and
commentaries reveal complex perspectives from different periods, locales, cultures and influences.[12] Different rabbinic texts will be examined
from different periods. Although the different rabbinic texts from the
Mishnah through the Babylonian Talmud are inter-related, they will
also be examined independent of one another to determine the individual perspectives present in each text. Often the circumstances and
views of each text are different than the interpretation attached to it at a
later time. This is particularly important in the case of the rabbinic myth
of the life and times of Jesus. In addition, manuscript traditions come
into play since manuscript scribes in Europe (so called Ashkenazic Jews)
under the watchful eye of Christian censors had different issues to deal

with than did manuscripts scribes in North Africa (so called "Oriental" Jews—outside of Europe).

The first printed complete edition of the Talmud was done by a Christian, Daniel Bomberg, in Venice between 1520-1523. Erratic censorship of manuscripts of the Talmud and other rabbinic literature had beed exercised during the Middle Ages, but the printings of the sixteenth and seventeenth centuries systematically and often non-sensically replaced certain words of the Talmud which were seen by Christian (European) censors as offensive. Many of these texts which were censored involved sections concerning Jesus, (Jewish-Christian) sectarians and various words for "non-Jews" which were seen as offensive by the censors. Replacements of words was one way of compensating for the deletion, but often, blanks or new cognates were produced to replace the censored words or materials. Jewish printers in the eighteenth and nineteenth centuries continued this institutionalized censorship. Although some small and often anonymous works which include the changes made by the censors were produced in the eighteeth and nineteenth centuries, they are far from complete and often are only restoring the sixteenth- and seventeenth-century wordings which themselves had been censored.[13] Even Sephardic Jews outside of Europe were not immune to this censorship since manuscripts from European scribes often circulated among Sephardic Jews. In short, trying to reconstruct the myth of Jesus in rabbinic literature in the second half of the twentieth century is a very difficult task. One must begin with Tannaitic literature, look at the development of the myth in early Amoraic literature, and see how these Amoraic sources from the fourth through sixth centuries C.E. understood the earlier first- through third-century C.E. traditions.

The Myth of Jesus in Rabbinic Literature: Tannaitic Literature and the Search for the Lost Myth of Jesus

In his book *Christianity in Talmud and Midrash*, R. Tavers Herford collected all the possible references to Christianity from the Talmud and Midrash. His work, which when it appeared in 1903 was a landmark achievement, provides a good point of departure. Since this work will deal with the development of the myth in rabbinic literature, it is important to begin with the references to Jesus in the earliest layer of rabbinic literature, namely the Tannaitic level, which contains traditions and is date-able from approximately the first century B.C.E until its editing in the mid-third century C.E. On page 351, Herford states the following:

> Considering, for the present the traditions of the Tannaite period, it will be noticed that the Mishnah does not contain the names Jeshu, or Ben Stada, or Ben Pandira. Tosephta contains all three, but not the for Jeshu ha-Notzri. Neither Siphri, Siphra, nor Mechilta contain, so far as I know, any allusion to Jesus. Tosephta contains covert reverence to Jesus in certain questions put to, and answered by, R. Eliezer ben Horquenos. These scarcely add any details to the tradition, because they are so obscure that their meaning is very uncertain.

In short, there is no mention of Jesus of Nazareth (by name) in any Tannaitic literature. In addition, Herford noted that in the Palestinian Talmud, there is also no mention of Jesus of Nazareth traditions.[14] This is an enormous corpus of work encompassing hundreds of pages and the absence of any mention of Jesus of Nazareth in this contemporary literature of the rabbis is rarely mentioned. The Mishnah (and Tosefta), according to Neusner, do not contain any "sustained narrative whatsoever, a very few tales, and no large-scale conception of history. It organizes its system in non-historical and socially nonspecific terms, lacking all precedent in prior systems of Judaism or in any prior kinds of Judaic literature."[15] So perhaps to look to these literatures for information on Jesus is inappropriate. The halakhic Midrashim (*Sifra, Sifrei, Mekhilta*), however, do not contain any information on Jesus as well, despite the fact that sustained narratives are found there. Three different hypotheses can be advanced for the absence of named Jesus traditions in Tannaitic literature:

1. These traditions were censored either early on (first through third centuries), or later (medieval) by Jews or non-Jews because of ideological reasons (the traditions were inflammatory, would lead Jews astray, were against Jewish law or concepts, etc.).

2. There were no traditions concerning Jesus of Nazareth known to the (Palestinian) Tannaitic rabbis that were deemed worthy of preservation in these collections, or the type of literature was not appropriate for their preservation.

3. Jesus of Nazareth, as he was know by the Gospels, was not a sufficient enough topic for inclusion in Tannaitic literature.

The Problems of the BT and PT

While different traditions associated with a named "Jesus" are found in the BT and the PT, the ability to find a specific reference to cite is difficult since they have been expunged by censors and citations are usually from notes and pamphlets that are of a mixed quality. Some traditions have elements in them that suggest that the specific designation of "Yeshu HaNotzri," the specific "Jesus of Nazareth" is meant, but only scattered manuscripts preserve this designation in its entirety. It is, in short, difficult to know if Jesus of Nazareth is meant or some other person named "Jesus" (a very popular name of the period) is associated with a tradition.

One of the main questions for the differentiation of layers of rabbinic literature is the fact that the Babylonian Talmud (BT) deals with a myth of a person named Jesus of Nazareth (HaNotzri) in many different ways. Many of the passages cited below have been restored according to the fourteenth-century Munich 75 manuscript. In most cases, the printed editions do not have any of these references. The following are the parts of the story extant in the BT where Jesus ("of Nazareth" in some manuscripts) is named:

> 1. The BT Shabbat 103a: Jesus of Nazareth "burns his food" in public.

> 2. BT Sanhedrin 43a: V' haTanya (as it was learnt):[16] On the eve of Passover (the eve of the Sabbath and the eve of Passover) they hung Jesus (of Nazareth—according to one manuscript). Jesus (of Nazareth) was stoned because he practiced magic and deceived and led astray Israel. Ulla (fourth-century Babylonian source): Jesus was a revolutionary and he was near to the kingdom.

> 3. Same: Jesus had five disciples: Matthai, Nequai, Netzer, Buni and Todah.

> 4. BT Sotah 47a and BT Sanhedrin 107b: Rabbi Yehoshua ben Perahyah and Jesus escape to Egypt. Jesus of Nazareth practiced magic and led astray and deceived Israel.

> 5. BT Avodah Zarah 16b-17a: One of the disciples of Jesus of Nazareth walking in the upper street of Sepphoris taught....

These are the clearly named passages of Jesus (of Nazareth) in the BT. Other passages which do not contain the name "Jesus" but rather code names which correspond to Jesus do appear in the BT and else-where in Tannaitic literature. In the BT, transference of known traditions to new and often unimagined contexts is a part of the editing process. In one transferred passage, a parallel to #2, (in Sanhedrin 67a) "Jesus" is substituted with the name "Ben Stada" and the event takes place in Lod. In a parallel to #5 in the Tannaitic Tosefta Hullin 2.24, one of the disciples of Jesus "ben Pantiri" is mentioned instead of "Nazareth." Herford and others build much upon the fact that the Tannaim used "Ben Stada and Ben Pandira" and other cognates to in place the name Jesus. Herford and others held that even if Jesus of Nazareth is never mentioned, the implication is that these others are surrogates for the myth of Jesus in rabbinic literature. Many authors imply that the Jews did not write "Jesus'" name in their literature either because they were afraid that in the third century C.E. these references would have been offensive to Christians and not conducive to good relations. Some authors hold that the absence of Jesus' name was intended not to lend credence to the movement by referencing him in their literature. The use of such cognates is a common rabbinic technique. "Edom" (another term for the biblical Esau), for example, was a rabbinic code-word for the Roman empire in general.[17] Herford and others argue that such is the case with Jesus' name.

In passages cited by Herford from Tannaitic literature, Ben Stada and Ben Pandira are both referring to Jesus. The name Ben Stada was a Greek word, perhaps derived from (*ana*) *statos*, and for a "seditious" person,[18] and Ben Pandira (often written in manuscripts Ben Pantira/iri) may be derived from an elipsis of the Greek *parthenos*, which means "virgin" or appropriately "the son of a virgin."[19] Even if one accepts all the information from the Ben Stada and Ben Pantira stories in rabbinic literature, the following are the rest of the information held by the rabbis on the Jesus myth:

1. BT Shabbat 104b: Brought spells from Egypt used in healing.

2. Same: Ben Stada is Ben Pandira and he is the product of Miriam and Stada and another person other than her husband, named Pandira.

3. Tosefta Sanhedrin 10.11 and BT Sanhedrin 67a: Ben Stada stoned to death in Lod in front of a Beth Din, rabbinical court.

4. PT Avodah Zarah 40d-41a: Quotation in the name of Jeshu ben Pantira.

There is a total of five independent Jesus (of Nazareth traditions) and another four or five independent traditions which can be cited in the entire rabbinic literature where a named person can directly or indirectly be linked to Jesus of Nazareth.[20] The most remarkable part of these traditions is that none of them deal with the central issue of Jesus' teaching in the Gospels; i.e. the messianship and the imminent *eschaton*. The following is a summary of some of the clear Jesus traditions myths in the Babylonian Talmud:

The Jesus of Nazareth traditions in the Babylonian Talmud seem to have a view of man who was privy to teachings about magic and healing from (or in) Egypt. He taught this and other elements to others in public, was not accepted by the rabbis, apparently was put to death for a variety of different charges, and was seen as connected with the Roman Government.[21] These named (Ben Stada and Ben Pantira) traditions which associate with the already mentioned "Jesus" traditions add something about his uncertain birth, powers of healing and a trial in front of either/ or rabbinic and Roman courts. In short, the rabbis appear to have little or no knowledge of the normative Gospel accounts of Jesus' life but do have parts of some Gospel aspects such as healing stories as in Mark 8, unique birth accounts of Luke 2 and Matthew 1, a tradition of going to Egypt as in Matthew 2, and a trial in front of the court as found in Matthew 25, Mark 14, Luke 22, and John 18.

Differentiating "Jesus" from "Non-Jesus" Myths in Rabbinic Literature

The unearthing and collecting of the references cited by Herford is in itself an important task. In this case, however, it must be said that the work of Herford systematically produces an error of the grossest form in textual research. In the case of the Tannaitic period, it is obvious that Herford is reading the later and clearer references of the Amoraic period into the more obscure references of the Tannaitic period. In the case of two references found in the Mishnah, and three citations found in the Tosephta, this is especially true. In the first case, Herford cites a reference from the Mishnah in tractate *Yevamot* 4.13 as proof of the allegation that Jesus is a "*mamzer*" (bastard). Unfortunately, he fails to cite this mishnah in full, and ultimately misses the whole point.

The mishnah in *Yevamot* is translated as follows:

> Who is deemed to be a bastard? (The offspring of the union with) any
> consanguineous relative with whom cohabitation is forbidden. This is

the ruling of R. Akiba. Simeon the Temanite said: (The offspring of any union) the penalty for which is *Kareth* at the Hands of Heaven. And the Halacha is in agreement with his view. And R. Joshua said: (The offspring of any union), the penalty for which is death at the hands of Beth Din. Said R. Simeon b. Azzai: I found a role of genealogical records in Jerusalem. And therein was written, "So-and-so is a bastard (having been born) from (a forbidden union with) a married woman, which confirms the view of R. Joshua.

First, it is quite evident that the name of Jesus does not appear, in any form, in this mishnah. Second, judging from Herford's analysis of the mishnah, it is obvious that he was not sure that the reference was to Jesus. On page 44 he writes, "When, therefore, Shim' on b.' Azzai reported that he had found a book of pedigrees, in which it was stated that 'a certain person' (*peloni*) was of spurious birth, it is *certainly probable* that the reference is to Jesus (emphasis my own).

Finally, it is clear that because Herford only cites the latter part of the mishnah, he inadvertently misinterpreted the meaning. For as he states on pages 44 and 45: "And R. Joshua had laid it down that a bastard is one who is condemned to a juridical death." This is a complete misreading of the mishnah. The mishnah in fact states the R. Akiba defined a bastard as a product of the union of the Levitically prohibited relatives. Simeon the Temanite holds the opinion that a bastard is defined as the product of the union of a woman and a man whose crime can be punished by Divine Justice. R. Joshua, however, holds that a bastard is the product of the union of a woman and a man whose crime (of the woman and the man) is punishable by death at the hands of the earthly court. The mishnah is not speaking at all about the juridical death sentence of the child, rather the parents who were committing adultery! Herford, however, uses this mishnah, (and misinterprets it) in order to lend credence and longevity to the Amoraic traditions of the death sentence of Jesus. As he states on page 45, "Now Jesus undoubtedly had been condemned (though not on account of his birth) to a juridical death, as the Talmud recognizes (see passages given subsequently, pp. 80, 83)." It is obvious that even Herford recognized that Jesus was not given a death sentence because of his birth, but he obviously tried to find a basis for the sentence of death given in the Amoraic sources to Jesus. Additionally, it is clear that Herford is relating the concept of bastard found in the mishnah to the Amoraic tradition of the BT Shabbath 104b, which points to the illegitimate parentage of Ben Pandira. Unfortunately, these are the opinions of third and fourth-century Babylonian sources. Herford has read the late Amoraic concept of Jesus' illegitimate birth into a Tannaitic piece, and, in doing so, completely misinterpreted the mishnah.

In citing the mishnah Sanhedrin 10.2, Herford makes some interesting revelations. The mishnah states, "Three kings and four private men have no part in the world to come; the three kings are Jeroboam, Ahab, and Manasseh...the four private men are Balaam, Doeg, Ahitopel and Gehazi (translation by Herford, pp. 64-65). Herford states in his commentary to this mishnah (page 66):

> Moreover, Balaam was not an Israelite, and therefore could not logically be included in a list of exceptions to a rule which only affected Israelites. It is evident that Balaam here does not mean the ancient prophet of Num. XXII fol., but someone else for whom that ancient prophet could serve as a type. From the Jewish point of view there was considerable likeness between Balaam and Jesus. Both had led the people astray; and if the former had tempted them to gross immorality, the latter, according to the Rabbis, had tempted them to gross apostasy.

Herford then goes on to cite a talmudic section of the BT Gittin 56b, 57a. In this section, the Amoriam cite the examples of Titus, Balaam, and Jesus. What is obvious prima facie, is that Balaam and Jesus are not synonymous for the Rabbis, since the Rabbis themselves distinguish them. Similarly, Herford himself makes the statement that Balaam is not an Israelite, while Jesus is a Jew. Again, nothing about Christianity or its founder can be seen in these passages.

In the references to Jesus found in the Tosephta, two of the citations refer to a Ben Stada, two refer to Ben Pandira (Pantiri), and one to an unnamed man who was crucified. Though it is quite possible to link the events as recorded in those citations to events in the life of Jesus, i.e. healing powers, crucifixion, etc., the fact remains that these were elements of ancient society which could be connected to any religious or philosophical movement in antiquity. The names of the individuals involved in these citations also gives rise to many questions. Herford, himself, is forced to admit (p. 40), "I cannot satisfy myself that any of the suggested explanations solve the problem; and being unable to propose any other, I leave the two names Ben Stada and Ben Pandira as relics of ancient Jewish mockery against Jesus, the clue whose meaning is now lost."

Though Herford readily admits that the meanings of the names are lost, he links the different accounts in the Tosephta using these names with other accounts in the Talmudim. In a footnote on page 345 (note 1), Herford recognizes that the Tannaitic source, R. Eliezer, differentiates between the two figures Ben Stada and Ben Pandira; yet, Herford persists in presenting the later Talmudic account of BT Shabbat 104b and BT Sanhedrin 67a to connect the two.

Unfortunately, Herford deals with Talmudic materials as if they all represent one continuous historical tradition. The Talmud does unify multi-period traditions in an associative method which is not always sensitive to their historical origins. The traditions concerning Ben Pandira and Ben Stada, however, cannot easily be considered as a contemporaneous Jewish recognition of or polemic with early Christianity since the connection of these names to a NT events is tenuous and not found at all in Tannaitic literature. Furthermore, the citation which Herford used concerning the crucifixion of Jesus in the Tosephta, (Sanhedrin 9.7) does not even mention Jesus, Ben Stada, or Ben Pandira. To be fair, the Talmud mentions cases of crucifixions, but they are not directly related to Jesus, Ben Pandira and Ben Stada. In the Talmudic references which Herford relates to Jesus' crucifixion, there is in fact no crucifixion (supplicium), but rather a hanging. This is not to say that the Rabbis of the Amoraic period are not alluding to Jesus' crucifixion or other events surrounding it. At the time of the redaction of these events into the Babylonian Talmud, however, it seems that they had only a passing connection with actual historical events. In Babylonia, where Christianity was not the state religion these accounts may have had other meanings as well.

The Gnostic Gospels, the Babylonian and Palestinian Rabbis and Jesus

So what were the sources of the Rabbis' information in the Babylonian Talmud? It is clear that some of the information could have come from the canonized Gospels, but the lack of any of the major themes of these Gospels, i.e. the imminent *eschaton* and messianship of Jesus are troubling. Another source of early Christian information does provide additional source material. Up until 1945, it was possible to assume that the rabbis possessed oral accountings which were passed in a piecemeal way to Babylonia on trade routes. In light of the discovery of the Nag Hammadi materials in that year, however, it is possible to demonstrate that other non-canonized Christian works may have circulated in non-Christian lands such as Babylonia. A number of elements in the rabbinic accounts lend themselves to this view:

1. The Gospel according to Nicodemus contains the charge of uncertain birth against Jesus, and that Jesus lived in Egypt and learned signs and wonders in the Land of Egypt just as Moses had (*The Other Bible*, p. 364-365);[22] Nicodemus is one of the apostles of Jesus (p. 366); includes stoning and then crucifixion by Pilate apparently with the agreement of the Jews.

2. The Talmud lists the five disciples in the BT Sanhedrin 43a. They are: Matthai, Nequai, Netzer, Buni and Todah. Nequai could correspond to Nico(demus). The Rabbis also have a tradition in the BT Taanit 19b-20a of a man named Naqdimon ben Gurion, a rich individual of Jerusalem, whose nick-name was Buni.

3. In the Gnostic Gospels (The Second Apocalypse of James),[24] the father of James is referred to as Thuda or the equivalent of our BT Todah.

4. The BT Gittin 57a account about "Jesus in Hell" is a parallel to the Gospel of Nicodemus' account of Christ's descent into Hell. (*The Other Bible*, p. 374-6).

5. The Gnostic Gospels also contain a strong tradition (continued in the Syriac church) about Didymos Judas Thomas, Judah the twin brother and apostle of Jesus.[23] In the Gospel of Thomas and in the Book of Thomas the Contender, traditions about the two different careers of Jesus and Judah Thomas are set out. The Tosephta Sanhedrin 9.7 has a possible parallel with this. Rabbi Meir states:

> What is the meaning of (Deut. 21.23); 'For a curse of God is he that is hung' ? [It is the case of] two brothers, twins, who resembled one another. One ruled over the whole world, the other took to robbery. After a time the one who took to robbery was caught, and they crucified him on a cross. And every one who passed back and forth said: 'It seems that the king has been crucified.' Therefore it is said; 'For a curse of God is he that is hung.'

The Rabbis seem to have some heterodox traditions of Jesus in general. These traditions may have been Gnostic traditions which may have circulated through Syrian and Alexandrian Christianity through the rest of the Middle East. It is not surprising, therefore, to discover this information in the Apocalypse of James, considering its connection with James and Syrian Christianity. The importance of a physical resurrection of Jesus to some Synoptic writers in the canonized NT or normative Christianity is apparent. This is clear in Matthew and Luke, although they do not agree about the number or place of these resurrections. Matthew, for example, has physical resurrections of Jesus in Jerusalem and Galilee, while Luke has only an appearance of Jesus in Jerusalem. The original Mark manuscripts did not contain a resurrection scene at all (although it was added in later medieval manuscripts). In Gnostic Christianity, it also appears that this main tenet of the Church is not seen as central. In fact, the *Treatise on Resurrection*, the *Exegesis on the Soul*, and the *Gospel of Philip*, demonstrate that for these Gnostic Christians resurrection was a spiritual idea and not a physical reality. Instead of the NT *eschaton*, these Gnostic texts offer a telos of history and the return of the "human sparks" to the Kingdom of Light. The exclusive messianship of Jesus is part of a Gnostic larger scheme in which the different counterparts of the unknown God are manifested in a number of different forms. Basilides taught, for example, the existence of six spiritual powers of which the Christ was only one.

These issues may explain, in part, why the Rabbis in Babylonia commenting on the myth of Jesus have no references to the central issues of the NT, i.e. the messiahship of Jesus and the *eschaton*. Their sources may have been heterodox Christians and Christianity and the details of the Gospel of Nicodemus provide enough context for many of the events mentioned by the Rabbis.

Conclusions

The mythic proportions of Jesus in Jewish tradition should be sought not in the text of the rabbis and Josephus but certainly in the Greco-Roman interpretations which emerged in the Hellenistic Judaism of Asia Minor, Babylonia, Palestine and Alexandria. The investigation of these myths should rightly begin with the Hellenistic underpinnings of these interpretations, such as the metaphysical systems of philosophy, views of ancient Greco-Roman heroes, semi-gods and the demiurge, etc., all of which contributed to the creation of a cultural milieu into which " the Jesus' myth fit in Hellenistic Judaism. The myth of Jesus in Jewish tradition seems to have been accepted in different ways by differing Jewish groups of the period, but the closer proximity to a certain type of hybrid Hellenistic civilization, language and ideas, the more mythic the Jesus myth became. Asia Minor and parts of Roman and

Palestinian Jewish literature bear witness to this tendency. The relative silence of traditions concerning the Jesus myth in Jewish literature of the period, however, is disturbing. Certain issues about the sources of the rabbinic myth of Jesus are clear:

> 1. The rabbis do not seem to be aware of the Josephus materials nor Josephus of the rabbinic materials relating to the life of Jesus. Some of the information of Josephus is at odds with the information of the rabbinic texts and vice versa.

> 2. The clear references to a named "Jesus of Nazareth" in rabbinic texts are not necessarily from canonized Gospel information.

> 3. The "encoded" references or allusions to a "Jesus" myth in rabbinic texts appear to be primarily from uncanonized (and/or Gnostic) Gospel sources and only secondarily from canonized NT sources.

> 4. Little or nothing seems to have been preserved of a Jesus myth in early Tannaitic literature despite its close geographic and time proximity. The overall myth of Jesus which emerges from the encoded and named traditions of Jesus in later (Amoraic Babylonian) sources do not present a positive, rabbinic, heroic image of Jesus.

A conclusion one might reach from the *argumentum ex silencio* (from the absence of Jesus materials in Palestinian Tannaitic literature) is that while certain Jewish groups may have been attracted to the Jesus movement in the first century, others were not. These "other Jewish groups" were apparently the ones responsible for the Tannaitic literature and therefore the Jesus materials do not appear in their canonized literature. The absence of a Jesus myth in Tannaitic rabbinic writings may also represent a silent polemic as well, but it is impossible to know. By the time the Tannaitic literature was codified and committed to writing in he third century C.E. the Jesus (Christian) movement is no longer a Jewish movement. Different considerations may have made whatever materials the Rabbis did possess inappropriate in a third-century Rabbinic code.

The inclusion of a Jesus myth in Josephus, whether spurious or not, may indicate that it was important to a segment of the population who read Josephus to have the Jesus myth contextualized in Jewish literature of the period. Since the early Church maintained, quoted, recopied and used the Josephus writings throughout the Middle Ages, it is not surprising to find a "formula-like" myth of the heroic proportions. The obvious absence of a Jesus myth in Philo's writings and in ancient Jewish papyri and manuscripts of the period is not as problematic as it might sound. The timing of the transmission of the myth and the writings of Philo (first half of the first century) and his location in Alexandria may be the question. While clearly there were "Jesus followers" in Alexandria by the second half of the century, the timing of Philo's writing may be crucial. Josephus, on the other hand, wrote in the second half of the first century when the myth was being circulated to a much larger audience than in the first half of the century. If a myth of Jesus developed among the Jews (especially outside of Israel), its importance must be relegated to the second half of the first century, coinciding with the missions of Paul.

The absence of the named Jesus myths in parallel readings from the Palestinian Talmud is also perplexing. Since the PT is a product of fifth-century Galilee (close to the centers of Christianity in Jerusalem, Caesarea and Antioch until the academy was closed in the fifth century C.E.) one might expect information. The absence of expected parallels may represent, however, the state of relations between Christians and Jews in the fourth- and fifth-century in Palestine rather than being a commentary on relations between the Rabbis and Jesus and the first-century followers of Jesus.

Finally, the Rabbis of Babylonia, writing as they were in the fourth and fifth century in a land that was only indirectly informed about the Jesus myth, are particularly unreliable sources of "real" information on Jesus for a couple of reasons. As Neusner has stated:

> It was the convention of rabbinic historiography to invent dramatic "incidents" out of the evidence of conflict, and so to represent as a clash of personalities what was originally a difference, of some seriousness to be sure, in matters of law.[25]

The use of the "Jesus" myths as a BT literary vehicle to express certain conflicts or clashes which were part of the struggle for the correct interpretation of Jewish law would be in keeping with the literary make up of the BT. This technique, however, would make it nearly impossible to recover any "real" information about a historical Jesus from BT texts. The stylized and symbolic references in the narratives (even to named "Jesus" traditions in the Babylonian Talmud) are used only insofar as they provide some background to a larger legal issue (adultery, capital punishment, idolatry, etc.) under discussion. These Jesus narratives in the Babylonian Talmud do not appear to be of interest because they are about Jesus but rather because they provide the Babylonian rabbis an opportunity to talk about indirectly related legal issues.

The other reason why BT information on Jesus in inherently problematic has to do with the political and social life of the Jews of Babylonia in the time of the redaction of most of the BT. The negative references to Jesus which may have been circulating among non-Jews of Babylonia (non-Christians in Babylonia may have been the real source of information about Christianity) might not be the most reliable sources of information on Roman or Eastern Christianity. These sources of information themselves may have been oral and heterodox written sources which understood the meaning of Jesus in a very different way than did the normative/canonized sources of the developing Nicean ante-Church.[26] The traditions which they impart may well tell us more about what non-Jews and eventually Jews in Babylonia had come to think about this movement which did not directly confront them in Babylonia but which they realized was indirectly related to them. The tone of the BT narratives may well reflect the rabbinic need in the fourth and fifth centuries to be anti-Roman in sentiment. The Babylonian Jews lived in a non-Christian/Roman territory and there may have been a need to distance itself from the Christians which by that time was a Roman (Christian) movement. The tone of the BT narratives may well reflect the rabbinic need in fourth and fifth century to be anti-Roman in sentiment. The negative statements about Rome and its leadership found in the BT (in encoded and unencoded narratives) as well as the Jesus stories may be an attempt by Babylonian Jews to distance themselves from a perceived Jewish-Christian-Roman connection. To be sure, these BT narratives, rather than being a reflection of the religious realities of the "true" myth of Jesus in first century Palestine, may better represent political and social concerns of Jews living in fourth- and fifth-century Babylonia under non-Christian/Roman rulers.

Notes

1.   Three works from different periods of the vast library of Neusner's writings on this subject will suffice. J. Neusner, *A Life of Yohanan ben Zakkai* (Leiden: Brill, 1962); *Development of a Legend: Studies on the Traditions Concenring*

Yohanan ben Zakkai (Leiden: Brill, 1970); *In Search of Talmudic Biography* (Chico: Scholars Press, 1984) .

2. J. Neusner, *Understanding Seeking Faith,* Volume Two (Atlanta: Scholars Press, 1987), 143-4.

3. M. Eliade, *Cosmos and History,* (New York: Harper, 1959), 39-41.

4. Ibid., 43-44.

5. M. E. Hardwick, *Josephus as an Historical Source in Patristic Literature Through Eusebius,* (Atlanta: Scholars Press, 1989).

6. *Josephus, Judaism, and Christianity* Ed. L. H. Feldman and G. Hata (Detroit: Wayne State University Press, 1987), 55-58.

7. The Arabic version of S. Pines contains a re-(w)orded version of this text. See: Feldman and Hata, Ibid., 58. The medieval manuscripts of the work, *Josippon,* which did circulate among rabbinic Jews in the Middle Ages and is linked to the texts of Josephus, did not generally contain this passage. See D. Flusser's chapter, "Josippon, A Medieval Hebrew Version of Josephus," in Feldman and Hata, Ibid., 386 ff. and footnote #29.

8. See S. Cohen's "Alexander the Great and Jaddus the High Priest According to Josephus," in *AJS Review* 7-8 (1982-3): 41-68 for some insights on how traditions of the period were used by Josephus. But not necessarily with legal materials. D. Goldenberg, "The Halakhah in Josephus and in Tannaitic Literature," *JQR* 67 (1976): 30-43.

9. This period is generally from the fourth century B.C.E. through first century C.E.; although this historical designation itself is not uniform. This period can be distinguished from the former biblical period by the use of Greek in textual traditions but not exclusively so. Many Jewish writers use the designation "Second Temple" period to distinguish different designations. Some refer to the period from the return to Judea after the Babylonian Exile (536 B.C.E. or more specifically from about 516 B.C.E.) until the destruction of the Second Temple in 70 C.E. by the Romans. D. Golan, in his book entitled *A History of the Hellenistic World* (Jerusalem: Magnes Press, 1983), 788-805, for example, dates the beginnings of the Hellenistic period from the birth of Alexander the Great in 356 B.C.E. and ends his chronological table with the death of Cleopatra in 30 B.C.E. For more on the controversy of this designation and the limitations of its use see: M. Hengel, *Judaism and Hellenism.* Trans. J. Bowden, (Philadelphia: Fortress Press, 1981), 1-5.

10. The Oxford Bodeleian Library manuscript is from the twelfth century and is incomplete.

11. At present, no completed critical edition of the Babylonian Talmud exists. Because of its wide-spread use during the Middle Ages throughout Jewish communities, many hundreds of thousands of variant readings could easily be established from the comparison of the extant manuscripts. R. Rabbinovicz, in a work entitled *Sefer Dikdukei Soferim (Variae Lectiones in Mischnam et in Talmud Babylonicum),* actually began to collect some of the

variants in fifteen volumes published between 1868-1886 (a sixteenth volume was completed later). This work contains only a part of the entire Babylonian Talmud and while certainly a ground-breaking labor at the time it contains serious methodological problems by current standards.

Many of the manuscript fragments pre-date the complete manuscripts, and their deciphering and recording are only recently underway. Although critical editions of the Hebrew Bible and New Testament exist, only partial attempts have been made (individual tractates) to create a critical edition of the Babylonian and Palestinian Talmudim. Extensive research and comparison is needed to determine if the text has been corrected, censored, "updated," and/or is just difficult to understand. Hundreds of thousands of medieval fragments of manuscripts (eighth through fifteenth century) have been found in various parts of the world which preserve readings that differ from the standard printed edition.

The Palestinian Talmud (so called "*Talmud HaYerushalmi*" or "Jerusalem Talmud," although not written in Jerusalem) exists in one almost complete manuscript, Codex Scaliger #3 from Leiden. It is medieval in origin even though internal evidence in the Palestinian Talmud assumes completion in the fifth century C.E. Although completed before the Babylonian Talmud, the Palestinian Talmud is shorter and was not historically viewed as authoritative as the Babylonian Talmud. Sometimes its Aramaic dialect is obscure; sometimes it is just not intelligible. It, too, contains many problematic elements of redaction and language and it is missing many books of commentary for unexplained reasons. For details see: H. L. Strack, *Introduction to the Talmud and Midrash* (New York: Atheneum, 1974), 65-66. Presently the Palestinian Talmud has complete discussions (gemara) on only thirty-nine tractates. The Babylonian Talmud has only gemara for thirty-six and one-half tractates, but the scope of the Babylonian Talmud's discussions is much greater that of the Palestinian Talmud.

Finally, a complex editing (or better "additions") process of the Babylonian Talmud seems to have been practiced even after the sixh century. During the Geonic and medieval period, from the eighth through the eleventh century, the text of the Talmud seems to have been added to, directly or indirectly (in the form of commentary, for example). In short, Jewish ethics using only selected rabbinic texts, and especially the Talmudim, in an uncritical form makes the information gleaned from such an analysis almost unintelligible.

12. Another definition of the type of critical analysis of rabbinic texts being suggested here is presented in D. Weiss Halivni's article in the *Encyclopedia Britannica*, (Chicago: William Benton, 1963), Vol. XXI, 645 s.v. TALMUD: Source Criticism. The article states: "Source criticism seeks to differentiate between the original statements as they were enunciated by their authors and the forms they took as a consequence of being orally transmitted; that is, between the sources and their later traditions...Source criticism claims

that the transmission of the Talmud was not, and perhaps could not have been verbatim, and that the text became altered in transmission, with the result that many statements in the Talmud have note come down in their original form. Instead, what survives is the form assumed in the last phase of transmissional development. While such a study is pertinent to most ancient texts, it is particularly relevant to the Talmud, which primarily consists of quotations and their interpretations."

13. Strack, Introduction, p. 279 note #27 reads: In the year 5391 of Creation (1631 C.E.) a Jewish Assembly of Elders in Poland issued a circular letter which reads as follows: "Having learned that many Christians have taken great pains to master the tongue in which our books are written, we enjoin you under the threat of the great ban to publish in no new edition of the Mishnah or the Gemara anything that refers to Jesus of Nazareth...If you will not diligently heed this letter, but run counter thereto and continue to publish our books in the same manner as heretofore, you might bring over us and yourselves still greater sufferings than in previous times...We therefore command you that when you publish a new edition of these books the passages referring to Jesus of Nazareth be omitted and the spaces be filled out by a small circle. The rabbis and teachers will know how the youth will be instructed by word of mouth."

14. Ibid., Strack, 280, notes #34 and #35.

15. R. Travers Herford, (Reprint) *Christianity in Talmud and Midrash* (New York: Ktav: 1975), 354.

16. J. Neusner, *In Search of Talmudic Biography* (Chico: Scholars Press: 1984), 91.

17. Y. N. Epstein in his book, *Mavo LeSifrut HaTannaim*, states that Tanya is an indication of a Babylonian Baraita or a tradition which has undergone significant revision in Babylonia, 244-246 (Jerusalem: Magnes Press: 1955).

18. Probably based on the similarity of the (D) and the (R) noted above and the letters of the word Edom and Roma were similar. The designation of Edom, mostly used in a negative sense in rabbinic literature both before the advent of the Roman Christian empire and after. Shir HaShirim Rabbah 2.2, Qohelet Rabbah 5.15, Genesis Rabbah 6.3, 16.2.

19. Herford, 345.

20. Ibid., 39.

21. For obvious reasons, Herford also includes even anonymous individuals which are parallel to NT traditions. Ibid., Herford, 62, 75, and 348.

22. One of these anonymous passages is used by Herford to demonstrate that the Rabbis had a tradition that Jesus was put to death by Pontius Pilate and not by the Jews. Ibid., Herford, 79 and 349. The other traditions also indicate that Jesus was put to death by the Jewish Beth Din.

23. *The Other Bible*. Ed. W. Barnstone, (New York: Harper and Row, 1984). Pages are indicated after citation information.

24. *The Nag Hammadi Library*. Ed. J. M. Robinson, (New York: Harper and Row, 1977), 117-130 and 188-194. In the *Second Apocalypes of James*, p. 249, the

connection is made. The connection between James and Syrian Christianity is made by Robinson on p. 242.

25. J. Neusner, *In Search of Talmudic Biography* (Chico: Scholars Press, 1984), 91.

26. An example of this phenomenon is the information about Christianity found in the Quran some hundred years later. Although this information may have been presented by partisan believers, it does not conform to the views of the normative/canonized views of the Nicean Church of the same period.

Melchizedek: King, Priest, and God

James R. Davila

Introduction

The priest-king Melchizedek is one of the most mysterious and elusive figures in the biblical tradition. He first appears in an epic narrative in the book of Genesis, then resurfaces periodically not only in the Hebrew Bible and the New Testament, but also occasionally in early Jewish literature and in the Coptic Gnostic texts. He appears to undergo weird transformations between these appearances and we can scarcely doubt that the enigmatic mythic fragments about him preserved in our sources are only tattered remnants of a long and very complex stream of tradition. The purpose of this paper is to reconstruct the outline of this stream of tradition from the pre-Davidic royal cult in Jerusalem to saviour theologies of late antiquity.

Melchizedek in the Hebrew Bible

The first mention of Melchizedek is in Gen 14:18-21. Here he appears as the king of "Salem" (שָׁלֵם) and the priest of God Most High (*El Elyon*) who blesses Abram when the latter returns from defeating the four kings and rescuing his kinsman Lot, and who apparently accepts a tithe from the patriarch. The source-critical and redactional issues for this chapter are particularly difficult. All commentators agree that Genesis 14 did not come from any of the generally proposed sources of the Pentateuch (J, E, D, P, or any variation of one of these). Most scholars believe that the narrative of the battle of the four kings against the five in 14:1-11 existed before it was incorporated into the Abraham cycle, and some argue that the verses about Melchizedek are a still later addition to the chapter.[1] Since my interest in this paper is in the passage on Melchizedek, I will focus on the question of the date and origin of the final form of the chapter. Space permits only an illustrative, not an exhaustive, discussion of previous scholarship.

E. A. Speiser, on the basis of doubtful cuneiform parallels, dates the contents of the chapter to the mid-second millennium B.C.E. and treats it as an essentially historical description of a campaign in the eighteenth century.[2] At the other end of the spectrum, John Van Seters argues that Genesis 14 is a late story similar to the cuneiform chronicles and dates it in the post-exilic period. For him, Melchizedek represents the priesthood of the Second Temple period after the exile.[3] The position of J. A. Emerton falls between these two extremes. He holds that the final form of the narrative (including the passage on Melchizedek) was edited during the reign of David in the tenth century and was meant to encourage the native "Canaanite" population to adopt the worship of Yahweh in the form of El Elyon.[4]

My own position is that the epic materials in Genesis, including the JE material and Genesis 14, reached their more or less final written form sometime during the monarchy (between c. 1000 and 586/7 B.C.E.). Speiser's cuneiform excesses are to be rejected, but Van Seters errs in the opposite direction. I see no reason for the post-exilic priesthood to hold up a non-Israelite priest-king as an example unless he had already been firmly established in the traditions of the First Temple period.[5] Various elements of the tale may well have a prehistory, but I doubt that they had a separate literary history. The story of David's rescue of hostages in 1 Samuel 30 is another example of the same epic theme.[6] Like Genesis 14, it begins with an account of the military assault that resulted in the hostage taking. David's consultation with the priest Abiathar in vv. 7-8 before the battle may correspond to the welcome of Abram by the priest Melchizedek after the battle in Genesis 14. David, like Abram, follows the enemy and takes them by surprise, defeating them utterly. In both accounts the hostages and all the spoils are recovered. Both passages close with a dispute over the booty. I read Genesis 14 as an epic tale of the heroic exploits of the patriarch Abram that, in its present form, serves to show the ancient roots of the priesthood held by the line of Davidic kings. This, which seems to me to be the most natural reading, logically places the composition of the text during the period of the Judean monarchy.

Another critical question is important for this inquiry: the identification of the city Salem. Ancient references to these verses in the Genesis Apocryphon from Qumran, the first-century Jewish historian Josephus, and the Targumim, explicitly identify Salem with Jerusalem.[7] In addition, a reference in Psalm 76:3 sets "Salem" in poetic parallelism with "Zion," another name for Jerusalem. Some of the force of the latter point, however, has been weakened by Fred Horton, who points out that the previous verse of the psalm sets the countries of Israel and Judah in contrasting parallelism. Horton thus argues that Salem could be a site in the northern kingdom of Israel that is contrasted with Jerusalem.[8] Nevertheless, his overall case is weak. The larger context of Genesis 14 sets this episode in the south, near Sodom, and in verse 17 the meeting of Melchizedek and Abram is located in the "Valley of the King," which in turn is placed in the environs of Jerusalem in 2 Sam 18:18 and by Josephus.[9] It is conceivable that Salem was originally another city, but we may at least affirm that Genesis 14 is the earliest source to associate it with Jerusalem. Moreover, Psalm 110, to be discussed below, unambiguously associates the priesthood of Melchizedek with the king in Zion. To sum up, then, in Genesis 14 Melchizedek is portrayed as the king of Jerusalem, the priest of the god El Elyon (which god, of course, was later identified with Yahweh), and an ally to Abram, the ancestor of the nation of Israel.

The only other mention of Melchizedek in the Hebrew Bible is found in Psalm 110, a royal psalm that most scholars agree had its life situation in the pre-exilic Judean royal cult located in Solomon's temple during the period of the Judean monarchy.[10] The royal terminology and the reference to Zion strongly indicate that this is a correct understanding. Some scholars have associated it with an annual New Year celebration, one that may also be reflected in other psalms in the Psalter. Because of its corrupt state, much of the psalm is obscure, but the passage that concerns us is clear enough. Verse 4, addressing the Davidic king, asserts "Yahweh has sworn and will not change his mind: you are a priest forever, after the order of Melchizedek." As has been noted by many scholars, there are other indications that the Davidic line of kings also carried out priestly functions. In 2 Samuel 6 we are told that David himself wore a priestly ephod and danced before the ark of the covenant when it was brought into Jerusalem. The list of David's court officials in 2 Sam 8:15-18 also informs us that "David's sons were priests" (v. 18). Thus, Psalm 110 associates a priesthood of Melchizedek with the Davidic royal cult in the Jerusalem temple.[11]

A reasonably clear picture of the Melchizedek tradition comes into focus around these two texts. Genesis 14 purports to preserve a tradition about Melchizedek, a pre-Davidic king of Jerusalem who, like many kings in the ancient Near East, was also a priest to the high god of the pantheon. Of course, we have no way of knowing if there even was such a person. His association with Abram is probably secondary, but it certainly helps present him in a positive light. Psalm 110 explains the positive portrayal of Melchizedek. It indicates that he was adopted by the Davidic dynasty as a founder of its royal priesthood. Given what we know about both King David and West Semitic royal cults, there is nothing unlikely in this conclusion. The succession narrative in 2 Samuel indicates that David, who founded the Judean dynasty, made creative use of the various religious traditions at his disposal in order to solidify his hold on power. He conquered Jerusalem as a neutral capital city, brought the ark of the covenant into the city, associated the ark with the tent-shrine of the wilderness traditions, and perhaps drew on two of the most powerful Israelite priestly houses for his high priests.[12] It is entirely in character that he should have adopted the Melchizedek priesthood of the Jerusalem kings in order to consolidate his own position in the city. Furthermore, as we shall see, the pre-Davidic Ugaritic dynasty of kings in Syria included pre-Ugaritic kings in their own royal cult.

Melchizedek in Later Texts

Melchizedek is not mentioned again in the Hebrew Bible. Our sources are silent for some centuries, and it is not until near the end of the Second Temple period in the closing centuries B.C.E. that further references to him appear. Yet the Melchizedek of the Second Temple period and later is a strangely transmogrified and, indeed, often virtually unrecognizable figure. Because my focus is the transmogrified Melchizedek, I will concentrate on the sources that present him as such. Due to limits of space, texts that present him essentially as in the Hebrew Bible (e.g., the Genesis Apocryphon from Qumran) will, for the most part, not be addressed.

Only one New Testament book, the Letter to the Hebrews, mentions him. Hebrews 7:1-3 reads:

[1]For this Melchizedek, king of Salem, priest of the Most High God, met Abraham returning from the slaughter of the kings and blessed him; [2]and to him Abraham apportioned a tenth part of everything. He is first, by translation of his name, king of righteousness, and then he is also king of Salem, that is, king of peace. [3]He is without father or mother or

genealogy, and has neither beginning of days nor end of life, but resembling the Son of God he continues a priest forever. (RSV)

It is then argued that Melchizedek was greater than both Abraham and the Levitical priesthood, and that Jesus is a high priest according to the order of Melchizedek as described in Psalm 110. For the writer of Hebrews, Melchizedek is a preexistent and immortal priestly divine being "like the Son of God."

This picture of Melchizedek is, if not exactly illuminated, at least supplemented by a number of texts. Probably the earliest come from Qumran. I begin with the fragmentary document known as 11QMelchizedek, written in an early Herodian hand and thus presumably composed in the second half of the first century B.C.E. or earlier.[13] The following passages are relevant to this inquiry:

> 6. . . this matter 7in the first week of the Jubilee after [the] ni[ne] Jubilees. And the d[ay of aton]ement is the e[nd of] the [t]enth [Jub]ilee, 8to atone in it for all the sons of [El and] the people of the lot of M[elchi]zedek . . . upon them . . . their . . . for 9it is the designated time for the year of favor for Melchize[de]k . . . holy ones of El for a reign of justice, as it is written 10concerning him in the songs of David, that which He said, "God stands in the as[sembly of El.] In the midst of the gods he judges." (Ps 82:1) And concerning him He said, "Above it 11on high, return! El judges the peoples." (Ps 7:8-9) . . .
>
> 23. . . with the judgments of El, as it is written about him, "saying to Zion, 'Your God reigns.'" (Isa 52:7). Zion is . . .
>
> 24. . . he who establishes the covenant, the turners away from walking in the way of the people. And "your God" is
>
> 25[Melchizedek (?) who will sa]v[e them from] the hand of Belial. And that which he said, "You shall sound the trumpet [in] all th[e la]nd." (Lev 25:9?)[14]

The text is an eschatological tractate that seems to give a chronology leading up to the eschaton and then describes the final judgment as administered by a divine being named Melchizedek. Using the "pesher" method of interpretation found frequently among the Dead Sea Scrolls, it presents quotations from Deuteronomy, Leviticus, Second Isaiah, and perhaps Daniel, and gives them a new interpretation. The first column of the work seems to be destroyed, although traces of a line written vertically between the two columns is generally assigned to column one. In column 2, lines 1-8, Melchizedek is closely tied to the Day of Atonement that marks the end of the tenth

Jubilee, on which atonement will be made for the sons of God and the people of the lot of Melchizedek. The issue here seems to be the chronology of the final judgment. Apparently it is to come at the end of the "tenth Jubilee," that is, after a period of ten times forty-nine years, perhaps comparable to the seventy weeks of years in Daniel 9. The fact that the culmination comes on the Day of Atonement may be connected with Melchizedek's priestly status in the Bible. This final period (beginning with line 9) "is the designated time for the year of the favor for Melchizedek," who is identified with the god mentioned in Ps 82:1. The function of the next quotation (of Ps 7:8-9) is not en‐tirely clear, but may serve to distinguish Melchizedek's judgment of the gods from God's (El's) judgment of "the peoples." In any case, the second verse of Psalm 82 is then applied to the diabolical figure Belial and his minions. Then we are told in lines 12-14 that, with the help of the gods and sons of El, Melchizedek will bring the vengeance of God on the forces of evil. In lines 15-22 another figure, the herald of good tidings of Second Isaiah, is introduced and discussed in what is, unfortunately, a badly broken passage. Melchizedek seems again to be the subject of discussion in lines 23-25, where, if the generally accepted reconstruction is correct, he is identified with "your God/*elohim*" of Isa 52:7. Another scriptural quotation, perhaps of Lev 25:9, is introduced at the end of the column. Only a few words of the following column survive, which are not of interest to us in this dis‐cussion.

Thus in line 10 of this text Melchizedek is called a "god" (*elohim*), and is taken as the protagonist of the judgment scene in Psalm 82, where God judges the other gods and sentences them to death.[15] Here Belial and the wicked angels take the part of the judged gods. Melchizedek is aided by other divine beings, and is probably called *elohim* again in line 25. So in this document from Qumran Melchizedek is pictured as an angelic or divine being (an *elohim*) who may have priestly associations and who is an eschatological judge.

Another Qumran document, the Songs of the Sabbath Sacrifice probably mentions Melchizedek twice (in both cases the name is damaged). This composition is especially concerned with describing the physical structure of heaven as the writer understood it, along with vivid and detailed descriptions of the angelic priesthood on high. Both fragments come from the same manuscript (4Q401), which appears to preserve material from the first half of the work.[16]

Fragment 11

כו]הן כוהנים	. . . pries]t of priest[s . . .
א]לוהי דעת וכן	. . . God of knowledge and . . .
מלכי] צדק כוהן בעד]ת אל	. . . Melchi]zedek, priest in the asse[mbly of God . . .

Fragment 22

[קדושי] [מם	. . . holy one[s . . .
[ש מלו ידיהם	. . . they filled their hands . . .
מל]כי צדק	. . . Mel]chizedek . . .

Given the broken state of the names, certainty is impossible. But the singular "priest" in fragment 11, line 3 argues fairly strongly that the preceding word was the name of a heavenly priest. Priestly ordination is also involved in fragment 22, where the name is better preserved but still not certain. The likelihood, then, is that Melchizedek appeared in the Songs of the Sabbath Sacrifice as an angelic priest. He may also have been associated with the eschatological battle, although the relevant fragments are in a different manuscript of the work.

Melchizedek is also an important figure in the Gnostic documents of late antiquity, both from Nag Hammadi and elsewhere. In the Second Book of Jeu, Melchizedek again appears as an angelic priest (Zorokothora Melchizedek) who brings the waters of baptism in a wine pitcher for a ritual involving Jesus and his disciples.[17] The text known as the Pistis Sophia contains a good bit of information about Melchizedek as a divine being. In the supernatural universe he is in charge of draining light from the "archons," the divine emanations that inhabited the Pleroma. This light is gathered by Melchizedek or his assistants, with or without resistance from the archons, and the dross left over was gathered together and made into human and animal souls.[18] Melchizedek is also a rescuer of souls in this document, one who, with the help of his assistants, delivers human souls from the "dragon" or the "judgments of the archons" and takes them to the "place of the Midst to the presence of the Virgin of the light."[19] Another passage supplements this description:

Now the souls which Hekate carries off by theft, she gives to her demons which are under her, and they torment them with her dark smoke and her wicked fire, and they (the souls) are greatly afflicted by the demons. And they spend 105 years and six months being punished in her wicked punishments. But they begin to perish and to be destroyed. . . . And Zorokothora Melchisedek looks forth from the height, and the world with the mountains moves, and the archons are in agitation. And he looks upon all the places of Hekate, and her places are dissolved and destroyed. And all the souls which are in her punishments are carried off and returned once more to the sphere, because they were perishing in the fire of her punishments.[20]

Here we are told that the underworld goddess Hecate captures some souls, which stay in her power for a set period of time. But Melchizedek "looks forth from the height," thus disturbing the archons and the world. Then he looks down on the realm of Hecate, which releases the souls imprisoned by her.

In addition, a whole Coptic Gnostic tractate is both named for and devoted to Melchizedek. Unfortunately, like many of the other texts, it is in a very fragmentary state (slightly less than half is recoverable, even with reconstruction). In this tractate Melchizedek is not only high priest of God Most High, as in Genesis 14 (e.g., IX.I.15.8-12), but he is directly identified with Jesus Christ, apparently in a pre-incarnate manifestation (e.g., IX.I.18.4-7; 25.1-14). Near the end of the document he defeats the archons in an eschatological battle reminiscent of the descriptions in the Qumran material (IX.I.26.1-14; cf. 13.9-18?).[21]

Finally, it is also worth noting that some of the early church fathers, such as Jerome and Epiphanius, mention groups of heretical Christians ("Melchizedekians") who hold an exalted view of Melchizedek to the point of calling him a god or divine being (*theos*) or identifying him with the Holy Spirit.[22]

This, then, is in outline the flow of the Melchizedek tradition as preserved in our sources. He begins as a king and priest of pre-Davidic Jerusalem and then, some centuries later, is described also as a divine heavenly being, a god (*elohim* or *theos*) who defeats and destroys the forces of evil at the last judgment and delivers souls from the underworld. I submit that the problem of the development of this tradition has never been squarely faced by scholars. How do we get from Melchizedek the priest-king to Melchizedek the god? My proposal is this: his divinity was not invented in the Second Temple period; rather it was suppressed in the Hebrew Bible. In other words, the apparent change from man to god is a matter of suppression of older traditions that were excluded from the biblical canon, not of innovation in the Second Temple literature.

West Semitic Funerary Cults

To support this proposal I must return to the world of West Semitic religion in the pre-Davidic period. In Genesis 14 Melchizedek is presented as a Canaanite king of Jerusalem. I suggest that the relevant question is that of the religious and cultic place of a deceased king in pre-Davidic West Semitic religion. The Ugaritic alphabetic cuneiform texts (most of the texts date from between 1400 and 1200 B.C.E.) are our main source of information on West Semitic religion in this period. The mythological and ritual texts are of special interest here and, in fact, a number them speak directly to our question.

The first of these is the so-called Ugaritic King List (KTU 1.113), a badly broken tablet whose verso side gives a long list of the kings of Ugarit in retrograde order and whose recto once contained a ritual text. Kenneth Kitchen has suggested that the complete tablet originally presented a hymn or ritual requesting favor from Baal for the reigning king and invoking the king's ancestors.[23] The important point to note for our purposes is that the names of the ancestral kings in the list are all preceded by a divine determinative (*'ilu*), which indicates that dead kings were deified in Ugaritic religion (a practice very common in the ancient Near East).

Indeed some striking examples occur in the later West Semitic documents. A Phoenician inscription inscribed on a gold plate, excavated in Pyrgi, Italy, and dating to approximately 500 B.C.E., has been interpreted by Gary Knoppers as a funerary inscription referring to an event "on the day of the burial of the deity" (*bym qbr 'lm*; lines 8-9), apparently a deceased member of the royal family.[24] Another case is found in the much later, more or less West Semitic kingdom of the Nabateans. Our epigraphic evidence indicates that the Nabatean king Obodas I, who ruled approximately 93-85 B.C.E., was deified. He is referred to in Nabatean inscriptions as "Obodas the god" (עבדת אלהא) and "Zeus Obodas" (vocative Ζεῦ Ὀβοδα), and his cult, which involved the Marzeah celebration, is attested into the third century C.E.[25]

There is an interesting parallel to the Ugaritic King List in the Genealogy of the Hammurapi Dynasty, published by J. J. Finkelstein. It begins with a listing of early West Semitic tribal names, which appear to be broken up into three *palûs* or dynasties, culminating in the First Dynasty of Babylon in the first half of the second millennium B.C.E., during which the document appears to have been written. The text concludes with an invitation to these deceased kings and others: (in Finkelstein's translation) "come ye, eat this, drink this, (and) bless Ammiṣaduqa the son of Ammiditana, the king of Babylon." The text appears to have been composed for use in the *kispum* ritual, a Mesopotamian ceremony in honor of dead royal ancestors, in which said ancestors were invoked, fed, and propitiated.[26] The parallels between the Amorite genealogy and the Ugaritic King List are striking: both give a list of royal ancestors ending apparently with the current dynasty, and both conclude with a ritual. It is probable that the Ugaritic King List was also related to some form of the *kispum* ritual.

The second Ugaritic document, generally known as the Ugaritic Funerary Text (RS 34.126), is in some ways closely related to the king list. Though well preserved, it is philologically very difficult.[27] This document describes itself as a "book of the sacrifice of darkness" and begins with a series of invocations of the *rapi'ū 'artsi* ("hale ones of the underworld," or the like) or *rapi'ūma qadmiyyūma* ("the ancient hale ones"), who are also called "the departed ones of Didanu" (lines 1-12). Four of these *rapi'ūma* are summoned by name, followed by two recently deceased kings, Ammi-tamru and Niqmaddu. Next (lines 13-17) is a very obscure ritual lamentation involving the throne of Niqmaddu. Then the sun goddess Shapshu, who has strong underworld connections elsewhere in Ugaritic literature, is invoked (lines 18-26). Seven offerings are then made and a blessing is invoked over the living king Ammurapi, his family, and the whole city of Ugarit (lines 27-34).

This mortuary ritual gives us a great deal of important information. First, it shows that the divine deceased kings had a significant role in the royal cult of Ugarit. The specific occasion of this particular text is uncertain, but it may be the funeral rite for Ammurapi's father, Niqmaddu, who is the last deceased king mentioned. Second, it shows that the Ugaritic royal cult involved very ancient pre-Ugaritic kings as well as the previous kings of Ugarit. The first group of deceased ancestors mentioned, the "departed ones of Didanu," is also associated, in the form Ditanu, with the Ugaritic patriarch Kirta in the Kirta epic (*CTA* 15.3.2-4, 13-15) and appears in at least one other rather obscure context in an Ugaritic text.[28] The name Ditanu is found in a traditional list of West Semitic ancestors common to the Genealogy of the Hammurapi Dynasty and the Assyrian King List. Kitchen tries to date this eponymous ancestor to approximately 2160 B.C.E.[29] It is perhaps more prudent simply to assign the tribal group

Didanu to roughly the end of the third millennium. The name appears as a tribal designation beginning in the Ur III period and appears to represent an important West Semitic group west of the Euphrates that was parallel to, rather than a subset of, the tribal group MAR.TU or Amurrum, from which we get the term Amorite.[30] In any case, it is likely that the four figures named as part of this group in our Ugaritic text are pre-Ugaritic kings of the Didanu tribe.

Third, it shows that deceased and presumably divinized kings were considered, at least eventually, to have entered the ranks of the so-called *rapi'ūma*, which I have translated, on the basis on etymology rather than usage, as the "hale ones." The same word appears in biblical Hebrew as *repha'îm* and refers in some cases to the giant inhabitants of Canaan before the Israelite conquest and in other cases to the ghosts of the dead. The word is found many times in the Ugaritic texts, but its exact meaning is still debated. As far as I am aware, all commentators accept that some of the *rapi'ūma* mentioned in the funerary text are deceased royal ancestors. Conrad L'Heureux argues that this is a late meaning and that the primary senses of the word were first, a human "aristocratic warrior guild under the patronage of El," and second, a group of gods. Both groups participated in the, respectively, heavenly and earthly celebration of the Marzeaḥ festival with El.[31] Baruch Margalit has argued for taking the term *rapi'ūma* as originally an early West Semitic tribal designation.[32] Other scholars, such as Marvin Pope and, most recently, J. N. Ford, argue that the *rapi'ūma* at Ugarit are always the divinized and, at least in some cases, royal dead.[33] I find the last position most convincing. That there may indeed be some connection between these dead and certain high gods or living human aristocrats is not to be excluded, but it has not been demonstrated adequately.

All of this is relevant, because the *rapi'ūma* texts are our only source for establishing the kind of afterlife envisioned for the royal dead at Ugarit. The Ugaritic Funerary Text makes clear that the *rapi'ūma* had an existence as underworld deities. The question is whether they also had, at least to some degree, a "beatific" existence, defined by Klaas Spronk as "being forever with God (or the gods) in heaven." Spronk takes a very radical position on this question. He argues that according to Ugaritic religion the *rapi'ūma* arose from the dead each year with Baal during the New Year celebration and feasted with him.[34] It is doubtful that the Ugaritic evidence can actually bear the weight of this whole theory. Nevertheless, the *rapi'ūma* do at times seem to be described as feasting with the gods. In particular, in the complex of texts in CTA 20-22, they are called *'ilāniyyūma* and *'ilūma*, "gods" (and so they are presumably the divinized dead), they are closely associated with the high gods Baal, El, and Anat, they are welcomed by the Ugaritic hero Danel, and they drive their chariots to a seven-day feast.[35] This is fairly strong evidence that the *rapi'ūma* at Ugarit were regarded as having something of a beatific afterlife, at some point, under some circumstances.

A somewhat later Syrian text from the West Semitic religious world is widely cited as further evidence that deceased kings looked forward to some form of beatific afterlife, and has also been compared to the *kispum* ritual. This text, generally known as the Hadad inscription, was written by a certain king Panammu in an Aramaic dialect in the mid-eighth century B.C.E. Panammu describes his own career, which he considers blessed by the gods. He instructs his successor to give proper veneration to the god Hadad, then adds:

> [17]. . . Then let him say, "May [the s]oul (נבש) of Panammu [ea]t with you (Hadad) and may [the s]oul of Panammu dri[nk] with you. May he keep on invoking the soul of Panammu with [18][Had]ad . . . [and may H]e accept it as an offering to Hadad and to El and to RKB'L and to Shemesh . . ."

He continues a bit later:

> [20]. . . if any of my sons shall take hold of the scepter and sit on my throne as king [21]over Y'DY and confirm (his) power and sacrifice [to this Hadad, yet does not invo]ke the name of Hadad, saying, "May the soul of Panammu eat [22]with Hadad and may the soul of Panammu drink with Hadad," he . . . his sacrifice and may He not accept it. And whatever [23]he asks, may Hadad not give (it) to him and may Hadad pour out wrath . . . may He not permit him to eat out of perturbation and may He deprive him of sleep at night and may He give him fear . . .[36]

So at least one Syrian king of the biblical period envisioned an afterlife for himself that involved his feasting with a high god.[37]

To return then to our main topic, we can use the West Semitic evidence as a framework to reconstruct a likely royal cult of Melchizedek in pre-Davidic Jerusalem. Melchizedek would have been a divinized royal ancestor who would have been invoked on occasion in the royal funerary cult. He would have been an underworld deity, but, as one of the royal dead, he would have been pictured as feasting with the heavenly gods, at least under some circumstances.

It is this cult of Melchizedek, I propose, that was absorbed into the Davidic royal cult of the Jerusalem temple, along with the Melchizedekan priesthood. Melchizedek in the Davidic cult would have been invoked and honored as precursor and patron of the Davidic dynasty, just as the much earlier Didanite kings were invoked and honored by the kings of Ugarit. Such an ancestor cult may seem irregular from a post-Deuteronomistic perspective, but it has no necessary conflict with a monotheistic cult that honored Yahweh, the God of Israel, as the high god of the dynasty. Melchizedek would have been seen as a much inferior, albeit quasi-divine, patron.

Conclusion

If we reconstruct such a cult of Melchizedek in the Jerusalem temple, the traces of a divine Melchizedek in the Second Temple period and later make good sense. He was a god in the Davidic royal cult and, hence, a god in the Qumran literature and to the early Christian fringe groups, an immortal figure like the Son of God in Hebrews, and Jesus Christ himself in the Gnostic Melchizedek tractate. As a divinized dead king he would have been pictured by the pre-exilic royal cult as an underworld divinity who also had a beatific afterlife, at least in some circumstances. The balance for the later Melchizedek is a bit different, but the same elements are present. He is basically a heavenly figure but still has strong underworld connections. He sentences the wicked divine beings to death in the Qumran Melchizedek text, redeems souls from the underworld in the Coptic Gnostic Pistis Sophia tractate, and causes his enemies to be swallowed up by Hades in the Story of Melchizedek.

Why, then, is there no trace of Melchizedek the god in the Hebrew Bible? Simply because the literature of pre-exilic Israel passed through the hands of the Deuteronomistic school, the editors of the book of Deuteronomy and the Deuteronomistic History. Funerary cults were strictly forbidden by this group, whose monotheism was extremely rigorous. An object lesson was also made of King Saul of Israel, who received severe condemnation in 1 Samuel 28 for calling up the shade or *elohim* of the prophet Samuel. Any attempt to communicate with the dead was utterly proscribed and necromancy was listed among sins that are considered by the Deuteronomists to be "abominable practices" before God (Deut 18:9-12). It is not surprising that all references to the cult of Melchizedek were suppressed in the biblical canon.

Thus, Melchizedek was allowed to remain in the Hebrew Bible only as a human priest and king and the patron of a Davidic priesthood. Nevertheless, Melchizedek the god survived in the apocalyptic, esoteric, and gnostic transformations of the royal cult, in which he became an angelic redeemer figure.

Notes

1. For bibliography and a summary of scholarship see G. J. Wenham, *Genesis 1-15* (Waco, Texas: 1987), 301-22.
2. E. A. Speiser, *Genesis* (Garden City, N.Y.: 1964), 99-109. For a critique of Speiser's position see N. 4 below.
3. Van Seters, *Abraham in History and Tradition* (New Haven/London: 1975), 296-308. For a critique of Van Seters's overall approach in his publications see Z. Zevit, "'Clio, I Presume.' Expanded Review of *In Search of History* by J. Van Seters," *BASOR* 260 (1985): 71-82.
4. J. A. Emerton, "Some False Clues in the Study of Genesis XIV," *VT* 21 (1971): 24-47; "The Riddle of Genesis XIV," *VT* 21 (1971): 403-39. Emerton's position is criticized by Van Seters in the reference in N. 3 above.
5. It is perhaps worth mentioning here that the cult of *['ē]l qōnê 'arṣ*, "El creator of the earth," appears to be attested on an ostracon containing a dedicatory blessing. This ostracon was discovered in Jerusalem and dates from the Iron Age (8th-7th centuries B.C.E.). Thus the cult of El was found in Jerusalem. See P. D. Miller, "El, the Creator of Earth," *BASOR* 239 (1980): 43-46.
6. For the application of the concepts "epic" and "epic theme" to the Pentateuchal literature see F. M. Cross, "The Epic Traditions of Early Israel: Epic Narrative and the Reconstruction of Early Israelite Institutions," in *The Poet and the Historian: Essays in Literary and Historical Biblical Criticism*. Ed. R. E. Friedman (HSS 26; Chico, CA.: 1983): 13-39; and R. S. Hendel, *The Epic of the Patriarch: The Jacob Cycle and the Narrative Traditions of Canaan and Israel* (HSM 42; Atlanta, GA.: 1987).
7. J. A. Fitzmyer, "'Now This Melchizedek . . .' (Heb 7:1)," in *Essays on the Semitic Background of the New Testament* (SBLSBS 5; n.p.: Scholars Press: 1974), 221-43, esp. 227-33.

8. F. L. Horton Jr., *The Melchizedek Tradition: A Critical Examination of the Sources to the Fifth century A.D. and in the Epistle to the Hebrews* (SNTSMS 30; Cambridge: 1976), 48-50.

9. Emerton, "The Riddle of Genesis XIV," (N. 4) 412-13.

10. For bibliography and discussion see L. C. Allen, *Psalms 101-150* (WBC 21; Waco, TX: 1983), 78-87. For a recent statement of another view, that the poem was composed in the Hasmonean era, see M. C. Astour, "Melchizedek (person)," *ABD* IV 684-86. The argument that an acrostic of the name Simon (Maccabeus) is to be found in this psalm has not been widely accepted (see Allen, above).

11. Horton, *The Melchizedek Tradition* (N. 8), 45-48.

12. F. M. Cross, *Canaanite Myth and Hebrew Epic: Essays in the History of the Religion of Israel* (Cambridge: 1973), 229-37.

13. `11QMelchizedek was first published by A. S. Van Der Woude in "Melchisedek als himmlische Erlösergestalt in den neugefundenen escha tologischen Midraschim aus Qumran Höhle XI," *Oudtestamentische Studiën* 14 (1965): 354-73. The text was reexamined and republished by E. Puech in "Notes sur le manuscrit del XIQMelchîsédeq," *RQ* 12 (1987): 483-512, which includes a drawing of the fragments on pp. 486-87. For additional bibliography see Puech's study, pp. 284 nn. 2-4. An especially helpful edi tion, by P. J. Kobelski, is found in *Melchizedek and Melchireša'*; (CBQMS 10; Washington DC: 1981), 3-23. The transcription given in N. 14 below is based on the photograph published in the editio princeps, with some help from Puech's drawing, and is provisional and fairly conservative. I was unable to obtain a copy of the better photograph, PAM 43.979, in time to consult it for this article. The passages relevant for my discussion here are either well preserved or can be reconstructed with confidence.

14. Hebrew text:

6. . . . :הדבר הזה

7. בשבוע היובל הראישון אחר תשׁ[ע]ת ה[יו]בלים ויׄום הכפ[ו]רים ה[וא]ה סׄו[ף ה]יו[ב]ל ה[ע]אשירי

8. לכפר בו על כול בני [אל ו]אנש[י] גׄורל מל[ו]כי צדק]וׄם עלי[המ]ה התן]לׄם[ ]ותמה כיא

9. הואה הקץ לשנת הרצון למלכי צד[ק ממם]]ם קדשי אל לממשׁלת משפט כאשר כתוב

10. עליו בשירי דויד אשר אמר אלוהים [נ]צ̇ב בעׄ[ד]ת אל]ב̇קורב אלוהים ישפוט ועליו אמ[ר] עׄליה

11. למרום שובה אל ידין עמים. . .

23. [   ] [במשפטי]ן] אל כאשׄר כתׄוב עליו [אומר לציׄ]ון מלך אלוהׄיך] ציׄׄון ה[י]אה

24. [   ] מקים הברית הסרים מלכת] בד[ר]ך העם ואל[ו]ה[י]ך הואה

25. [   ] מלכי צדק אשר יצי[ל]מה מ[י]ד בליעל ואשר אמר והעברתמה שופ[ר בׄ]כׄו̇ל ארׄ[ץ

15. For bibilography and a discussion of the ancient Near Eastern background of Psalm 82 see M. E. Tate, *Psalms 51-100* (WBC 20; Dallas, TX: 1990), 328-41. For reasons that will become clear below, I do not

think that the association of the *elohim* of Psalm 82 with death was lost on the author of 11QMelchizedek.

16. C. Newsom, *Songs of the Sabbath Sacrifice: A Critical Edition* (HSS 27; Atlanta: 1985). Newsom's tentative evaluation of the contents of this manuscript is on pp. 126-27. Fragments 11 and 22 are presented and discussed on pp. 133-34 and 143-44, pls. II-III. It is interesting to note that fragments of an account of the final judgment are found in another manuscript of this work (4Q402, fragments 1 and 4, in Newsom's edition, pp. 148-50, 154-62, pl. III). These fragments seem to have belonged to the fourth and fifth songs of the work, respectively. I hope to discuss in a future study the accounts from Qumran and elsewhere of the participation of Melchizedek/Michael in the eschatological battle.

17. Second Book of Jeu, chs. 45-46. See C. Schmidt and V. Macdermot (eds.), *The Books of Jeu and the Untitled Text in the Bruce Codex* (NHS XIII; Leiden: 1978), 142-49. For a recent discussion of the Coptic Gnostic texts that mention Melchizedek see B. A. Pearson, "The Figure of Melchizedek in Gnostic Literature," in *Gnosticism, Judaism, and Egyptian Christianity* (Studies in Antiquity and Christianity 5; Minneapolis, MN.: 1990), 108-23.

18. Pistis Sophia, book I, chs. 25-26. See C. Schmidt and V. Macdermot (eds.), *Pistis Sophia* (NHS IX; Leiden: 1978), 68-75.

19. Pistis Sophia, book III, chs. 128-29 (Schmidt and Macdermot, *Pistis Sophia* [N. 18] 648-53).

20. Pistis Sophia, book IV, ch. 140 (Schmidt and Macdermot, *Pistis Sophia* [N. 18] 726-29). Cf. book III, chs. 112, 131; book IV, ch. 139 (Schmidt and Macdermot, *Pistis Sophia* [N. 18] 572-83, 664-73, 718-25). I have omitted the italics in the translation from this edition, which indicate Greek words embedded in the Coptic text. Zorokothora or Melchizedek is also mentioned in book II, ch. 86 and book IV, ch. 136 (Schmidt and Macdermot, *Pistis Sophia* [N. 18] 382-93, 706-707).   The name Zorokothora appears to be a meaningless *nomen barbarum* (Pearson, "The Figure of Melchizedek" [N. 17] 114 n. 36). It appears with different spellings in two Coptic magical texts. See M. Meyer and R. Smith (eds.), *Ancient Christian Magic: Coptic Texts of Ritual Power* (San Francisco, CA: 1994), 91, 284, 391.

21. B. A. Pearson et al., *Nag Hammadi Codices IX and X* (NHS 15; Leiden: 1981), 19-85.

22. Horton, *Melchizedek Tradition* (N. 8) 87-114; Pearson, *Nag Hammadi Codices IX and X* (N. 21) 38-40. Another text may bear on this discussion. The Story of Melchizedek, preserved in Greek and daughter translations and composed in its extant form in late antiquity, retells the biblical story of the encounter between Abraham and Melchizedek. This episode is prefaced by a life of Melchizedek that borrows Jewish traditions about

Abraham and applies them to Melchizedek. In one of these traditions, found in the Apocalypse of Abraham 7-8, Abraham argues with his father Terah over idolatry, then leaves his father, who along with his house is promptly consumed by divine fire from heaven. In the Story of Melchizedek, after Melchizedek's town performs a massive sacrifice of children, including his own brother, Melchizedek prays "'that as many as were present at the sacrifice of my brother Melchi, may Hades come and swallow them up.' And God heard Melchizedek, and immediately the earth gaped open and swallowed them . . ." When Melchizedek is made the hero of the story, divine vengeance comes from Hades rather than heaven. This change seems to support his special relationship with the underworld. For the text see S. E. Robinson, "The Apocryphal Story of Melchizedek," *JSJ* 18 (1987): 26-39, esp. 29-30, 31-32. The quotation is on p. 31. The Apocalypse of Abraham is translated by R. Rubinkiewicz and H. G. Lunt in *OTP* 1, 681-705. It is also interesting to note that in 2 Enoch 71-73 Melchizedek is a priestly redeemer figure who was born from his mother's body after her death. See the translation of 2 Enoch by F. I. Anderson in *OTP* 1, 91-221, esp. 204-13.

23. K. A. Kitchen, "The King List of Ugarit," *UF* 9 (1977) 131-42, esp. 139-40. For further discussion and bibliography see T. J. Lewis, *Cults of the Dead in Ancient Israel and Ugarit* (HSM 39; Atlanta, GA.: 1989), 47-52.

24. G. N. Knoppers, "'The God in His Temple': The Phoenician Text from Pyrgi as a Funerary Inscription," *JNES* 51 (1992): 105-20.

25. A. Negev et al., "Obodas the God," *IEJ* 36 (1986): 56-60, pl. 2b. For the Nabateans and king Obodas I, see D. F. Graf, "Nabateans," *ABD* IV 970-73.

26. J. J. Finkelstein, "The Genealogy of the Hammurapi Dynasty," *JCS* 20 (1966): 95-118. The quotation is on p. 97.

27. For discussion and bibliography see Lewis, *Cults of the Dead* (N. 23): 5-52. Excellent photographs of the text have been published by W. T. Pitard in "RS 34.126: Notes on the Text," *Maarav* 4 (1987): 75-86, 111-55.

28. D. Pardee, "Visiting Ditanu: The Text of RS 24.272," *UF* 15 (1983): 127-40.

29. Kitchen, "The King List of Ugarit" (N. 23): 142.

30. G. Buccellati, *The Amorites of the Ur III Period* (Publicazioni del seminario di semitista richerche 1; Naples, Italy: 1966), 235-36, 243-44, 333.

31. C. E. L'Heureux, *Rank among the Canaanite Gods: El, Ba'al and the Repha'im* (HSM 21; Missoula, MT.: 1979), 109-230; "The Ugaritic and Biblical Rephaim," *HTR* 67 (1974): 265-74. The quotation is on p. 272 of the latter study.

32. B. Margalit, "The Geographical Setting of the AQHT story and Its Ramifications," in *Ugarit in Retrospect: Fifty Years of Ugarit and Ugaritic*, ed. G. D. Young (Winona Lake, IN.: 1981), 131-58, especially 151-58.

33. M. H. Pope, "Notes on the Rephaim Texts from Ugarit," in *Essays on the Ancient Near East in Memory of Jacob Joel Finkelstein*. Ed. M. de Jong Ellis (Memoirs of the Connecticut Academy of Arts and Sciences XIX; Hamden, CT.: 1977), 163-82; "The Cult of the Dead at Ugarit," in *Ugarit in Retrospect*, ed. Young (N. 32), 159-79; J. N. Ford, "The 'Living Rephaim' of Ugarit: Quick or Defunct?" *UF* 24 (1992): 73-101.

34. K. Spronk, *Beatific Afterlife in Ancient Israel and in the Ancient Near East* (AOAT 219; Kevalaer: 1986), 145-206. The quotation is on p. 85. For critical reviews of this volume see M. S. Smith and E. M. Bloch-Smith, "Death and Afterlife in Ugarit and Israel," *JAOS* 108 (1988): 277-84; K. van der Toorn, "Funerary Rituals and Beatific Afterlife in Ugaritic Texts and in the Bible," *BO* 48 (1991): 40-66.

35. Again, Pitard has published superb photographs of these texts (taken under the auspices of the West Semitic Research Project of the University of Southern California) in "A New Edition of the 'Rāpi'ūma' Texts: KTU 1.20-22," *BASOR* 285 (1992): 33-77. He includes transcriptions of the fragments, along with an epigraphic commentary. Pitard does not include a translation or philological commentary and refrains from suggesting an overall interpretation of the texts.

36. *KAI* 214.17-18, 20-23. With one exception I have translated the passage as transcribed in *KAI*. The text is badly damaged and other readings and restorations have been proposed, but none of them affect the substance of my argument here. In line 21 I restore ולא, "and yet does not," with J. C. L. Gibson, *Textbook of Syrian Semitic Inscriptions*, vol. II, *Aramaic Inscriptions* (Oxford: 1975), 66-67, 74. The lack of negation before the following verb יאמר is difficult (cf. *KAI* p. 220), but this restoration seems to make the best sense in the context. On this passage see also J. C. Greenfield, "Un rite religieux araméen et ses parallèles," *RB* 80 (1973): 46-52.

37. J. F. Healy, basing his case on a critical analysis of some of the work of Mitchell Dahood, has argued that some Psalms (especially Ps 21) reflect a royal ideology of beatific afterlife for the Judean king. See "The Immortality of the King: Ugarit and the Psalms," *Or* 53 (1984): 245-54.

The Face of Jacob in the Moon: Mystical Transformations of an Aggadic Myth

Elliot R. Wolfson

As in other religious cultures, in traditional Jewish law and lore the moon occupies a central position. With respect to the former, one need only mention the obvious fact that the Jewish calendar is lunar. Within the constructed edifice of rabbinic halakhah the specific commandment of sanctification of the moon, *qiddush ha-levanah*, assumes a dispropor- tionate weight inasmuch as the liturgical demands of each day revolve around the proper determination of the lunar cycle. The weightiness of this obligation is captured in the hyperbolic utterance attributed to R. Yohanan: "He who blesses the new month on time it is as if he received the face of the *Shekhinah*."[1] The "as if" construction is employed in rabbinic texts with the obvious intent of emphasizing or even exagger- ating a point. But it is also the case that in rabbinic rhetoric this construction denotes the comparison of dissimiliar things. The equation thus renders two seemingly disparate matters equivalent by bringing them into an homologous relationship. Simply put, the "as if" formula signifies bond and disjunction in one. Applying this to the specific case at hand, the equating of the act of blessing the moon (*birkat ha-levanah*) and receiving the face of the divine Presence (*qabbalat pene ha-shekhinah*) does not suggest that for rabbinic authorities the ontological division between God and the moon is blurred, but rather that the moon is so significant in the life of halakhic Judaism that sanctifying it bestows upon an individual the same merit as seeing the face of the divine Presence. The mythic correlation of the blessing of the moon and the reception of the face of the Presence gave rise to specific religious conduct, as may be seen, for example, in the statement attributed to Abbaye in the Babylonian Talmud to the effect that the blessing is recited in a standing position since it involves the act of *qabbalat pene ha- shekhinah*.[2] The supreme value accorded the rite of sanctification of the moon stems from the fact that this particular act is the temporal basis for all other religious activities. Indeed, according to another dictum attrib- uted to R. Yohanan, the sole purpose for the creation of the moon was to sanctify new months and new years since the sun alone was sufficient to illuminate the physical universe.[3]

Sacred time in Judaism is determined by the revolution of lunar rhythms.[4] In this regard Judaism reflects an element of human experience expressed in diverse religious cultures: the very cycle of life and death is tied in an intrinsic way to the moon. It is likely that the most primordial measurement of time as a recurrent sequence of creation and destruction is patterned after the periodic waxing and waning of the lunar disc. Time in its most primitive sense is marked by a *circulus mythologicus*, the cyclical appearing and disappearing disclosed by the phases of the moon. The symbolism of the moon, therefore, valorizes for *homo religiosus* the transient and ephemeral quality of human existence, for in the nature of the cosmic process birth culminates with death, but death is followed by rebirth. In that sense we can speak of the moon as the archetype of cosmic becoming, which is connected in religious consciousness with a mythic rite of passage.[5] In classical Judaism, however, salvation does not consist of deliverance from the cycle of time, as one finds in some other religions, but rather by the ongoing participation in the life of ritual that reflects the movement of the lunar dance. The reenacment of sacred time in traditional Judaism, a process that ensues from the essentially lunar character of the liturgical calendar, does not entail the overcoming of historical time through myth and ritual.[6] On the contrary, ritual time is both cyclical and linear, for the circular pattern of repetition reenacted through ritual is linked to specific moments in Israel's linear history.[7] The convergence of liturgical time and historical time, I submit, is encapsulated in the symbol of the moon, which represents the paradoxical union of two polar currents, linearity and circularity.

With respect to traditional Jewish lore it should be noted that time and again rabbinic sources emphasize the special connection between the Jews and the moon. Many texts could be cited to illustrate this point, but in this context I mention only one representative example. The ontic connection of the moon and the Jews is epitomized in the prayer recited during the blessing of the moon first mentioned in the Babylonian Talmud: "To the moon [God] says, 'Renew yourself, crown of splendor, for those who have been carried since birth,'[8] for in the future they will be renewed like it, to glorify their Creator for the sake of the glory of His kingdom."[9] Significantly, the moon is here described metaphorically as the "crown of splendor," *'ateret tif'eret*. Bracketing the question of whether or not there is contained in this metaphor a residual of a mythical notion regarding the hypostatization of the moon as the divine crown,[10] it is evident that this philological resonance served as the impetus for precisely such an interpretation in a variety of medieval Jewish mystical texts to be discussed below.

The linkage of the fate of the Jews to the moon is based, moreover, on the implicit and at times explicit characterization of the moon as feminine. Although the feminine character of the moon is implied already in Joseph's dream wherein the image of the moon metaphorically represents his mother,[11] the more elaborate depiction of the moon as female in Late Antique Judaism seems to be due to Hellenistic influence.[12] The supposedly effeminate aspect of the moon underlies the lunar symbolization of Israel inasmuch as the Jewish people occupied a socially and politically inferior status and, given the more or less standard gender stereotypes in Late Antiquity and the early Middle Ages, the female typically represents the weak, passive, and dominated force. The feminization of the moon is apparent in the rabbinic mythologem regarding the diminution of the moon and particularly in those aggadic passages that speak of the compensation of the moon's reduction in size as consisting of its becoming a symbol of Israel and the pious whereas the sun represents Esau and the wicked.[13] The symbolic conception of the ecclesia of Israel in terms of the lunar image enabled the rabbis to invert the hierarchical relations in the socio-political realm. That is, when judged from the standpoint of the material world Israel is weak vis-à-vis the other nations, especially Rome or Christianity identified as the biblical Edom, but in terms of the otherworldly values the Jews well outshine the other nations, a theme exegetically connected to the eschatological hope expressed in Isa. 30:26. Precisely this point underlies the following rabbinic pericope that is linked redactionally to the verse, "God made the two great lights, the greater light to dominate the day and the lesser light to dominate the night, and the stars" (Gen. 1:16):

> R. Levi said in the name of R. Yose bar Ilai: It is appropriate that the big one counts according to the big [light] and the small according to the small [light]. Esau counts according to the sun, which is big, and Jacob according to the moon, which is small. R. Nahman said: This is a good sign, Esau counts according to the sun, which is big. Just as this sun rules in the day but does not rule at night, so too Esau has this world but not the world-to-come. Jacob counts by the moon, which is small. Just as this moon rules in the night and day, so Jacob possesses this world and the world-to-come. Furthermore, R. Nahman said: As long as the

light of the big one exists the light of the small one is not known. When
the light of the big one sets the light of the small one is known. Thus, as
long as the light of Esau exists the light of Jacob is not known; when the
light of Esau sets then the light of Jacob will be known, as it is written,
"Arise, shine, for your light has dawned" (Isa. 60:1).[14]

The lunarization of Israel, therefore, represents a distinct departure from
a common element in the structure of heroic mythologies in which the
powerful figure is assimilated to the sun.[15] In the rabbinic texts, by
contrast, what appears to be physically strong is associated with what is
spiritually weak and what appears to be physically weak is spiritually
strong. When the march of history is viewed eschatologically, lunar
Israel triumphs over solar Edom.[16] The cycle of birth and death associated with the moon symbolically represents the assurance that Israel will
be redeemed after years of exile and servitude.[17] According to another
talmudic passage, it is more precisely the endurance of the Davidic
kingdom that is linked to the image of the rejuvenated moon, a motif
most probably suggested by the connection of the moon and David
made in Ps. 89:38.[18] The eschatolgical valence accorded the moon in
traditional rabbinic lore is underscored in the following comment of the
fourteenth-century Spanish exegete and homilist, Judah ben Solomon
Campanton: "The kingdom of David is hidden in exile as the moon
breaks forth and it is hidden (*ha-levanah nifretset we-nisteret*), and this is
the matter of Perez and Zerah, which you should comprehend,[19] and the
matter of their saying in the renewal of the moon, 'May David, king of
Israel, endure forever.' Therefore there is no king except from David and
this is the king Messiah, may he be revealed speedily."[20]

The particular motif that I wish to concentrate on in this study, the
face of Jacob in the moon, is a more specific application of this larger
symbolic nexus. As Louis Ginzberg already intimated, this aggadic
motif may be referred to as the Jewish version of the myth of the man in
the moon.[21] The association of Jacob and the moon is expressed in
classical rabbinic sources as we have seen already in the aforecited
passage from *Genesis Rabbah*. Semantically this connection is buttressed
by the use of the word *qatan*, "small," to refer to the moon (Gen. 1:16) and
to Jacob (Gen. 32:11; Amos 7:2). According to one talmudic passage, a
righteous person receives the epithet *ha-qatan*, "the small one," on
account of the moon, the "smaller light," *ha-ma'or ha-qatan*. The specific
names mentioned in support of this general claim are Jacob, Samuel, and
David.[22] In different rabbinic sources other biblical figures are compared

to the moon, including Aaron and Joshua,[23] but no figure received as much attention in this regard as Jacob. Indeed, there is an essential connection between Jacob and the moon insofar as this symbolic linkage is rooted in the more general imaging of Israel in terms of lunar symbolism.[24]

The relation of Jacob and the moon was greatly expanded in medieval Jewish sources. The impact of this mythic conception can be seen, for instance, in a substantial change in one of the liturgical formulations recited after the blessing on the moon. In *Masekhet Soferim*, the apocryphal talmudic work generally thought to have originated in eighth-century Palestine, the form of this passage is *barukh bor'ekha, barukh yotserekha, barukh meqaddeshekha*, "Blessed be the One who created you, blessed be the One who formed you, blessed be the One who sanctified you."[25] By contrast, in various halakhic compendia of the thirteenth and fourteenth centuries, for example, the *'Orhot Hayyim* of Aaron ben Jacob ha-Kohen of Lunel,[26] the *Tur* of Jacob ben Asher,[27] and *Sefer Abudarham* of David ben Joseph Abudarham,[28] we find evidence for a variant formulation than the one preserved in *Masekhet Soferim*. According to this variant the liturgical refrain is *barukh yotserekha, barukh 'osekha, barukh qonekha, barukh bor'ekha*, "Blessed be the One who formed you, blessed be the One who made you, blessed be the One who shaped you, and blessed be the One who created you," for the first letters of the four words, *yotserekha, 'osekha, qonekha*, and *bor'ekha*, spell the name *ya'aqov*. This variant is obviously a ritualized concretization of the mythic identification of Jacob and the moon. So powerful was this identification that some later authorities upheld the liturgical order *yotserekha, 'osekha, qonekha*, and *bor'ekha*, and rejected the new order, *'osekha, yotserekha, bor'ekha*, and *qonekha*, which clearly reflected the hierarchical chain of the four worlds in standard kabbalistic ontology, *'asiyyah* (making), *yetsirah* (formation), *beri'ah* (creation), and *'atsilut* (emanation).[29] Not even the attribution of this alternative formulation to the charismatic figure of Isaac Luria could totally supplant the older tradition since the latter encapsulated the potent mythical association of Jacob and the moon.[30] The point is epitomized in the following comment of Isaiah Horowitz:

> "Jacob then got fresh shoots of polar" (Gen. 30:37), [the expression *maqqal livneh*] alludes to the moon (*levanah*), for the two countenances are joined as one. Then the face of Jacob is engraved in the moon. Thus [the blessing is fixed] *barukh yotserekha, barukh 'osekha, barukh qonekha, barukh bor'ekha*, [which spells] according to the first letters *ya'aqov.*

There four [expressions] allude to the chain of [the four worlds] *'atsilut,*
beri'ah, yetsirah, and *'asiyyah.*…Thus *'osekha* alludes to the world of
'asiyyah, yotserekha to the world of *yetsirah, bor'ekha* to the world of
beri'ah, and *qonekha* to the world of *'atsilut.* The reason that this is not
mentioned according to the order [of the four worlds] is so that it could
allude to the name of Jacob.[31]

The symbolic connection of Jacob and the moon evolves in medieval
Jewish mystical sources into a mythological conception of the image of
Jacob engraved on the moon, a conception that is based on another motif
widely attested in earlier midrashic, liturgical, and mystical sources: the
image of Jacob engraved on the throne of glory.[32] The point is underscored in the following marginal note on the blessing for the new moon
in one of the manuscript witnesses of the commentary on the liturgy of
Eleazar of Worms: *"Barukh yotserekha, barukh 'osekha, barukh qonekha,*
barukh bor'ekha, and the sign [made of the first letter of these four words]
is *ya'aqov,* for his form is engraved upon the throne and the moon."[33]
Although this notation is not the work of Eleazar himself, it can be
illustrated from other textual evidence that the conflation of the two
mythic depictions first occurs in the esoteric writings of the Rhineland
Jewish Pietists of the twelfth and thirteenth centuries. Thus, for example,
in the commentary on the forty-two-letter name of God, falsely attributed to Hai Gaon and included in Eleazar's *Sefer ha-Hokhmah,* we read as
follows: *"PZQ* is numerically equal to *yofi ha-nikhbad* ('glorious beauty')
as well as the numerology of *'al kiss'o* ('upon His throne') as well as *'al*
levanah ('upon the moon') for He sits on His throne and the beauty of His
Presence (*yofi shekhinato*) illuminates the image of Jacob that is engraved
on His throne in the image of the moon."[34] Two aggadic traditions are
here combined—one concerning the image of Jacob engraved on the
throne and the other concerning that image engraved in the moon. The
word *PZQ,* one of the combinations of the forty-two-letter name of God,
is numerically equal to the expression *yofi ha-nikhbad* ("glorious beauty"),
i.e., both equal 187, which is also the numerical equivalence of the
expressions *'al kiss'o,* "upon His throne" and *'al levanah,* "upon the
moon." The use of the term *yofi* here reflects the technical connotation of
that term in the *Hekhalot* literature and hence its signification is the
luminous beauty of the enthroned form of the Presence.[35] The latter two
expressions, *'al kiss'o* and *'al levanah,* convey the notion that the luminous
splendor of the *Shekhinah*—the glorious beauty—shines upon the image
of Jacob that is said to be engraved upon the throne in the image of the
moon.[36]

The Pietistic conception is expressed succinctly in the fifteenth century by Naftali Herz Treves whose commentary on the prayer book, *Mal'ah ha-'Arets De'ah*, is a repository of citations and paraphrases from Eleazar's writings, other Pietistic and mystical texts, including works of theosophic kabbalah. Thus, reflecting on the hymn *'el 'adon 'al kol ha-ma'asim*, recited during the *yotser* of the Sabbath morning service, Treves writes: "The form of the moon is in the throne and that is the form of Jacob…'and He diminished,' *we-hiqtin*, the form of Jacob the small one (*ha-qatan*) who is called according to her name." In a second passage from this work, the author comments on the blessing on the moon: "The form of Jacob is in the moon, and it alludes to the Community of Israel that is under the throne of glory." In this context Treves has appropriated a more standard kabbalistic symbol for the divine Presence, the Community of Israel, to designate the image of Jacob engraved on the moon. However, as will be seen below, already in the Pietistic sources one may assume that the image of Jacob, the moon, and the throne, all refer to the divine Presence and thus they function hermeneutically in a way that is identical to the kabbalistic symbols.

The full mythical significance of this text can only be appreciated if one bears in mind that in the esoteric theosophy of the German Pietists the image of Jacob engraved on the throne is transformed into a mythical symbol for the lower, feminine glory that is also identified as the cherub or throne upon which the upper, masculine glory sits. The moment of enthronement is treated by Pietistic authors as one of the most recondite doctrines for it involves a sacred union between the upper and lower glories. This union is depicted as well in terms of the relationship between the *Shekhinah* and the image of Jacob, related especially to a passage in *Hekhalot Rabbati* that characterizes the erotic embrace of the glory and that engraved image. Against this background one can appreciate the mythic proportions of the symbolic correlation of the moon and the image of Jacob. That is to say, in the esoteric teaching cultivated by the Pietists, the moon assumes a hypostatic character for it symbolizes the lower divine glory, the visible feminine Presence vis-à-vis the upper invisible glory. The symbolic connection made between the *Shekhinah*, the moon, and the image of the throne is especially highlighted in the following passage in Eleazar's commentary on the secrets of the liturgy:

> It is said in Sanhedrin [42a]: He who sanctifies the moon it is as if he received the face of the *Shekhinah*. Therefore we leap as [it is written] "the creatures ran to and fro like the appearance of lightning" (Ezek.

1:14). Therefore we bless the moon until midnight when her blemish is filled[37] and the rainbow is formed. The throne is [in the shape of the letter] *kaf*, thus is [it written] "the appearance of the splendor like the appearance of the image of the throne." "The secret of the Lord is with those who fear Him" (Ps. 25:14).[38]

In this passage, as one finds in many other passages in his corpus,[39] Eleazar builds on the idea first expressed in the quasi-mystical work, *Midrash 'Otiyyot de-R. 'Aqiva'*, the throne is symbolically associated with the letter *kaf*, obviously based on the linguistic fact that the Hebrew word for throne, *kisse'*, begins with that letter.[40] In the Pietistic writings, however, the symbolization of the throne by the *kaf* signifies a decidedly feminine character.[41] The throne is hypostasized as a feminine potency in the divine realm. It should be noted that the female hypostatization of the throne is found in earlier Jewish esoteric sources, including most importantly *Hekhalot Rabbati*, as well as other mystical currents more or less contemporary with the Pietists. It is evident, therefore, that the Pietists are elaborating on an older motif rather than innovating and creating new symbols. What is new, however, is the further connection of this symbolic nexus with the image of the moon. The association of the moon and the throne is facilitated by the fact that the shape of the lunar crescent is that of the *kaf*, the very letter that symbolizes the throne.[42] As Eleazar explicitly puts it in another one of his writings: "The letter *kaf*: Thus stands the moon for the throne is a circle behind Him like a *kaf*, and it is made like a half moon, the cloud and water surrounds the *Shekhinah*, and so too [concerning] the moon [it is said] 'Dense clouds are around Him' (Ps. 97:2)."[43] For Eleazar the moon has been fully hypostasized; hence, his hyperliteral reading of the rabbinic dictum, "He who blesses the moon it is as if he received the face of the Presence." Blessing the moon results in the receiving of the face of the Presence because the moon symbolizes that Presence.[44] Here we have traversed the sphere of metaphorical discourse and entered the domain of symbolic myth.

The mythic symbolization of the *Shekhinah* as the moon invests new meaning into the ritual of leaping (*riqqud*) before the moon first mentioned in *Masekhet Soferim*. According to that source one is to leap three times facing the moon and repeat three times: "Just as I am leaping before you but I do not touch you so too if some people should leap towards me they should not touch me. 'Terror and dread shall descend upon them' (Exod. 15:16)." The leaping, therefore, is emblematic of the fact that one is spared real harm at the hands of one's enemies. For

Eleazar, by contrast, the leaping is an emulation of the motion of the celestial beasts who bear the throne. To leap before the moon is to assume the posture of those beasts and hence this gesture must be understood as a sign of angelification.[45]

It is likely, moreover, that the leaping motion has implicit sexual overtones insofar as the moon is characterized in explicitly feminine terms.[46] The purpose of leaping before the moon, according to Eleazar of Worms, is to enact the unification of the worshiper and the moon, which in turn emulates the process above whereby the masculine potency unites with the feminine. The *hieros gamos* is intimated in Eleazar's statement, "Therefore we bless the moon until midnight when her blemish is filled and the rainbow is formed." The fullness of the moon represents the feminine in a state of completion, associated more specificaly with sexual union, and the formation of the rainbow is an obvious phallic symbol.[47] The worshiper has an active role in facilitating that union by blessing and leaping before the moon.

Support for my interpretation may be gathered from Eleazar's remark that Judah the Pious would say the verse, "Hark! My beloved! There he comes, leaping over mountains, bounding over hills" (Song of Songs 2:8),[48] when he leapt three times before the moon.[49] One may presume that through the performance of this ritual Judah assumed the persona of the male beloved addressed by the female lover who symbolically represents the *Shekhinah*.[50] Through his leaping, therefore, Judah mimics the leaping above that symbolizes the unification of male and female in the divine pleroma. The secrecy that surrounds this nexus of symbols, underscored by Eleazar's citation of Ps. 25:14 at the end of his explication of the blessing on the moon, is related to the erotic implications that emerge from the feminine quality of the divine hypostasis represented concomitantly as the throne and the moon. One of the salient components of the esoteric teaching of the German Pietists is based on the assumption that there is a sacred union in the divine realm, which is depicted in several ways, but most pervasively in terms of the myths of coronation and enthronement. The esoteric quality of the vision of the divine glory, a central component of the religious life of the Pietist, embraces the erotic union above. I note, parenthetically, that the nexus of eros and vision underlies the following passage in *Sefer Hasidim*: "The hair of a woman is a lewd matter, as it says, 'your hair is like a flock of goats' (Song of Songs 4:1). [He who looks at the hair of a woman] will not merit [to see] 'the hair of His head that is like lamb's wool' (Dan. 7:9). If he is careful not to look at a woman he will see the glory, as it says,

'When your eyes behold the king in his beauty' (Isa. 33:17)."[51] Building on the statement attributed to R. Sheshet in B. Berakhot 24b, "a woman's hair is a lewd matter," the author of *Sefer Hasidim* notes that the punishment for looking at a woman's hair is being denied a vision of the hair of the glory related in the verse from Daniel. The correlation of seeing the divine Presence and abstaining from looking at women is enunciated in a second passage from *Sefer Hasidim*:

> The essential strength of pietism is that, even though [people] insult him, he does not abandon his piety, and his intention is directed to God and he does not look at women whereas others apart from him do look. Thus he merits the abundant goodness that is hidden and his eyes will be satiated by the splendor of the Presence, 'when your eyes behold a king in his beauty' (Isa. 33:17), [that is] whoever does not look at women in their nakedness or at a virgin, as it says, '[I have covenanted with my eyes] not to gaze on a maiden' (Job 31:1)....Every one whose [sexual] impulse does not derive pleasure from lewdness will merit to see the splendor of the Presence in the future.[52]

The very essence of the pietistic lifestyle is here linked to the overcoming of visual temptation.[53] The point is reiterated by Eleazar of Worms in his laws of penitence included in his *Sefer ha-Roqeah*:

> I should not restrain my spirit for the sake of my Creator for even a short while, and I should not take pleasure for even a short while in matters of adultery and impurity. I must accustom my eyes to [not] look at the face of a woman for she is fire[54]....Everyone looks at the face of women, but he does not and this is the worship of the Creator in truth. One must avoid all physical pleasure with women, seeing them, touching them, sitting with them, seeing their lovely garments, hearing their voices in speech or song, speaking with them, whether married or single, with the exception of his wife.[55]

The link between an eschatological vision of the *Shekhinah* and refraining from looking at a woman's nakedness is not a mere rhetorical trope, but rather it is rooted in a mythical conception of the glory that imputes gender (in intensely erotic terms) to the divine. Eleazar's understanding of the ritualistic greeting and blessing of the moon presupposes the unfolding of precisely such a mythic drama. The reception of the face of the *Shekhinah* on the part of the worshiper below signifies a union of man and God, but at the same time the blessing of the individual triggers a process above that results in the union of the masculine and feminine potencies. Although the mystical and theurgical elements are conceptually distinct, experientially they are inseparable.[56]

The motif that I have examined in this study is yet another indication of the phenomenological and textual links connecting the esoteric traditions of the German Pietists and the emerging theosophy of the Provençal and Spanish kabbalists in the twelfth and thirteenth centuries. An especially important text that serves as a bridge connecting the Ashkenazi lore and the kabbalistic symbolism is the following comment of Judah ben Yaqar on the words *motsi' hamah mimeqomah u-levanah mimekhon shivtah* ("He brings forth the sun from its place and the moon from its dwelling") in the standard morning liturgy for Sabbath, *ha-kol yodukha we-ha-kol yeshabbehukha*:

> It says "its place" (*meqomah*) by the sun and "its dwelling" (*mekhon shivtah*) by the moon to allude to the fact that the nations count [days and months] according to the sun... but Israel count according to the moon for the image of Jacob is engraved in it. Even though we have not found in the aggadah that his name or form is engraved in the moon, still it must be said that the moon is called *ma'or qatan* (the "lesser light"), and on account of her name the verse says, "How will Jacob survive? He is so small," *mi yaqum ya'aqov ki qaton hu'* (Amos 7:2). It says in the *Hekhalot*[57] that there is a creature whose name is Israel and engraved upon its forehead is Israel, and it stands in the middle of the firmament, and it says, "Bless the Lord who is blessed." All the archons above respond after it, "Bless the Lord who is blessed forever." Each and everyone of the angels, hosts, and all the camps utters to this creature while standing, "Hear, O Israel, the Lord our God, the Lord is one" (Deut. 6:4). Therefore, it is explained that the creature, whose name is Israel and upon whose forehead is inscribed Israel, sees the moon upon which is engraved the image of Jacob. She is called small (*qatan*) on account of Jacob who is Israel, and the moon draws the name Jacob to her and unites with it, and the moon sits next to the creature. This is [the meaning of the expression] "its dwelling" (*mekhon shivtah*). Similarly, it is written there, "what I do to the visage of Jacob, your father, that is engraved upon the throne of glory, for when you say before the Holy One, blessed be He, 'Holy, holy, holy,' I bend down over it, embrace it, fondle it, and kiss it, and My hands are on My arms." All this is by way of parable and secret (*derekh mashal we-sod*).[58]

This passage accentuates all the mythical and symbolical elements already operative in the writings of the German Pietists. However, one important change is discernible in Judah ben Yaqar, a shift in focus that reflects an approach that became dominant in subsequent kabbalistic literature. Following his Pietistic sources Judah identifies the moon upon which the image of Jacob is engraved with the feminine *Shekhinah*, a symbol that became quite prevalent in subsequent kabbalistic texts.[59] Moreover, in consonance with his sources Judah interprets this aggadic motif in terms of a sacred union in the divine realm. For Judah, however, the focal point of that union is between the moon and the icon of Jacob and not simply between the glory and the moon upon which Jacob's image is engraved. Thus, Judah states explicitly that the moon draws the name of Jacob to her and unites with it. The name "Jacob" symbolizes the celestial angel who is also called Israel insofar as that name is inscribed upon his forehead. The supreme position of that angel is underscored by the fact that the recitation of the traditional confession of monotheism, "Hear, O Israel, the Lord our God is one," is directed to him. It is plausible, although it is not stated explicitly, that Judah ben Yaqar accepted the further identification of the angel named Israel as Metatron. In any event, the union represented by the image of Jacob engraved upon the moon is between the feminine *Shekhinah* and the highest angel.

In subsequent kabbalistic texts the image of Jacob engraved upon the moon symbolizes the unification above between the masculine Jacob and the feminine moon. For example, Todros Abulafia thus comments on the aggadah in B. Hullin 91b regarding the setting of the sun at the death of Jacob:

> The plain meaning of these words in this passage is known, but I will inform you of the hidden secret that is concealed within it. Know that the sun mentioned here is the sun of righteousness in truth that will shine in the future on those who fear God, for they said that the image of the likeness of Jacob is engraved on the sphere of the sun, and there are those who say the sphere of the moon. Everything is true for he is engraved even on the sphere of the sun and this resplendent light shines and emanates upon the light of the moon from the splendor that is opposite her.[60]

According to Todros Abulafia, there is no conflict between the two traditions regarding the location of Jacob's image, for, on the one hand, Jacob is symbolically equivalent to the sun, i.e., both refer to the masculine *Tif'eret*, and, on the other, this emanation shines on the moon, which represents the feminine *Shekhinah*. The synthesis of the two traditions expresses the idea of the sacred unity above.

This very point is articulated in the following relatively early kabbalistic text extant in manuscript:

> That which the rabbis, may their memory be for a blessing, said concerning the image of Jacob engraved upon the moon bears two explanations, but it all amounts to one thing. The rabbis, may their memory be for a blessing, suggested to us in this statement that the efflux that comes to the world from 'Atarah derives from Tif'eret. Therefore they said that the form of Jacob is engraved upon the moon, for Tif'eret is called Jacob inasmuch as it took his portion and the moon is called 'Atarah inasmuch as she is the power of the moon. Or you can say that the light that comes from the moon is from the sun, for the splendor of the sun enters the moon and the moon shines. Therefore they speak of the form of Jacob insofar as it is the power of the moon. Or you can say that the light that comes from the moon is from the sun, for the splendor of the sun enters the moon and the moon shines. Therefore they speak of the form of Jacob insofar as the sun receives from Tif'eret who is called Jacob.[61]

Needless to say, the ritual of birkat ha-levanah was transformed by this change in symbolism. The primary purpose of the blessing of the moon—as related specifically to the image of Jacob engraved upon the moon—was to facilitate the hieros gamos in the Godhead.[62] The profoundly mythical nature of this basic Jewish ritual is duly expressed in the following explanation of the ritual of sanctification of the moon given by the sixteenth-century kabbalist, David ben Solomon ibn Abi Zimra:

> According to the way of secret the rabbis, blessed be their memory, said, "If Israel merited to receive the face of the Shekhinah only one time every month, it would have been enough for them."... You already know that the physical moon and sun, which are visible, are in the pattern of the spiritual sun and moon. Just as the physical moon receives from the light of the sun, and sometimes it is revealed and sometimes hidden, sometimes it is full and sometimes wanting, and it is small in size in relation to the sun... so are the moon and sun in actuality above in the supernal world. Therefore, the ritual of sanctification of the month was given to Israel, [for it is] like the betrothal of the bridegroom and the bride.... Know that by means of sanctifying the moon and the intercalation of the year below the bride who is comprised [of all] above is sanctified and she is joined to her husband, and from this union the new, pure souls of the righteous and pious burst forth into this world as well as the groups of angels of lovingkindness

and mercy…. That the physical moon is in the pattern of the spiritual moon is attested by the fact that if you contemplate the face of the moon when it is full you will see in it something like the form of a human. I asked the sages who gaze upon the stars [concerning this phenomenon] and not one of them knows the reason or explanation. In my opinion it is an allusion to what the rabbis, blessed be their memory, said, "the form of Jacob, our father, is engraved on the throne of glory." The throne is the name of the last attribute, the Matrona, and the form of Jacob is Jacob the elder, the secret of the king who sits on the throne. He dwells in her midst and is united with her, betroths her and illuminates her face. As an allusion to this the form of a human face is inscribed on the physical moon.[63]

The physical phenomenon of apparently seeing a human face in the moon is symbolic of the process above that involves the inscription of Jacob's image upon the moon. Interpreted kabbalistically, this inscription signifies the sacred union of the masculine and the feminine in the Godhead. The attainment of this union, which is symbolically depicted by the aggadic image of Jacob's icon engraved on the moon, is the ultimate mystical intent of the ritualistic blessing of the moon and the sanctification of the month.

Many other texts could have been cited to illustrate the point, but here I will mention specifically two others given their standing as authoritative halakhic works. The erotic implication of the iconic inscription of Jacob's image on the moon is underscored in the gloss of Moses Isserles[64] to the Joseph Karo's *Shulhan 'Arukh, 'Orah Hayyim*, § 426:

> It is customary to say [in the blessing of the moon] "David, king of Israel, may he long live," for his kingship is compared to a moon, and in the future it shall be renewed like it, and the Community of Israel shall again cleave to her husband, who is the Holy One, blessed be He. This may be compared to the moon that is renewed with the sun, as it says, "For the Lord God is sun and shield" (Ps. 84:12). Therefore, they perform acts of joy and they dance in the sanctification of the month like the joy of a wedding.[65]

In a similar vein, Joel Sirkes writes in his commentary, *Bet Hadash*, to the *Tur, 'Orah Hayyim*, § 281:

> It must be explained, moreover, that the form of Jacob is seen in the moon. Therefore, they established in the blessing of the moon, *Barukh yotsrekha* [*barukh 'osekha, barukh qonekha, barukh bor'ekha*], the first letters

are *ya'aqov*. ... Thus, according to this it is said [in the liturgical poem recited on Sabbath, *'el 'adon 'al kol ha-ma'asim] qara' la-shemesh wa-yizrah 'or* ["He called to the sun and it shone forth in light"], for the light of the *Shekhinah* dwells on the splendor of the icon of Jacob whose name is sun (*shemesh*). *Ra'ah we-hitqin tsurat ha-levanah* ["He saw and established the form of the moon"] in order that the light of the sun will strike and illuminate the moon, so that by means of this the form of Jacob will take shape in the moon, for the moon receives its light from the sun that is verily the form of Jacob.

According to Sirkes, reflecting a longstanding kabbalistic tradition, the sun and the moon correspond symbolically to the masculine and feminine potencies of the Godhead.[66] When the light of the (male) sun strikes the (female) moon, the (phallic) image of Jacob is formed within the lunar disk. Thus, in a second passage in his *Bet Hadash* to the *Tur, 'Orah Hayyim,* § 426, Sirkes comments: "Jacob is called 'sun'...and the moon is illuminated from the light of the sun. Therefore the form of the moon is adorned with the form of Jacob (*tsurat ha-levanah metuqenet be-tsurat ya'aqov*)."

The theurgical interpretation of the myth of the image of Jacob engraved in the moon is clearly the predominant one in kabbalistic literature, but the mystical dimension was not totally eclipsed. That is to say, one still finds in kabbalistic treatments of the blessing of the moon the notion that the mystics are themselves crowned by the splendor of the *Shekhinah*. Indeed, the image of the crown associated with the moon in the traditional blessing was interpreted by kabbalists as a reference to the *Shekhinah* that crowns the heads of the righteous. Thus, for instance, Moses de León comments on the liturgical expression in the blessing on the moon, "crown of splendor, for those who have been carried since birth," in the following manner:

> The moon is the crown that stands in the secret of her splendor, to establish her dwelling-place, and she is the crown that will rest on the heads of the righteous who have been carried since birth. This is [the import of the rabbinic statement that] the righteous sit with their crowns upon their heads for there each one is bound according to his level and his intellect "to gaze upon the beauty of the Lord, to frequent His temple" (Ps. 27:4).[67]

In line with what I said above in conjunction with the German Pietistic material, it can be surmised that in the kabbalistic material as well the theurgical and mystical elements are experientially inseparable. Conceptually, it is possible to distinguish the two but when judged from the perspective of the texture of the religious experience the distinction is not that significant. In terms of the specific focus of this study, the blessing of the moon concomitantly facilitates and celebrates the mythic union of the masculine and the feminine aspects of the divine. This unification, however, also signals the union of the mystic and the divine. In particular, the convergence of the theurgical and the mystical poles of the experience is represented by the regnant symbol of the crown.[68] This image, as I have argued elsewhere, signifies the restoration of the feminine to the masculine, for the female crown is itself the corona of the phallus.[69] The union of the male mystic and the *Shekhinah* thus constitutes the ontic reintegration of the female in the male.

The ontological assimilation of the feminine into the masculine is applied by some kabbalists to the blessing of the new moon, which is understood as the rectification (*tiqqun*) of the primordial blemish of the moon. Thus, for example, the following explanation of the blessing of the moon is attributed to the disciples (*haverim*) of Isaac Luria:

> The blessing of the moon: It is known to all who enter the gates of wisdom that all the turns that a person takes to ascend, the supernal ones above and the lower ones below, arouse the forces below in deed and in speech, and these are called the female waters that arouse the male waters above, one after the other, one above the other, until it reaches [the state such that] the overflow comes forth from the Cause of Causes, blessed be His name. Therefore, in every prayer and blessing that a person prays there must be a great intention, for speech is considered as an action, and the intent that he intends is the speech. If we are obligated to do such in all blessings, how much more so with respect to the blessing of the moon, for at first we avenge her insult, a double portion, and speak somewhat of her praise in front of her, to elevate her to the supernal level....In this blessing that we bless we elevate and exalt the moon. We receive a beautiful gift, the face of our Father in heaven, for we appease her in His place regarding the fact that she was diminished.[70]

Echoing the same sentiment, we read in the continuation of this text:

> "To the moon [God says]," that is, the Holy One, blessed be He, promised *Malkhut*, which is the moon, that she would be renewed and that she would rise to the place of *Tif'eret*. ... "In the future they will be renewed like it," that is, [the countenances of] *Ze'eir 'Anpin* and *Nuqba'* in the future will be renewed and they will be like [the countenances of]

'*Abba*' and '*Imma*', and '*Imma*' too will be renewed and she will rise in this manner, for '*Imma*' and *Tevunah* are one countenance (*partsuf*) and similarly *Yisra'el Sabba'* and '*Abba*' will become one countenance (*partsuf*), and the world will be perfected.[71]

The blessing of the moon, kabbalistically understood, thus involves the ascension of all the divine configurations (*partsufim*), *Nuqba'*, *Ze'eir 'Anpin*, '*Imma*' and '*Abba*', which may be viewed as the construction of the exclusively male persona. The reconfiguration of the divine potencies that occurs as a result of the traditional blessing of the moon restores the moon to a state of fullness, which is essentially the union of the male and the female that results in the ontological transformation of the female into a male.[72] The masculinization of the full moon is explicitly affirmed in the technical language of Lurianic kabbalah in the following passage from Hayyim Vital:

> The extent of her diminution was not less than a single point that is comprised of ten, which is the point of the final *Malkhut* within her, as was mentioned above, and the extent of her aggrandizement is that all the ten *sefirot* will be in her, and she will be face-to-face with *Ze'eir 'Anpin*, entirely on a par, and the two kings will make use of one crown, [the very situation] concerning which the moon complained, as is known. The matter, as is known, is that from *Tif'eret de-'Imma'* a crown was made for *Ze'eir 'Anpin*, and when she ascends to there, and her crown will be from *Tif'eret de-'Imma'* like him, their crowns will be equal, and the two of them will be one for the two of them will be in the aspect of *Tif'eret de-'Imma'*, which is one *sefirah*. At that point she will not need to receive her illumination by means of *Ze'eir 'Anpin*, but rather the two of them will receive their illumination from '*Imma*', each one by itself, and the one will not need the other. *Ze'eir 'Anpin* and *Nuqba'* will be equal in their being like '*Abba*' and '*Imma*'....This is the extent of her aggrandizement and as a result all the worlds will be in the ultimate rectification.[73]

Precisely such a process underlies the kabbalistic understanding of the motif of the image of Jacob engraved upon the moon. By the complex transposition of gender symbolism the face of Jacob in the moon signifies the ontic assimilation of the moon into Jacob. The point is enunciated by David ben Solomon ibn Abi Zimra in a passage from another one of his compositions that basically parallels the text of his that I cited above:

Thus you have learned that the *yod* is called "moon," [as it says in the blessing of the moon] "To the moon [God] says, 'Renew yourself, crown of splendor, for those who have been carried since birth,'" which refers to Israel who have been carried since birth. Therefore, we do not bless it except when it has an increase of light, that is, when its blemish is filled, but not in the time of its deficiency, for one does not bless over that which is a disgrace. Here I will inform you about a matter concerning which I have been in doubt since I became mature: When you look at the form of the moon when it is full you will see in it the likeness of the form of a human face in actuality. Concerning this I asked the philosophers and the astrologers, but none of them knew how to explain how this form takes shape in it, for at that time it is filled with the light of the sun and it is appropriate for it to be shining and glowing completely. In my opinion this is a wondrous secret from the mysteries of nature, and it alludes to what the rabbis, blessed be their memory, the sages of truth, said regarding the image of Jacob that is engraved on the throne of glory, and the throne is the crown of splendor of which we wrote above,[74] and Jacob is Jacob the elder, and the moon is the image of the throne, as I have written. Therefore, the image of Jacob, our father, and his icon are engraved and take shape within the lower moon. Thus, the rabbis, blessed be their memory, established [in the liturgical hymn *'el adon 'al kol ha-ma'asim]* ra'ah we-hitqin tsurat ha-levanah* ["He saw and established the form of the moon"]. It does not say, *ra'ah we-hitqin ha-levanah* ["He saw and established the moon"], but rather *tsurat ha-levanah* ["the form of the moon"]. You will not find them speaking of the form (*tsurah*) except with respect to the moon, but not with respect to the sun, and this is to allude to this secret. Understand it well.[75]

The moon, or more specifically the full moon, is symbolized by the letter *yod* for the latter is the mark of the covenant of circumcision, the corona of the penis. In her fullness, when she receives the light of the masculine sun, the moon becomes a crown of splendor, reflected liturgically in the expression *'ateret tif'eret*, that is, the crown of the divine splendor, which is the phallus. According to David ibn Zimra, the mystical significance of this process is related to the aggadic tradition of the icon of Jacob being engraved on the moon, which he further relates to the physical phenomenon of the apparent image of a human form in the face of the moon. Translated into theosophic symbology, the inscription of Jacob's face transforms the feminine moon into the masculine crown. This secret of male androgynization holds the key to unlocking the myth of the man in the moon as it evolved in kabbalistic literature.[76]

The deep resonance that this mythic structure had on the religious psyche of Jews through the Middle Ages is well-attested by the rituals and liturgical formulations that surround the blessing of the moon in medieval codes of law and custom that still influence traditional forms of piety. This particular example illustrates a much larger point expressed by Mircea Eliade: "a living myth is always connected with a cult, inspiring and justifying a religious behavior."[77] To be sure, a ritualistic practice in a given religious society can long outlive the mythical belief that gave rise to it, but in the absence of that myth one of two responses is inevitable: either the potency of the ritual is significantly diminished (if not totally abolished) or the particular way that it is practiced must be modified. It is too constricting to insist that demythicization of ritual necessarily implies the abrogation of ritual—on the contrary, it is evident that rituals play a significant role without myth—but I think it is accurate to say that in traditional religious cultures, including Judaism, the link between myth and ritual has been a vital one.[78] At the very least, the particular motif that I have studied in this essay supports the approach of Eliade: the living myth of the image of Jacob in the moon brought about certain forms of religious behavior that in turn reinforced that very myth. If in the current existential situation of Jewish communities the mythical pulse of these rituals no longer beats, that does not change the fact that it was precisely this mythical pulse that first gave life to these rituals.

Notes

1. B. Sanhedrin 42a.
2. Ibid. Subsequent codes of Jewish law and religious custom reiterate the view of Abbaye and the normative halakhic practice required a standing position for the recitation of the blessing.
3. Cf. *Genesis Rabbah* 6:1. Ed. J. Theodor and Ch. Albeck, 2nd edition (Jerusalem: 1965), 39; *Pesiqta de Rav Kahana*. Ed. B. Mandelbaum (New York: 1962), 5:1, 78; *Pesiqta Rabbati*. Ed. M. Friedmann (Vienna: 1880), 15, 66a. The midrashic view may be an elaboration on the biblical verse, "He made the moon to mark the seasons; the sun knows when to set" (Ps. 104:19).
4. The hackneyed perception that classical Jewish sources affirm a conception of linear (historical) time as opposed to cyclical (mythical) time has been challenged recently by P. Steensgaard, "Time in Judaism," in *Religion and Time*. Ed. A. N. Balslev and J. N. Mohanty (Leiden: 1993), 63-108. See also Y. H. Yerushalmi, *Zakhor: Jewish History and Jewish Memory* (Seattle and London: 1982), 108-109 n. 7. Although Yerushalmi clearly rejects the Eliadean

conception of the abolition of historical time through myth and ritual (102 n. 2) as inappropriate for classical forms of Judaism insofar as the latter exhibits a fundamentally historical orientation (5-26), he nevertheless recognizes that the commonplace distinction between the linear character of Hebrew thinking about time (or history more generally) and the cyclical thinking of the Greeks may be oversimplified. It is beneficial to consider sacred time from both vantage points, and indeed what is most curious about Judaism is the historicization of agrarian festivals, a process that results in the merging of the linear and cyclical views of time. Yerushalmi himself comes to just such a conclusion when he reflects on how medieval Jews related to historical time: "Neither the usual 'linear' nor 'cyclical' category alone will suffice to describe their experience....Having already underscored the importance of the public reading of Scripture in impressing the biblical past upon the consciousness of Jews, we must also realize that the very incorporation of those ritualized public readings had also endowed that same past with the inevitably cyclical quality of liturgical time....A similar merging of historical and liturgical time, of verticality and circularity, was obviously present also in the historical festivals and fasts... To be sure, all this is still far removed from any notion of an 'eternal return' or of mythic time. The historical events of the biblical period remain unique and irreversible. Psychologically, however, those events are *experienced* cyclically, repetitively, and to that extent at least, atemporally" (41-42; author's emphasis). See below, n. 7. After having completed this study I received a copy of an unpublished paper by M. Idel, "Some Concepts of Time and History in Kabbalah," presented at a conference sponsored by the Center for Jewish Studies, Harvard University, on "Jewish Attitudes Toward and Conceptions of History," October 4-5, 1994. Idel proposes a model of "complex" time by which he attempts to avoid the dichotomy of the cyclical and the linear views of time that have dominated the history of religions. Idel's discussion of the relationship of time, history, and ritual in Judaism bears some similarity to my own thesis briefly outlined in this study and elaborated in much greater detail in a monograph on kabbalistic conceptions of time that I am presently writing. In particular, Idel too notes, contra Eliade, that in the case of traditional Judaism rituals helped shape the linear (or historical) conception of time by means of a cyclical (or mythical) conception.

5. See M. Eliade, "The Moon and Its Mystique," in *Patterns in Comparative Religion*. Trans. R. Sheed (New York: 1958), 154-187; idem, *The Sacred and the Profane: The Nature of Religion*. Trans. W. R. Trask (New York and London: 1959), 156-157, 180; idem, "Time and Eternity in Indian Thought," in *Man and Time*. Ed. J. Campbell (Princeton: 157), 185; idem, *Images and Symbols: Studies in Religious Symbolism*. Trans. P. Mairet (Princeton: 1991), 72-73. For a summary, and somewhat popular, account of the depiction of the moon as the measure of time, see K. Cain, *Luna: Myth & Mystery* (Boulder: 1991), 108-127. See also M. Mokri, "La Lumiere en Iran ancien et dans l'Islam," in

La Thème de la lumière dans le judaïsme, le christianisme, et l'islam. Ed. M.-M. Davy, A. Abécassis, M. Mokri, and J.-P. Renneteau (Paris: 1976), 358-361.

6. This is the position articulated by Eliade in various studies. See, e.g., M. Eliade, *Cosmos and History: The Myth of the Eternal Return.* Trans. W. R. Trask (New York: 1959), 34-48; "Time and Eternity in Indian Thought," 173-175, 186-188, 195-200; *Myths, Dreams and Mysteries: The Encounter Between Contemporary Faiths and Archaic Realities.* Trans. P. Mariet (New York: 1960), 30-31, and passim; *Myth and Reality.* Trans. W. R. Trask (New York: 1963), 75-91; *Images and Symbols,* 73, 88-89. A succinct summary of Eliade's views is given by L. Kolakowski, *The Presence of Myth.* Trans. A. Czerniawski (Chicago and London: 1989), 48-49.

7. This very point was made by Eliade, *Myth and Reality,* 168-170: "Christianity had to keep at least one mythical aspect—liturgical time, that is, the periodical recovery of the *illud tempus* of the 'beginnings'....However, though liturgical Time is a circular Time, Christianity, as faithful heir of Judaism, accepts the linear Time of History: the World was created only once and will have only one end; the Incarnation took place only once, in historical Time, and there will be only one Judgment....As for Judaism, it gave the Church not only an allegorical method of interpreting the Scriptures, but, most importantly, the outstanding model for 'historicizing' the festivals and symbols of the cosmic religion. The 'Judaization' of primitive Christianity is equivalent to its 'historicization,' that is, to the decision of the first theologians to connect the history of Jesus' preaching and of the earliest Church to the Sacred History of the people of Israel. But Judaism had 'historicized' a certain number of seasonal festivals and cosmic symbols by connecting them with important events in the history of Israel...The Church Fathers took the same course: they 'Christianized' Asianic and Mediterranean rites and myths by connecting them with a 'Sacred History.'" Although there is much to disagree with in Eliade's comments, the essential point for the purposes of my analysis is his recognition that already in the case of Judaism the liturgical time of myth and ritual is correlated with historical time, and that this correlation is part of the legacy that Judaism imparted to Christianity. A similar position is taken by Eliade in other writings, e.g., *The Sacred and the Profane,* 110-112. See above, n. 4.

8. That is, an epithet for the people of Israel based on Isa. 46:3

9. B. Sanhedrin 42a; *Masekhet Soferim.* Ed. M. Higger (New York: 1937), 19:10, 339. This formulation is lacking in the blessing of the moon mentioned in P. Berakhot 9:2, 12d.

10. The expression *'ateret tif'eret* is used in a technical way to designate the *Shekhinah* in *Song of Songs Rabbah* 4:25. Ed. S. Dunasky (Jerusalem and Tel-Aviv: 1980), 122: "'A splendid crown on your head,' *wa-'ateret tif'eret be-ro'shekh* (Ezek. 16:12), this is the *Shekhinah,* as it says, 'You shall be a glorious crown in the hand of the Lord,' *we-hayyita 'ateret tif'eret be-yad yhwh* (Isa. 62:3), and it is written, 'The king marches before them, the Lord at their head,' *wa-ya'avor malkam lifnehem wa-yhwh be-ro'sham* (Micah 2:13)." The

designation of Israel as the crown of splendor in *Song of Songs Rabbah* 8:5, 170, may also have hypostatic connotations: "Israel also said before the Holy One, blessed be He, 'Let me be a seal upon your heart, like the seal upon your arm' (Song of Songs 8:6). The prophets said to them: You have not asked properly. The heart sometimes is seen and sometimes is not seen, but His seal is not revealed. What would have been proper? 'You shall be a glorious crown in the hand of the Lord,' *we-hayyita 'ateret tif'eret be-yad yhwh* (Isa. 62:3)." It seems to me that in this text the phallus is displaced by the crown: the seal (*hotam*) of God, which is the phallus, can never be disclosed, but in its place the glorious crown is revealed in God's hand. The essential hiddenness of the phallus in Israelite religion and in rabbinic Judaism based thereon has recently been emphasized by H. Eilberg-Schwartz, *God's Phallus and Other Problems for Men and Monotheism* (Boston: 1994). I have adopted a similar approach in my *Through a Speculum That Shines: Vision and Imagination in Medieval Jewish Mysticism* (Princeton: 1994).

11. Cf. Gen. 37:9-10. Perhaps one may surmise a vestige of a mythical conception of the moon as a goddess in ancient Israel from various passages that criticize Israel for practicing such idolatry as well as in certain rituals that were sanctioned as part of the official Israelite cult, including the Sabbath and the Paschal sacrifice. See M. Petit, "La Lune en canaan et israel," in *Sources Orientales* 5 [*La Lune: Mythes et rites*] (Paris: 1962), 129-150. (I thank Steven Wasserstrom for drawing my attention to this collection of studies on the symbol of the moon in various religious cultures.) Conversely, the literary evidence of the Bible attests that ancient Israelites, assimilating Canaanite mythology, depicted Yahweh in solar images, a point corroborated by archaeological evidence. See J. Glen Taylor, "The Two Earliest Representations of Yahweh," in *Ascribe to the Lord: Biblical and Other Studies in Memory of Peter C. Craigie*. Ed. L. Eslinger and G. Taylor (Seffield, 1988), 557-566. (I thank Victor Hurwitz for pointing out this study to me.).

12. See L. Ginzberg, *The Legends of the Jews* (Philadelphia: 1968), 5:40-41 n. 112: "The statement made in the Greek Apocalypse of Baruch 9 to the effect that the moon has the likeness of a woman (in the original myth she must have been the wife of the sun) is unknown in Jewish sources." See also comment of H. E. Gaylord, Jr., in his translation of 3 Baruch 9:3, "[The moon] is like a woman, sitting on a chariot. ... The form of the moon is like a woman," in *The Old Testament Pseudepigrapha*. Ed. J. H. Charlesworth (New York: 1983), 1: 672 n. 9b: "This representation of the moon is hellenistic and has no parallel in Jewish literature of the period." On the image of the moon riding a chariot, without any gender specification, see 2 Enoch 16:7 cited by Gaylord *ad locum*. In this connection it is of interest to note that in Mesopotamian culture the basic gender of the moon is masculine, the symbol of male virility and sexual prowess being the crescent, but the full moon displays the feminine gender, representing female fecundity. See T. M. Green, *The City of the Moon God: Religious Traditions of Harran* (Leiden: 1992), 22-43. On the moon as a symbol of fecundity in Islam, see Mokri, "La

Lumiere en Iran ancien et dans l'Islam," pp. 378-386. In other mythological and folkloristic traditions the full moon represents masculinity on account of the fact that the fullness is associated with impregnation and fertility. See Cain, *Luna: Myth & Mystery*, 73. On the lunar qualities of the Greek goddess Demeter, see C. Kerényi, *Eleusis Archetypal Image of Mother and Daughter*. Trans. R. Manheim (Princeton: 1967), 30, 32, 130-131. See also P. Friedrich, *The Meaning of Aphrodite* (Chicago and London: 1978), 32-33, 79-80. The symbolic correlation of the moon and the feminine, particularly the archetype of the mother, is known from a variety of religious societies. See Eliade, "Moon and Its Mystique," 163-169; T. Harley, *Moon Lore* (London: 1885), 53-68; C. G. Jung, *The Archetypes and the Collective Unconscious*. Trans. R. F. C. Hull (Princeton: 1969), 81. On the appropriation of this symbolism in alchemical literature, see R. Bernoulli, "Spiritual Development as Reflected in Alchemy and Related Disciplines," in *Spiritual Disciplines: Papers from the Eranos Yearbooks*. Ed. J. Campbell. Trans. R. Manheim (Princeton: 1960), 316-318, 337; C. G. Jung, *Alchemical Studies*. Trans. R. F. C. Hull (Princeton: 1967), 79 n. 64, 161; idem, *Psychology and Alchemy*. Trans. R. F. C. Hull (Princeton: 1968), 383 and 404.

13. Cf. B. Hullin 60b; Shavu'ot 9a; *Midrash 'Aggadah*. Ed. S. Buber (Vienna: 1894), 3; *Zohar* 1:46b, 252a; *Legends*, 5:34-36 n. 100. The symbolic correlation of the gentile and the sun, on one hand, and the Jew and the moon, on the other, underlies the statement in B. Sukkah 29a: "The rabbis taught: When the sun is eclipsed it is a bad sign for idolaters (literally, worshipers of the stars); when the moon is eclipsed it is a bad sign for the enemies of Israel, for [the people of] Israel count [the months] according to the moon and the idolaters according to the sun." Cf. *Sefer Hasidim*. Ed. J. Wistinetzki and J. Freimann (Frankfurt am Main: 1924), § 289. On the use of solar and lunar imagery in early Christian literature and iconography, which may have some bearing on the rabbinic materials, see H. Rahner, "Das Christliche Mysterium von Sonne und Mond," *Eranos-Jahrbuch* 10 (1943): 305-404. An interesting comparison of Israelite history from Abraham to Yehoyaqim is charted in terms of the monthly lunar cycle in *Exodus Rabbah* 15:26. (For a different version of this passage see Abraham bar Azriel, *Sefer 'Arugat ha-Bosem*. Ed. E. E. Urbach [Jerusalem: 1939], 1:164 and the editor's comments in n. 11 *ad locum*.) Significantly, spiritual perfection occurs fifteen generations after Abraham when Solomon was enthroned in the Temple. The moment of enthronement thus parallels the fifteenth of the month when the disc of the moon is full. It would appear that in this context the full moon symbolizes the impregnated female who, through the insemination of the male, becomes a fecund and fertile being. The nexus of the full moon and the building of the Temple in the reign of Solomon is elaborated in kabbalistic literature. Cf. *Zohar* 2:145b; Moses de León, *Shushan 'Edut*. Ed. G. Scholem, *Qovets 'al Yad* 8 (1976): 368. Needless to say, countless other examples could have been cited. The symbolically feminine character of the moon also underlies the special connection of women and the celebration of Rosh

Hodesh in rabbinic literature, expressed in some sources in terms of
women's refraining from labor on the new month. Cf. P. Pesahim 4:1, 30d;
Ta'anit 1:6, 64c; B. Hagigah 18a, Megillah 22b; Rosh ha-Shanah 23a; *Pirqe R.
'Eli'ezer* (Warsaw, 1852), ch. 45, 107a; Asher bar Saul of Lunel, *Sefer ha-
Minhagot*. Ed. S. Assaf, *Sifran shel Ri'shonim* (Jerusalem: 1935), 170; Judah ben
Yaqar, *Perush ha-Tefillot we-ha-Berakhot*. Ed. S. Yerushalmi, 2nd edition
(Jerusalem: 1979), pt. 2, 59; Eleazar of Worms, *Sefer ha-Roqeah* (Jerusalem:
1967), § 228, 130; *The Book of the Pomegranate: Moses de León's Sefer ha-Rimmon*.
Ed. E. R. Wolfson (Atlanta: 1988), 190 (Hebrew section); *Tur*, '*Orah Hayyim*,
417; *Sefer Rabiah*, 2:209; Isaac bar Moses of Vienna, '*Or Zaru'a* (Zitomir:
1862), pt. 2, § 454, 91c; Meir ben Baruch of Rothenburg, *She'elot u-Teshuvot*.
(Ed. Praque-Budapest, reprint Jerusalem 1986), 3:2b, § 13; Seligmann of
Bingen, *Maharaz Bingen: Hiddushim, Be'urim, u-Fesaqim* (Jerusalem: 1985),
116; Israel ibn al-Nakawa, *Menorat ha-Ma'or*. Ed. H. G. Enelow (New York:
1930), 2:201-202. Cf. Tosafot, B. Shabbat 24a, s.v., '*o dilma' kevan de-lo' 'asur
be-'asiyyat mela'khah*. See Y. Liebes, "De Natura Dei: On the Development of
the Jewish Myth," in *Studies in Jewish Myth and Jewish Messianism*. Trans. B.
Stein (Albany: 1992), 50. The matter is explained in terms of the ontic
allignment of the divine emanations in Hayyim Vital, *Sha'ar ha-Kawwanot*
(Jerusalem: 1902), 76b: "On Rosh Hodesh there is no ascent at all [of the
feminine] to [the masculine] *Ze'eir 'Anpin*, but the feminine (*neqevah*) alone
ascends from gradation to gradation. By means of this you can understand
the reason why women are forbidden to work on Rosh Hodesh and not
men." Cf. *Peri 'Ets Hayyim* (Jerusalem: 1980), 19:1, 452. (The association of
women and the moon also has negative connotations in kabbalistic literature related specifically to menstruation and the monthly cycle; see below,
n. 59.) It is of interest to note that, according to the kabbalistic explanation
of this custom in *Hemdat Yamim* (Kushta: 1735), 2:23d-24a, by abstaining
from work the women unite with their ontic source, the *Shekhinah*, which is
the divine feminine. Conversely, if women do not heed this custom they
create a blemish above in the supernal realm. On the special connection of
women and the celebration of the festival of the New Moon in a contemporary traditional community of women from Kurdistan and Yemen, see S.
Sered, *Women As Ritual Experts: The Religious Lives of Elderly Jewish Women
in Jerusalem* (New York and Oxford: 1992), 28-29.

14. *Genesis Rabbah* 6:2, 42-43; *Pesiqta de Rav Kahana*, 5:14, 103-104. Esau and
Jacob, who typologically represent Christianity and Judaism, are thus
contrasted by the respective solar and lunar calendars. By contrast, Ishmael
and Jacob, i.e., Islam and Judaism, share in common the marking of time by
the moon. The significance of lunar symbolism in Islam is obvious and need
not be elaborated here. See M. Rodinson, "La Lune chez les arabes et dans
l'islam," in *Sources Orientales* 5 [*La Lune: Mythes et rites*] (Paris: 1962), 153-
215, and the study of Mokri cited above, n. 4. It is, however, of interest to
consider the following comment in *Zohar* 3:281b (*Ra'aya' Mehemna'*): "The
moon is good and evil, good in its fullness and evil in its deficiency. Since

it is comprised of good and evil, both Israel and the sons of Ishmael count by it. When it is eclipsed in its fullness it is a bad sign for Israel and when it is eclipsed in its deficient state it is a bad sign for the Ishmaelites." On the dual nature of the moon in alchemy, related to the hermaphroditical character of Mercurius, see below n. 59.

15. See Jung, *Psychology and Alchemy*, 381-382; idem, *Archetypes and the Collective Unconscious*, 6.

16. Cf. *Pirqe R. 'Eli'ezer*, ch. 7, 17b; ch. 51, 123a. See, however, *Exodus Rabbah* 15:31. The midrashic parable in that context assumes that the linkage of Israel and the moon is only a temporary situation that will be rectified in the messianic era when Israel will receive all the celestial luminaries. The present situation is compared to an engagement and the future to marriage itself. According to another aggadic comment when the people of Israel are meritorious their computation follows the moon in its fullness, but when they are not it follows the moon in its eclipsed state. See *Pesiqta Rabbati*, ch. 15, 77a; *Pesiqta de Rav Kahana* 5:12, 101. Cf. Eleazar ben Moses ha-Darshan, *Sefer Gimatri'ot*, MS Munich 221, fol. 115a: "'For the sun had set' (Gen. 28:11). The crownlets over 'the sun' (*ha-shemesh*) alludes to the fact that Jacob was the sun and it intimates all of the royalty of the house of David that was compared to the sun that will set in the future and will cease in the time of the destruction [of the Temple]." In this case the association of Jacob (or Israel) with the sun has negative connotations. Finally, it should be noted that on occasion one finds in rabbinic sources traces of the more typical heroic mythos according to which the righteous and magnanimous soul is compared to the sun. Cf. B. Yoma 38b; Qiddushin 72b. For a later kabbalistic appropriation of this symbolism, cf. G. Scholem, "A New Section from the *Midrash ha-Ne'elam* of the *Zohar*," *Festschrift in Honor of Louis Ginzberg* (New York: 1946), 443 (in Hebrew): "R. Hiyya said, what is [the import of] what is written, 'he stopped there for the night, for the sun had set' (Gen. 28:11)? Rather the sun is [a reference to] Jacob, and when he gave his power to Esau the sun, which was the power of Jacob, was taken away and given to Esau, as it is written, 'for the sun had set.' Until this day the splendor and glory of the sun have been removed from Jacob and given to Esau. In the future the Holy One, blessed be He, will restore him to his power and no others will receive his power." Cf. Joseph of Hamadan's commentary on the *sefirot*, MS Oxford, Bodleian Library 1628, fols. 69a-b: "The light actually illuminates the righteous whose face is like the sun and moon. Moreover, they have said [B. Baba Batra 75a] that the face of Moses is like the face of the sun and the face of Joshua is like the face of the moon. The reason that the face of Moses our master, peace be upon him, is like the face of the sun is [related to] what he receives from the sun, for he has received the Torah from the attribute called 'day' (*yom*) and Joshua received from the attribute called 'moon' (*levanah*)." Underlying this comment is the rather widespread kabbalistic identification of the sun as the masculine principle, particularly the sixth

gradation or *Tif'eret* (represented by Moses), and of the moon as the feminine principle, the tenth gradation or *Malkhut* (represented by Joshua). See below, n. 23.

17. This is precisely how the matter is explained in a host of medieval sources. To cite some relevant examples: Asher bar Saul of Lunel, *Sefer ha-Minhagot,* 171; *Mahzor Vitry.* Ed. S. Hurwitz (Nurenberg: 1923), 183; *Shibbole ha-Leqet ha-Shalem.* Ed. S. Buber (New York: 1959), 134; the commentary of R. Asher to the blessing on the moon in *'Orhot Hayyim* (Florence: 1754), 70a; *Siddur of R. Solomon ben Samson of Garmaise.* Ed. M. Hershler (Jerusalem: 1971), 196; Judah ben Yaqar, *Perush ha-Tefillot we-ha-Berakhot,* pt. 2, 59-60; *'Arugat ha-Bosem,* 1:164; Eliezer ben Natan, *Siddur ha-Raban* (Bene-Beraq: 1991), 431; *Menorat ha-Ma'or,* 2:203.

18. See B. Rosh ha-Shanah 25a (and cf. commentary of Rashi *ad locum,* s.v., *david melekh yisra'el,* where Ps. 89:39 is mentioned explicitly); *'Arugat ha-Bosem,* 1:163, 241, 298.

19. That is the twin boys that were born to Judah and Tamar; cf. Gen. 38:27-30. According to the lineage given in Ruth 4:18-22, David is a direct descendant of Perez. Insofar as the Messiah is thought to derive from David, it follows that the illicit sexual relation of Judah and Tamar produced the messianic seed. This dimension underlies the connection made by Judah ben Samuel Campanton between the names of the twins, on the one hand, and the waxing of the moon, on the other. Cf. Bahya ben Asher, *Be'ur 'al ha-Torah.* Ed. H. D. Chavel (Jerusalem: 1981), ad Gen. 38:30, 1:316-319. Bahya emphasizes that Zerah and Perez correspond respectively to the sun and the moon, a correlation that is interpreted in terms of the standard kabbalistic symbolism of the masculine and the feminine aspects of the divine.

20. MS JTSA Mic. 2532, fol., 17b. Cf. *Zohar* 1:192a.

21. See *Legends,* 5:275, n. 35. On the image of the man in the sun, see below n. 23. For a wide-ranging discussion of the motif of the man in the moon in ancient, medieval, and modern writers, see Harley, *Moon Lore,* 5-53. On p. 21 Harley refers to the motif of the visible face of Jacob in the moon as a "Talmudic tradition."

22. B. Hullin 60b. See *'Avot de-Rabbi Natan.* Ed. S. Schechter (Vienna: 1887), version A, ch. 36, 107; *Midrash 'Aggadah,* 3; *'Arugat ha-Bosem,* 3:42. On the connection of the righteous and the moon, exegetically linked to Ps. 89:38, cf. *Midrash Tehillim.* Ed. S. Buber (Vilna: 1891), 11:6, 51a; 16:12, 62b. In other midrashic sources the comparison of the countenance of the righteous (or, more specifically, the seven groups of the righteous who in the eschatological future will receive the face of the *Shekhinah;* cf. P. Hagigah 2:1, 77a) to the moon is linked exegetically to Song of Songs 6:10. See *Sifre Deuteronomy.* Ed. L. Finkelstein (New York: 1969), 10, 18 and 47, 105; *Wayyikra Rabbah.* Ed. M. Margulies (New York and Jerusalem: 1993), 30:2, 693; *Pesiqta de Rav Kahana,* 27:2, 405; *Midrash ha-Gadol on Leviticus.* Ed. A. Steinzhaltz (Jerusalem: 1976), 654.

23. See *Legends*, 3:75, 441, 4:4, and sources given in 5:28 n. 170 and 6:170 n. 6.
    Although in both instances the figure is male it is obvious that the symbolic
    image of the moon has a feminizing effect insofar as the two personalities
    are contrasted with Moses whose visage is compared to the sun. That is to
    say, the solar image symbolized the higher, more powerful force and the
    lunar image the lower, weaker force. It is evident that, according to standard
    gender hierarchies, the former is masculine and the latter feminine. This
    motif is further developed in kabbalistic literature. For example, compare
    the citation of Isaac the Blind in *Be'ur Sodot ha-Ramban* (attributed to Meir ibn
    Sahula) to Exod. 17:16 (Vilna: 1927), 14a. The gender implications of this
    aggadic tradition are well drawn in the following passage from *Tseror
    Hayyim*, attributed to Shemayah ben Isaac ha-Levi, extant in MS Oxford,
    Bodleian Library 1781, fol. 103a: "Understand what [the rabbis] blessed be
    their memory, said, 'the face of Moses is like the face of the sun and the face
    of Joshua is like the face of the moon,' and consider precisely what is said,
    'the face of Joshua is like the face of the moon,' for just as the moon receives
    the light of the sun and from its light it shines so Joshua received from
    Moses. This is what is said in *Sefer Yetsirah*, that which receives force from
    something else is referred to in feminine terms. Comprehend that in Song
    of Songs God, blessed be He, designated Israel by feminine terms…because
    Israel receives the force and influx from God, blessed be He." See above, n.
    14.
24. On the connection of the moon and the heart of Jacob, compare the
    kabbalistic tradition in MS Munich 56, fol. 202b.
25. *Masekhet Soferim*, 19:10, 339.
26. *'Orhot Hayyim*, 70a. Cf. *Kol Bo*, § 43
27. *Tur*, *'Orah Hayyim*, 426; cf. *Maharaz Bingen: Hiddushim, Be'urim, u-Fesaqim*,
    169-170; *Menorat ha-Ma'or*, 2:204.
28. *Sefer Abudarham ha-Shalem* (Jerusalem: 1963), 344.
29. Cf. *Peri 'Ets Hayyim*, 19:3, 463; *Siddur ha-'Ari* (Zolkiew: 1781), 136b; Moses
    Cordovero, *Tefillah le-Mosheh* (Przemysl: 1892), 285b; Shabbetai of Rashkov,
    Siddur ha-'Ari (Korets: 1788), 92b; *Siddur Nehora' ha-Shalem* (Slavuta: 1827),
    190a. This order is attributed to Menahem Tsiyyoni is MS Oxford, Bodleian
    Library 1651, fol. 23a.
30. Cf. Samuel Vital, *Siddur Hemdat Yisra'el* (Munkacs: 1901), 182a; Moses
    Zacuto, *'Iggerot ha-Remez* (Livorno: 1780), § 10, 7a; *Hemdat Yamim*, 25b; Jacob
    Emden, *Siddur 'Amude Shamayim* (Jerusalem: 1993), 976; Hayyim Joseph
    David Azulai, *Mahaziq Berakhah* (Livorno: 1785), 426:3; Jacob Koppel
    Lipschitz, *Siddur Qol Ya'aqov* (Slavuta: 1804), 53b; Shalom Sharabi, *Sefer 'Or
    ha-Levanah* (Jerusalem: 1925), 34-35.
31. *Siddur Sha'ar ha-Shamayim*, 220b-221a.
32. See E. R. Wolfson, "The Image of Jacob Engraved Upon the Throne: Further
    Speculation on the Esoteric Doctrine of the German Pietism," in *Massu'ot:
    Studies in Kabbalistic Literature and Jewish Philosophy in Memory of Prof.
    Ephraim Gottlieb.* Ed. M. Oron and A. Goldreich (Jerusalem: 1994), 131-185

(in Hebrew); a revised and expanded English version appears in E. R. Wolfson, *Along the Path: Studies in Kabbalistic Myth, Symbolism, and Hermeneutics* (Albany: 1995), 1-62, and relevant notes on 111-186. Some of the sources discussed here have already been cited in my study on the motif of the image of Jacob engraved upon the throne.

33. MS Paris, Bibliothèque Nationale 772, fol. 144b. The text of Eleazar itself in the body of the commentary follows the formulation of *Masekhet Soferim*. See also Eleazar's *Sefer ha-Roqeah*, § 229, 131. In addition to the image of Jacob in the moon there is evidence in the Pietistic writings for the idea of the form of man in the sun. See MS Paris, Bibliothèque Nationale 772, fol. 130a; *Perushe Siddur ha-Tefillah la-Roqeah*. Ed. M. Hershler and Y. A. Hershler (Jerusalem: 1992), 2:524.

34. MS Oxford, Bodleian Library 1812, fol. 59a. The passage is cited in *Merkavah Shelemah* (Jerusalem: 1971), 30a. See Farber, "Concept of the Merkabah," 406. Cf. Abraham Saba, *Tseror ha-Mor* (Jerusalem: 1985), 129: "They said that the form of Jacob is engraved on the throne of glory and it is engraved on the moon." This source was already noted by Ginzberg, *Legends*, 5:291 n. 134.

35. See R. Elior, "The Concept of God in Hekhalot Mysticism," *Jerusalem Studies in Jewish Thought* 6:1-2 (1987): 27-31 (in Hebrew; English translation in *Binah: Studies in Jewish Thought*. Ed. J. Dan [New York: 1989], 106-108). See also S. Leiter, "Worthiness, Acclamation and Appointment: Some Rabbinic Terms," *Proceedings of the American Academy of Jewish Research* 41-42 (1973-74): 137-168, esp. 143-145. It is possible that the term *yofi* in this context also has a phallic connotation. For other references in which this usage is implied, see Wolfson, *Through a Speculum That Shines*, 85-86 n. 50.

36. Reflecting the Ashkenazi tradition Abraham Abulafia writes in '*Otsar 'Eden Ganuz*, MS Oxford, Bodleian Library 1580, fol. 9b: "The secret of His throne (*kiss'o*) is the moon (*levanah*) [i.e., both terms equal 87]. Thus the sages said that the form of Jacob is engraved on the throne of glory and it is engraved upon the moon." I have referred to this text and other pertinent Abulafian sources in "Image of Jacob," 145 n. 190. The influence of the Ashkenazi material is also discernible in a passage from *Midrash ha-Ne'elam* published by Scholem, "A New Section from the *Midrash ha-Ne'elam* of the *Zohar*," 431. For an English rendering of this passage, see Wolfson, "Image of Jacob," 177 n. 347.

37. Cf. B. Sanhedrin 41b.

38. MS Paris, Bibliothèque Nationale héb. 772, fol. 144b; text printed in a slightly different version in *Perushe Siddur ha-Tefillah la-Roqeah*, 2:605. Cf. *Sode Razayya*, ed. Weiss, 68.

39. Cf. *Perush ha-Merkavah*, MS Paris, Bibliothèque Nationale héb. 850, fol. 67a; *Sode Razayya'*, ed. Kamelhar, 23; *Perush Sodot ha-Tefillah*, MS Paris, Bibliothèque Nationale héb. 772, fols. 90b, 123a.

40. *Batte Midrashot*, 2:406.

41. See Farber, "Concept of the Merkabah," 116, 571-574, 581, 618-627.

42. Cf. *Zohar* 3:248b (*Ra'aya' Mehemna'*) where the form of the moon is described as a letter *kaf*. It is interesting to note that in *Sefer Yetsirah* the letter *kaf* is associated with the sun and the moon with the letter *taw*. See I. Gruenwald, "A Preliminary Critical Edition of Sefer Yezira," *Israel Oriental Studies* 1 (1971): 159.

43. *Sode Razayya'*. Ed. Weiss, 68.

44. For a different approach to the image of the moon in the Ashkenazi material, see Liebes, "De Natura Dei," 51.

45. Cf. Eleazar's *Perush ha-Merkavah*, MS Paris, Bibliothéque Nationale héb. 850, fol. 56a: "'The legs of each [living creature] were [fused into] a single rigid leg,' *we-raglehem regel yesharah* (Ezek. 1:7): the last [letters spell] *millah* to tell you that by the dancing of the feet they utter song." The ontic emulation of the beasts who bear the throne, or the cherubs, on the part of human beings, is a theme that Eleazar affirms on a number of occasions in his writings. See, e.g., *Hokhmat ha-Nefesh* (Bene-Beraq: 1987), ch. 51, 88. The use of the description of the celestial creatures' feet to justify recommended bodily gestures for prayer is well-attested in rabbinic literature. Cf. B. Berakhot 10b; see E. Zimmer, "Poses and Postures during Prayer," *Sidra* 5 (1989): 107-108 (in Hebrew). Cf. in particular the explanation of Solomon ben Abraham ibn Aderet to this talmudic passage in his *Perushe ha-Haggadot*. Ed. by L. A. Feldman (Jerusalem: 1991), 25-26. According to the Rashba, the secret of the aggadic tradition alludes to the necessity of the human worshiper to be transformed into an angel when he stands before God.

46. For a later attestation of this symbolism see J. Zwelling, "Joseph of Hamadan's *Sefer Tashak*: Critical Text Edition with Introduction," Ph.D. diss., Brandeis University, 1975, 454: "And He leaps over the hills to unify with the Matrona." Cf. the explanation of the ritual to leap three times during the blessing of the moon attributed to Hayyim Vital in *Peri 'Ets Hayyim*, 19:3, 461: "Sometimes *Malkhut* is underneath *Yesod*, and in order for body to be joined to body, which is in the *sefirah* of *Tif'eret*, one must leap three times, for *Netsah, Hod*, and *Yesod* leap and they ascend to *Hesed, Gevurah*, and *Tif'eret*. There are the three leapings of the blessing of the moon to join her to her husband, and this is the ascent of *Netsah, Hod*, and *Yesod* to *Hesed, Gevurah*, and *Tif'eret*." It is evident that later kabbalists associated the ritual of leaping before the moon with that of leaping before the bride. The conceptual underpinning here is that the sanctification of the moon is an occasion for the sacred union of male and female. Thus, for example, compare the explanation of leaping before the moon in Emden, *Siddur 'Amude Shamayim*, 976: "(And one does not bow down [to the moon], and there is a great secret in this, like the leaps that we make in the *qedushah* of the prayer), and this is in the pattern of a wedding in which dancing and [acts of] joy are performed." It is evident that the leaping or dancing (*riqqud*) is a euphemism for a sexual act. (The phallic nature of dance in diverse religious cultures has been noted by various scholars; for example, see G. van der Leeuw, *Sacred and Profane Beauty: The Holy in Art*. Trans. D. E. Green

[New York: 1963], 22.) On the prohibition of bowing down to the moon, cf. Isaiah Horowitz, *Siddur Sha'ar ha-Shamayim*, 220a: "In the blessing of the moon one leaps three times, and one must be careful not to bow down, rather one lifts up one's fingers. And one should not look at [the moon] except for one time so that one will see her position." Cf. Abraham Abele ben Hayyim ha-Levi Gombiner, *Magen 'Avraham*, commentary on *'Orah Hayyim* 428:8.

47. With respect to the gender symbolism of the moon and the rainbow there is a similarity between the German Pietistic literature and the theosophic kabbalah. See Wolfson, *Through a Speculum That Shines*, 334 n. 39 and 337-338 n. 40. On the significance of the image of the rainbow in the mystical theosophy of Haside Ashkenaz, cf. Eleazar's *Sefer ha-Shem*, MS London, British Museum 737, fol. 346b: "The letters of the name of the Holy One, blessed be He, are letters of fire, and their splendor is like the splendor of the rainbow in the cloud. Moreover, the Torah that preceded the world was written black fire upon white fire." In this connection it is of interest to consider the statement in *Sefer Hasidim*. Ed. R. Margaliot (Jerusalem: 1957), § 18, 78 (the relevant passage in this version, which follows the standard edition first published in Bologna in 1538, is lacking in the Parma manuscipt that served as the basis for the Wistinetzki-Freimann edition) that at the conclusion of the standing prayer (*'amidah*) the worshiper must bow down in such a way that he makes himself into the shape of a rainbow. I do not know if a deeper esoteric significance should be attributed to this recommended bodily posture, but it is a matter worthy of further reflection.

48. In classical rabbinic sources Song of Songs 2:8 is interpreted variously as a reference to God's activities. Cf. *Mekhilta' de-Rabbi Ishmael*, Pisha 7, 22; *Sifre Numbers* 115, 125; *Sifre Deuteronomy* 314, 357; *Song of Songs Rabbah* 2:19, 65-66; B. Rosh ha-Shanah 11a. In some rabbinic passages the juxtaposition of Song of Songs 2:8 and Exod. 12:2 suggests that the former was interpreted as a reference to the sanctification of the moon. Cf. *Pesiqta de-Rav Kahana*, 88-89; *Pesiqta Rabbati*, 70b-71a; *Exodus Rabbah* 15:1.

49. MS Paris, Bibliothèque Nationale héb. 772, fol. 144b. In his *Siddur Sha'ar ha-Shamayim*, Isaiah Horowitz cites a tradition (*qabbalah*) from Judah he-Hasid to say Song of Songs 2:8-9 when one leaps before the moon. Cf. Gombiner, *Magen 'Avraham*, commentary on *'Orah Hayyim* 428:10.

50. Cf. *Sefer ha-Shem*, MS London, British Museum 737, fol. 281a, where Song of Songs 6:3 is cited by Eleazar as a prooftext to support the notion that the prophet knows the supernal mind (*da'at 'elyon*) through the anthropomorphization of the glory as related in Ezek. 1:26. The citation of the verse, "I am my beloved's and my beloved is mine," in this context clearly indicates the erotic nature of theosophic gnosis.

51. *Sefer Hasidim*, § 59. On the association of a woman's hair and the demonic in zoharic literature, see I. Tishby, *The Wisdom of the Zohar*. Trans. D. Goldstein (Oxford: 1989), 1358-1359. I have discussed this theme, particularly in the writings of Joseph of Hamadan, in "Crossing Gender Boundaries

in Kabbalistic Ritual and Myth," in *Circle in the Square: Studies in the Use of Gender in Kabbalistic Symbolism* (Albany: 1995), 211 n. 85. For a more general discussion of the shaving of hair in zoharic texts, see Y. Liebes, "How the Zohar Was Written," in *Studies in the Zohar*. Trans. A. Schwartz, S. Nakache, and P. Peli (Albany: 1993), 121-126.

52. *Sefer Hasidim*, § 978. See ibid., § 979, where the connection again is made between withstanding visual temptation and meriting a vision of the divine. On the necessity to avoid gazing at the the face, breasts, and genitals of women, cf. *Sefer ha-Roqeah*, § 5, 26. On the linkage of sexual desire and the eyes, a much older motif in Jewish sources that has many parallels in non-Jewish material, cf. *Hokhmat ha-Nefesh*, ch. 20, 35. The parallel drawn between seeing the glory and abstaining from looking at a woman should be compared to the connection between transmission of the divine name and abrogation of sexual desire made elsewhere in Pietistic literature. For references, see Wolfson, *Through a Speculum That Shines*, 239 n. 202. The common denominator is the ontic identification of the name and the glory. See Wolfson, op. cit., 245-247. To be sure, the connection made between the vision of the glory and gazing upon women must also be understood in terms of the German Pietists' objectification of women as mere sex objects that arouse the desire of men. See the recently published study of J. R. Baskin, "From Separation to Displacement: The Problem of Women in *Sefer Hasidim*," *AJS Review* 19 (1994): 1-18. Pietistic attitudes toward sexuality have been discussed by various scholars; see M. Harris, "The Concept of Love in *Sepher Hassidim*," *Jewish Quarterly Review* 50 (1959): 13-44; I. G. Marcus, *Piety and Society: The Jewish Pietists of Medieval Germany* (Leiden: 1981), 42-43, 46-47, 79; D. Biale, *Eros and the Jews: From Biblical Israel to Contemporary America* [New York: 1992], 72-82. Also relevant is E. Kanarfogel, "Rabbinic Attitudes Towards Nonobservance in the Medieval Period," in *Jewish Tradition and the Nontraditional Jew*. Ed. J. J. Schacter (Northvale, N.J.: 1992), 3-35, esp. 17-26. On the more general status of women in this cultural context, see I. G. Marcus, "Mothers, Martyrs, and Moneymakers: Some Jewish Women in Medieval Europe," *Conservative Judaism* 38 (1986): 34-45; and K. Stow, "The Jewish Family in the Rhineland in the High Middle Ages: Form and Function," *American Historical Review* 92 (1987): 1085-1110. One could argue that the Pietists' obsession with illicit sexuality is translated into the realm of theosophic speculation such that one can speak of the tendency "to transform human sexualiy into erotic theology" (Baskin, 14; this position adopted by Baskin, as she acknowledges, 17, is in part influenced by Biale's discussion of displacement of sexual desire from the human to the divine in eighteenth-century Polish Hasidism; see *Eros and the Jews*, 141-145). In some measure this is true, but it must be borne in mind that recent scholarship tends to view the social reality presented in *Sefer Hasidim* (and, to some extent, other Pietistic works) as a product of cultural construction rather than a literal depiction of historical fact. (For recent discussion of this methodological issue, see I. G. Marcus, "The Historical Meaning of *Hasidei*

Ashkenaz: Fact, Fiction or Cultural Self-Image?," in *Gershom Scholem's Major Trends in Jewish Mysticism 50 Years After: Proceedings of the Sixth International Conference on the History of Jewish Mysticism.* Ed. by P. Schäfer and J. Dan [Tübingen: 1993], 103-114.) If that is the case, then, the social reality itself is shaped by certain religious beliefs and practices. Hence, to appreciate fully the comments of the Pietists about earthly women one must have a grasp on the construction of the feminine in the esoteric teachings of the Pietists. I too subscribe to the view that theological reflections must be understood in terms of social reality, but in the case of the German Pietists I see no reason to privilege the social reality over the theological reflections insofar as the social reality itself is a product of cultural self-reflection in which theology plays a prominent role. Thus, in my opinion, it would be more accurate to say that the erotic theology is transformed into human sexuality. Finally, let me emphasize that the eroticized spirituality of the German Pietists does not only involve man's intense relationship with God, as Baskin argues, following the position of Joseph Dan, but it also involves the assumption that within the divine realm there is a male-female polarity.

53. The moralistic imperative not to gaze at women expressed in the Pietistic literature is based on earlier rabbinic statements. Cf. B. 'Eruvin 18b; Nedarim 20a; 'Avodah Zarah 20a-b; Zevahim 118b.

54. Eleazar playfully relates the word *'ishshah*, "woman," to the expression, *'esh hi'*, "she is fire." The implication, of course, is that the woman has a latent destructive, even demonic, force that causes harm to the man who looks upon her lustfully.

55. *Sefer ha-Roqeah*, § 20, 30. The causal relation between control of sexual lust and the dwelling of the divine glory is also underscored in the following comment of Eleazar in *Sefer ha-Shem*, MS London, British Museum 737, fol. 310b: "[God] chose the small *yod* for His name [i.e., YHWH] for there is no place devoid of Him, as it says, 'for I fill both heaven and earth' (Jer. 23:24), and He constricts His presence on that which is small, on the Ark and on the covering. [He dwells a distance of] ten handbreadths above the Ark to indicate that the *Shekhinah* dwells on the one who subdues his lust." Cf. *Hokhmat ha-Nefesh*, ch. 80, 136.

56. On the inseparability of the mystical and theurgical elements, cf. *Sefer ha-Shem*, MS London, British Museum 737, fol. 359b: "Just as He created the heart of the guide [i.e., Metatron] in the likeness of the *hashmal* with fire and hail to guide the beasts, for the *hashmal* needs the beasts since the spirit [of the beasts] was in the ophanim [cf. Ezek. 1:20-21], and everything was unified like a man's heart. Therefore, one should greet someone to the left of a person, as it says in the tractate Yoma [53b], for this is the right of the glory, 'I am ever mindful of the Lord's presence; He is at my right hand; I shall never be shaken' (Ps. 16:8). The one who gives charity should give the charity with his right hand to the right hand of the poor person, as it says, 'because He stands at the right hand of the needy' (ibid., 109:31)."

57. *Synopse zur Hekhalot Literatur*, §§ 296, 406.

58. *Perush ha-Tefillot we-ha-Berakhot*, pt. 1, 97-98.

59. On the erotic symbolism of the moon as the vulva, connected especially to the spiral shape, see Eliade, "Moon and Its Mystique," 156. On the feminization of the moon in various religious cultures, see ibid., 163-169. Particularly significant is the connection between the moon and the snake discussed by Eliade. Compare also the comment of the alchemist, Michael Maier, cited by Jung, *Alchemical Studies*, 79 n. 64: "For whenever the heavenly sun and moon meet in conjunction, this must take place in the head and tail of the dragon; in this comes about the conjunction and uniting of sun and moon, when an eclipse takes place." The androgynous nature of the moon is also represented in alchemy by the identification of Mercurius, who is both masculine and feminine, and the moon. See Jung, *Archetypes and the Collective Unconscious*, 311; idem, *Psychology and Alchemy*, 65-67, 371-372, 464; idem, *Alchemical Studies*, 226-227. The motif of the image of Jacob engraved in the moon conveys the same androgynous quality as the convergence of the serpent and lunar imagery. The demonic valence implied in this convergence is also emphasized in the association of the moon and a woman's menstrual cycle affirmed in some kabbalistic sources, especially Lurianic material. Cf. *Peri 'Ets Hayyim*, 19:3, 458-459: "The blood of menstruation is in the woman from the place of the chaos (*tohu*), and from there came to be the serpent who had intercourse with Eve and inseminated her with filth [cf. B. Shabbat 146a]. Thus it is intimated with respect to the moon that it will not give off its light that comes from the sun except for a moment, for she is in an abundance of light and she is purified for her husband. Her light ceases for fourteen days, which are the days of impurity, and after twenty-eight days we do not see her for she is beneath the earth. But the deficiency of her light is for a moment, and this is that very moment alluded to in the verse, 'For a little while I forsook you, but with vast love I will bring you back' (Isa. 54:7), and this is the secret of 'for a moment I hid My face from you' (ibid., 8)." On the symbolic connection of the periodic waxing and waning of the moon and a woman's menstrual cycle, cf. *Sefer Hasidim*. Ed. Margaliot, § 1148, 571-572 (the relevant passage is lacking in the Parma manuscript). On the correlation of the moon and the menstrual cycle in other religious cultures, see G. van der Leeuw, "Primordial Time and Final Time," in *Man and Time*, 327; Eliade, "Moon and Its Mystique," 165; Jung, *Archetypes and the Collective Unconscious*, 184; Friedrich, *The Meaning of Aphrodite*, 79. On the association of menstrual blood and the demonic in medieval kabbalistic sources, cf. *Zohar* 1:126b; 2:111a; *Book of the Pomegranate*, 345; M. Recanati, *Sefer Ta'ame ha-Mitswot*. Ed. S. Lieberman (London: 1962), 79c-d, 80d-81a. See Tishby, *Wisdom of the Zohar*, 1358-1359; P. Giller, *The Enlightened Will Shine: Symbolization and Theurgy in the Later Strata of the Zohar* (Albany: 1993), 152 n. 102. The demonic aspect of the moon, related to menstruation, seems also to underlie the following passage in *Zohar* 3:248b (*Ra'aya' Mehemna'*): "Why is it called *levanah*? On account of the *libbun ha-halakhah* [purification of the law], for she is within, 'all the glory of the

princess is inward' (Ps. 45:14). Through the fire of *Binah* that rests on her she is purified, and the secret of the matter is, 'Be your sins like crimson, they can turn snow-white' (Isa. 1:18)." The demonological association of the moon and the serpent, related to the primordial sin of Adam and Eve and the consequent diminution of the moon, is a motif affirmed in kabbalistic sources as well. See Tishby, op. cit., 462. On the evil side of the moon, symbolically associated with Islam, see the passage from *Ra'aya' Mehemna'* cited above, n. 14. The satanic quality of the moon is underscored in the comment in *Zohar* 1:34a to the effect that when the moon shines infants must be guarded against the forces of judgment that roam the world. The association of the demonic and the moon, which symbolizes the feminine aspect of the Godhead, is implied in the following statement of Nathan Spiro, *Matstsat Shimmurim* (Venice: 1665), 82b: "If you join the letters [of the name] Laban [i.e., *lamed*, *bet*, and *nun*] and the final *he'* of the Tetragrammaton, which refers to Rachel, you form the letters [of the word] *levanah*, which is Rachel who is called the holy moon, as is known." It should be mentioned that the connection of the moon and the demonic is also underscored in the kabbalistic explanation of the goat that is sacrificed as the new month offering. Cf. *Zohar* 1:64a, 65a, 252a; 2:269a; 3:248b; M. Recanati, *Perush 'al ha-Torah* (Jerusalem: 1961), 41a-b, ad Exod. 12:2; David ben Solomon ibn Abi Zimra, *Metsudat David* (Zolkiew: 1862), 24c-d. The demonic aspect of the moon is implied as well in the fact that the astrological sign of Cancer, symbolized by the crab and associated with malignancy, is the house of the moon. See Jung, *Archetypes and the Collective Unconscious*, 342-343.

60. *'Otsar ha-Kavod ha-Shalem* (Warsaw: 1879), 32a.

61. MS Vatican, Biblioteca Apostolica ebr. 228, fol. 19a. For other kabbalistic sources that affirm the notion of Jacob's image engraved upon the moon, see Wolfson, "Image of Jacob," 144-146 n. 190.

62. This is the underlying reason for the comment of the author of *Hemdat Yamim*, 24d: "The later authorities have written that women should not sanctify the moon, and the explanation is simple for those who understand. Everyone should be careful not to look at [the moon] except for the single vision before one begins to make the blessing, and after that one should not look at her at all." The kabbalistic reason for why women are exempt from blessing the moon is that as a result of the blessing there is the sacred union above and it is not proper for women to behold the exposure of the phallus that ensues as a result of that union. Similarly, male Jews should not look at the moon except prior to uttering the blessing. That is, it is necessary for the males to look at the feminine persona prior to the act of coitus. Underlying the prohibition of looking at the moon is the taboo of gazing upon the divine phallus, a theme that I have discussed at length in *Through a Speculum That Shines*.

63. *Metsudat David*, 24b-d.

64. The impact of kabbalistic ideas on this sixteenth-century Polish rabbi has been well documented by J. Ben-Sasson, *The Philosophical System of R. Moses Isserles* (Jerusalem: 1984; in Hebrew).

65. See above, n. 46.

66. This standard kabbalistic symbolism is implicit in the interpretation of the rabbinic legend of the diminishing moon found in Moses Isserles, *Torat ha-'Olah* (Praque: 1570), 3.22, 90a-91b. Cf. ibid., 2:37, 62c.

67. *Book of the Pomegranate*, 191. This passage from *Sefer ha-Rimmon* is copied anonymously in an anthology of kabbalistic secrets preserved in MS JTSA Mic. 1804, fol. 68b.

68. David ben Judah he-Hasid, in his *'Or Zaru'a*, MS JTSA Mic. 2203, fol. 55a, thus comments on the liturgical refrain in the blessing on the moon, "To the moon [God] says, 'Renew yourself, crown of splendor, for those who have been carried since birth,'": "'To the moon [God] says,' that is, *Tif'eret* says to the moon, which is *'Atarah*, when the time of the new moon arrives *'Atarah* is renewed [in relation to] *Tif'eret* in glorious garments (*bi-levushe kavod*) like a man who says to his wife, 'Adorn yourself, purify yourself, and prepare yourself for me to come to you [in sexual intercourse] for this is the time of ritual immersion.' In a similar manner *Tif'eret* speaks to *'Atarah*. 'For those who have been carried since birth,' for she bears all the souls that she renews in the sabbatical year." The symbol of the crown of splendor signifies that the divine crown (*'atarah*), which is the tenth *sefirah*, is united with the divine splendor (*tif'eret*), the sixth *sefirah*. At the same time this image conveys the notion that the divine crown encompasses the souls of Israel.

69. See *Through a Speculum That Shines*, 357-368.

70. *Peri 'Ets Hayyim*, 19:3, 462.

71. Ibid., p. 463. Cf. MS Oxford, Bodleian Library 1651, fol. 22b.

72. On the elevation and masculinization of the moon, i.e., the *Shekhinah*, by means of *Yesod*, cf. Moses Cordovero, *Pardes Rimmonim* (Jerusalem: 1962), 18:5, 86b.

73. *'Ets Hayyim* (Jerusalem: 1910), 36:1, 55a.

74. The convergence of the symbolism of the throne and the crown is expressed in much older esoteric sources. For some references, see E. R. Wolfson, "Images of God's Feet: Some Observations on the Divine Body in Judaism," in *People of the Body: Jews and Judaism from an Embodied Perspective*. Ed. H. Eilberg-Schwartz (Albany: 1992), 161-162.

75. *Magen David* (Munkacs: 1912), 24b-c.

76. In my opinion the masculinization of the moon underlies the following description of Sabbatai Zevi given by Nathan of Gaza, *Derush ha-Taninim*, in G. Scholem, *Be-'Iqvot Mashiah* (Jerusalem: 1934), 44: "You already know that he is the secret of the Torah and the essence of the Torah will not be revealed except through him, and he will rectify the blemish of the moon that is in each and every month, in the secret of 'And the light of the moon shall become like the light of the sun' (Isa. 30:26). There are twelve months, and in each and every month this name is revealed and the moon is

renewed, and this is the name Shaddai, which in its plene form equals *ro'sh hodesh* and the numerical value of the name and the appellations of our master and teacher, may his glory be elevated, and he rectifies the twelve months by means of the letters *bet* and *yod* [which together equal twelve] of [the name] Shabbetai." The messianic figure, Sabbatai Zevi, has the ability to perfect the blemish of the moon through his mystical name Shaddai, which corresponds to the phallus. In her rectified state the moon shines with the light of the sun, which indicates the union of the moon and the sun that results in the transformation of the moon into the sun. That transformation signifies the redemptive moment. See Wolfson, "Crossing Gender Boundaries," 231-232, n. 198.

77. M. Eliade, *The Quest: History and Meaning in Religion* (Chicago and London: 1969), 73. For a critique of the correlation of myth and ritual, which is so central to Eliade's thought, see J. Z. Smith, *To Take Place: Toward a Theory of a Ritual* (Chicago and London: 1987), 101-102.

78. For a recent attempt to shift the emphasis from myth to ritual, see M. Idel, "Some Remarks on Ritual and Mysticism in Geronese Kabbalah," *Journal of Jewish Thought and Philosophy* 3 (1993): 111-130.

Sabbatai Zevi, Metatron, and Mehmed: Myth and History in Seventeenth-Century Judaism

David J. Halperin

Introduction

The argument I am about to set forth is a complicated one. I can convey most clearly the point I intend to make by calling the reader's attention to two texts. I will compare the two; I will argue that they resemble each other strongly and that the resemblances are not coincidental, and I will proceed to draw the implications of these resemblances for the history of Judaism in the seventeenth century.

The two passages derive from sources that seem to have little in common. The first is taken from an ill-defined text that is properly titled *Sefer Hekhalot*, but which modern scholars have preferred to call *3 Enoch*. This text is itself part of a fluid and amorphous mass of Hebrew materials called the *Hekhalot*, a literature defined partly by its obscure and elusive style, partly by its dominating concern with the angelic realms and (occasionally) how human beings may penetrate those realms.[1] We know nothing about the author of *3 Enoch*, and can only guess at the date of its composition: late in the Talmudic period, or perhaps very early in the Middle Ages. The passage itself is part of a story set in the mythic past, the remote and hazy time before Noah's Flood. The narrator is the patriarch Enoch, who describes how he ascended to heaven and was there transformed from a man into a being superior to the angels: a lesser divinity, in fact, who shares the name *Yahveh* with his senior partner. The actors are supernatural beings, and the story may reasonably be designated a Jewish myth.

The story told in the second passage, by contrast, transpires within historical time—Thursday, 16 September 1666, the day that the would-be Messiah Sabbatai Zevi converted to Islam in Adrianople, in the presence of Sultan Mehmed IV, thereby climaxing more than a year of Messianic excitement that had engulfed the entire Jewish world.[2] The passage is drawn from the earliest surviving hagiography of Sabbatai Zevi, written early in the 1680s (that is, about five or six years after

Sabbatai's death) by one Baruch of Arezzo.[3] The event it describes unquestionably took place, though, just as unquestionably, it is grossly disfigured in this account by the writer's wishful thinking.

3 Enoch:

R. Ishmael said: Metatron, Prince of the Divine Presence, said to me: Out of the love which he had for me, more than for all the denizens of the heights, the Holy One, blessed be he, fashioned for me a majestic robe [*levush shel ge'ah*], in which all kinds of luminaries were set, and he clothed me in it. He fashioned for me a glorious cloak [*me'il kavod*] in which brightness, brilliance, splendor, and luster of every kind were fixed, and he wrapped me in it. He fashioned for me a kingly crown [*keter malkhut*] in which 49 refulgent stones were placed, each like the sun's orb, and its brilliance shone into the four quarters of the heaven of 'Arabot, into the seven heavens, and into the four quarters of the world. He set it upon my head [*kesharo al roshi*] and he called me, "The lesser YHWH" in the presence of his whole household in the height, as it is written, "My name is in him."[5]

Baruch of Arezzo:

Our Lord ... did not arrive [in Adrianople] until two days after they had expected him; and he arrived in the evening, too late to receive an audience [with the sultan]. The next morning, he stood before the king. "Peace be upon you," he said to him. And he answered, in the Turkish language: "Upon you be peace." A eunuch stepped forward, one of the king's intimates, carrying a robe [*levush*] that the king had worn. A second eunuch held the king's turban [*miznefet*]. With these garments they clothed him. They called him by the king's own name, Mehmet. The king decreed a large sum for his allowance. Thus it was that the rumor spread that he had changed his faith and become a Muslim ... .[4]

In both stories, the hero undergoes a promotion that involves at least an apparent transformation. The promotion is marked by the granting of a robe (*levush*), of distinctive headgear that may be designated "crown" (*keter*) or "turban" (*miznefet*), and of a new name: "Yahveh" in the ancient myth, "Mehmed" in the Sabbatian hagiography.

Looking deeper—as we will, in the course of this paper—we will discern the following shared theme: A human being undergoes a transformation that recreates him in his very essence, and yet, paradoxically, leaves him the same being that he was before. With this transformation comes a promotion from powerlessness to near-supreme power. Most important: the hero commits a grave violation of religious taboo, without which his transformation and elevation would have been impossible.

As we watch this theme play itself out, we will observe myth transforming itself into history, or, perhaps, history being reconceived (by its actors and its narrators) as myth. We will find ourselves at the end with a fresh clue to the psychology of Sabbatai Zevi, the apostate Messiah, and to the psychology of those Jews who remained convinced he was Messiah in spite of, or perhaps because of, his apostasy.

Sabbatai's Conversion

What happened when Sabbatai Zevi converted to Islam? Did his conversion change him? Did he perceive himself as transformed? Did others perceive him as transformed?

At first sight, these questions seem absurd. Modern historians have naturally seen the event of 16 September 1666 as the critical turning point of the Sabbatian movement. Gershom Scholem has vividly described the shock and the consternation the news created.[6] Contemporary sources bear out the judgment that some momentous change was seen to have occurred on that day. Writing in November 1666, Rabbi Joseph Halevi of Livorno describes how Sabbatai, faced with the threat of death,

> began grovelling on the ground before the sultan, begging that he might be allowed to take refuge in the sultan's religion. He threw his cap on the ground, and spat on it. He insulted the Jewish faith and profaned God's name, in full public view.[7]

The Muslim turban, which Sabbatai assumed in place of his Jewish cap, became for his supporters and his opponents alike the key symbol of the otherness of his new status. Thus, Halevi mockingly points out how the Messianic crown (*keter*) that Sabbatai's enthusiasts had envisioned for him has turned out to be a turban (*zenif*),[8] while Sabbatian writers use "donning the turban" as a fixed phrase for his conversion.[9]

By 1668, two of the most creative and articulate Sabbatian thinkers, Nathan of Gaza and Abraham Cardozo, had both come to espouse a theory of the apostasy that insisted on the Messiah's absolute alienation from Judaism as the essence of his salvific act. They understood Isaiah 53:5, *vehu mehullal mippesha'enu*, to mean: *he was profaned for our sins*. To atone for the sins of the holy people, the Messiah must become *profane*; which means, utterly other than they. He must (in Nathan's words) "*give up* what he once was *in exchange* for becoming something else." This dreadful "exchange" is symbolized by the "evil garment"—the turban, that is—the Messiah is compelled to wear.[10]

Sabbatai himself knew that he was not as he had been. Eight days after his conversion, he wrote to his brother Elijah Zevi:

> Now leave me be, for the Creator has made me into a Muslim [literally, "Ishmaelite"]. I am your brother, Mehmed *kapici bashi oturak* [that is, according to Scholem, honorary gate-keeper for the sultan]. He spoke and it was, he commanded and it was established.[11] I am oppressed for my beloved, and he for me; the ninth day of his having created me anew, according to his will.[12]

A year or two later, Sabbatai wrote how God had "willed that I enter *din Islam*—that is, the Ishmaelite religion—with all my heart ... to invalidate the Torah of Moses until the end time."[13] Not that Sabbatai wholly abandoned Judaism. All sources agree that he continued to behave both as a Jew and as a Muslim until the end of his life; only periodically did he "turn himself entirely toward *torat hesed* [that is, Islam] ... for [he said] thus God willed."[14] But he was hardly a Marrano, a Jew acting as a Muslim under coercion (as Cardozo liked to imagine him[15]), and, extensive as his self-delusions were, this was not one of them.

Yet all this evidence, for the perception that Sabbatai's conversion had radically transformed him, is only one side of the story. There existed in Sabbatian thought a contrary trend, which held that the conversion did not mark a break in Sabbatai's career as Jewish Messiah, but was a logical extension of what had gone before.

Writing from Livorno, shortly before 16 February 1667, Joseph Halevi reports that the news of the apostasy has split Sabbatai's loyalists into a number of factions. One of them holds that the Messiah "must enter among the demonic entities [*kelippot*] in order to make himself their master, and he has thus assumed them as his garment [*nitlabbesh bahem*]." This is plainly an early version of the theory that Scholem has stressed as the primary Sabbatian rationalization of the apostasy: that the Messiah must descend into the demonic realms of Gentile-dom in order to rescue the sparks of holiness that (according to the Lurianic Kabbalah) are held captive there.[16] This of course presupposes that the Messiah has changed himself. But others offer a different explanation, which

> denies that he apostatized at all. ... What really happened, they say, is that the sultan hugged and kissed him as soon as he saw him. He placed the royal crown [*keter*] on his head; and, on top of his cap, a grass-green turban [*zenif*]."[17]

"Crown" and "turban" are here complementary, and they supplement rather than replace Sabbatai's Jewish cap.

Halevi scoffs at the various explanations as "all equally idiotic," and we must concede he has a point. At the same time, there was some justice in the view that, by taking the turban from the sultan's hands, Sabbatai had done exactly as his supporters had expected. In September 1665, Nathan of Gaza had prophesied that Sabbatai would peacefully assume power from the sultan.[18] He did not use the language of crowning. But, about the beginning of December, the Hamburg rabbi Jacob Sasportas— who was then a cautious skeptic—paraphrased Nathan as saying that the sultan "will remove his turban [*miznefet*], lift off his crown [*atarah*], and place it on the Messiah's head."[19] Following Ezekiel 21:31, from which he draws his language, Sasportas identifies turban and crown; a link that takes added significance from the context of Ottoman practice, which treated the turban as distinctively Muslim headgear, forbidden to Jews.[20] Replying to Sasportas a few weeks later, the "believing" Amsterdam rabbi Aaron Sarfatti accepts and echoes his formulation of Nathan's prophecy.[21] Halevi represents the prophecy in the same way (November 1666),[22] and in Sasportas's subsequent letters, as well as in the narrative with which he holds together his various documents, the expectation that the sultan will "crown" Sabbatai becomes almost a cliché.[23] I see no reason to doubt that Halevi and Sasportas, hostile unbelievers though they were, accurately reflect the anticipation they heard from the mouths of the faithful. They would have had no reason to invent it, precisely because, in a sense, the anticipation came true.

Needless to say, this had no consequences in the real world. If the turban Sabbatai wore was indeed a Messianic crown, the power that ought to go with the crown was conspicuously absent. It cannot long have remained a realistic option that, on 16 September 1666, Mehmed IV had indeed made Sabbatai his deputy or his heir; better to transfer the sphere of the Messiah's salvific activity to the intangible Kabbalistic world of sparks and *kelippot*. And yet the notion that the apostasy was not apostasy at all, but promotion, hung on. It perhaps regained some of its influence after Sabbatai's death. The two earliest authors of lives of the Messiah, Baruch of Arezzo and Abraham Cuenque, make use of it in their accounts of the event.

We have already quoted Baruch's description of Sabbatai's interview with the sultan, and need only to add its context. What happened, according to Baruch, is this: The sultan had summoned Sabbatai to appear before him in Adrianople. The Muslims and Christians of Adrianople "assumed that his head was to be cut off and that all the Jews were to be murdered," and accordingly "sharpened their knives, all ready to work their will on the Jews." But, far from executing Sabbatai, the sultan greeted him in a friendly manner, and went on to share with him his robe, his crown, and even his name. Sabbatai was thus able to induce the sultan to cancel the planned pogrom;[24] and Baruch invites us to reflect that the Lord's mercies are plainly no thing of the past. The apostasy, as such, has practically disappeared; Baruch only touches on it by noting it as a misunderstanding. He will go on to contradict himself on this point, and tell us how Nathan "knew for certain that our Lord had handed himself over to the *kelippot* in order to extract the sparks of holiness from them"; but this does not cancel out that he knew a version of the event in which it was not apostasy but promotion.

Abraham Cuenque of Hebron, who (according to Scholem) wrote his account of Sabbatai's life about 1690, follows the same line.[25] Like non-Sabbatian writers, Jewish and Christian, he attributes a key role in the event of 16 September to a highly placed Jewish apostate in the sultan's court. This apostate, says Cuenque, told Sabbatai that the sultan was in terror of him, and that the smallest act on his part (*davar katan*) would induce the sultan "to seat you on his throne, and you can set the royal crown [*keter*] on your head." Sabbatai refuses; the time is not yet ripe. "Then said the apostate: 'You must take the turban [*miznefet*] upon your head; for, if you do not do so, not a single Jew will survive in the entire Turkish Empire, and the rest of the kingdoms will follow the Turks' example.'"

Is the suggestion that Sabbatai assume the turban an alternative to the suggestion he assume the crown, or a repetition of it? Cuenque hints that the latter is the case. In the sequel, the sultan asks Sabbatai if he is the man said to be the Jews' Messiah. Sabbatai affirms that he is. "I like you very much," the sultan says; "do you wish to be my friend?" Sabbatai says he does. The sultan removes his turban and his robe (*malbush*), and clothes Sabbatai with them. Like Sasportas, Cuenque uses the language of Ezekiel 21:31, *hesir ... hammiznefet*; he shows thereby that he regards the sultan's action as a transfer of power. This would suit what follows: the sultan listens humbly as Sabbatai sternly lectures him on Jewish superiority, and tells him that the Turks' power and their very existence derive from God's blessing of Ishmael in Genesis 17:20.[26]

> The sultan could not restrain himself. He burst into tears. *What is your name?* he asked him.[27] *Sabbatai Zevi*, he replied. *I now*, said the sultan, *give you the name Mehmed Effendi, which means, my wise friend Mehmed.*

Is it possible that Sabbatai himself shared the perception that his biographers were later to express? Let us look again at his letter to his brother Elijah, written right after the apostasy. There is more to it than meets the eye. "I am your brother, Mehmed *kapici bashi oturak.*" The translation masks an incongruity. Sabbatai does not write, *ani ahikha*, "I am your [Elijah's] brother," but *ani ahikhem*, "I am your [plural] brother." We may suspect an allusion to Genesis 45:4, where Joseph reveals himself to his astonished brothers with the words *ani yosef ahikhem*, "I am Joseph your brother."[28] Eight days after beginning his life as a Muslim, Sabbatai has begun to envision that life in terms of the Biblical paradigm of Joseph. Mehmed *kapici bashi oturak* is a high official at a Gentile court, gifted with new clothing (cf. Genesis 41:42) and a new name (cf. 41:45);[29] he is lord of Jews and Gentiles alike, second only to the Pharaoh who has elevated him; he is entirely unrecognizable to his Jewish brothers. Yet he remains *Joseph your brother*, now Muslim and (he imagines) therefore powerful; though his brothers will not yet recognize it, his elevation is part of God's plan (cf. Genesis 45:8). He is transformed, yet remains the same.

This "Joseph paradigm" recurs in other letters written after 1666. In his circular letter of Nisan 1676, which we will presently examine in

some detail, Sabbatai promises to send "a messenger before you, to ...
tell you all my honor in Egypt, and something of what he has seen."[30] The
allusion to Genesis 45:13, and to Joseph's honor in Egypt, is plain. At
about the same time, Sabbatai writes to Joseph Karillo to "come before
me, *for God has made me lord of all Egypt. Come down to me without delay!*"[31]
The italicized words are taken directly from Joseph's speech in Genesis
45:9.

Sabbatai again designates himself as *ahikhem*, in a letter written
evidently before the end of 1672: "Thus speaks your brother Me'emet—
the faith of the Lord God of truth [*ahikhem me'emet emunat adonai el
emet*]."[32] We shall need presently to unpack the significance of the
Hebrew pun by means of which Sabbatai interprets his Muslim name.
For the moment, let us note that the key to understanding it is in a remark
made earlier in the letter: that "the truth of the Lord God of truth [*amittat
adonai el emet*] ... is concealed from everyone, yet destined to be revealed
to heavenly and earthly beings alike, by that servant of his whose name
is like his master's name [*avdo she shemo keshem rabbo*]." With this last
phrase, Sabbatai points toward a paradigm for his self-understanding
that both incorporates and supersedes the more obvious Joseph paradigm. Only when we examine it will we understand who Sabbatai's
"master" was, and what living under that master meant to him.

Metatron and Lucifer

The Hebrew phrase *sheshemo keshem rabbo* is quoted verbatim from
the Babylonian Talmud, Sanhedrin 38b. The Talmud has raised the
question of why Exodus 24:1 represents God as telling Moses to *ascend
to the Lord*. He should have said, *Ascend to me!* And the reply follows:
"This is Metatron, whose name is like his master's name [*she shemo
keshem rabbo*]. So it is written, *For my name is in him* [*ki shemi bekirbo*;
Exodus 23:21]. But if so, we ought to worship him! It is written, *Do not
rebel against him* [*ibid.*], [which the Talmud understands to mean] *Do not
exchange me for him*." For the Talmudic rabbis, the danger of *exchanging*
Metatron for God was a real one: in Hagigah 15a, Rabbi Elisha ben
Abuyah sees Metatron in heaven, mistakes him for a second divinity,
and is damned in consequence.

The rabbinic literature provides no further direct information of
significance on Metatron. But the *Hekhalot* materials, which may be
assumed contemporary at least to the later strata of the rabbinic litera-

ture, have a great deal to say about him, and their evidence supplements and clarifies what can be gathered from the Talmud. Metatron is "Prince of the Divine Presence" (*sar happanim*), a near-divine being who actually shares the name of the supreme divinity, and is thus called "Lesser Yahveh." Curiously, he is also called *na'ar*, "youth," a designation that seems to me to point to the psychological roots of the Metatron myth (below), but which the *Hekhalot* themselves explain as referring to Metatron's being a Johnny-come-lately in the heavenly realms.

For Metatron was once a human being. "I am Enoch son of Jared," he tells Rabbi Ishmael,

> whom God took up ... to serve the Throne of Glory ... my flesh was turned into flame, my sinews and bones into fiery coals, my eyelids to the sheen of lightning, my eyeballs to flames of fire, my hair to flame, all my limbs to wings of burning fire, and my entire body to consuming flames.[33]

Thus elevated and transformed, Enoch-Metatron sits on a throne like God's (*3 Enoch* ch. 10), lord over those angels who had once tried to prevent his ascension (ch. 6). We have already examined one stage of his transformation, and seen it to involve receipt of a robe, of a crown, of a name like his master's.[34]

This story, remarkable as it is, is hardly isolated in ancient Jewish tradition. It is part of a much larger mythic complex, the identity of whose protagonist may shift but whose fundamental themes remain constant.[35] The complex includes the older stories, preserved in the Pseudepigrapha (notably, *1 Enoch* 71:11-16), of Enoch's elevation and transformation into a supernatural being.[36] But the nearest cognates to the Metatron traditions of the *Hekhalot* are the midrashic accounts of how Moses ascended to heaven, over the violent opposition of the angels, to seize the Torah for Israel. Much older variants of the Moses-ascension theme, such as that preserved in the *Exagoge* of the Alexandrian Jewish writer Ezekiel, must also be taken into account.

When all these variants are taken into account, the essential mythic theme emerges as follows: *A human being forces his way into heaven, against the opposition and to the detriment of those already entrenched there. He takes for himself the emblems and instruments of power, and is thus transformed into a higher being who wields near-supreme power.* We are obliged to qualify the adjective *supreme* with the adverb *near*, in deference to the monotheistic system that imposes itself on the myth: God is eternally supreme and cannot be dethroned by an ascending human; the human can therefore triumph only with God's collusion, and he cannot hold power higher than God's own. Yet here and there are traces of a latent conception that ignores this boundary, and has the ascending hero take the place of God himself.

So conceived, this complex—which we shall call, for convenience, the *Metatron complex*—proves to be the reverse image of another complex, nearly identical to it except in its perspective on the protagonist, which reverses the end of the story. In the Metatron complex, the ascending being is the hero, who must triumph; the reverse complex makes him a demonic rebel who must be defeated. As Paul D. Hanson has shown, this reverse complex was fairly widespread in ancient Near Eastern mythology.[36] It is given classic formulation in Isaiah's taunt-song against the rebellious *Morning-star, son of Dawn*, who *said in your heart, I will ascend to heaven, I will lift up my throne above the stars of God ... I will ascend upon the heights of cloud, I will be like the Most High*, yet who must be *thrown down to Sheol, to the depths of the pit* (Isaiah 14:12-15). We may, accordingly, give this shadow-side of the Metatron complex a name drawn from the Latin translation of Isaiah 14:12: the *Lucifer complex*.

The mythological roots of the Lucifer complex show themselves clearly in the Christian tradition, which identified Isaiah's "Lucifer" (="Morning-star") with the devil, and which transferred the most important features of the Lucifer complex to the figure of Antichrist. In the rabbinic tradition, they remain latent. Rabbinic exegesis of Isaiah 14:12-15 identifies the ascending rebel with wicked Nebuchadnezzar, who proposed, after destroying Jerusalem, to "climb to the lofty heavens and destroy the celestial chambers; I will make war with the exalted holy ones and will set my royal throne over the cherubim."[37] One effect of this identification is that the demonic overtones of the "Morning-star" figure are transferred to Nebuchadnezzar, and from there to anyone who becomes identified with Nebuchadnezzar. The importance of this point will become clearer as we go on. Another effect is that the Lucifer complex does not have a life of its own in Jewish tradition, but persists as the shadow-side of the Metatron complex. We shall presently see direct evidence of this.

The Metatron and Lucifer myths can be interpreted at several levels. Most basically, they can be understood psychologically as representing what Ernest Jones has called "the world-old conflict between father and son, between the younger and the older generation, the favourite theme of so many poets and writers, the central *motif* of most mythologies and religions."[38] (The designation of Metatron as *na'ar*, "youth," points to this origin for the myth.) The Metatron complex views the struggle from the perspective of the rising generation, the Lucifer complex from that of the entrenched generation. Just as the generational struggle renews itself endlessly, so do the myths.

We must add to this, however, that the precise form the myths take, as well as the importance that is attached to them, will vary with historical circumstances. There are times when one form or another of the myth provides an answer to some pressing need of the believing community, and at such a time, the myth will come strongly to the foreground of the community's expression. And there may be times when an actual person appears who seems to enact the themes of the myth. When these two circumstances intersect, the person in question will be invested with all the power of the myth that he or she represents, and will become the focus of the community's faith and energy. This is what I believe to have happened in 1666.

The continuing vitality of the Metatron myth is evident from the Zohar. He was basically irrelevant to the sefirotic system that dominates this Kabbalistic classic, and could not well be assimilated into its theosophy. And yet the Zohar assigns him a substantial role.[39] He is still Enoch transformed; he is still the *na'ar*; he still partakes of "his master's name."[40] By the later Middle Ages, this last claim had taken on a new dimension. Rashi, commenting on Exodus 23:21, had explained that *my name is in him* refers to the numerical equivalence between *Metatron* and the divine name *Shaddai* (which normally appears as "the Almighty" in English Bible translations). The Zohar takes for granted this association[41]—which we will see to have been highly significant for Sabbatai Zevi and his followers—and advances it a step further. In the Zoharic system, the name *Shaddai* is specifically associated with the *sefirah Yesod*, the divine phallus that binds together the male and female aspects of the system. Metatron thus becomes a manifestation (in the inferior realm of the angels) of this *sefirah*.[42] His link with *Yesod* further connects him with Joseph, who, in Kabbalistic Bible exegesis, invariably stands for *Yesod*.[43] Sabbatai's Joseph paradigm thus shades into a Metatron paradigm—a point to which we must return.

It is not only the divine aspect of Metatron that is represented in the Zohar. His dark, "Lucifer" side is also in evidence. Several passages in the later strata of the Zohar, *Raya Mehemna* and *Tikkunei Zohar*, identify him with the rod of Moses in Exodus 4, which can change into a snake and back again. (The writer finds *matteh*, the Hebrew word for "rod," within the name Metatron.) "When he is a *rod*, then he is a *helper* from the domain of good; when he turns into a snake, then he is an *opponent* from the domain of evil, and *Moses flees from before him* [Exodus 4:3]."[44] He is further equated with the *tree of the knowledge of good and evil*,[45] whose *good* aspect is Metatron and whose *evil* aspect is Samael, "king of the demons."[46] In these passages, written around the beginning of the fourteenth century, the demonism latent in the figure of Metatron comes to the surface. We will see it emerge yet more strongly in the self-identifications of Sabbatai Zevi.

Metatron, as we have seen, is the *sefirah Yesod*; Joseph is also *Yesod*; therefore Metatron is Joseph. The Polish Kabbalist Nathan Shapira of Krakow—who died in 1633, when Sabbatai was a child of six or seven—dwells upon this equation in his treatment of the Joseph story in his magnum opus *Megalleh Amukkot*.[47] One element of his interpretation, in light of Sabbatai's fate, is particularly striking. "The entire essence of our holy patriarchs," he writes, "was to gather the holy sparks that had been driven out into the demonic realms [*sitra ahra*], [symbolized by] *the land of Canaan* [Genesis 37:1]." This is essentially the task of Joseph-Metatron, "to gather them and bring them into holiness."[48] "Joseph went down into Egypt in order to raise the sparks of purity that had descended there … for the righteous [*zaddik* = *Yesod*; referring to Joseph] brings out of Sheol—that is, the *kelippah*—the sparks of purity … the *kelippah* swallowed some elements of holiness and will vomit them up. … The Lord … brings the righteous [Joseph] down to Sheol so as to raise him back up with the spark."[49] I cannot invoke any direct evidence that Sabbatai or his followers were familiar with Nathan Shapira's interpretations of Genesis.[50] But, if they were, Shapira's exegesis will have seemed to them an extraordinary foreshadowing of the role played from 1666 onward by their Messiah, who was Joseph, who was Metatron.

Sabbatai as Metatron

There can be no serious doubt that Sabbatai Zevi and his followers had access to the Metatron traditions, both in their Zoharic versions and in their original formulations in the *Hekhalot*. *3 Enoch*'s account of Metatron's elevation and transformation—which Moses Cordovero had quoted, presumably from manuscript, in the 1540s[51]—was printed, under the title *Derush Pirkei Hekhalot*, about the year 1650. Extracts from it appear in both the 1660 and 1681 editions of *Yalkut Re'uveni*. A distinct but parallel version was published as part of the *Alphabet of Rabbi Akiba*, in Krakow in 1579 and again at some date after 1600.[52] The Zohar, according to the testimony of Moses Pinheiro, was the staple of Sabbatai Zevi's Kabbalistic studies,[53] and it is hardly thinkable that he was unaware of its treatment of Metatron. We may add that the *Book of Zerubbabel*, a seventh-century Hebrew apocalypse whose prophecies played a substantial role in Sabbatian propaganda from the early days of the movement,[54] knows Metatron as a stand-in for the Biblical God, for God had "made my name like his" (*vayyasem shemi kishemo*).[55]

Let us grant—as we must—that Sabbatai *could* have modelled himself after Metatron, and that his followers *could* have applied the same paradigm to him. We must now ask what positive evidence there is that they *did* do so.

Writing a few years before his death in 1706, the eccentric Sabbatian Abraham Cardozo quotes the testimony of one "Rabbi Ezra Halevi":[56]

> If Sabbatai Zevi told us once he told us a hundred times—"us" meaning "I and all the rabbis who were in his presence"—if he told us once he told us a hundred times that he was destined to be administrator of the upper and the lower realms, raised higher than Metatron.[57]

Sabbatai thus anticipates for himself an exaltation that replicates Metatron's, yet surpasses it. (His supersession of Metatron in no way precludes his identification with Metatron. We know from Christian typology that the One who fulfills the type can easily be superior to the type itself.)

In the same document, Cardozo sketches a Messianic theology which he attributes to the malignant spirits who, in 1683, seduced the Jews of Salonica into mass apostasy:

> They said ... that the Messiah is fully divine; [that he is] Metatron as well; all the more so that he is an absolute Samael; that the divine sefirot of the Malkhut of the World of Emanations have become incorporated within him, and through them he has achieved his exalted greatness.[58]

All the language of this passage points to Sabbatai as Metatron.[59] His simultaneous equation with Samael, baffling at first, is surely rooted in the late-Zoharic teaching that Metatron and Samael are two aspects of the same being. We may suppose that Cardozo attributes to his evil spirits an ideology that he in fact owes to his Sabbatian opponents, an ideology that elevates Sabbatai, *qua* Metatron, to absolute divinity and absolute demonism at the same time. We have no reason to deny that the germ of the idea may go back to Sabbatai himself.

There is in fact very strong evidence, from the heyday of the Sabbatian movement, that at least one element of the Metatron paradigm was operative in the minds of Sabbatai and of his followers, from the most to the least sophisticated of them. This is the repeated claim that Sabbatai partakes of the divine name *Shaddai*, and the interpretation of this claim through two key catch-phrases of the Metatron myth: the Biblical *my name is in him*, and the Talmudic *his name is like his master's name*.

Rashi, as we have seen, had pointed out that *Metatron* has the same numerical value as *Shaddai*, and had interpreted Exodus 23:21 accordingly. Now at some point—probably very early—it occurred to Sabbatai or to one of his adherents that *Shaddai* could equally be brought into numerical equivalence with *Sabbatai Zevi*: all one had to do was spell out the three letters of the name *Shaddai* (*shin-dalet-yod*), and count up the value of this full spelling. (In the eyes of early modern Kabbalists, this form of *gematria*, known as *millui*, was just as valid as the more straightforward technique.[60]) *My name is in him*, and *his name is like his master's name*, were therefore as true of Sabbatai as they were of Metatron, and true in precisely the same way.

Hence:

> God's faithful prophet, Rabbi Nathan Ashkenazi [of Gaza] the prophet … has written that our Lord has the same name as his master [*shemo keshem rabbo*]: *Sabbatai Zevi* has the numerical value of *Shaddai* when spelled out in full as *shin-dalet-yod* [Hosea Nantawa, writing from Alexandria in September 1666].[61]

It was certainly for this reason that Sabbatai, while still in Gaza in 1665, had made for himself a ring inscribed with the full spelling of *shin-dalet-yod*;[62] though we cannot be sure whether Sabbatai got the idea from Nathan or the other way round. Early in April 1666, Raphael Supino writes that a woman of Aleppo, one of a number of illiterate prophetesses who have attested to Sabbatai's Messiahship, has explained "that *my name is in him* [Exodus 23:21] refers to the name *Shaddai*; which, when given its full numerical value, corresponds to the value of *Sabbatai Zevi*."[63] Supino is pleased to suppose that the woman's discovery was miraculous; we may prefer to reflect that it is a straightforward extension of the interpretation of the verse given by Rashi, whose Bible commentary was accessible to any Jew with a smattering of education.[64] At the end of September, the members of a newly founded Messianic yeshiva in Amsterdam—most of them unlearned men, as Scholem has observed[65]—write to Sabbatai expressing the hope that they may find renewal in his protective "shade, which is the shade of *shin-dalet-yod;*[66] for his name is in him [*ki shemo bekirbo*]."[66]

Joseph Halevi (in Livorno) reinforces the impression we have gained: that the *Shaddai*-Sabbatai association, and its background in the Metatron myth, were widespread among the believers in 1666. All the Jewish rabble,[68] he writes to Nantawa at the beginning of November (after the news of the apostasy had begun to spread), had come to conceive that Sabbatai was divine. When the pious rabbis rebuked them, "the people one and all"[69] insisted that Sabbatai had religious authority to permit that which had hitherto been forbidden, "inasmuch as his name is like his master's name [*sheshemo keshem rabbo*]."[70]

But November 1666 was a bad time for the believers. Writing to Sasportas later in the month with a full account of the apostasy, Halevi howls for revenge against "these imbeciles, these credulous nincompoops" who had so cruelly slandered him:

> But tell them, all the same, not to lose hope. For Mehmed their savior has now returned to his school days; a pupil, now, of the Muslim religion [*dat ha yishma'elim*]. Yes, indeed; the sultan has enrolled him in one of their abomination-houses, there to receive instruction in their faith. He will no doubt study hard, and will grow up to be quite a scholar. He will then come to save them, and raise them to the spiritual level of their prophet—his master, whose name is like his—their prophet Mehmed [*sheshemo keshem rabbo mehmed nevi'am*].[71]

Halevi thus effects a stunning reversal of the claims of Sabbatai and his propagandists. They are right; Sabbatai's name is indeed like his master's—now that he has fused himself to the demonic world of Islam,[72] and taken on the name of the Muslim prophet. (Mehmed is the Turkish pronunciation of Muhammad.) The true identity of Sabbatai's master is revealed in his new name.

We will now be able to understand the full meaning of Sabbatai's signing himself (at some point after the apostasy, but before the end of 1672) "your brother Me'emet—the faith of the Lord God of truth [*ahikhem me'emet emunat adonai el emet*]." With this signature, Sabbatai answers

Halevi's reversal of his claim to be the servant "whose name is like his master's name," with a counter-reversal even more stunning than Halevi's.

Sabbatai describes the addressees as "my brothers and my friends, who love my king and my God, the Lord God of truth" (*malki velohai adonai el emet*). He uses the phrase "Lord God of truth" (from Psalm 31:6) a second time in the body of the letter, and a third time in the signature. In the meantime, he has declared himself to be "that servant of his whose name is like his master's name" *avdo sheshemo keshem rabbo*). Who is his master? God, presumably; for his Muslim name *Me'emet* contains within it the Hebrew word, *emet*, by which God designates himself as "God of truth." But it is also *Mehmed*, the Muslim potentate who has given Sabbatai his own name, and thereby established a kinship between the two of them. Sabbatai's opening formula, "those who love my king and my God," now takes on a new meaning. King and God are one: the Jewish God is Sabbatai's king, but the Muslim king is also Sabbatai's God.

The Sabbatian and anti-Sabbatian interpretations of Metatron's *name like his master's name* thus unfold in a sort of dialectic. Sabbatai and his followers begin by asserting: *Sabbatai Zevi has within himself the essence of the divine, for he shares the name of his master Shaddai*. His enemies retort: *Sabbatai Zevi has within himself the essence of the demonic, for he shares the name of his master Mehmed*. And Sabbatai, synthesizing the two, gains the last word: *I have within myself the essence of divine power, for I share the name common to God and the sultan*.

Sabbatai, in his role of Metatron, thus throws himself as a bridge over the gulf between the divine and what his contemporaries had regarded as demonic. The once-forbidden realms have now become open for Jews to enter.

This, I suggest, was the crux of Sabbatai's salvific work, which made it possible for him to be called Messiah. The salvation he brought had one disadvantage: it took place entirely within the realm of fantasy. But the times demanded it; and, insofar as he could, Sabbatai Zevi tried to answer their call.

Sabbatai in Context

Considering the Sabbatian movement, historians must try to resolve the questions *Why then?* and *Why him?* What was there about the middle of the seventeenth century that made the time particularly ripe for a major outbreak of Messianic activity? And why did the unlikely figure of Sabbatai Zevi seem an appropriate focus for that activity?

The conventional explanation for Messianic outbreaks—they come when conditions seem intolerable, when people are miserable and desperate and will grab at anyone who claims to be their savior—does not work very well for Sabbatianism. For it is difficult to think of the 1660s as a particularly miserable or desperate time for the Jewish people.[73] True, the Chmielnicki uprising of 1648-49, with its accompanying slaughters of Polish and Ukrainian Jews, had been traumatic. True, Spain remained a land of terror for any "new Christians" unlucky enough to be suspected of holding on to some traces of their Jewish past. But the Chmielnicki horrors were receding into the past,[74] while in the present, Inquisitorial Spain was visibly declining as a world power. The tolerant Netherlands had taken its place.

How did contemporary Jews view their present? Sasportas preserves an exchange on the subject, between himself and the Moroccan rabbi Jacob ibn Sa'adun (summer 1669). Ibn Sa'adun denies that we now live in a time of religious persecution (*shemad*); Sasportas affirms that we do.[75] (At issue is the legal question of whether a community may choose to disregard the fast of the Ninth of Av.) Sasportas's evidence is remarkably sporadic. The strongest part of his argument rests on conditions in Spain and Morocco. (He had earlier declared the state of Jewry in Morocco to be the worst in the world by far.[76]) Ibn Sa'adun had praised Jewish freedoms in Amsterdam, Hamburg, and England. Sasportas retorts that Jews in Amsterdam and Hamburg are not *that* free, and that he knows a case when the Hamburg authorities had forced a synagogue to close. He complains about restrictions on Jews in Italy. He does not respond to Ibn Sa'adun's mention of England, nor does he say anything whatever about persecution in the Ottoman Empire. There seems to have been rather little he could have said.[77] This is apparently the best case Sasportas can mount for regarding 1669 as a time of persecution, and it does not add up to much.[78]

Jonathan I. Israel writes that

> in some respects Jewry, from the end of the sixteenth century onwards, was being reintegrated into the life and civilization of the west. It may be true that this reintegration was more economic than cultural, yet the rifts and disintegrative tendencies within western Christendom had placed the age-old confrontation of Christianity and Judaism on a

totally new basis. … It was precisely this which enabled European Jews to become part of western civilization.[79]

This reintegration was most visible in Amsterdam, where Jews enjoyed freedom, toleration, and a measure of acceptance unprecedented in Jewish history, at least since the rise of Christianity.[80] But Amsterdam, if exceptional, was no isolated freak. Intellectual exchanges between Jews and Christians, on terms approaching equality, had become reasonably normal by the middle of the seventeenth century, in Holland and elsewhere; and sympathetic Christian approaches to understanding Jews and Judaism were no longer unheard of.[81] We will recall that two Amsterdam Jews, the orthodox Manasseh ben Israel and the not-so-orthodox Spinoza, both managed to achieve international celebrity among European Christians.

Amsterdam provides us with a check for evaluating the relation between the Sabbatian movement and Jewish misery and desperation. For if there were some causal connection, surely we would expect the "Dutch Jerusalem" to be the least likely place in the world for Sabbatai Zevi to have found adherents. Yet the opposite was the case. To judge from Sasportas and from the documents he preserved, Amsterdam was one of the main European centers of Sabbatian enthusiasm. "Our world," wrote one "believing" Amsterdam rabbi at the end of 1665, "has been turned topsy-turvy; people have forsworn the dicing-houses and the lotteries … day and night do they contemplate God's Torah, meanwhile undertaking perfect penance" in anticipation of the coming redemption.[82] I have already mentioned the Messianic yeshiva founded in Amsterdam the following summer. This evidence will encourage us to consider the possibility that there was something precisely in the new freedom of the Jews in Amsterdam—and, to a lesser extent, elsewhere in the world of the seventeenth century—that encouraged them to receive Sabbatai Zevi as Messiah.

For this freedom had its problematic aspects. To begin with, it would be difficult to imagine a time when the dominant ideology of Judaism was less equipped to provide religious legitimation or regulation to the reality of Jewish integration into non-Jewish culture. This ideology was, or was in the process of becoming,[83] the Kabbalah; and the Kabbalah insisted, with a radicalism unprecedented in the history of Jewish thought, on the absolute abyss that separates Jews from Gentiles. The Kabbalists saw Jews and Gentiles as practically two different species, gifted with qualitatively different souls.[84] As Jews were moving socially and intellectually closer to non-Jews and finding reason to believe in their common humanity, they found themselves committed to an ideology that taught them that such rapprochement was unnatural, evil, impossible. The tension must have been at least as acute and painful as at any time in Jewish history.

To this we must add that the rapprochement itself was very much limited. A century later, European thinkers would evolve conceptions of nationhood that would make it possible (at least in theory) for a Jew to become a free and equal member of the nation while remaining a Jew. In the seventeenth century, such conceptions had barely begun to be formulated.[85] A more appropriate image for Jewish-Gentile relations had been proposed in the 1590s by the Maharal of Prague. The Gentiles

> treat us as a man does his wife in this third watch of the night,[86] when the woman talks with her husband. They who are called our masters [=husbands] ... just as a man draws his wife near when he loves her and divorces her when he hates her, so the nations expel us when they hate us.[87]

We may paraphrase: the Jewish people, collectively, is an Esther taken to Ahasuerus's palace and bed,[88] powerful only to the extent that she can placate and manipulate her lord.

I do not think this had changed fundamentally by 1650. Jews were tolerated or even welcomed in many places, secure and powerful in none. Even in Amsterdam, Jews had to be extremely careful not to offend Protestant sensibilities lest they find their welcome withdrawn; this may be part of the reason why they excommunicated Spinoza.[89] As for the Ottoman Empire, it would be hard to think of a crueler or more pointed statement of Jewish powerlessness than the reply the kaimakam is supposed to have given (in 1667) to those rabbis who warned him against the seditious activities of Nathan of Gaza:

> Why are you so worried? If this prophet Nathan comes here and becomes a Muslim, he will be shown the same honor as was Sabbatai Zevi Kapici Bashi Oturak. And if not, you have nothing to be anxious about. For he, and all the Jews in the Turkish Empire with him, are incapable of the slightest action, or any rebellion against the emperor's will. It is idle foolishness; what can they do?[90]

The Gentile can be so tolerant, because the Jew is so helpless. This is certainly better than persecution, but it remains painful and humiliating.

The "Emancipation" of later centuries presented Jews with the difficult challenge of finding ways to be French, English, American and so forth without ceasing to be Jewish. The "reintegration" of the seventeenth century presented them with the impossible challenge of *finding some way to be Gentile without ceasing to be Jewish*. This was the only alternative to either cutting themselves off from their past or settling for a reality that was a frustrating and humiliating tease. The world around them offered no exit from this dilemma. Their own Kabbalah, by turning the world into a cosmic duality of holiness on the one side and absolute otherness on the other, made it vastly worse. A gaping abyss stood before them, and it might be crossed only by a Metatron.

My thesis is that the myth of Metatron took on crucial significance in the middle of the seventeenth century, because Metatron had performed the impossible feat that the Jews of the seventeenth century yearned to replicate. *While remaining identifiably human, he had transformed himself into a divinity*. By committing the sin of Lucifer—that is to say, by violating the fundamental taboo that declares God's deity unique and inimitable—he had crossed the boundary that separated the human from the divine, and had integrated both in himself. He thus moved from the remote fringes of power to its center. Once he had been a feeble human intruder in the heavenly realms, to whom the natives had given the most grudging welcome possible. Now he was a divinity, sharing the name of the supreme divinity; he was their lord and master.

Superimpose the Metatron myth on the seventeenth-century reality, and the following correspondences emerge: "Jew" stands in the place of "human," while "Gentile" stands in the place of "divinity." The second equation is a fantastic offence against the entire Kabbalistic theosophy, for which the opposing realms are "divine" and "demonic," with Jews in the first and Gentiles in the second. If therefore Metatron is to enable Jews to achieve the godlike power that inheres in the Gentile world, he must transcend this dichotomy with a second great integration: of the divine and the demonic. For this task Metatron was eminently well suited. At the root of his myth we find Metatron and Lucifer together, as positive and negative images of the same being. This dual entity re-emerges in the later strata of the Zohar, where the supreme angel Metatron and the demon king Samael appear as one being in two aspects.

Metatron is the mythic figure that has the power to span all the categories, to resolve the contradictions that plagued the Jews of the seventeenth century. He, or his surrogate, will therefore be the savior of Israel.

The question of why Sabbatai Zevi seemed a plausible Messiah to seventeenth-century Jews will become more tractable if we ask it as: why did he seem a plausible Metatron?

Never in his life did Sabbatai display the qualities of a great leader. In his actions before the apostasy he showed himself to be grandiose, erratic, given to despotic cruelty, and to arbitrary tampering with hallowed traditions.[91] None of this was secret; Sabbatai's enthusiasts must have known his failings as well as we do. They did not, of course, expect their Messiah to convert to Islam. But they well knew his propensity for "strange acts"—peculiar and seemingly purposeless violations of Jewish law—which must have conveyed clearly enough even before the apostasy that Sabbatai would not recoil from breaking the tradition's most august taboos. The "unbelievers" kept insisting on such a man's unworthiness to be Messiah, and were driven to distraction that their arguments had no impact.[92] The futility of their protests, which were obviously reasonable, demands some explanation. We may find it in the hypothesis that Sabbatai's adherents believed in him, not in spite of his well-publicized flaws, but because of them.

In Sabbatai's willful and impulsive behavior, there is something that suggests Metatron and the larger mythic complex of which the Metatron stories are part. The notorious episode at the Portuguese synagogue at Smyrna, on 12 December 1665, is a case in point. The congregation had barred the synagogue doors to him; Sabbath though it was, he hacked his way in with an axe. Once inside, he proceeded to harangue and terrorize the worshippers, forcing them to pronouce the tabooed four-letter Name of God. He distributed the kingdoms of the earth to his followers: his brother Elijah he pronounced sultan of Turkey, his second brother emperor of Rome, and so forth.[93]

The atmosphere of the episode is one of exultant despotism, redolent of the *Hekhalot* traditions of Metatron's exaltation (e.g., *3 Enoch* ch. 14). Sabbatai's forcing his way into the synagogue suggests the ascending hero (notably, the midrashic Moses) who battles his way into heaven over the angels' resistance. His allotment of the kingdoms will remind us of Metatron's having been granted power over the seventy nations of the earth, "to elevate the humble to the height at the utterance of his lips; to smite kings at his command … to remove kings from their kingdoms, and to exalt rulers over their dominions …. "[94] And his high-handed violation of Jewish religious norms, on this and countless other occasions, calls attention to what is perhaps Sabbatai's most strongly Metatron-like feature: his unabashed representation of himself as one who is, in significant part, a being of evil.

Sabbatai as Lucifer

He is, to begin with, a snake.[95] At least as far back as July 1666, he was signing his letters with a sketch of a twisting serpent, and he kept up the practice until near the end of his life. His followers pointed out that the numerical value of *nahash*, "snake," is the same as that of *mashiah*, "Messiah."[96] A few years after the apostasy, Nathan of Gaza declared, evidently on Sabbatai's authority,[97] that Sabbatai is the "holy serpent" whose "crooked" acts of cosmic restoration had been foreseen by Moses in Exodus 4. "When Moses saw all these things, and the acts of restoration to be performed by the spark from his seed ... that [his rod] had turned into a mighty serpent, *he fled from before it* [4:3]."[98] The allusion to Moses[99] is very reminiscent of the Zoharic passage (above) that demonstrates, from Exodus 4, Metatron's propensity for changing from rod into snake and back again, and it seems likely that Sabbatai had this passage in mind. When declaring himself a snake, therefore, he is identifying himself with Metatron in his serpentine, demonic aspect.[100]

He is also Lucifer. Even in his youth he had begun to identify himself with the rebellious "Morning-star" of Isaiah's prophecy. People in Smyrna could remember how, in his early twenties, he had been wont to recite Isaiah 14:14, *I will ascend upon the heights of cloud, I will be like the Most High*; and that he had once uttered these words:

> with so special an emphasis that he imagined, was indeed convinced, that he was lifted into the air. He therefore dared once to ask his comrades, whether they had not seen him being lifted up from the earth? and when they answered truthfully that they had not, he answered them: *You are nt worthy of so glorious a sight, for you are not purified as I am.*

It was afterwards—according to the Dutch minister Coenen, to whom we owe this anecdote—that Sabbatai began to reveal to his followers, "often while repeating the above-mentioned verse from Isaiah," that he was the Messiah son of David.[101]

These youthful fantasies of exaltation recur, in vastly more grandiose form, in a circular letter that Sabbatai dispatched about six months before his death (Nisan 5436 = March-April 1676) to his adherents in at least two communities, Sofia and Arnaut-Belgrade.[102] The version that went to Arnaut-Belgrade—which seems to survive in Sabbatai's own autograph—is appended to a brief request for High Holy Day prayer books, which is treated as a distinct letter by itself. This letter has its own signature: "Thus speaks the man lifted up on high [II Samuel 23:1], above all the host of heaven in heaven and above all the kings of earth on earth [Isaiah 24:21], the Messiah of the God of Israel and Judah, Sabbatai Zevi." This declaration, with its indirect allusion to Lucifer's *I will lift up my throne above the stars of God*, is grandiose enough. But the circular letter that follows it is yet wilder.[103]

> I am sending a messenger before you [Exodus 23:20], **the one mentioned above, to bring you good news.**[104] He will tell you all my honor in Egypt, and something of what he has seen [Genesis 45:13]. Be careful of him, and obey him. Do not rebel against him concerning anything he tells you in my name, for I will not forgive your iniquity [Exodus 23:21] **when God arises to judge and the Lord of hosts is exalted in judgment** [Psalm 76:10, Isaiah 5:16].[105] **And who is the God who can save you from my hand?** [Daniel 3:15] **for aside from me there is no God** [Isaiah 44:6].[106] But if you obey him and do all I tell you [Exodus 23:22],[107] I will surely ascend and will fill your treasuries [Proverbs 8:21].
>
> So speaks the man lifted up on high [II Samuel 23:1], **upon the heights of the Father** [*al bamote av*; Isaiah 14:14];[108] Lion of the Exalted Dwelling, Gazelle of the Exalted Dwelling; the Messiah of the God of Israel and Judah—**Sabbatai Mehmed Zevi.**[109]

At least nine Biblical passages are compressed into this brief manifesto.[110] The dominant text is obviously Exodus 23:20-22, the description of the mighty angel who bears God's name within him, which the Metatron traditions from the Talmud on understood to refer to their hero. In using the passage, Sabbatai steps into the role of God, who is the speaker in the Biblical text. But he is also the one described, the divine "messenger" Metatron. This will explain the otherwise puzzling reference, in the Arnaut-Belgrade version of the circular letter, to the messenger's having been "mentioned above." The only person who has been "mentioned above" is Sabbatai himself, in the signature affixed to his request for prayer books. It follows that the "messenger" Metatron, and the God who sent him, are united in the person of Sabbatai Zevi.

Sabbatai, then, is God. He is also Metatron. As we have already seen, he is Joseph (evident from the allusion to Genesis 45:13). In his signature, as in the signatures of several earlier letters, he identifies himself with David, "the man lifted up on high" (*haggever hukam al*; II Samuel 23:1).

He goes yet further, and carries his self-identifications into the sphere of the demonic. In the fuller version addressed to Sofia, he extends the *al* of II Samuel 23:1 into Isaiah 14:14, so that he becomes *the man lifted up on the heights*—not *of cloud*, as Isaiah originally had it—but *of the Father*. (The two words are nearly identical in Hebrew.) As in his youth, so in his approach to death: he understands his quest for elevation as that of Isaiah's "Morning-star," who ascends on high to challenge and to become the Father.

As Sabbatai is the "Morning-star," so he is the "Morning-star's" earthly avatar: Nebuchadnezzar, in accord with rabbinic interpretation of the Isaiah passage (above). That is how he can combine Nebuchadnezzar's blasphemous challenge—*Who is the God who can save you from my hand?*—with the divine declaration that *aside from me there is no God*, and adopt both together as his own words. He thus synthesizes Biblical God and demonic Gentile tyrant, as effectively as in his interpretation of his Muslim name *Me'emet*.

The synthesis was foreshadowed even before the apostasy. Nathan of Gaza had prophesied (September 1665) that Sabbatai would come "mounted on the Lion of the Exalted Dwelling, having as his bridle a seven-headed snake";[111] and, as one "believing" rabbi pointed out to Sasportas a few months later, these details were very suggestive of Talmudic legend about Nebuchadnezzar.[112] Sabbatai could also be identified with Biblical analogues to Nebuchadnezzar. In Nathan's writings, beginning from the spring of 1665, Sabbatai is Pharaoh.[113] Nathan identifies him as Ahasuerus, and this self-identification can be traced in Sabbatai's behavior both before the apostasy and afterward.[114]

These identifications, which at first sight seem so strange, rest on a fundamental equation of the divine with the alien and the despotic. Sabbatai Zevi made this equation his life's principle, and embodied it in his most important acts. When he took the robe, turban, and name of Mehmed IV, we may suppose that he was moved by something more than the threat of death. We may suppose that he saw himself presented with the opportunity that had been given to Metatron, of entering into the power-filled and godlike world that Judaism had defined as alien. Like Metatron, he defied religious taboo and took his chance.

Sabbatai and Mehmed

Sabbatai Zevi, if I am right, was a historical person who saw himself as a figure from ancient Jewish myth, and behaved accordingly. His success was that many of those who shared the myth were ready to share his belief that he was indeed enacting it on earth. His failure, and the deep tragedy of his followers, was that the myth had almost nothing in common with the reality of the mid-seventeenth-century. Sabbatai's "honor in Egypt," so proudly announced in his circular letter, had no real existence. His extraordinary talent for using himself as a mythical symbol to bridge cosmic realms carried with it (apart from a few months in 1666) little or no corresponding power in the real world. This is why his movement failed, and why the literature its followers created is so overwhelmingly sad and defeated.

One point remains to be considered. Contemporary realities, as we have seen, did much to shape the problems for which Sabbatai offered himself as a mythic resolution. Might they also have colluded with the ancient myth in shaping the solution he proposed? That is to say, can we find in the events of his lifetime anything that could have suggested to him that he might act out the role of Metatron, stepping into Ottoman power as Metatron stepped into celestial power?

1648 was an important year for Sabbatai Zevi. It was the year, it would seem, in which he first proclaimed himself Messiah. It was the year for which the Zohar had promised redemption, and which saw instead the Chmielnicki disaster. It was also the year when, less than two weeks after Sabbatai's twenty-second birthday, the Sultan Ibrahim was deposed from the Ottoman throne, and replaced by his six-year-old son Mehmed IV.[115]

"Ibrahim the Mad," as his contemporaries called him,[116] had ruled since 1640. He had made himself drastically unpopular by his military failures, his corruption, his extravagance, and his use of his power in an unrestrained and brutal hunt for sexual gratification.[117] On 8 August 1648, his opponents approached the Mufti with the question "whether that according to their law, Sultan Ibrahim as a fool, a tyrant, and unfit for government ought to be deposed?" and received an affirmative answer. The Janissaries forced Ibrahim to flee to his mother for protection; and "taking forth his eldest son Sultan Mahomet, set him on the throne of his father, and planting the *sargouch*, or imperial feathers, on his head, saluted him for emperor with loud acclamation."[118] Nine days later, Ibrahim was strangled.

Thus far the account, more or less contemporary, of the English consul Paul Rycaut. Joseph von Hammer-Purgstall, drawing upon Turkish sources, represents Ibrahim's mother as having yielded (on 8 August) to the rebels' demand: "So be it. I shall fetch my grandson, Mehmed, and place the turban on his head."[119] On 16 August, in the Mosque of Eyub, "the saber was buckled upon" the young Mehmed IV

> amid the customary ceremonies. ... He was clothed in an undergarment the color of sulfur, interwoven with gold; above it, a purple outer garment interwoven with gold. The turban, wound about his head after the fashion of Sultan Selim's, was adorned with two diamond herons, above which an emerald the size of an egg radiated the light of hope and the splendor of youth.[120]

Did Sabbatai know the details of the episode? It is hardly conceivable that he did not. His father was a broker and agent for English merchants in Smyrna.[121] A European merchant can hardly have survived the cutthroat international competition in Smyrna without prompt and exact information on what was going on at the Ottoman court.[122] Surely his father's employers knew precisely what had happened; surely they told his father; surely his father told him.

We know that the child sultan made his way into the dreams of at least one of his Jewish subjects. This was Abraham Yakhini, a Constantinople Kabbalist and preacher who was later to become one of the Sabbatian movement's most prominent and dedicated leaders.[123] *I dreamed yesterday that I had the king's, Sultan Mehmed's, cap on my head, and also the king's scarf in my sash. I saw also beds mde up in royal fashion, with coverlets [woven] of gold and silver. I saw also a woman's nipples and I pressed one of them, at which milk came forth. I awakened and realized it was a dream. And I further saw the king among children like himself.*[124]

Unfortunately, Yakhini does not record the date of his dream. But it is obvious from the last sentence that it cannot have been more than a few years after Mehmed's accession, and we may suspect that it dates from a time when the excitement of that event was still fresh. (It was, in any event, well before Yakhini had met Sabbatai or come to take any interest in him.) The distinguished preacher, then in his thirties, evidently entertained an unconscious fantasy in which he identified himself with the royal child and thereby satisfied his yearning for maternal nourishment. He expressed this identification by transferring to himself Mehmed's headgear.

What, then, of Sabbatai? We know too little about his Messianic activities in 1648 to gauge what effect Ibrahim's deposition and Mehmed's accession may have had on them. Scholem infers from Dönmeh tradition that Sabbatai believed himself to have been anointed by the prophet Elijah (or by the patriarchs) on 21 Sivan 5408 = 11 June 1648.[125] If this is correct, it cannot have been the transfer of power that inspired his Messianic claim. But it is hard to believe that a momentous event like the deposition and execution of a sultan, coming two months after he had begun to imagine himself Messiah, can have seemed to him insignificant or fortuitous, or that it can have failed to influence his own conception of what his Messianic future might be. Surely it stirred in him fantasies that were more grandiose versions of those expressed in Yakhini's dream.[126] Mehmed had received robe and turban from Ibrahim; someday he, Sabbatai, would do the same from Mehmed.[127]

Eighteen years later, when his private myth had become the collective fantasy of the Jewish world, Sabbatai Zevi stood in Mehmed's presence. True to his dream, he was offered robe and turban. Metatron would not have refused. Neither did he.

Notes

1. D. J. Halperin, *The Faces of the Chariot: Early Jewish Responses to Ezekiel's Vision* (Tübingen: J.C.B. Mohr, 1988), especially chapter IX; P. Schäfer, *The Hidden and Manifest God: Some Major Themes in Early Jewish Mysticism* (Albany: State University of New York Press, 1992); these two books cite the extensive prior literature. The Hebrew text of *3 Enoch* was published, with English translation and extensive notes, by H. Odeberg, *3 Enoch; or The Hebrew Book of Enoch* (originally published 1928; republished, with a prolegomenon by J. C. Greenfield, New York: Ktav Publishing House, 1973). It was again published, in the context of several major *Hekhalot* manuscripts of which it is a part, in P. Schäfer, *Synopse zur Hekhalot-Literatur* (Tübingen: J.C.B. Mohr, 1981). P. Alexander has prepared a new translation for J. P. Charlesworth, *The Old Testament Pseudepigrapha*, 2 vols. (Garden City, NY: Doubleday, 1983-85), 1:223-315.

2. Most modern accounts of the Sabbatian movement are based on the magisterial work of Gershom G. Scholem: *Major Trends in Jewish Mysticism* (New York: Schocken Books, 1954), 287-324; *Sabbatai Sevi: The Mystical Messiah, 1626-1676* (Princeton: University Press, 1973); *Kabbalah* (New York: New American Library, 1974), 244-286. See, for example, S. Sharot, *Messianism, Mysticism, and Magic: A Sociological Analysis of Jewish Religious Movements* (Chapel Hill, NC: University of North Carolina Press, 1982), 86-

129; J. I. Israel, *European Jewry in the Age of Mercantilism: 1550-1750* (2d edition; Oxford: Clarendon Press, 1989), 209-216.

3. Baruch of Arezzo, *Zikkaron Livene Yisra'el*, in A. Freimann, *Inyanei Shabbetai Zevi* (Berlin: Itzkowski, 1912), 43-78. I am currently preparing English translations of this and other Sabbatian texts.

4. Freimann, 58 (my translation).

5. *3 Enoch*, chapter 12; translation by Alexander, in Charlesworth, *Old Testament Pseudepigrapha*, 1:265; Hebrew text in Odeberg and in Schäfer, #15 (see note 1, above). The closing Biblical quotation, which we shall presently discuss at greater length, is from Exodus 23:21.

6. Scholem, *Sabbatai Sevi*, 693-705.

7. J. Sasportas, *Zizat Novel Zevi* (ed. Isaiah Tishby, *Sefer Zizat Novel Zevi Lerabbi Ya'aqov Sasportas* [Jerusalem: Bialik Institute, 1954]), 172.

8. Sasportas, 191.

9. E.g., Baruch of Arezzo (Freimann, 46): *ad ahar shessam hazzenif hattahor al rosho.* Yehuda Liebes cites a Donmeh text that uses the phrase *lehikkanes bammiznefet*, "to enter the turban": Liebes, "Yahaso shel Shabbetai Zevi Lehamarat Dato," *Sefunot* n.s. 2 (1983), 297 n 208.

10. Nathan of Gaza, letter of 7 February 1668, quoted in Sasportas, 260-262, and Baruch of Arezzo (Freimann, pages 59-61). (The allusion to the "evil garment" is from *Tiqqune Zohar*, *tiqqun* 60.) Cardozo, letter to his brother Isaac (1668; precise date uncertain), in Sasportas, 289-297; cf. Yosef H. Yerushalmi, *From Spanish Court to Italian Ghetto* (New York & London: Columbia University Press, 1971), 314-320.

11. From Psalm 33:9.

12. Hebrew text in T. Coenen, *Ydele verwachtinge der Joden Getoont in den Persoon van Sabethai Zevi …* (Amsterdam: Joannes van den Bergh, 1669), 86; Leyb b. Ozer, *Sippur Ma'asei Shabbetai Zevi: Beshraybung fun Shabbesai Zevi.* (Ed. Z. Shazar; Jerusalem: Merkaz Zalam Shazar, 1978), 108; J. Emden, *Sefer Torat Hakkena'ot* (Jerusalem: Makor, 1971; facsimile of the first edition, Amsterdam, 1752), 10a; and, wih a brief discussion, in Liebes, "Yahaso," 295. Translation in Scholem, *Sabbatai Sevi*, 686.

13. Liebes, "Yahaso," 271; I have followed Liebes's dating of the letter.

14. Y. Fenton, "A Document from the Internal Circle of Shabbateans in Adrianople" [Hebrew], *Pe'amim* 44 (1990), 31-40. The quotation, from a contemporary observer, is on 38.

15. Sasportas, 291.

16. Scholem, "Redemption Through Sin," in *The Messianic Idea in Judaism And Other Essays on Jewish Spirituality* (New York: Schocken, 1971), 94-99.

17. Sasportas, 247. The language describing the turban's color is drawn from M. Sukkah 3:6; I am not sure how to explain it, since Halevi elsewhere (in his November letter to Nantawa) makes a point of the turban's being white. It is presumably related to Stanford J. Shaw's observation that, in the Ottoman Empire, "the color green was reserved for Muslims since it was considered

particularly sacred by Islamic tradition" (*The Jews of the Ottoman Empire and the Turkish Republic* [New York University Press, 1991], 79).

18. Letter to Raphael Joseph, in Sasportas, 10.

19. Sasportas, 13.

20. J. von Hammer, *Des osmanischen Reichs Staatsverfassung und Staatsverwaltung*, 2 vols. (Hildesheim: Georg Olms Verlagsbuchhandlung, 1963, reprint of 1815 edition), 1:440-441. I owe this reference to my research assistant, Pamela E. Kinlaw.

21. Sasportas, 27-28.

22. Sasportas, 189.

23. Letters: Sasportas, 114, 153-154. Narrative: 1, 75, 137.

24. Halevi also mentions a massacre having been planned against the Jews. But he blames Sabbatai for instigating it, and claims that it was cancelled due to the intercession of the queen mother and two high court officials (unnamed), Sasportas, 173.

25. Emden, *Sefer Torat Hakkena'ot*, 20a.

26. This detail is perhaps not wholly fantastic. The chronicle of Jacob Najara, which reports Sabbatai's doings in Adrianople during part of the year 1671, twice represents him as quoting this verse in the sultan's presence (Abraham Amarillo, "Te'udot Shabbeta'iyyot Migginzei Rabbi Sha'ul Amarillo," *Sefunot* 5 [1961], 255, 259-260).

27. The question perhaps alludes to Genesis 32:27, where the angel asks it of Jacob as a prelude to giving him a new, better, truer name.

28. So Emden's text (above, n. 12). Coenen's *m'hykm* (followed by Leyb b. Ozer) is presumably an error, like his misspellings of *yishma'eli* and *yom*.

29. And, like Joseph (Genesis 41:45), a new Muslim wife: Scholem, *Sabbatai Sevi*, 685; Sasportas, 198, 202, 304 (using the phrase *ba'al bat el nekhar*, taken from Malachi 2:11, which has a long history in the demonological xenophobia of the Zohar; see I. Tishby, *The Wisdom of the Zohar*. Trans. D. Goldstein 3 vols. [Oxford: University Press, 1989], 3:1370). It is significant that Halevi dates his letter recounting Sabbatai's apostasy to "the week of the Torah portion [containing the verse] *Esau went to Ishmael, and took Mahalath to wife* [Genesis 28:9]" (Sasportas, 174); this surely refers to Sabbatai's Muslim wife, identifying her with the Kabbalistic demoness Mahalath (Zohar, 3:111a [*Ra'ya Mehemna*]; I. Hurwitz, *Shenei Luhot Habberit*, 3:38c). Sabbatai himself will have had a different perspective on the matter.

30. Sources cited below.

31. Quoted in Baruch of Arezzo (Freimann, 68). I infer the date of the letter from its context in Baruch's narrative.

32. To rabbis David Yitzhaki and Benjamin Rijwan; text in Baruch of Arezzo (Freimann, 64); cf. Scholem, *Sabbatai Sevi*, 864.

33. *3 Enoch*, chapters 4 and 15. The passage is quoted by Moses Cordovero from *Sefer Hahekhalot: Pardes Rimmonim, Sha'ar Hahekhalot*, chapter 12 (Munkacz, 1906 [reprinted Jerusalem, 1962], 2:51c).

34. I have discussed the Metatron traditions and their significance in some detail in *Faces of the Chariot*, chapter IX.

35. The observations that follow are based on *Faces of the Chariot*, and on my article "Ascension or Invasion? Implications of the Heavenly Journey in Ancient Judaism," *Religion* 18 (1988), 47-67.

36. Hanson, "Rebellion in Heaven, Azazel, and Euhemeristic Heroes in 1 Enoch 6-11," *Journal of Biblical Literature* 96 (1977), 195-233.

37. Targumic Tosefta to Ezekiel 1:1; in S. Wertheimer, *Batte Midrashot: Twenty-Five Midrashim Published for the First Time From Manuscripts Discovered in the Genizoth of Jerusalem and Egypt*, 2 vols. (2d edition; Jerusalem: Ktab Wasepher, 1968), 2:135-140; discussed in Halperin, "Ascension or Invasion," 50.

38. E. Jones, *Hamlet and Oedipus* (London: Victor Gollancz, 1949), 75-76.

39. I. Tishby, *Mishnat Hazohar*, 2 vols. (3d edition; Jerusalem: Bialik Institute, 1971-75), 1:451-455; = *Wisdom of the Zohar* (English translation), 2:626-31; R. Margaliot, *Malakhei Elyon* (2d edition; Jerusalem: Mossad Harav Kook, 1964), 72-108; H. Odeberg, Introduction to *3 Enoch*, 111-125.

40. *Shema demareh*: Zohar, 1:149a (*Sitre Torah*); cf. Cordovero's comments in *Or Ha hammah* (Przemysl, 1896-98; reprinted Bnai Brak: Yahadut, 1973), 1:130c.

41. Passages quoted by Margaliot, *Mal'akhe 'Elyon*, 88. Nachmanides, commenting on Exodus 23:20, quotes this explanation of *my name is in him* from Rashi (ed. H. Chavel, *Perushe ha-Torah l'Rabbenu Mosheh ben Nahman* [Jerusalem: Mossad Harav Kook, 1959-60], I, 441).

42. E.g., Zohar, 3:229b, 231a (both from *Raya Mehemna*).

43. Margaliot, *Malakhei Elyon*, 74n, cites several passages from the Lurianic writings identifying Metatron with Joseph. Genesis 37:2, which calls Joseph a *na'ar*, encouraged this identification. On Joseph-Metatron in Nathan Shapira's *Megalleh Amukkot*, see below.

44. Zohar, 1:27a (from *Tikkunei Zohar*). The opposition of *helper* and *opponent* is based on midrashic exegesis of Genesis 2:18. See also the texts collected in Margaliot, *Malakhei Elyon*, 97; and cf. Tishby, *Mishnat Hazzohar*, 1:453 = *Wisdom of the Zohar*, 2:629.

45. Zohar, 3:255a (*Raya Mehemna*).

46. Zohar, 2:115a; 3:282b-283a (*Raya Mehemna*).

47. E.g., *Megalleh Amukkot* to *parashat Vayyeshev* (Lvov, 1795, reprinted, n.d.), 42d, 43d, 45a, 46b, 47b.

48. Ibid., 42d.

49. Ibid., 49c-d; expounding I Samuel 2:6, *The Lord kills and brings to life, brings down to Sheol and raises up*. The idea that the Israelites went down to Egypt in order to rescue the captive sparks goes back at least to Moses Cordovero: *Pardes Rimmonim, Sha'ar Hashe'arim*, ch. 3 (1:70a-b). Shapira's treatment of Joseph-Metatron foreshadows yet another aspect of Sabbatai's experience: his imprisonment in the fortress of Gallipoli, as it was interpreted by Sabbatai's followers; for they represented the fortress as the "tower of strength" of Proverbs 18:10, "into which the righteous runs and is safe [*bo yaruz zaddik venisgav*]" (Scholem, *Sabbatai Sevi*, 460). Shapira identifies the

"righteous" of the Proverbs passage with Joseph-Metatron, pointing out that *Metatron* and *bo yaruz* have the same numerical value (*Megalleh Amukkot*, 47a, 57b).

50. Scholem (*Sabbatai Sevi*, 299n) proposes that Nathan of Gaza was familiar with *Megalleh Amukkot*—but he speaks only of that portion (on *parashat Va'ethannan*) that had been published in 1637. *Megalleh Amukkot* on the rest of the Pentateuch did not appear in print until 1795. (*Ofan 111* on *Va'ethannan* [*Sefer Megalleh Amukkot*, Bnai Brak: Torat Shomrei Emunim, 1992, 174-178] quotes Proverbs 18:10 and I Samuel 2:6 in the course of a discussion of Metatron, but this will work against rather than for my suggestion, since the interpretations Shapira gives here are different from those in *parashat Vayyeshev*.) It hardly seems unthinkable, however, that the ideas expressed in the unpublished portion of Shapira's work might have circulated orally or in manuscript before 1665, or perhaps, that the highly eclectic Shapira was not innovating, but drawing on Kabbalistic associations that were already current.

51. See above, n. 33.

52. P. Alexander, introduction to *3 Enoch*, 224-225; H. Odeberg, introduction to *3 Enoch*, 17-23. (Full references above, n. 1.) On the *Alphabet of Rabbi Akiba*: A. Jellinek, *Bet ha-Midrasch*, 6 vols. (reprinted Jerusalem: Wahrmann Books, 1967), 2:xxx-xxii; I. A. Benjacob, *Ozar ha-Sepharim* (Vilna: Romm, 1880), 32. (The *Alphabet* was printed again in Amsterdam, 1708, but that is obviously too late to be relevant.)

53. Scholem, *Sabbatai Sevi*, 115-118; Liebes, "Yahaso" (above, n. 9), 289-290; M. Idel, "'One from a Town and Two from a Family'—A New Look at the Problem of Dissemination of Lurianic Kabbala and the Shabbatean Movement" (Hebrew), *Pe'amim* 44 (1990), 11.

54. Scholem, *Sabbatai Sevi*, index, s.v. *Zerubbabel, Book of.*

55. So the first edition of *Zerubbabel* (Constantinople, 1519), as reproduced by Y. Even-Shemuel, *Midreshei Ge'ullah* (2d edition; Jerusalem: Bialik Institute, 1954), 380. Cf. Wertheimer, *Batte Midrashot*, 2:498, based on the Constantinople edition. The text of this passage is extremely uncertain, and Even-Shemuel may be right in supposing that the speaker was originally not Metatron but Michael (69-70). Our concern, however, is not with the hypothetical original of *Zerubbabel* but with the text that Sabbatai and his contemporaries would have known. The Sabbatian "Zerubbabel" apocalypse, composed about 1667 and inserted into the text of *Hekhalot Rabbati* (Wertheimer, 1:118-134; Even-Shemuel, 352-370; discussed by Scholem, *Sabbatai Sevi*, 737-740), seems to presuppose a text very much like that of Constantinople. It takes for granted, at any rate, that Metatron is the speaker.

56. Cf. Scholem, *Sabbatai Sevi*, 861, 909.

57. I. R. Molho and A. Amarillo, "Autobiographical Letters of Abraham Cardozo" (Hebrew), *Sefunot* 3-4 (1960), 203. Yehuda Liebes's skepticism about statements attributed by Cardozo to Sabbatai Zevi (*Studies in Jewish Myth and Mysticism* [SUNY Press, 1993], 109) does not seem justified in this

instance. The grandiose notion of his own importance that Sabbatai expresses here is (as Cardozo explicitly recognizes) far better suited to the purposes of his extremist opponents than to his own. There is no reason for him to have fabricated it.

58. Molho and Amarillo, 211: *shehammashiah hu elohut gamur vekhen mt"t [=metatron] vmk"v [=umikkal vehomer] ss"m [=shessama'el] gamur shennitlabbeshu bo hassefirot ha'elohiyyot shel hammalkhut de' azilut uvahem nitgaddel venitromem.*

59. According to Cordovero's *Pardes Rimmonim* (*Sha'ar Abi'a*, ch. 4; 1:79a), Metatron "is the garment [*levush*] of the Shechinah, and the Shechinah conceals herself within him and demonstrates her actions through his agency. When this happens, his name becomes *Metatron* with a *yod*; the letter *yod* [=ten] indicating the Shechinah that is constituted of ten [*sefirot*]. ... All the *sefirot* become incorporated [*mitlabbeshot*] within Metatron, in order to act in this world through Metatron's agency, and that is why the Shechinah must be included within him ..." (Cf. also *Sha'ar Erkhei Hakkinnuyim, s.v. ken.*) Cardozo's Sabbatian opponents had evidently adopted this view, for he represents them as defending their belief in the Messiah's divinity on the ground that "Metatron is often a deity, inasmuch as the Shechinah incorporates herself within him [*mitlabbeshet bo*]" (quoted in Scholem, "Hadashot Lidi'at Avraham Cardozo"; reprinted in *Researches in Sabbateanism* [edited and annotated by Y. Liebes; Tel Aviv: Am Oved, 1991], 415-416).

60. Scholem, *Kabbalah*, 337-343.

61. Sasportas, 156.

62. Scholem, *Sabbatai Sevi*, 234.

63. Sasportas, 73.

64. J. Katz, *Exclusiveness and Tolerance: Studies in Jewish-Gentile Relations in Medieval and Modern Times* (Oxford University Press, 1961), 137. In Baruch of Arezzo's story of Joseph ibn Tzur, the hero declares that "I did not possess even enough knowledge to study Rashi"; meaning, "I was an absolute ignoramus" (Freimann, 73).

65. Scholem, *Sabbatai Sevi*, 542.

66. Alluding to Psalm 91:1, *Zel shaddai.*

67. Freimann, 111-112. We may add to this file the letter written in June 1666 from Gallipoli by Samuel Primo (on Sabbatai's authority): following Job 11:7, it declares that "none can probe the depths of *shin-dalet-yod*, who is our Lord, Redeemer, and Savior in one" (Baruch of Arezzo; in Freimann, 55-56; cf. Scholem, *Sabbatai Sevi*, 510-513).

68. *Kol ammei ha'arez.*

69. *Kol ha'am mikkazeh,* from Genesis 19:4.

70. Sasportas, 186.

71. Ibid., 173.

72. The Biblical quotation that Halevi uses to date his letter—*Esau went to Ishmael, and took Mahalath to wife*—points to the demonological subtext that he read into Sabbatai's conversion. See above, n. 29.

73. Israel (above, n. 2), especially chapters VI-IX.

74. Ibid., 152-154. Any suggestion of a causal connection between the Chmielnicki massacres and the Sabbatian movement must reckon with the fact that no Messianic movement developed in the wake of the massacres themselves—this in spite of the Zoharic prophecy that 1648 would be a year of salvation (Idel, "One From a Town ..." [above, n. 53], 21-22; Scholem, *Sabbatai Sevi*, 88-93). It is true that Sabbatai Zevi seems first to have declared himself Messiah in Smyrna in 1648; his stimulus may perhaps have been the news from Poland, or perhaps events closer to home which we have presently to consider. But, in 1648, no one paid much attention (Scholem, *Sabbatai Sevi*, 138-143). If it had been the Chmielnicki massacres that sparked the Sabbatian movement, it makes no sense that Sabbatai would have been able to attract a following in 1665 but not in 1648.

75. Sasportas, 336, 353-354.

76. Ibid., 323.

77. S. J. Shaw, The *Jews of the Ottoman Empire and the Turkish Republic* (New York University Press, 1991), 77-86.

78. We must concede that, if Sasportas had written a year or so later, he could have added to his dossier the expulsion of the Jews from Vienna (1669-70).

79. Israel, 207-208.

80. S. Schama, *The Embarrassment of Riches: An Interpretation of Dutch Culture in the Golden Age* (University of California Press, 1988), 587-595.

81. Israel, 224-231.

82. Aaron Sarfatti to Sasportas; Sasportas, 29.

83. I add this qualification in deference to the reservations of Moshe Idel, who—against the position held by Gershom Scholem and most of his followers, that Kabbalah was the dominant stream of Jewish thought beginning with the sixteenth century—has questioned the extent to which it had penetrated the popular Jewish consciousness prior to the end of the seventeenth century. See Idel, *Kabbalah: New Perspectives* (New Haven and London: Yale University Press, 1988), 257-259; "One from a Town ... " (above, n. 53), 9-20.

84. In the sixteenth century, for example, the Kabbalistic schema moved the Maharal of Prague to suppose not only that Jewish and Gentile souls are different in quality, but that even "the body of the Jew consists of a more refined variety of matter than that of the Gentile." It followed that Jews must, as far as possible, segregate themselves socially and culturally from Gentiles (B. L. Sherwin, *Mystical Theology and Social Dissent: The Life and Works of Judah Loew of Prague* [Rutherford/Madison/Teaneck: Fairleigh Dickinson University Press; and London and Toronto, Associated University Presses, 1982], 98-99, 116). Jacob Katz discusses this exclusivist trend in early modern Judaism, without, however, putting much stress on the role of Kabbalah in promoting it (*Exclusiveness and Tolerance*, 143-155).

85. Thus, Salo Baron sees a foreshadowing of Emancipation in Grotius's *Remonstrantie*, at the beginning of the seventeenth century: *A Social and Religious History of the Jews*, 2d edition, 18 vols. (New York: Columbia/JPS, 1952-83), 15:25-33.

86. The image is drawn from the Talmud, Berakhot 3a.

87. Quoted by J. Katz, "Bein Tatnu Letah-tat," in *Halakhah and Kabbalah: Studies in the History of Jewish Religion, its Various Faces and Social Relevance* (Hebrew; Magnes Press, 1986), 321; from *Derush al Hattorah ve'al Hammizvot* (delivered at Posnan in 1592, according to Sherwin [above, n. 84; 34, 41]; and published, apparently in expanded form, in 1593).

88. An image that Sabbatian apologists were later to use in explaining the Messiah's apostasy: he had become a new Esther, ready to bring salvation to his people (e.g., Nathan of Gaza's letter of 7 February 1668, in Sasportas, 262).

89. A. Kasher and S. Biderman, "Why Was Baruch de Spinoza Excommunicated?" in D. S. Katz and J. I. Israel eds., *Sceptics, Millenarians and Jews* (Brill, 1990), 98-141.

90. Leyb b. Ozer, *Sippur Ma' asei Shabbetai Zevi*, 136; paraphrased in Emden, *Torat Hakkena'ot*, 11b.

91. His cruelty appears in his enthusiastic justification of the brutal beating of a skeptic, on the Sabbath, by his followers in Venice: *They kept the Sabbath strictly and well, for our Lord King is himself the Sabbath* (letter of June 1666, quoted in Baruch of Arezzo, Freimann, 55-56). As to "arbitrary tampering," it is hard to discover rhyme or reason in the demands reported by Joseph Halevi, *that Sabbath be observed on Monday instead of on Saturday. ... He planned, similarly, to shift God's festivals from their appointed dates: to observe the Day of Atonement on Thursday this year, and so forth* (Sasportas, 174). The point seems to have been to show his absolute control over the sacred calendar.

92. Sasportas and Baruch of Arezzo both quote a letter sent by the rabbis of Constantinople to certain individuals who had protested the Messiah's "strange deeds." The rabbis try to rationalize Sabbatai's acts—"certain actions which on the surface may seem peculiar, but which in fact are wondrous"—suggest that the reports have been exaggerated, and end up by excommunicating the protesters (Sasportas, 133-135; Freimann, 53-55). This response to the unbelievers' objections seems to have been fairly typical.

93. Scholem, *Sabbatai Sevi*, 396-405.

94. *3 Enoch* ch. 48C, from the *Alphabet of Rabbi Akiba* (Alexander's translation; in Charlesworth [above, n. 1], 312).

95. Scholem, *Sabbatai Sevi*, 235-236, 308-309, 807, 813, 915; I. Einhorn, "Three Shabbatean Plates" (Hebrew), *Pe'amim* 44 (1990), 72-75.

96. Sasportas, 78.

97. *Zeh gillah amirah.*

98. *Derush Hammenorah* (in Scholem, *Be'ikvot Mashiah* [Jerusalem: Tarshish, 1944], 124); cited by Scholem, *Sabbatai Sevi*, 813. On the dating of the text, see

Scholem's introduction (*Be'ikvot Mashiah*, 89). Earlier in the same paragraph, Nathan—again, on the basis of Sabbatai's own claim?—identifies
Sabbatai with the *na'ar* of Isaiah 65:20, "whose root is in *Yesod*," and he goes
on to link Sabbatai with the triad Moses, Joseph, and David. (Nathan had
made a similar claim, though with less detail, back in the summer of 1666
[*Derush Hattanninim*, in *Be'ikvot Mashiah*, 16-17]: Sabbatai's rank is that of
the *sefirah Yesod*; as such, he couples with the Shechinah; he is the *na'ar* of
Isaiah 65:20.) We have seen that Metatron bears the title *na'ar*, that he is the
angelic manifestation of the *sefirah Yesod*, and that he is identified with
Joseph.

99. Similarly in *Derush Hattanninim*: *Be'ikvot Mashiah*, 21; partially translated in
     Scholem, *Sabbatai Sevi*, 310.

100. The expression *hannahash hakkadosh* also occurs in Nathan's commentary on
     (his own) *Vision of Rabbi Abraham*, *Be'ikovt Mashiah*, 63. Similarly, Israel
     Hazzan of Kastoria, who was a companion of Sabbatai's after the apostasy,
     declares Sabbatai the "holy serpent" (*nahash hakkadosh*) that he finds men-
     tioned in the Zohar (3:119b). This snake travels with raised tail and *strikes all
     who are in its presence*; that is (Israel Hazzan explains), when Sabbatai is "in
     a state of illumination ... he wants to convert everyone around him to the
     Muslim religion" (*Commentary on Psalms*; ms Budapest-Kaufmann 255, 8b;
     cf. Scholem, "Perush Mizmore Tehillim Mihugo shel Shabbetai Zevi
     Be'adrinopol," *Alei Ayin: The Salman Schocken Jubilee Volume* ... [Jerusalem,
     1948-52], 162-163; reprinted in *Researches in Sabbateanism* [above, n. 59], 94).

101. T. Coenen, *Ydele verwachtinge der Joden* ... (Amsterdam, 1669), 9. I am
     grateful to Professor Petrus Tax (University of North Carolina, emeritus) for
     his help in reading and translating the Dutch text. Cf. the English version
     in *Sabbatai Sevi*, 127.

102. Three versions of the letter survive: (1) The *longer "Sofia" version*, addressed
     to "my brothers and friends, all the men of faith in the city of Sofia,"
     published, from a copy of the manuscript made by Yitzhak Ben-Zvi, by
     Zalman Rubashov (Shazar), "Te'udot Shabbeta'iyyot Me'aram Zovah,"
     Meassef Zion 6 (1934), 54-58. (2) A briefer version of this document, with the
     same address at its beginning, quoted by *Baruch of Arezzo* in his *Memorial to
     the Children of Israel* (Freimann, 68). (3) The *"Arnaut-Belgrade" version*,
     addressed to "my brothers and friends, the residents of Arnaut-Belgrade,"
     published by A. Amarillo, "Te'udot Shabbeta'iyyot Migginzei Rabbi Sha'ul
     Amarillo," *Sefunot* 5 (1961), 249-250 (evidence for its being an autograph,
     238-239). As to the date of the letter: The request for prayer books to which
     the "Arnaut-Belgrade" version is appended ends with a note identifying
     "Alkum" as the place of writing, and dating the document to Sunday, 1
     Nisan, while the longer "Sofia" version bears the date Monday, 23 Nisan.
     Neither source gives the year. But the only possible year is 5436 (=1675-76):
     according to E. Mahler's tables (*Handbuch der jüdischen Chronologie*, origi-
     nally published 1916, and reprinted Hildesheim: Georg Olms, 1967), 5436

was the first year after 5423 (=1662-63) in which 1 Nisan fell on a Sunday and 23 Nisan on a Monday, and Sabbatai died at the end of 5436. (Rubashov infers the date 5436 for the "Sofia" version on the basis of the context in which Baruch of Arezzo quotes it; and this is confirmed by Sabbatai's presence in "Alkum"—that is, Dulcigno in Albania—to which he was exiled at the beginning of 1673.) 1 Nisan 5436 = 15 March 1676; 23 Nisan 5436 = 6 April 1676.——In giving the date, both the "Arnaut-Belgrade" version and the longer "Sofia" version play on the name "Nisan" and the language of Exodus 17:15, where Moses is said to have built an altar and *called its name the Lord is my standard—nissi*, replaced in both versions by *nisan*. The allusion is explained (though in a puzzling enough fashion) in a note, evidently written by a copyist, which begins the longer "Sofia" version: *Sabbatai Zevi made a snake of silver and placed it upon the standard* (*nes*; following Numbers 21:9, where Moses is the actor). Sabbatai's link with the snake, which we have already observed—and which is repeated in the serpentine signatures of the "Arnaut-Belgrade" version—is here stressed.

103. In the translation that follows, I mark in bold type those words and phrases that are not shared by all three versions. Scholem (*Sabbatai Sevi*, 914-917) has plausibly suggested that Baruch of Arezzo deliberately censored his quotation of the "Sofia" text. If I have correctly interpreted the "Arnaut-Belgrade" version's reference to the "messenger ... mentioned above" (see below), it will be evident why the latter phrase was inappropriate for the version sent to Sofia. We may credit the remaining divergences to Sabbatai's shifting moods, and rely upon a combination of the "Arnaut-Belgrade" and "Sofia" texts to give us our fullest picture of his self-representation.

104. "The one mentioned above" is found only in the "Arnaut-Belgrade" version; "to bring you good news" is omitted by Baruch of Arezzo.

105. Omitted from the "Arnaut-Belgrade" version.

106. Omitted by Baruch of Arezzo.

107. Baruch of Arezzo: "all he tells you."

108. Found only in the longer "Sofia" version.

109. Omitted by Baruch of Arezzo; the longer "Sofia" version has "Sabbatai Zevi Mehmed."

110. Aside from the passages noted in brackets, *aloh a'aleh* ("I will surely ascend") may reflect Genesis 46:4 or Numbers 13:30. The titles *arya deve illa'e vetavya deve illa'e* ("lion of the Exalted Dwelling, gazelle of the Exalted Dwelling") are drawn from the Babylonian Talmud, Hullin 59b; Sabbatai had been applying them to himself at least since the summer of 1666 (Sasportas, 78). (The Sabbatian Passover plate published by Itzhak Einhorn in *Pe'amim* 44 [1990], 72-75, brings together lion, gazelle, and snake as emblems for Sabbatai Zevi.)

111. Letter to Raphael Joseph, Sasportas, 12.

112. Aaron Sarfatti to Sasportas (end of 1665 or beginning of 1666), Sasportas, 27. The Talmudic description of Nebuchadnezzar is on Shabbat 150a (top), in

the context of interpretation of verses from Isaiah 14. Cf. also Sasportas, 61, which represents Sabbatai's followers as applying to him Daniel 5:19, the original referent of which is Nebuchadnezzar.

113. Scholem, *Sabbatai Sevi*, 225, 296-297, 308-309. But Sabbatai is also the suffering Job, whom the Zohar identified as "one of the servants of Pharaoh" (2:34a, following rabbinic exegesis of Exodus 9:20). As Job, therefore (Nathan argues), Sabbatai "is called *servant of Pharaoh* [*eved par'oh*]. For *Pharaoh* is the name of the true King Messiah, so called ... from his act of entirely *tearing* [*peri'ah*] the foreskin of the *kelippah*. When he achieves this, he will ... no longer be called *Job*, but *Pharaoh*; whereas he had previously been called *servant of Pharaoh*, like the snake who acts in the service of the spirit [?]" (*Derush Hattanninim*, in Scholem, *Be'iqvot Mashiah*, 20-21; cf. *Sabbatai Sevi*, 308-310). Yet again, Sabbatai is a servant whose name is like his master's.

114. *Sabbatai Sevi*, 296-297, 393, 851.

115. For the details that follow, I am indebted to the work of my research assistant, Pamela E. Kinlaw.

116. S. Shaw, *History of the Ottoman Empire and Modern Turkey: Volume 1: Empire of the Gazis: The Rise and Decline of the Ottoman Empire, 1280-1808* (Cambridge and New York: Cambridge University Press, 1976), 201.

117. Ibid.; P. Rycaut, *History of the Turkish Empire from the Year 1623 to the Year 1677* (London: John Starkey, 1680), 19, 29, 33; R. Dankoff, *The Intimate Life of an Ottoman Statesman: Melek Ahmed Pasha (1588-1662); As Portrayed in Evliya Celebi's Book of Travels* (Albany: SUNY Press, 1991), 39; N. Barber, *The Sultans* (New York: Simon and Schuster, 1973), 89-94.

118. Rycaut, 33.

119. J. von Hammer-Purgstall, *Geschichte des Osmanischen Reiches*, 2d edition, 4 vols. (Pesth: Hartleben, 1834-36), 3:319. I quote the English version of Lord Kinross, *The Ottoman Centuries: The Rise and Fall of the Turkish Empire* (New York: Morrow Quill Paperbacks, 1977), 317, which is presumably translated from Hammer-Purgstall.

120. Hammer-Purgstall, 3:324. The translation (from the German) is my own.

121. Scholem, *Sabbatai Sevi*, 107-109.

122. D. Goffman, *Izmir and the Levantine World, 1550-1650* (University of Washington Press, 1990), 93-137.

123. Scholem, *Sabbatai Sevi*, esp. 166-171.

124. Abraham Danon, *Études Sabbatiennes* (Paris: A. Durlacher, 1910), 43; from an autograph manuscript of Yakhini's which (according to Scholem, *Sabbatai Sevi*, 168n) has since disappeared. I am not sure why Yakhini speaks of Mehmed's "cap" (*kova*, a term appropriate for Jewish headgear; see above, nn. 7, 17), or what he means by his "scarf" (*sudar*). I suspect that both *kova* and *sudar* are parts of Mehmed's turban, the former being the felt cap that was the core of the turban, the latter the length of cloth that was wound around the cap. (It was the cloth that gave the turban its distinctive shape,

and also its name.) See Raphaela Lewis, *Everyday Life in Ottoman Turkey* (London: B. . Batsford, and New York: G. P. Putnam's Sons, 1971), 92; and, in more detail, Hammer, *Staatsverfassung*, 1:440-447.

125. Scholem, *Sabbatai Sevi*, 140-142.

126. This postulate, that the two men's unconscious processes were much akin, will help explain how it was that Yakhini fell under Sabbatai's spell, became his fervent devotee, and could not be shaken from his conviction by either the apostasy or the death of his Messiah.

127. There is perhaps some echo of this expectation in the strange *tikkun* that, according to *Sefer Merivat Kodesh* (in Freimann, 17-18), some of Abraham Cardozo's disciples performed at the tomb of the Sultan Ibrahim: its purpose was apparently to get Ibrahim to appear to his son Mehmed in a dream and drive him insane, so that he would abdicate in favor of the Messiah. (Cf. Scholem, "Avraham Mikhael Cardozo: Derush Kodesh Yisra'el La'adonai," in *Researches in Sabbateanism* [above, n. 59], 428.)

Contributors

Michael Berkowitz is Assistant Professor of History at Ohio State University.

S. Daniel Breslauer is Professor of Religious Studies at the University of Kansas.

Richard A. Freund is Professor of Religion at the University of Nebraska at Omaha.

James R. Davila is Lecturer in Early Jewish Studies at the Divinity School of the University of St. Andrews, Scotland.

Joel Gereboff is Professor of Religious Studies at Arizona State University.

David J. Halperin is Professor of Religious Studies at the University of North Carolina at Chapel Hill.

Ronald S. Hendel is Associate Professor of Religious Studies at Southern Methodist University.

Howard Schwartz is Professor of English at the University of Missouri-St. Louis.

Deborah Sills is Assistant Professor of Religion at California Lutheran University.

David Norman Smith is Assistant Professor of Sociology at the University of Kansas.

Steven M. Wasserstrom is the Moe and Izetta Tonkon Associate Professor of Judaic Studies at Reed College.

Elliot R. Wolfson is Professor of Jewish Studies at New York University.

Index